GROWING PAINS

by Wanda Gág

MILLIONS OF CATS

SNIPPY AND SNAPPY

THE FUNNY THING

WANDA GÁG'S STORY BOOK

THE ABC BUNNY

GONE IS GONE

TALES FROM GRIMM

SNOW WHITE AND THE SEVEN DWARFS

Photo by Robert Janssen, 1940

Wanda Gág

Wanda Gág

GROWING PAINS

DIARIES AND DRAWINGS

FOR THE YEARS

1908-1917

NEW YORK COWARD-McCANN, *Inc.* PUBLISHERS

NC
139
G2
A2
19901

10/24/40 $2.50 H. S. News

To My Mother and Father

FOREWORD

The impulse to set down one's intimate thoughts and feelings in sequence is a universal trait of long standing. Almost every one has started a diary at some time or other. Yet it is seldom consistently carried on. The effort is too great. "Nothing requires a rarer intellectual heroism," said Santayana, "than willingness to see one's equation written out." Frank self-projections of a complete human being are even more uncommon. I am not referring to the Confessions of a Rousseau, Casanova, or Mabel Luhan, which are self-created legends written with only a modicum of inhibitions. Nor the voluminous Journals of the Concord Philosophers, Emerson, Alcott, Thoreau, or of Leonardo da Vinci, which are notebooks of thoughts, speculations, and observations. Nor the Journal of the Brothers de Goncourt, which caused such a scandal in their time. Pepys approaches it, in that he wrote for himself alone, yet whatever there is of revelation remains indirect, for he was concerned almost entirely with external things. The febrile diary of Marie Bashkirtseff is revealing if one were sure that the original has not been tampered with. *Maud* is an amusing if somewhat superficial piece of youthful Americana. Van Gogh in his almost day-to-day letters to his brother approaches the ideal rather closely; and so does Delacroix in portions of his Journal, which begins thus in his twenty-fourth year: "I am carrying out my plan, so often formulated, of keeping a journal. What I most keenly wish is not to forget that I am writing for myself alone. Thus I shall always tell the truth, I hope, and thus I shall improve myself."

To the literature of self-appraisal must now be added *Growing Pains* by Wanda Gág. It is a faithful transcript of her diary from her fifteenth to her twenty-fourth year, covering her life in New Ulm, Minnesota, where she was born, and in St. Paul and Minneapolis, where she went to art school. The great virtue of the diary form is the immediacy of impression: the thoughts and feelings are set down from day to day as they occur. Try as we may, we can not later capture their spirit and flavor, for our recollections are inevitably colored by all impressions subsequent to the event. Authentic impressions of childhood and youth have seldom been recorded. It is this that makes *Growing Pains* such an invaluable chronicle, a veritable case-history in adolescent psychology. Here are recorded with the greatest candor, the thoughts and feelings, the joys and sorrows, the turbulence and the egotisms, the vague gropings toward maturity of an adolescent girl. To be sure, she was an exceptional girl —exceptional in determination and intelligence, exceptional in the honesty of her self-revelation, exceptional also, in the fact that she had a genuine creative gift in art. It is the record of the early development of an artist, and it thus speaks to still another audience. She reveals in her pages the trials and tribulations that beset every sincere creative artist in quest of self-realization, the numerous false by-paths that must be explored and retraced before the true way is found, and last but not least, the sheer unremitting labor of learning the metier. As an artist she has developed much further than the work illustrated in her diary. Indeed, if she had not matured far beyond the efforts of her student days, and worked out her own personal and distinctive style, she would not be the great artist she is today. She is beyond question one of the outstanding print-makers in America. Artists are enthusiastic over her originality and her mastery of form and design; and the layman is attracted by the vividness and intensity with which she depicts the every-day things of life: a kitchen table, cats, flowers, trees and hills. In everything she does one feels the impress of a powerful and sensitive individuality. The books she has written and illustrated, *Millions of Cats, The Funny Thing,* and *Snippy and Snappy,* have become veritable children's classics, for they have all the simple and memorable qualities of a folk tale.

Wanda Gág started her diary in her fifteenth year and has kept it up to the present day, a period of over thirty years. Thus, *Growing Pains* represents but a small fragment of the whole. No one outside herself has ever seen the diary in its entirety and probably no one ever shall. Judging by the part that she has allowed to be published, it must be an amazing document—no less than the complete and full-rounded delineation of one woman's life, presented without reserve or scruple, in all the complex relationships and experiences of modern life. I know of nothing like it in literature. I once asked her why she wrote a diary. She had no reason except that she "must"—a force as compelling as the "drawing fits" she talks about in her diary. It is a compulsion that must at times have caused her no end of suffering to carry out, for the analysis of feeling and the probing of motives, if performed with unequivocal honesty, the very re-living of painful experience, are harrowing indeed, and call for the utmost detachment, will power, and integrity. In this devotion to the wise Delphic maxim "Know Thyself" she has captured some of the insight of the mystics and initiates; likewise in her distinction between "Myself" and the "Me's." I suspect that her self-appraisal has been somewhat in the nature of an emotional catharsis for her. She has set down, projected, externalized the experiences of an eventful and exciting life and thereby avoided psychological aberrations. Her consistent practice of this art, though entailing considerable effort, has given her an exceptional maturity and a rarely integrated personality. She is a curious combination of spiritual humility and expansive egotism.

It has required no little courage on her part to allow *Growing Pains* to be published. It is, after all, a very limited exposition of her mature personality, a partial impression further heightened by the storm and stress of adolescence. That she can issue it to the world as a contribution to the understanding of art and psychology, is a measure of her adult and enlightened point of view.

CARL ZIGROSSER

CONTENTS

FULL PAGE ILLUSTRATIONS

CONTRASTS

INTRODUCTION

Thirty-one notebooks originally comprised this diary. They are full of diagrams, self-portraits and other sketches, with many crossed-out words, ink spots—even tear blots. Several of the books are wrinkled and blurred from being stored in a damp cellar, and a few are lost.

I carried my diary around with me wherever I went, and so any time, any place, in would go another batch of "chicken scratches untidy," or a quick sketch of whatever happened to be on hand, be it a child, a leaf, or (to my victim's unfailing embarrassment) someone's feet. Often indifferent to sentence structure, neatness, and accuracy of dates, I was mainly concerned with "getting things down"—sometimes an immediate recording of an episode or conversation, or of my thoughts and emotions. Since my pen was always racing with my thoughts, the writing is scribbled and often all but illegible.

These "scribbly" old notebooks, unopened, unread, and more or less carelessly stored in Minnesota for many years, were eventually sent on to me in New York. I had often wondered how I would feel upon re-reading them and had even speculated about it in my diary at times. "Perhaps some day," I wrote, "I shall be coward enough to tear up all these anguished writings." I found, instead, that I was able to regard my youthful outpourings, while with a natural interest and hence not complete detachment, still with considerable objectivity. True, all the usual juvenilities were there: the slang and silliness, the girlish gush-and-crush, the introspection, the agonizing over love, the youthful arrogance and turgidity; but, recognizing these traits as typical of the various age groups of which I was successively a part, I saw myself as only one of many going through the normal phases of adolescence.

It was with this detached attitude that I approached the preparation of my material for publication. I had little difficulty in deciding to retain incidents which showed *me* in an unflattering light, but what about the many good friends appearing in the diary? Ought I to omit passages which might be interpreted as being slightly unfavorable to them? This, after careful consideration, I decided against as being only sentimentally kind and not truly fair to them as the mature, intelligent individuals I know them to be.

Some editing had to be done, of course. Any diary is apt to be unbalanced in some respects. In the first place, unimportant items are often given too much space, and to remedy this I have eliminated unnecessary repetitions and a mass of clogging detail. In the second place, a real diary, spontaneously written, cannot by its very nature possess narrative completion. No matter how thoroughly day-by-day episodes may be recorded, a certain amount of background material, such as preceding events, environment, and family conditions—so obvious and familiar to the diary-keeper—is never touched upon or, at best, is revealed very gradually and imperfectly. It seems necessary, therefore, to include here the following sketch in order to supplement this diary and to set the stage for the opening pages of *Growing Pains*.

I was born in this country, but often feel as though I had spent my early years in Europe. My father was born in Bohemia, as were my mother's parents. My birthplace—New Ulm, Minnesota—was settled by Middle-Europeans, and I grew up in an atmosphere of Old World customs and legends, of Bavarian and Bohemian folk songs, of German *Märchen* and *Turnverein* activities. I spoke no English until I went to school.

In our home artistic expression of all kinds was taken for granted. Our father, Anton Gág, was an artist; and in our mother's family the creative urge took the form of painting, modeling and fine cabinet work. We children—six girls and a boy—all drew and most of us wrote stories and poems.

Anton Gág, though always in delicate health, worked hard and kept his large family in modest comfort. During the week, for his livelihood, he decorated houses and churches; but on Sundays, for his inner satisfaction, he painted pictures in his attic studio. We children had learned early how to behave when someone was "making something" and were sometimes allowed in his studio while he painted there. I liked this—there was a silent, serious happiness in the air which, although I had no words for it then, I recognized as the ineffable joy of creation. I had already experienced this exaltation myself at times, so I knew that on Sundays my father was happy in his soul.

What I did not know then, but realized later, was that a conflict existed in his soul as well. As the head of a beloved family, he had a responsibility which he never neglected; as an artist, he had a responsibility to an inner compulsion which was never entirely satisfied. Always yearning for a formal art education, he cherished the dream of some day studying under able teachers—perhaps even in Europe!—but in this great hope he was doomed to frustration.

When I began my diary in October, 1908, I was fifteen years old and there were eight in our family—my mother and seven children. My father had died in May of that year. Our savings depleted by his long illness, our mother sick and weak from a year's nursing and anxiety, we felt dazed and helpless. Besides our home, there was left to us some twelve hundred dollars insurance money which, with the addition of eight dollars a month from the county, was made to stretch over the next six years.

Through all this, my schooling had suffered several setbacks. In the fall of 1907 I had entered high school but, because of much extra work at home, I was able to attend afternoon sessions only. As my father's illness became critical I was needed at home all day, and at his death my school days seemed to be at an end forever. Along with the small county relief allowance, along with the personal charity of many kindly neighbors, came the community advice, almost an ultimatum: education was a fine thing if one could afford it . . . to have a talent for drawing was very nice but art didn't pay . . . therefore, Wanda as the oldest child had better forget about school, stop drawing, and clerk in a local store to help support the family.

These suggestions were well meant, I knew, but there is more than one kind of hunger in the world, and the question "What is to become of us?" assumed in my mind proportions far beyond our immediate material future. Were we all to be satisfied with a grammar school education, with jobs as clerks, bookkeepers or hired girls? And then as to myself—suppose I *could* stop drawing, had I a *right* to do so? Only Mama and I knew what had happened that day in May when Papa, calling me to his bedside and taking my hand, had said faintly, *"Was der Papa nicht thun konnt', muss die Wanda halt fertig machen."* (What papa couldn't do, Wanda will have to finish.) I had nodded my head, speechless with the sudden realization that he was dying, and overwhelmed by the trust which had been placed in my keeping.

Here was a justification for the ideas which were dimly but surely taking form in my mind; and in its wake came the youthful, rebellious resolve: "I have a right to go on drawing. I will not be a clerk. And we are *all* going through high school!" Mama understood perfectly, and had no objection to this course if a way could be found to accomplish it. I had no definite plan of action but I made a start. I drew postcards and place cards, and instead of writing and illustrating stories and poems for pleasure, I now did so with the purpose of turning them into cash. This would have been impossible had it not been for the *Journal Junior,* bless its pink pages! This juvenile supplement to the *Minneapolis Journal,* which I had but recently discovered, encouraged the creative efforts of grammar and high school students by actually paying for accepted material, and I immediately deluged them with my work.

At about this time I came across an old half-empty ledger of my father's. In our household anything which could be drawn or written upon was in great demand; a notebook of any kind was a positive treasure. I pounced on the old ledger and, prompted perhaps by the fragmentary business accounts in my father's handwriting, I began recording my earnings and expenditures, what drawings I had sent where and when, and other notes pertaining to my new business ventures. I was never able to limit myself to plain figures and facts in keeping accounts; and so reports on the weather, new additions to the baby's vocabulary, family incidents, even youthful thoughts and yearnings, found their way into my "ledger." And that, to the best of my memory, is how I came to start this diary.

New York, N. Y.
August, 1940

GROWING PAINS

Part One

NEW ULM, MINNESOTA

1908-1910

Monday, Oct. 12, 1908

I sent one of my pictures to the Journal Junior, "Toddie's Hanged Our Dollies," and forgot to put my address on it so I sent another envelope with my address on it. The same day I sent a story, "Lou's Soap Bubble Party," and a picture to illustrate it, to McCall's. Some time ago I sent these three articles to the Youth's Companion—

> Story—Golden Brooch
> Picture—Great Grandmother's Chest
> Poem—   "   "   "

I wonder how the whole thing will turn out.

A few days ago Margaret Kelly told me that Martha Schmid didn't believe I drew free hand. She thinks I trace. Trace indeed! When I don't even care much for copying.

Tuesday, Oct. 13

Some time ago I got a check for $1.00 prize from the Woman's Home Companion for a drawing. It had 14 children on it. I got the dollar at the Citizen's Bank.

I'm thru reading "Kristy's Rainy Day Party" and quite done with the Orange Fairy Book.

It is a beautiful day.

I do hope Mae Harris Anson [editor of the Journal Junior] will not throw away my picture before my second letter with my address reaches her.

The baby can say Deya for Stella, Dudi for Tussy, Adda for Asta, Deyi for Dehli, and all kinds of other words that she learns every day.

1

The same day I was at the bank I got our Fair money for this and last year, $3.25 in all.

1907	Wanda drawing—1st		$.50
	Dehli and Asta drawing—1st		$.50
	Tussy pillow slip—2nd		$.25
1908	Wanda drawing—1st		$.50
	Dehli	" —1st	$.50
	Wanda	" —3rd	$.25
	Stella Splasher—2nd		$.25
	Tussy centerpiece—1st		$.50

My money from the Fair and the one dollar from the Woman's Home Companion will go for shoes, I think.

School is going out now. We'll have pot pie for dinner.

Wednesday, Oct. 14. A fine day.

Mama went to Hasenclever's today.

Tussy, Asta, and Dehli made some pictures yesterday evening but Asta only carried out her idea on paper, "Taking a picture with a Kodak." It's as cute as it can be, and if she gets it as nice on the drawing paper I'm sure it'll be pretty good, for her at least. I didn't know she could do so well. Dehli and Tussy have theirs on drawing paper already, in India ink. Tussy's is called "Getting ready for Hallow e'en," and Delhi's is called "Eating Egg-O-See."

I started a story last night and I'm going to write some of it now——

Thursday, Oct. 15. A splendid day.

I finished the story yesterday and started another one.

Mama lay down this afternoon, and is still in bed.

The baby can say these words: Bugga for buggy, baba for baby, plll for please, Oh Gaka for Oh jiminy cracker, mama, bu for *bub,* mi for *mich; heis, horch,* and *guck da,* and can smack for driving. Abba for apple, gaggak for duck, *ch ch* and *doot doot* for a train, and a great many more.

I made supper tonight. We had fried potatoes, left over cabbage, and a little bit of veal-stew. We took mama's supper up on the waiter. The baby slept twice. I ironed a little today.

Saturday, Oct. 17. A dreary day.

Made another picture, "When sister makes the candy."

"when sister makes the candy."

By WANDA-HAZEL
1919.
NEW-ULM-MINN.

Yesterday grandma sent up two chickens, some cabbage, carrots and three cheese-cakes.

Stella made up a poem about a leaf last night, and Thursday night I wrote 2 poems, "The Snowstorm" and "A Mother Goose Party." Here is "The Snowstorm."

> 1. I go to bed with my candle-light.
>   Outside the world is solemn and white,
>   And quietly, softly, hushed and slow,
>   Come the pretty, white little flakes of snow.
>   And leaving the world so calm and so white,
>   I creep to bed in the peaceful night.
>
> 2. In the morning when I get up, Oh ho!
>   The world is full of the drifting snow!
>   The little red house way down by the hills,
>   Is drifted with snow to its window sills.
>   I meet the world in the early morn,
>   In a jolly, frollicky wild snowstorm!

I'm making an everyday jumper out of one of mama's wrappers. It isn't going to be pretty, I think. As far as I know it's going to be *horrid*. I'll have to get new shoes. My others are too small. We gave Ritschl's grandmother a picture of herself and her husband which papa painted.

I was at Ione Dekker's and got the Oct. Woman's Home Compan-

ion. Am writing the story of a Hallowe'en party to send them. Asta
wrote a story too. It's just too funny! The baby is still up. She isn't
sleepy yet. We have to laugh so much at her. She can say book, Aggaga
for Egg-O-See, and wawa for water. She can chew gum nicely.

Tussi, Stella + Asta   Bobbing for Apples.

Monday, Oct. 19. Sunny at times but smoky and windy.

They say the biggest mill in Minneapolis is burning. They also say
that the woods in Michigan are burning.

I sketched the baby tonight after school, and just a little while before,
I sketched Asta 4 times and Dehli 3 times. I sketched them in a dark
room. They wore a night gown and held a candle. I want one for "The
Snowstorm." 2 of them are in India Ink. The others are in pencil.
I wish I had a decent pencil. The one I got from Karl Ritschl has disappeared. I have a faint Idea of seeing it in the desk-drawer last but
search as I will, I can't find it.

Today was "leaf-searching" day. I got the *most* leaves and the prettiest
ones, too; plum leaves, apple tree leaves, raspberry bush leaves, rose bush
leaves, maple leaves and any number of other kinds. I have two shoe
boxes full and a capful, and one of the buggy pockets is full too. Aunt
Magdalene was here.

I like "Merrylips" but "Roberta & her brothers" isn't as good as I
thought. Had sago pudding tonight. Good night.

Oct. 21, Wednesday. Rainy, dark day.

Aunt Mary was here yesterday and brought me 2 waists and a skirt.

She told me Erna Rosen wants half a dozen postals. That makes a dozen I've got to make because Miss Brown wants 6.

Rec'd (for painting postals) $3.95	1907 Fair Money .... $ .50
Cost ...... .51½	1908 Fair Money .... .75
Gain 3.43½	Prize from W. H. Companion 1.00
$1.69	$1.75
3.43½	6 cts. stamps for sending .... .06
.10 for stamping table cover	$1.69
Total gain $5.22½	

The baby thinks she can draw!—"ma guck grrrrr," she says.

Oct. 23. Rain, Rain, Rain.

Fern Fischer and Judy Dekker were over here last night. I made Judy a paper doll and Fern a picture. Washed and dried the breakfast dishes today and washed the dinner dishes. Today is ironing day and ironing night too it seems.

I made the first illustration to "The Snowstorm" tonight, that is, put in the shadings, etc. Wish I had somebody to tell me what they think about it. Somebody that knows about art. Stella is too young to criticise. No mail for me. It's perfectly discouraging. Wish I could draw like Mary True Ayer.

Oct. 26, Monday. Rain, Rain, Rain.

Rain since Friday *more* or *less*. Saturday we worked most of the time. Not much time for reading, drawing or anything like that. Yesterday I was over at Dekker's in the evening with Stella. Wore the white and pink lawn dress. We had apple dumplings for our Sunday dinner, and sour fish for supper tonight. We bought him of Mr. Schmid for 15 cents. For dinner we had beef steak fried in the furnace. Copied pretty many stories and poems * the day before yesterday, and Sunday I started to copy a fairy story.* No drawing worth mentioning.

Mama was up at Helk's today. I cleaned up part of the children's side of the attic today. They've mussed it all up. I gave Tussy a bundle of cloth to sew with today.

Nov. 2. A fine, warm, sunny day.

My hopes are shattered some. Got a letter from the Youth's Companion with my stuff in it & a letter from one of the Co.

* My own.

Fern Fischer was here yesterday and she said that somebody told her that I don't do anything but read and draw. I guess so! I wonder if washing dishes, sweeping about 6 times a day, picking up things the baby and Howard throw around are reading. And I've never heard of taking care of babies, combing little sisters, cleaning bed rooms & attics as being classed as drawing! I wonder what else people will say about me.

Yesterday night I drew and inked 12 postals and today I colored them. They are all for Thanksgiving & I think I'll ask Eggen's Drug Store if they don't want to buy any of me.

Made a picture not long ago called "The Bonfire."

I've got my new shoes now. They cost $1.75.

I've read "Betty Wales Junior" and it's splendid! Stella got "Miss Petticoats" but I didn't read it because I haven't much time & I've read it when I was in the 8th grade.

Dehli's drawing pictures all the time for her friends.

Nov. 11, Wed. A cold, bright day.

Miss Meadows * asked me whether I was going somewhere to study art later, and I told her I'd like to go to high school first. "All right, come in January," she said. But I don't know whether I can. To be sure I'd like to but—. Ione Dekker said that I should take 4 half subjects & so get 2 credits.

I've got Tussy's Christmas presents done—two of them—bookmarks.

I and Stella and Asta were out at Aunt Klaus's. We got a lot of pretty milkweeds & rose berries & autumn leaves, besides some apples which Aunt Klaus gave us along. We had a splendid time.

* A high-school teacher.

I drew a heading in india ink for Aunt Janet's Pages * but I don't know whether I'll send it—the stamps are giving out, that's why. My india ink is quite gone too. I don't see how I'm to get some when it's gone.

I phoned to Eggen's Drug Store several days ago and asked what they intended to do about the postals and they said they'd keep them. He said they'd sold quite a number already.

November 12. A cold day. It's snowing.

Mama didn't feel well so I made supper. We didn't have much to make anyway, just bacon and potatoes to fry. Made a Fireplace Picture last night. I'd like to send it to the Journal Junior, but the stamps—.

Nov. 13. A cold snowy day. Friday.

Great good luck! I found an old book with 5 stamps—2 cent stamps —in it! I'm so glad. Now I'm going to send the Heading for Aunt Janet's Pages, and one or two pictures to the Journal Junior. I sorted all our labels today. We've got 90 covers of Fleischmann's Compressed Yeast—50 of Lion Coffee heads—30 of 9 O'clock Washing Tea. That's how I found the stamps. The baby can say *dümp* for *strümpf*. Asta is copying a story tonight which she wrote some time ago. It's called "The Girl who didn't Obey her Mother." I found the big eraser again today.

Nov. 15, Sunday

Good luck!!!!!!!!

I just got the Journal Junior from Fern, and my picture, "Toddie's Hanged Our Dollies," is in it! I suppose the dollar prize will come pretty soon. Oh I'm so glad. That makes another dollar for mama.

* A juvenile feature of the *Woman's Home Companion*.

I promised to draw Miss Brown a picture and she promised to give me a 2 cent stamp to send the Heading for Aunt Janet's Pages away. I'm glad. Asta's drawing a picture tonight. The baby can hug, kiss, show us where her heart is, and show us her tongue.

"Toddie has hanged our dollies"

Nov. 16, Monday

I got the check for one dollar from the J.J. today. Otherwise no mail. I got the stamp from Miss Brown today. Copied Miss Brown's sheet music called "Dreaming." It's a pretty piece.

Nov. 17, Tuesday

I got a letter from a little eight year girl in Minneapolis complimenting me on my picture in the J.J. Stella got the "Prisoner of Zenda" today. I've read over half. It's splendid. We had our storm windows made on today. I found the pencil I got from Karl Ritschl, today. I'm writing with it. It was a beautiful day.

Nov. 18

A beautiful day but oh! so twisted! Mama bought wood today—$8½ a cord. I wasn't good today, I read too much and didn't work enough. But really I wish I hadn't been so bad.

Stella, Tussy & Asta are over by Fischer's this evening, and I and mama cried.

November 19. A nice day. Thursday.

Today was wash day. I and Stella rung out and hung up nearly all the wash (which was not so very much). The baby is getting cuter all the time.

Nov. 27

I have been down at grandma's. We came home yesterday in time for the Thanksgiving dinner. We had pumpkin pie, potatoes, goose & apples. Oh I was homesick the last day I was at grandma's.

Vivian Ritschl wants 2 dozen place cards painted, a cupid holding a package of rice. She's going to marry soon and I think her mama gives her a party next Tuesday.

I went down to Eggen's to get some paints. I got *Devoe* with 2 yellow, 1 blue, 1 red, & also 5 Calendars at 1 cent a piece. I sell postals to Eggen's, 6 for 25 cents & they sell them for 5 cents straight thru. That makes $.75 credit for our school books, the cost of all was $1.13 I believe. I'll have that paid off pretty soon.

Aunt Magdalene was here. She brought me a blue velvet hat and promised me a black and white checked jumper. I'm so glad!

No mail! We've got the baby up quite late tonight & she's so foxy!* She mocks just everything we do. I was at Ione's tonight & she gave me 2 great sheets of drawing paper. I'm glad of that too.

November 30. A cold windy day.

Fern Fischer came over in the afternoon and brought the Journal Junior. Ione's story is in it. That's the second one she has had in. Perhaps I'll send one pretty soon too.

December 1. A cold, windy, sunny day.

It was zero this morning. Inked 6 postals while the baby was sleeping

---

* Full of tricks—from the German word *faxen*, meaning tomfoolery, tricks.

this afternoon and inked 4 tonight. No mail for me. I wonder when I'm going to hear from McCall's? Stella got "Dotty Dimple at School" today. I've read nearly all of it. It's good.

Dehli's wearing Asta's coat, Asta's wearing Tussy's, and Tussy's wearing the one which used to be Stella's. All of us have coats now except I & mama.

December 2, Wednesday

The baby can say gatz for *katz* which means cat. Sometimes when she has something she oughtn't to have, then we try to take it from her, she says, "Da bow-wow gomt da," for *"Der bow-wow kommt da,"* meaning "There comes the dog." She tries to scare us that way but we can't scare her. She simply isn't afraid of anything.

The baby slept in the morning. In the afternoon I went down to Eggen's to bring a dozen postals down. I took some pretty heavy drawing paper along home too. You get 2 great big sheets for a nickel so I got a nickel's worth. I asked Eggen's clerk whether they had any India Ink in bottles and he told me they had only the sticks. He asked me what kind of bottles they were and I described them to him and he said he could write it down on the order list and get one for me. He is very nice and obliging to customers. I had on my hat that I got from Aunt Magdalene. Eggen's have a great many nice books that I'd like to have. I wish I had a little more money. I hope I'll get a book for Christmas.

No mail at all for me. I do hope McCall's got my story and illustrations, but it almost seems as if they didn't because I haven't heard from them for so long.

We had chicken pot pie for supper. I'm drawing postals again tonight.

December 7, Monday. A cold but bright day.

December 4th was Dehli's birthday. She didn't get anything from us because we didn't have enough time & money to give her anything. Perhaps Asta and Tussy made her some pictures or cards tho.

Oh but I worked this afternoon. I was pegging away at copying a story with the *most horrid* pen. It scratched just like everything. It made me so cross and it was almost a thousand words long, too. I had the baby upstairs with me, too, while I was writing it. She kept climbing on my chair and begging for candy. Finally I had it done, it was the story about the "Punken Hunt" with two boys in it called Fletcher and Buster.

I sent it to the J.J. I wanted to illustrate it at first—because several years ago I sent one too, illustrated & the Editor said I should send another

one illustrated on unruled paper (I had my picture on ruled ink paper)
but I've never tried it since then—but I didn't have time enough so I sent
it off without.

Dear! I've such a lot to do! Xmas presents! (to make without any
money at all, as may be said) Miss Brown's picture! Postals! etc.! etc!

In the afternoon Stella went up to Hasenclever's. She got two big
pieces of cloth to choose from for the bag which they make in school.
Mama couldn't afford it so Mrs. Hasenclever was kind enough to give

her some. One is a piece of silk crepe and the other is cashmere or imitation. Stella will use the silk, I think, and mama gets the cashmere.

Saturday the *Stroh zempra** was at our house. Mama went (?) to
the butcher shop and suddenly a great rattling and clattering was heard
outside the door. The smaller children, (except baby) were in bed but
they came down thinking it was music. I & Stella made believe holding
the door so he (or she!) couldn't get in. Then all at once some candy
came dashing into the room by way of the door and we picked it up.
They were all so scared that they wanted to eat the candy next day! and
Tussy got a nigger baby without a head without noticing or caring in
the least, which she otherwise would have noticed. They were all very
anxious to get to bed (except I & Stella & the baby, of course) but soon

---

* Visits from the *Stroh zempra* were always expected at our house around Christmas
time. He carried candy for good children, and iron chains which he rattled ominously in
order to scare the naughty ones. For very bad children he had a sack full of straw with
which to stuff their insides after they had been cut open. Some adult played this role much
as an American father plays the part of Santa Claus. I do not know the origin of this
custom.

there was a knocking at the window too. Soon mama came with some meat which, by the way, had been bought the other day, and of course Tussy, Asta, Dehli and Howard were very glad to have her there again. They promised to be good. They were too scared to sing.

Tussy is to be a fairy in School for Christmas. We have some wings, twisted wire with cloth sewed over it. Stella had them once when she was in the 4th grade. Papa had painted them then. They are so pretty! Just like real wings.

December 13, Sunday. A fine warm day.

This is Howard's birthday. We had cookies for supper—a special treat —and he got some pictures from us children.

I was up at Dekker's today but Ione wasn't home. Tussy & the baby were with me. We stayed by Dekker's for a while and then I went up to Hasenclever's. None of the Hasenclevers were home either, so I went to Birnbaum's but Lieschen wasn't home either, so I went home again.

When I came home Aunt Magdalene was there. She had been up several days this week. She sewed Dehli and Asta a dress. She didn't quite finish them tho. She finished them down at grandma's and brought them up today, finished. She bought Dehli's cloth. It's a light blue and is a sort of Danish Cloth. Aunt Magdalene slept by us that night.

I've got quite a lot of Xmas Presents done. I've got Dr. Haftel's, Dr. Fraade's, Mr. Harrington's, Ritschl's, and some more are done.

Aunt Magdalene and I went to Eggen's. I asked whether they needed any more postals because if they had some yet I'd wait a while yet, and Mr. Eggen told me that they didn't need any just now, but perhaps later they'd need pretty many later, because there's usually quite a rush for Xmas postals when Xmas draws near.

Cousin Clara was here tonight with her little girl. She gave Howard a nickel & baby a nickel. She bought 2 postals of me too, so I got another 10 cents.

December 18, Friday. A bright sunny day.

It has snowed, and a great deal too, and it was cold, too, for several days. There are not very many wagons to be seen now, there are mostly sleighs. Today is the last day of school this year. Now come the Xmas holidays. They will have no school until January 4th, I think. I've got an order for 2 dozen postals from the Turn-verein and an order for 25 from Mrs. Schmiff.

December 23, Wednesday

Oh goody! goody! goody! We've gotten so many Xmas presents. Monday they started in coming. In the forenoon Henry Hack came over with about 15 cents worth of nuts, a nickel doll with 2 braids for Tussy, and a lot of ribbon "to make doll dresses," he said. But we are going to use the ribbon for hair-ribbons. I made a Christmas present for Mrs. Hack and sent it over with the children.

The same day I went down town to send Ritschl's Xmas presents off. On Monday, too, we got some apples but we haven't the least idea where they came from. The next day we got more apples, almost a bushel, from the Turn-verein and a great big box of underwear from Mrs. Graf. I had sent a present to her too. Today we got 100 lbs. flour from the Ladies' Turner Society. Yesterday I was downtown with Aunt Mary and she bought just piles of things for us. The others didn't see them tho, yet.

Afterwards I went to Eggen's. I bought 10 cents nuts and 15 cents candy. Oh yes, I forgot to say I bought 4 ink tablets and 3 pencil tablets at 3 cents each. Nobody saw these except Stella, I and mama. When I came home again, Mrs. Harrington rang up by phone. Stella went to the phone and Mrs. Harrington told her that I should come down Wednesday afternoon. I went to bed very happy.

Today we washed dishes and cleaned up a little and off I started for Mrs. Harrington's. Mrs. Joliffe was there when I came. Mrs. Harrington just wants me to go to school. It was almost noon when Mrs. Joliffe went so Mrs. Harrington asked me to stay to lunch. She told me to go to the music room. I went in and sat on the couch. Mr. Harrington came in too, and he asked me how old I was and other things. I had noticed several pretty oil paintings in the room and was quite sure that papa had made them. Mr. Harrington told me that papa had made them, and the decorations of the room too. He said he was sorry that papa was not living. He said it was so hard to get anyone to do the decorating. Of course I had to cry. I tried to keep the tears from coming but I couldn't. I sat as if in a dream. I don't know, I felt so funny, but I found Mr. Harrington leading me into the dining room with his arm around me. I managed to stop crying just enough that I could see straight but it took pretty long for the tears to clear away. Mr. Harrington didn't eat anything, I think. Mrs. Harrington said he wasn't feeling well, and he looked as if he were sick. They had mince pie but I didn't care for any. I liked the honey bread best of all.

Oh yes, before lunch I phoned to mama telling her that Mrs. Harrington wanted me to stay for lunch & that she wanted to buy me a coat. After dinner we went off. We got a nice red coat, half tight-fitting & butterfly sleeves. Then Mrs. Harrington got me a skirt, a woolen one to make shorter, 6 linen handkerchiefs, the baby a go-cart for 75 cents, and hair ribbons, a whole lot. She also got some outing-flannel, pink and blue, for petticoats for me. Then we went to Eggen's where Mrs. Harrington bought a wagon and horse for Howard. It cost 25 cents.

Coming out of Eggen's store I said to Mrs. Harrington, "How can we ever thank you enough?" And she said, "Oh, be a good girl and study all you can and be neat, that'll pay for it." I told her I'd send some of my pictures down too. She told me to come down often and see her, and phone any time I want. I'm so happy!

Oh yes, and Aunt Klaus was here—and she brought a great pat of butter, some milk and 2 cheese cakes! We had pea soup today. Tussy has been down at Nora's for two days to take care of Cousin Dolores. She got six cents yesterday.

December 25

This is Christmas day at last and we have the most presents! *

Asta, Dehli and Howard went to bed at 7 o'clock. They were very much excited. I & Stella fixed up the Christmas tree in the evening, and a good deal of trouble we had too. The tree was crooked and looked as if it would tumble over any minute. Finally we found some strong cord and got it all right. We put on apples, cookies, candy and candles. We hadn't hardly any ornaments but I like it better if the trees are decorated with eatables than all such things that can't be eaten.

December 30

Yesterday I took 12 postals for the Turnverein up to Hershl's. Paula Hershl showed me her presents. She's got some pretty ones.

Yesterday evening I sketched mine, Tussy's big doll, Asta's small doll, Dehli's small doll and Tussy's small doll, and I & Stella were just admiring Tussy's ten-cent doll's jacket when down went the doll and off went a leg. Oh but I was scared! Tussy cried over it this morning but I gave her some blue velvet which Mrs. Hasenclever had given to me and she was quite satisfied.

The wind is roaring around the house like everything. No mail.

* From friends and neighbors.

December 31. A Happy New Year!

This is Sylvester Eve, and we children have been dripping candle.

We got coal today and the whole house is black. In the cellar the whole table and floor are as black as ink.

I brought papa's oil painting of roses up to Hershl's for the Turnverein.

It is a New Year's present. We had oysters, crackers, coffee, apple cake, and cinnamon cake for supper as a special New Year's treat. I don't know whether we'll stay up until midnight.

1909

January 7

On New Year's I & Stella stayed up to 10 o'clock. We would have stayed up longer but it was so cold in the house. It's pretty cold too to-night in here, too.

Last Sunday Nora, Aunt Mary & Aunt Magdalene were here. Judy came too, & in the evening we acted "The Katzenjammer Family." I was "Fritz," Stella was "Hans," and Judy was "Mrs. Katzenjammer," she being the fattest.

On Monday Aunt Magdalene came and stayed for dinner. In the afternoon she started to sew Dehli's dress from the cloth she got from Ritschl's. The next day we sewed Asta's dress from the cloth, too, that she got from Ritschl's. We also made in the same day 2 aprons, one for Asta and the other for Dehli, and started a waist for Tussy. It is a party-colored plaid which Aunt Mary bought. The next day Aunt Magdalene started my blue dress. Oh it looks just as pretty! It's quite the prettiest dress I've had for a long, long time and I'm awfully glad.

I copied a story yesterday and illustrated it. I've only got 1 stamp left and that looks pretty bad unless I'll be so lucky as to get some or find some more pretty soon.

I made mama a hair receiver out of the yellow silk I got from Mrs. Hasenclever.

"Am I going to school or not?" I haven't the least idea. Oh dear, I do wish I could go to school. I believe I'd jump for joy if I only could.

February ? Friday

This is just an awful snowstorm, but beautiful! Why the world is a regular fairy land! Our garden house looks as clean and dainty as any fairy castle, I think, for the whole floor is covered with snow. The evergreens in Logan's garden are just laden down with thick ridges of pearly snow, and big white mountains can be seen almost everywhere. I & Tussy went to get the milk. We were dressed quite warm, with shawls over our faces, but still the wind took our breath away. I rather enjoyed it though, for some reason, I don't know why. I think it is because the landscape is so beautiful.

I'm writing this upstairs, the baby's sleeping. Mama's baking bread today. Yesterday we ironed and the day before we ironed and on Tuesday we washed. I stayed home Tuesday morning to help mama wash. The baby hasn't been feeling very well these last few days. She is a little feverish.

Today is the basket ball game I guess, the high school against some other team. They're going to write the high school yells on the board today. By the way, have I said already that I'm going to high school? I am, and what's more, I'm going in the forenoon and the afternoon! Last year I went only in the afternoon. I have Miss Meadows for Rhetoric, Miss Dillon for Ancient History & English Composition, and Mr. Jellick for physical Geography.

* * *

"Great Grandmama's Chest."

(NOTE:—Several months are unrecorded at this point. The old ledger which I had been using was filled and apparently I had nothing to write in for a while.

During this period my work had been appearing regularly in the Journal Junior, and the editor, Mae Harris Anson, had asked me to do a series of ten full-page drawings. I worked out a story called "Robby Bobby in Mother Goose Land," and with Miss Anson's acceptance of it came a package containing 20 sheets of Bristol board, several bottles of India ink, pencils, pens, erasers, a ruler and a draughtsman's triangle. The lack of these materials must have been evident to Miss Anson, for I used any paper I could find, had no way of drawing right angles and often cleaned off my pencil marks with bread crumbs. My father had been a painter, not a draughtsman, and I had never before seen a triangle, Bristol board or even art gum.)

* * *

April 8, Thursday

I didn't go to school today because mama wasn't well. Ione Dekker got herself a notebook just like this, and I bought this without telling Stella and the rest.

Mrs. Harrington phoned today and told us that if we'd come down to her house tomorrow, she would pay for us all to go to the "Scenic." I made 4 place cards for Mrs. Schmiff and she paid me 20 cents; 10 cents more than I asked for:—hence my boldness in buying this notebook without asking mama! Bought a pint of oysters and got a check for $1.50 from the J.J. for my "Lou's Soap Bubble Party."

April 9, Friday

Sent Prenzel Bros., Dr. Dressler, and Dr. Fraade an Easter present, and gave one to Mrs. Harrington. Stella, Tussy and I dyed eggs tonight and succeeded admirably.

April 11, Easter Sunday

Got up early this morning and hid eggs. We got the J.J today and I've got a picture in it again. I put all the prints of our drawings which were in the J.J. into a book.

April 13

Am at Ione's now. We've studied our Ancient and Rhetoric. We *"schnattered"* half the time tho.

Received $1.00 from Mr. Prenzel in return for the Easter present I sent him. I really didn't expect anything in return. I just sent the Easter present because they receipted our meat bill from last year.

April 15, Thursday

Miss Dillon gave us a "poetical" speech. She insisted that poets were necessary in the world; that their duty was to point out beauties of Nature, and that we would be too material-minded without them. Some of the kids simply wouldn't agree with her but I do.

Rocked the baby to sleep before I went to school and learned part of the memory work of Antony's funeral oration for this afternoon. Finished the 5th of my chart of Robby Bobby drawings for the J.J. tonight. $25 to get! If I could only keep it for myself, but such a thing is not to be thought of. Mama went to Turning School to-night.*

* Turning School—the free gymnasium classes conducted by the *Turnverein* at the Turner Hall.

April 18, Sunday Evening

The baby is wearing the green lawn panel-front dress I made for her. She can sing so many songs, "Oh you Pussy Willow," "Rock-a-by baby," "Be as still as any mouse," *"Mit den Füsschen trap trap trap,"* "Barber Shop," "Ring around the roses," and "Walking on the green grass."

Stella's Drawing

Stella has a picture in the Journal Junior; it's her first published picture.

April 20, Tuesday

Stella got her dollar check.

We had to write a literary description for English Composition today. Mine's perfectly silly. It's so sentimental at the end.

Splendid warm weather all the time. Spring beauties are out already. I feel like going in the woods tonight but I don't know whether I may. Got a yard of china silk to trim my hat with. I'm so tired I can hardly keep my eyes open. Goodnight.

April 22, Thursday

I trimmed Tussy's hat. It costs too much to have them trimmed at the milliners. Started Stella's the same evening and finished it this morning. I've got a temporary infatuation tonight, a "flower and plant" craze. Am collecting as many flower's and plant's names as I am interested in. Made baby a guimpe and hoodie, and am making her an apron.

April 24, Saturday

A stormy, sunny, calm, cool, and warm day. It's a regular April day, thunder, lightning, rain and sunshine. Trimmed Asta's and Dehli's hats this morning and trimmed mine this evening. Oh I'm tired, my back aches from standing so long. Sewed the baby's apron done. Guess I'll have a sailor dress made from the blue-checked cloth Aunt Mary gave me for my birthday. We got some rolls from the bakery but they were sugary mixed with salt and we couldn't eat them so we didn't have much for supper.

I think Mr. Winkler* would look better if he had whiskers. I don't know whether he would, but it seems so to me.

April 28, Wednesday

A dreary, cold, rainy day. I stayed home yesterday afternoon because mama didn't feel well. The baby had a whim today and ate molasses and salt together while mama wasn't looking. It's a wonder she didn't get sick.

Oh I think Lowell can describe nature beautifully, the June day and the morning on which Sir Launfal set out, for instance. Yesterday evening, while I was studying my Ancient, I fell asleep and had the most delicious dream about Miss Dillon! No wonder, when she is so delicious herself! I finished "Polly Oliver's Problems" last night. It certainly is a good book.

April 31, Friday

Yesterday Stella stayed home, and today Tussy did, because mama isn't feeling well.

May 5, Wednesday

This is a regular July day. I'm almost roasting. I got our bonnets and starched them. I guess I'll iron them this afternoon.

Mama is sick since last night. Dr. Fraade was here, and Mrs. Kirschner staid until about 11 o'clock. Tussy, Stella and I are staying home today because mama can't work. I was so scared I was trembling all over. Mama is up a little now but I guess she'll go to bed this afternoon again.

The first of May the children made paper flowers (for May baskets) because it was too cold for wild flowers. The next day was Sunday. I had the first of my Robby Bobby series in the J.J. and Tussy had a picture in it. Tussy received her check, $1.00.

* A high-school teacher.

Mama lay down in bed this afternoon and slept for about 2 hours. Howard came home from school because he didn't feel well. He's alright now, tho, and has gone with Tussy and Dehli to pick flowers. I and Stella washed up the dining room and the kitchen floors.

Aunt Magdalene was here the other day and brought a dress for baby and a white petticoat for me from Aunt Mary.

Tussy's Drawing

May 6, Thursday

I'm tired! I and Stella did the washing and we had the biggest wash! Tonight we spaded and raked and shoveled, making gardens. We bought 8 packets of flower seeds today, Candytuft, Nasturtiums, Mignonette, Petunia, Hyacinth beans, ageratum, portulaca and carnation.

Mama has been up part of the day but she feels almost worse than she did yesterday. Still I think she feels a little stronger on the whole. Tussy, Stella and I were home again today, again. I'd like to go to school tomorrow but I don't know whether I can.

The radishes and lettuce in our hotbed are growing nicely.

May 7, Friday

Mama's face is quite swollen and she hasn't slept at all today. She can't go to sleep, but a little while ago she lay down in bed and I guess she's sleeping now. We got a great lump of butter, and a pail of cheese and cream, mixed, and two pails of sweet milk from grandma this morning.

May 9, Sunday

Stella, Tussy, and Asta brought a great basket full of flowers yesterday.

There were marsh marigolds, violets, bloodroots, Dutchman's breeches, and yellow bells, and I sketched one or more of every kind. Dehli made some too, and Howard too.

Another one of the Robby Bobby charts is almost done. I worked on it yesterday. Made Dehli a paper doll and some dresses. We got the Journal Junior, and the second set of Robby Bobby is in it today. Tussy wrote a story to-night called "The Magic Parasol." Today's the first time for a long time that I drew something for my own pleasure. Otherwise it is always to sell. We've all got a cold from the sudden change of temperature several days ago.

May 10, Monday

Gave away paper doll furniture* for following:

Swing to Asta.................In return for writing a diary for 3 months.
Stove to Dehli................. "   "   "   "   "   "   "   "   "
Bed to Tussy.................. "   "   " washing dishes.
Washstand to Fern............. "   "   " 1 fashion book.
Piano to Kurt................. "   "   " 30 sheets writing paper.

   Then I promised:

Sewing machine to Dehli........In return for writing 10 stories.
   "   "   to Asta......... "   "   "   "   "   "
   "   "   to Tussy........ "   "   "   "   5   "
Swing to Fern.................In return for giving me comic papers.
Piano to Asta & Dehli...........In return for drawing a picture in their
                               diaries every day & for illustrating an
                               event of the day.
Piano to Tussy.................In return for cleaning upstairs, steps &
                               halls.
Washstand to Dehli & Asta.......In return for taking piano lessons from
                               me, provided they are good.
Stove to Asta.................For doing what I say.

Queer enough! But I want to see what they can do.

I got about 6 or 7 fashion books from Fern because I gave her about 3 pieces of paper furniture. Went to school again to-day. Got thru alright even if I did stay out 3 days.

May 12, Wednesday

Have all the pictures inked of Set 6 except one. That I have in pencil

---
* We made elaborate doll furniture out of cardboard.

but King Cole has to sneeze so I want to wait until I see somebody sneeze to get the expression.

Howard was playing band yesterday evening, playing on a stick, and he fell down. He ran the stick into his mouth, and we put him to bed. This morning we called for Dr. Fraade, and I stayed home from school. It looks just as if Howard had the mumps, his face is so swollen. Finished Howard's sailor blouse. Mama did most of it but I did the sleeves.

Dehli is writing her diary already.

May 13, Thursday

Went to school the whole day. Howard's cheek is still swollen. Not much doing, that is, not that I care to tell.

May 15, Saturday

Things do look a little brighter now, for as I only want to write of the brighter sides of every day, things haven't gone near as smooth as they look written out on these pages. The buzzing in mama's ears has quite stopped, tho of course she is not well yet; her nerves are still weak, nevertheless she can sleep better than usual. I think it is because she goes out in the fresh air so much. She cannot work much; we have to wash dishes almost every evening after school. Howard's cheek is gradually coming to its normal size. Otherwise we feel quite well.

It's perfectly splendid outdoors now. The trees have such dainty green leaves, and their branches look like sprays or plumes of downy green. The grass is green too, and some plum trees have actually started to blossom!

Yesterday when I came home from school mama lay down, and I started on my Robby Bobby Charts because I got a letter yesterday from Mae Harris Anson. She said I should send the rest soon. I worked at them today too, and have them almost done. Stella and Tussy scrubbed but I came off quite easy because I had the Robby Bobby sets. This ink seems to be getting lighter and lighter—and I intend to send them off Monday. Stella won't let me stay up any longer. She's scolding, so Goodnight.

May 17, Monday

I stayed home from school this morning doing my Robby Bobby sets. They are off at last. Now I can rest for a while, I hope.

May 18, Tuesday

Yesterday evening Fern practiced some duets with me. She can play pretty good. We had a thunder storm last night. Johnnie came last night and took off our storm windows.

Guess I'll study my rules of punctuation altho I don't see any sense in studying such rules. A person's common sense ought to tell a person, when a comma, semi-colon, dash etc. ought to be used. Yesterday I tried to sketch Mr. Winkler but every time I came about to the nose he moved. Fern brought three comic papers.

This evening after supper we watched the clouds. They were beautiful and looked like a giant popcorn kernel which had burst.

Thursday evening

Aunt Magdalene came this forenoon, stayed for dinner and started to sew Tussy's empire dress. It's quite far done now. Aunt Mary came after school and brought some light green cloth for Stella, and lawn and insertion for a dress for baby's birthday.

Dehli is writing in her diary quite regularly and I'm glad of it. It's such fun to read her queer accounts. Goodnight, Goodnight.

May 21, Friday

One nasturtium, 2 hyacinth beans, and a great many sweet peas have sprouted in our gardens. Everything is so beautiful out doors now, I just hate to be in the house. The trees are full of foliage, and apple and plum blossoms are opening everywhere so that the air is full of fragrance.

I do wish I could go to Summer Drawing School at Minneapolis altho it's not very likely to happen. It is from June 15 to July 17 and costs $15 for one Study. I think, if I had the chance, I'd take Composition. It includes or is composed of, I don't exactly remember which—drawing from nature and the figure. Wouldn't that be splendid? I'm thinking so much about that that I even dreamt of drawing last night. I was to pose, and I asked the teacher whether they couldn't draw me from the front because my profile was not good. Not that I mean to say I'm pretty from the front, but that the shape of my nose cannot be seen so well as from the side.

Fern and Kurt Fischer are here to-night playing paper dolls as usual. Aunt Magdalene is still at our house, sewing.

My head is so full of new ideas that I've got the beginnings of a great

ROBBY-BOBBY IN MOTHER GOOSE LAND

Drawn by Wanda Hazel Gag, Ninth Grade,
High School, New Ulm, Minn.

By and by, Robby-Bobby peeped through a fence and saw a pretty little girl, raking in the garden. He threw off his royal mantle and jumped over the fence. When he came near, he said: "Isn't it a beautiful day?"

The little girl threw down her rake, and with a pout turned her back on Robby-Bobby. "No," she said, with a stamp of her foot, "it isn't a beautiful day at all. It's perfectly horrid." "Oh!" said Robby-Bobby. And then, "Oh, I see—you're 'Contrary Mary'!"

"May I see your garden?" said Robby-Bobby most politely. "No," snapped Mary, and she turned away and began to sprinkle her flowers, as if no one were near. "Won't you give me a flower?" Robby-Bobby said again. "No, you shan't have a single flower," said Mary and went on sprinkling.

"How very, very contrary she is," said Robby-Bobby to himself. Then suddenly he laughed to himself, and said, "I know what to do." Then turning his back on Mary, he said with a truly royal air, "I don't want to see your gardens anyway. I don't s'pose they're worth showing to princes anyway."

"... dy are, too," snapped Mary. "You've got to see 'em now, anyway," and ... him around and showed him all her garden. "Well, anyway, I don't care for ... wers. We've splendid ones at ho——"

"You shall have some," said Contrary Mary. "Mine are the best in the world," and she filled Robby-Bobby's hands with blossoms. Robby-Bobby thanked her most politely and went on his way, whistling gaily.

A Robby-Bobby Page from the Journal Junior

many and the ends of hardly any! They whirl around at a great rate with
no destination seemingly; but they have anyhow. At least I hope so. Oh
I wish I wouldn't have to work and go to school for a day or two so I
could sketch and draw and paint, and paint and draw and sketch, until
I had pictures of spring landscapes, birds, and flowers before the chance
is over.

I'm thru with "The Real Diary of a Real Boy." Since Tussy's seen it
she's all fire and flame to keep a diary too.

May 25, Tuesday (in school)

Yesterday was baby's birthday. She was two years old and got 2 presents; a paper doll outfit from me and a bag of candy from Fern Fischer.
She took the paper doll to bed with her and this morning the head and
hands were bent, and a foot was off.

Mr. Winkler was here a moment ago watching me because I talked to
Daisy. I wish he'd come again. I want to see the shape of his face a little
better. I intend to draw a picture of all the teachers before vacation.

May 29 (in school)

I started to draw Mr. Winkler. I do wonder what he thinks. Almost
every time I looked at him he saw me. I could not help from smiling and
had much to do to keep from laughing.

Later:—I tried to sketch Mr. Winkler again and he must have noticed
something, his face had such a queer expression on his face.

June 3, Thursday

This afternoon I didn't go to school because mama didn't feel well. She
was in bed nearly all day. I'm hungry. We had only doughnuts, beefsteak and butter bread this evening, and I don't care for beefsteak.

June 6, Sunday

Tussy made a picture to send to the J.J. Stella's picture is in again, and
the 6th of my series is in too.

June 11, Friday

High School closed to-day. Gave back my 3 books to Mr. Jolliffe.* In
the evening mama and I went to the Commencement Exercises.

* Superintendent of Schools. He allowed us to use some of his school books.

June 17

There is to be a total eclipse of the sun at 6.15. We've smoked some glasses so we can watch it. They say it will be as dark as night.

June 21, Sunday

June 15 the Drawing School at Minneapolis began. Oh how I wish I could have gone! Stella got a letter from a girl in Minneapolis. She complimented Stella on her drawing. Ate only doughnuts and coffee for supper to-day. Stella had a picture in the J.J to-day. The 8th of my series was in too.

Beginning of summer. Guess Stella, Tussy and I are going to go down to grandma's to-night to stay for two or three days. Made 2 water-color sketches of roses, one yellow and one pink.

6:40:—Arrived at grandma's about an hour ago. It's awfully hot.

June 22, Monday

Got up at about 5:15 this morning. Aunt Mary went to Rosen's so we made the phonograph go, and we danced to the music to amuse ourselves. Had strawberry gelatine with oranges. I can drink all the milk I want. After our work was done Stella and I spent most of our time looking thru Uncle Josie's telescope.

July 7, Wednesday

We came home from grandma Thursday, June 24, because mama didn't feel well.

I have two rooms in the attic cleaned and am at the third. Stella and I are to have the middle room.* Talk of being glad. We're to have bookshelves, window seats and everything; Stella is our carpenter you know, very celebrated the world over. I am to have the contract of decorating everything, handpainted calendars, etc.

Perhaps I go to grandma's with baby this week. Then for cream, milk and good meals! Made 115 place cards in about 2 days. Wish I could keep the money to buy dresses with, but what's the use of dreaming all the time? Am reading "A Gentle Knight of Old Brandenburg." It's a peach. Went up to Ione's last night. Ione is embroidering some pretty centerpieces.

July 8, Thursday

Tussy and Dehli went down to Grandma. Fern, Stella, and I went out

---

* This had been our father's studio.

to the cemetary and worked for about two hours. We didn't have anything decent for dinner so I'm still hungry.

July 12, Monday

It was a bright and sunny day yesterday but an awfully miserable day for me on the whole. I wanted to go along up to the park but Asta wouldn't stay home so I had to stay. Then I got the plate-holders filled but the kodak wouldn't work. Later I had to take care of Howard and Baby. I was so provoked with them that I went upstairs and had a good long bawl.

Stella went down to grandma's with Uncle Josie. We have so much milk that we can't drink it all. We have some of Grandma's dairy butter. I like grandma's butter better than creamery butter. I work in the attic just about every day. I have four small centerpieces done. Fern gave me the Sunday papers and stayed over night.

July 19, Monday. At grandma's

This is a perfectly sweet day, summer breezes, little bits of windy sky, and fluffy strings and snatches of clouds. Got up at about 8:00 this morning. Was awfully tired. Had breakfast, dried dishes, combed myself and went down to the river with Dehli. Waded around for a while. That was fun, all soft mud and sharp stones outside—and the soft, warm, plashy water, so deliciously wet and smooth, in the river. After that we went up and sat around for a while until I had a notion to go and pick currants. We picked a saucer full and ate them with milk and sugar. After dinner I sat down and wrote this up, and here I am, with the dishes to be washed, Aunt Magdalene going to town to sew, and Dehli to be combed, so Goodbye for the time.

August 3, Tuesday

I'm learning to swim. We've been in the river Wednesday, Friday, Saturday and Monday. I can swim a little with a board. I must confess I am a little homesick for Baby.

For August 1, Sunday

Aunt Magdalene and I took a boatride for about an hour. Oh, it was perfectly splendid. A "moony, spooney" night. When we came back we sang, mostly Indian songs; and I put my hair down with a band across my forehead like an Indian maid's.

I am practicing to draw lady's heads. My tan dress is done except the hooks and eyes.

Aug. 9

Wednesday evening Aunt Magdalene, Asta, Dehli and I came home, and Stella and Tussy went along down the same evening.

Our room on the third story is quite done; except curtains, window seat etc., of course. They shall have to wait ever so long I suppose, because I can't get them without money and that's all there is to it. I've finished two centerpieces. One's perfectly awful and the other's awfully small. I wish I could have carried out the furnishings in one or two colors but that would have cost more, and I have to be satisfied with a rainbow-furnished room.

A picture of mine was in the J.J. last Sunday and I received the dollar check to-day. We washed and ironed to-day. Baby is wearing bloomers and she looks awfully sweet in them. I'm reading "The Virginian." It's perfectly splendid, especially *the* Virginian. I'm over half and I don't even know what his name is. Vivian Ritschl was here today and asked me to make about 50 cards.

August 30, Monday

Feel splendid tonight. First day of school and I'm really going to High School again. Could almost jump some twenty odd feet in the air for joy. Am going to take 5 subjects. Ancient by Miss Dillon, Agriculture and Commercial Arithmetic by Mr. Winkler, Algebra by Miss Lee, and Biology by Mr. Evans. I'm sure I don't know what to do tho, because I need two books, and one costs $1.25 and the other $.75.

Friday I walked out to Ritschl's. Stayed for supper and had an automobile ride—my first one—nearly to town and back.

August 31, Tuesday

Went to Jolliffe's after school and got four school books. Now I have all except the biology. *I denk ich gehe zu bett, goote nacht, Ladies und shentlemens.*

September 3, Friday

How-do-you-do, Diary; pretty cool weather, isn't it? I have a biology book now. Mr. Jolliffe gave me one to use. I like agriculture so far. Commercial Arithmetic is what I need. I'm awfully slow at adding etc. but I hope this will help my "mathematical genius" to get to work.

Impersonated an Indian maid Wednesday evening. Whoop! La! "I'll wear feathers on my head, Paint my face an Indian red—" I look pretty "Indianish" except my nose, of course. Please don't call this conceit, because my hair *is* black and straight, and my face and hands *are* dark without a doubt; and that's nothing to be particularly proud of, is it?

Miss Dillon asked me to make 2 dozen cards—with a Dutch girl or boy on each. Made 8 in pencil to-night. Easy as pie. Uncle Josie brought about 5 or 6 water melons, some mushmelons and ever so many apples today.

I am "composing" a " " " " "song" " " " ". Those quotation marks are there to show how far from a song it is. Have the accompaniment for both hands now. Suppose it sounds like sauerkraut mixed with cheese. Now I still have the words to get. Wish I had some cloth to make a Dutch collar with.

September 5, Sunday

How do you do? Fine day to-day. Drew 12 pictures in my birthday book. The birthday book is going to be one in which people write their names and birthdays.

Have asked mama to wake me early to-morrow morning so that I can paint Miss Dillon's place cards before school. I have noticed that Miss Dillon doesn't only smile with her eyes and mouth but with her whole face, even her eyebrows.

Baby and I studied biology to-day. She asked me the name of nearly everything she came across and pronounced it after me. She's certainly inquisitive enough. Wish I had a Dutch collar. Of course there are a great many more wishes; but that's the only one I wish to write of now. Oh yes, one more, I wish I had my angleworms studied. But I haven't, so here goes——! Goodnight.

September 8, Wednesday

Damp and cool this morning. Don't know my biology. Don't care a snap. I'll guess.

Stayed home this afternoon because mama was in bed. She didn't feel well. Hope I can keep on going to school all this year.

Two Pencil Drawings Made at the Age of Twelve

Wanda and Stella

Wanda at Ten Months

8:15 p.m.—Things went criss cross, but what's the use of "troubling trouble"? Besides this book is not supposed to contain the dark sides of things. Have learned my Ancient & Agriculture. Have my Algebra rules to learn. Algebra isn't only the simple "X" matter. Eight other letters of the alphabet have stepped upon the platform, waiting for recognition. (Pardon the poor metaphor.)

Have 19 pictures in my Birthday Book.

September 9, Thursday

Had a CAT-astrophe this morning at about 5 o'clock. Logan's cat always comes over to our house. This morning she went into the cellar (to catch mice perhaps) and she jumped on the stand we keep our butter and things on, and the result was—perfectly awful. A two-quart jar of pickles smashed, pail of molasses spilled, pail of milk spilled, about a half-dozen eggs smashed. About two pounds of butter, not injured. (Special report for the Diary Record)!

$$\text{Let } X = \text{cat}$$
$$\text{Let } 2X = \text{stand}$$
$$\text{Let } 3X = \text{food}$$
$$X + 2X + 3X = 6X \text{ or the catastrophe etc.}$$

Walked to school with Mr. Winkler.* He complimented me on Miss Dillon's place cards, and Miss Dillon gave me the money for them. He said when I'm a great artist *(when)* I shouldn't forget him.

My " " "song" " " is progressing. Have added another part. Have 3 different parts now, but words I have none.

September 10, Friday

Didn't study much last night. Just played piano, talked and sang. Practiced speed drawing, for fun. Made one girl in $2\frac{1}{2}$ min. another in $3\frac{1}{3}$ min. and another in $2\frac{3}{4}$ min.

XXX stands for the criss cross time we had at home this noon. Mama was in bed and we had the worst time getting dinner and giving the kids their things. To-day Mr. Evans really laughed. He is getting a little jollier, it seems.

About 10:30 p.m.—Had a fierce commercial lesson. Adding, + ding, + ding, + ding, just about all there was to it, but hard! I felt "flippety flop" and was glad when Mr. Winkler told me I might take my seat.

---

* Mr. Winkler and Mr. Evans roomed across the street from us at Logan's.

Worked like everything at home, and drew and painted after supper. My birthday book has 24 pictures in already. I intend to make a rhyme for every month. Monday is the beginning of the Fair, I believe. Want to hunt up some drawings, and paste them up by that time, too. If I had cloth I'd like to make myself a Dutch collar.

Asta is sleeping on her chair, and Dehli's blinking so that her eyes look like one of those worn out lanterns which flicker because the air whips thru the cracks. Stella has 30 examples to do to-night. If I were one of those kids I'd kick. Asta is toppling about like a May bug trying to get to bed without interrupting her dreams. Goodnight.

September 11, Saturday

A bitter-sweet day. Mama is still not feeling well. Worked and ran up and down town. The sweet part of the day is that one of my wishes is starting to grant itself—I'm going to get a Dutch collar. I have to make it myself. Cut the pattern and cut the goods to-day.

Practiced speed drawing to-night, in pencil. Made about a dozen. One took me 35 seconds.

I sorted drawings to-night for the Fair. I haven't hardly any that I made this year. That's because I did more painting and drawing for other people. Oh dear, I wish I could earn a pile of money so that I could draw a little for myself, and so that I could go to school without having to think of quitting. I can't see why some kids don't like school. I can scarcely wait for the Monday's.

I have often wondered whether I had a style of my own, in drawing. The other day a lady told me they could always tell when they saw my pictures that I drew them. I wonder if other people think so too. I wonder why all people can't draw. I don't see why they can't guide their pencil to draw just as easily as to write. I needn't be proud of my writing. Wonder whether I'll ever learn to write so that other people can read it. Guess I've wondered enough to-night. There is this room to clean up and that'll take some time, for Asta & Dehli have been cutting paper. Goodnight.

September 12, Sunday. Rainy day.

Some people are here to buy an oil painting. Why *do* we have to sell pictures? I feel as if I wanted to take all the paintings and put them somewhere so that no one could come and buy them. While I was at grandma's this summer, mama sold one too, and I just know we didn't get enough for it, so there! People seem to think because we have so many pictures* it doesn't matter to us whether we have a few more or less. But it does, for pictures are not like money.

Our Fair drawings are just about done. We'll have about 8 charts this year. Read over part of my diary and found the place where I wrote of Mr. Winkler's having a moustache (April 24). Oh Smiling Billikens! Such thoughts!

Uncle Frank came this evening and I asked him to play guitar, and he did. Such delicious music. Then we played the High School Song— I on the piano, of course—and Stella and I sang. Then we played another song—a Bohemian song, I guess—and that went a little better. Gee, I wish I could play guitar. Mr. Winkler ought to join us with his flute. I'm sure it would sound "dandiful"—almost as good as the Bohemian band down in Goosetown.** Oh glorious palm-trees, such conceit (?).

September 15

Yesterday the Agricultural class went out to the Fair. Daisy and I went to a tent in which was a real Japanese. Mr. Winkler bought Daisy and me an ice cream cone. While we were looking at some other things we met Asta and Dehli. Asta, seeing my cone said, "Aw!" I suppose she thought I bought it. Don't know whether Mr. Winkler heard her or not; anyway, he bought cones for Asta and Dehli too. It was awfully good of him, and besides mama told us we could have only a dime to spend between us 5 girls and that would have been pretty hard to manage. Got a first prize for my drawings.

Guess I'll study my agriculture. Don't want to get stuck tomorrow. To-day I stood there like the blank space in a bank note, feeling pretty cheap.

Sept. 17, Friday

I stayed home this morning—wash day. Went to school this afternoon. After supper I did my algebra. Then I started in to study my Ancient— and the rest is all a blur because I fell asleep right in the midst of the Assyrians.

Sept. 18, Saturday

Poor diary; nearly done with you, am I not? I'd write piles but I have

* Paintings done by my father.
** New Ulm's German-Bohemian settlement.

to save space, because I'd hate to quit writing for a time and I don't don't know whether I can get another book right away. Ironed to-day. My Dutch collar wish has granted itself. Am ever so glad.

Sept. 19, Sunday

I dressed up like an Indian maid again. It's piles of fun acting Indian-ish, with the "heap big chief" and "paleface" etc. Judy's here to-night. She promised to give me a nickel if I made two paper dolls. 5 cents toward my diary. Heigh-ho.

Sept. 20, Monday

Oh glories, joys, beauties, victory etc. etc. etc! I'll get a new diary! Talk of being glad! (Excuse silly language.)

Guess I'll try and make our apple tree bear fruit by pounding rusty nails in the trunk, and perhaps I'll graft or bud it too. I simply love Ag-riculture. Went to school all day to-day. Thought I'd have to stay home because mama didn't feel well, but I'm in school anyway. If I can only keep on going to school—. It looks dark and dreary outdoors, and I feel as blue as the old dress Stella wears at home. Talk *of* blues.

Sept. 23, Thursday

Governor Johnson's funeral is to-day. Observed the day in school.

Sept. 25, Saturday

Drew and inked 2 J.J. charts, $10. Let Miss Lee and Miss Dillon write in my birthday book. Miss Lee and Miss Dillon asked how much I'd charge for making another like it.

Am in the Glee Club. Talk of glee! I sing second soprano.

> Oh diary, ah diary,
> The sentimental end hath come.
> It hath come.
> Oft have I written in here, with scribblings and
> chicken scratches untidy——

That's enough. People will laugh at me if I go on this way. I bought the new diary so I'll have to quit in here. "Oh love, how can I leave thee?" But I'll have to whether I want to or not. The space is getting smaller. I dreamt Mr. Winkler played violin. Goodbye, dear darling Diary.

*   *   *

Sept. 26, Sunday

How do you do, my new Diary? I really must try to keep you a little neater than I did the old one. Perfectly splendid day. Went down town and got you and got the Journal Junior. Tried drawing with pastel yesterday. Wish I could knit good, so I could knit myself one of those high-necked sweaters. I have piles of things to do as usual, but never mind, I'm not likely to neglect *you*.

Sept. 27, Monday

After supper Fern and Judy came over and we acted our play. Dehli was Napanee and I was Arrah Wanna. We dressed up like an Indian, of course, and I acted "heap big Indian Chief's daughter."

Got awfully low in Algebra—62. Got 98 in Agriculture, that's one consolation. No wonder, that deals with material things while Algebra is vague x's and y's and z's. Ancient is a happy medium between those two; it's really true, but it's true in such a far-off mysterious way.

Programme next Friday. I'm in the Athena Literary Society. The other society is called the Thalian Society. The society who has the most points at the end of the year will get a banner. When I'm on the program I hope they'll give me an original story to write. I hate debates, and recitations 5 miles long are just as bad.

Howard had his hair cut. Looks so queer. Stella and I made supper to-night. Fried potatoes, and I put too much water in them and they got all wrong. They only ate about half of them, too. If I'd have an extra nickel I'd buy Dehli a diary, she writes such interesting things.

For want of anything else to do, I shall describe our High School teachers.

Miss Lee has beautiful dark hair. She teaches Algebra and is very "easy."

> She wears some glasses, "pinchers" too,
>   And is rarely ever seen
> On the street or up at school
>   Without wearing something green.

Miss Dillon has charge of the Glee Club. When she starts to sing her voice reminds me of a butterfly poising its quivering wings for flight. When I first saw Miss Dillon I thought she was one of the High School girls. She teaches Ancient and English Comp.

Miss Allen has light hair. She doesn't teach any of my subjects.

Mr. Winkler wears a curl at one side of his head on top, and he often wears green ties. He plays the clarionet and he's quite fond of farming. He teaches Agriculture, Commercial Arithmetic and Book keeping. He's got black hair and pale blue eyes, which looks rather queer.

Mr. Evans is certainly very "easy." When I first saw him he seemed as young as one of the High School boys, about 18. He teaches Biology.

Sept. 28, Tuesday

Gave Mr. Winkler my birthday book to write in. Miss Lee wants two such books, at $1.50 each, before Xmas. Uncle Josie was at our house today and brought a whole lot of apples. Fern brought over something which looked like a butterfly. I took it up to Mr. Evans, and it was a bat! Didn't know young bats were so pretty.

Oct. 3, Sunday

Yesterday I ironed and did other housework. Took the first step in crossing 6 flowers. If I had a notebook I'd keep a sort of agricultural diary, making records of all the experiments I made etc.

"Beverly of Graustark" is in the Brown County Journal as a serial story. Oh I'm so glad, I'm sure if I were a grasshopper or that sort of thing, I'd jump and skip and do every imaginable thing. Feel perfectly nutty, or beany or dippy or silly or anything you wish, for all I care. Things went straight as a nimrod this noon (whatever that is. I'm sure I don't know what it means, only nimrod sounds straight.)

Oct. 8, Friday

Things didn't go "nimroddy" yesterday. They went like this:

Looked up *nimrod* in the dictionary, or tried to at least, but it wasn't given at all. I suppose I made it up myself. If I did, I must have made it up a long time ago because it sounds so familiar.

Tussy has to wash dishes three times because I have to make her a paper doll. Fell asleep while studying my Ancient yesterday evening, consequently I didn't know my lesson today. I tell you I felt like a circle without any rim around it.

Guess Governor Eberhart will come here tomorrow and make a speech.

Dehli spilled ink over Stella's notebook. In a way I'm glad because now Stella will beg ma until she can get a new one and I can use hers. I really need one.

Oct. 9, Saturday

I've got the inky notebook and Stella will get a new one. Am excused from the Saturday house work to-day. Have to draw. Am in our room now in the attic. "Beverly of Graustark" in the paper again; 2 chapters (this is a pen-and-half again). Inked and painted 14 pictures in Miss Lee's Birthday Book.

The leaves are turning gay both in color and in action (don't care whether action explains my meaning or not; anyway I mean that they dance and jump about like rainbow fairies [by rainbow fairies I mean the colors of course { altho the leaves don't generally turn blue }]). Braces, Brackets & parentheses. Who can solve this algebra problem? Not I for one thing, not you, for another.

If I had an apple now—a great big red one, I'd start to draw again as soon as I were done eating it, but I haven't so I'll try to think of something more to write.

> Oh gee,
> How doth the busy bee
> Improve the shining hours
> By making honey sweet and good
> From all the pretty flowers.
> Oh my,
> How doth this lazy I,
> Improve (?) the shining hours
> By drawing things
> And painting things
> With my nimrodic powers.

I don't see what makes me feel inclined to write such perfectly silly things. Guess I'll peg down good and hard for work. Rain Rain Rain.

Oct. 10, Sunday

Stella and I are in our room again. Just love it up here. Have an addition to our room. A chair, only you can't feel safe on it, I had such weak tacks to fix it with.

Just made two pictures in pastel. It's pretty hard to anybody who is inexperienced. I am certainly inexperienced enough, but I've found out myself that in pastel drawing, lines and the way you manage these lines counts a good deal. I don't mean lines used as outlines, they count in any kind of drawing, of course. What I mean is the inside lines that you fill the drawing out with. I've tried to explain what I mean, but it seems to me nobody could understand so I'll let it go at that.

Am done with my Biology notebook work, also with my algebra. Now if Tussy and those would go to bed I could study my Ancient, but they won't go; and I simply can't study properly when they're around, talking as if they were clocks wound up for 14 days.

Oct. 11, Monday

Today the weather is not very agreeable—to put it in a mild way— damp & cool, and rain, rain, rain, rain, rain *and* rain. Skies dreary from one end to the other, ugh! just about makes me shiver to think of it.

I know what metaphysics means. Wouldn't want to study that. I'll bet I'd feel so mixed up and bewildered I wouldn't know whether my name started with beans or pickles, and whether I was standing on green cheese or air, and so forth, etc.

I can write names and things in Greek. Some you can read real easy.

Oct. 14, Thursday. Cold as ice.

Just arranged the High School song in Quartette form. It's awfully easy I think, to arrange, you know. Stella and I hung up the wash today— just a pile—our fingers were all stiff too, by the time we got done.

Guess Dehli will plant wheat. She's interested in High School work now already; how interested would she be if she were really *in* High School?

Stella and I raised a rebellion this morning because we have to clean up the kitchen every evening, and Tussy, Asta and those always make the muss.

Oct. 16, Saturday. Moderately cool (or warm)

Was excused from the Saturday work again because I worked on Miss Lee's birthday book, and besides, I had to go downtown twice. Went to the doctor with Howard. Howard's had that sore since last spring.* Ugh, such horrid-looking instruments. Howard almost cried, too, but he "bore it like a man."

Got a Harrison Fisher picture from Fern for making a paper doll. It's called "The College Girl after the May-day Hoop-rolling." It's perfectly sweet, which of course is needless to say. They're all "Dandies." This ink is just like the kind of embroidery thread that starts with a dark shade, grows lighter, runs into the dark shade, etc.

* The accident mentioned May 12. A splinter had pierced the inside of his cheek, had remained there and caused an infection.

Oct. 17, Sunday

Asta started a diary to-day. Here's one sentence:—"Ink is very fierce." If she keeps on saying such funny things as she did to-day, we ought to keep it for a grouch medicine.

I have two cold sores, and Stella has already remarked on my beauty(?). Wish I could play guitar. Am ever so glad tomorrow's Monday. I always am. Guess I'll prepare myself for an Ancient "cram." I'll study topsy-turvy, beginning at the middle and ending at the beginning, and when I have everything properly mixed up in my head, I'm ready for the test.

"Lena Rivers" at Turnhall to-night. "Beverly of Graustark" next Sunday I guess. Oh, if I could only, only go to that one. I just know it will be perfectly splendid.

Yesterday we had chicken for supper.

If $2-5=9$, then I knew my ancient lesson, if not, never mind.

Σο-Λονγ

Α Σπλενδιδ Δαν Τω-δαν

Oct. 20, Wednesday

I feel nimroddy. Drew Mr. Winkler's arm to-day, only I didn't get the hand. He had it too far behind his book. Glee Club practice to-night. I do hope there won't be so many discords.

Later:—In some queer way I happened to think of looking up "nimrod" in the Encyclopaedia, and Wonder of Wonders, Queerness of Queernesses, it WAS GIVEN. And what do you think it means? A man. Here:—"Founder of Babylonian and Later Assyrian Empire. Appears in art as engaged in combat with a wild beast." Isn't that the limit? And I put it to such perfectly silly uses, too. So I didn't invent the word after all, oh glory!

Thursday, Oct. 21

Yesterday evening I chopped wood, or tried to at least. That's hard. I chopped away until I was dizzy. Anyway, I don't want to freeze in the evening and we haven't anyone to chop it for us.

Oh gee, I feel fierce. When things go all mixed up it's pretty hard to keep your temper straight. I feel as if I could throw things around until my temper was cool. There's nothing in particular to be sore about but, on the whole, things are so unsatisfactory. Made a dozen and a half place cards to-night and its a wonder none were spoiled, there were so many standing around jogging my elbows, shaking the table, criticizing and making suggestions. This is just the sort of ink I need to-night, bold & black, it makes me feel a great deal better to write a fierce-looking page.

I feel a little better now that I have written out my troubles. It is only 8 p.m. now but I feel as if I'd like to go to bed and sleep off my troubles a little.

Oct. 22, Friday

Oh beans, things went crooked, crooked, crooked. I didn't go to school this morning because I didn't feel well. This afternoon we had a program. The Thalians won. When I came home I went up to our room and made place cards. After dinner I made some more. Then I read "Beverly of Graustark" while I was rocking the baby to sleep. That's just about the best book I've read; I can scarcely wait for the next chapter. Am going down to the doctor with Howard now.

Oct. 24. A bright sunny day, cold nevertheless.

My hands are all full of blisters & sores from chopping wood. I'm always trying to make firewood but I'm afraid I'm making only chips. Then Stella broke the ax. That was the culminating point. Just about all I could chop with the hatchet was splinters.

I have made almost 5 dozen Hallowe'en cards for Miss Gerber. I only, only hope that I may go to "Beverly of Graustark" when that comes. I'll bet I'd just about jump out of my slippers for joy if I could. They're so loose anyway, it wouldn't be impossible. I feel rather glum. Trouble before, and trouble beyond, and fun at the sides only. Dreamt about school last night. I could almost cry myself sick sometimes to think that so many girls who have the opportunity of going thru High School just hate school and look upon it as hard work; while I have to be afraid any time that I may have to stop school before I know it.

Oct. 25, Monday

This is the most beautiful day, warm and sunny as in early fall. Still I don't feel altogether happy. Stella went home from school earlier this morning because mama didn't feel well, but she didn't come home early enough to make a decent dinner so we didn't have near enough to eat except apples. Stella promised to make an early supper tho, so that's alright.

Oct. 26, Tuesday

Glee Club practiced "Ave Maria" last night. I chopped some more wood last night and this noon, consequently my fingers are more bruised and scratched up. Tussy is staying at home to-day because mama is still not feeling well. I didn't think Tussy could make such a good dinner as she did. Miss Lee payed me for the Birthday book.

Oct. 27, Wednesday

Things went a little better to-day. I stayed out of school this forenoon because mama wasn't well yet. We did have the worst time getting supper to-night. The kids couldn't get any ham and it took ever so long until they came with the lard and the wieners. But oh joy of joys! Uncle Frank came and chopped a whole lot of wood. I hope it will last long enough to give my bruised fingers a chance to heal.

Oct. 28, Thursday

Tussy was home this morning and made dinner. It would have been alright only she forgot to whip eggs into the soup, and the soup was all cold by the time we came home. Then, the kids wouldn't mind, and instead of getting crackers they got half-baked, doughy bread.

Just came back from Commercial Arithmetic. I found out a short method of subtraction, but I'm not the only one nor the first one, for when I told Mr. Winkler he knew it too. But that's always the case. I've found out things time and time again, and every time somebody else has found out the same thing before me. Isn't that queer? I know a short way of adding with nines, now I guess I'll tell Mr. Winkler about that too, and see whether he has noticed that too. I suppose he has. I had better do my lessons.

Oct. 29, Friday. A bitter-sweet day.

When I came home I painted some of Mrs. Fraade's Hallowe'en cards. She has ordered 7½ dozen. Then I went to the doctor with Howard. The doctor says Howard's sore is coming on nicely. Am ever so glad. Then I went upstairs and painted & read until it was dark—I mean I went up into our room in the attic, not upstairs. Then I watched the sunset. It was simply grand, first all strips of lavender, pink and white, and every imaginable variation of these colors, and the trees and hills for a foreground. Then later it changed into a rosy crimson all along the western horizon. The outlines of the trees became more distinct, and the inside more solid, a black mass like ebony, with their outlines cut sharp and clear against the fiery background; oh it was all too beautiful to explain. All I could do was to watch and get out as much as possible of the beauty of it all; and perhaps I did feel a little bit sentimental; a person generally can't help it in such cases. So much for the sweet part. Things went crooked, generally, after that, but it isn't the use of taking notes of your troubles. You're better off if you forget them. I know when I read my old diaries I nearly always skip those parts anyway. It seems to me this is rather sentimental but I can't help it. I always feel better after I've written my thoughts down. That's one reason why I keep a diary. I can read over the jolly parts and I remember that things went straight oftener than I had imagined. This whole paragraph hasn't much unity and coherence, but whats the dif?

Oct. 30, Saturday

Indian summer at last. The weather is perfectly grand, so beautiful that it quite makes up for all those dreary, cold days we had not long ago. The fairies must have been very busy spinning their magic pearl threads during the cold weather, for the air is all full of their wonderful floating creations. Some look like kites, others like miniature snakes gliding thru the air, and some look exactly like fairy washlines with a stray bit of cloth dangling here and there. There is only a very gentle breeze, but still those little strings whip and float up and down until they meet a friendly tree or wire to which they cling. There are some ever and ever so long—I guess some are long enough to reach from one side of the street to another. I wonder what causes them. My spirits are a little higher to-day too, on the whole.

This morning I drew and painted, and read "Castle Craneycrow" between times. I guess I had better draw a little again. "Castle Craneycrow" is just dandy.

Oct. 31, Sunday

I made 15 caricatures for Alberta Low's Hallowe'en party.

Today we played a few Hallowe'en games at home. I got "a boy with blue eyes and red rosy lips." Then I got "Move to Aberdeen, N.D." Then came the grand finale. I dressed like Napanee, Stella and Fern as witches, Kurt as a wizard, Tussy and Asta as Gretel and Hänsel Schpeiderwitz, respectively. Dehli went along to carry our wraps that we didn't need. Then we marched up to Low's. Alberta was certainly surprised and I'm sure we looked spooky —anyway they turned off the lights and the weird light of the pumpkins shone on us. They didn't know us until they caught sight of me and then they pulled me forward and said, *"Now do you know who they are?"* They knew me by my silly nose, of course, and possibly by my eyes and hair, a little. I for my part remember nothing distinctly. I felt like one of those witches with a sort of wheel spinning around me, everything was like a dream, vague and whirly, you know. Anyway, we had piles of fun and my spirits are a great deal higher than they've been for some time.

If I were a magic artist or something of that sort, I would paint the picture I saw to perfection; I remember distinctly how whirly and queer it was, so dreamy and yet so real, only as far as I know that's quite "unpaintable," isn't it? I'll have to work like everything if I want to get that 3½ doz. place cards done by Tuesday.

Hallowe'en

Nov. 2, Tuesday

To-night after school Mr. Ritschl gave us all a splendid ride in his new Kissel Kar. That's the second automobile ride I've had. Then I went up in the attic and painted place cards while Stella made supper.

Mr. Ritschl sent us about $2 worth of groceries to-day. Sweet potatoes too—I wonder if I like them. I never liked them before but it seems to me that I like them now. When we studied sweet potatoes in Agriculture I was so hungry for some that I'm quite sure that I like them now.

Nov. 3, Wednesday

Stayed home from school to-day. Washed my sailor dress. Wouldn't it be just splendid if we had enough money to live comfortably, and so we could have oysters and things? It's no use wishing, so we're trying to satisfy ourselves by imagining things. Isn't that quite "fairy tale-ish"? Just like the man in the Arabian Nights who imagined he was eating a fine meal—isn't it?

When I know the characteristics of a person I can generally tell where each particular one comes in, even if it's dark and I can't see the person well, or even if I can't exactly tell what he or she is saying. It's too queer to explain. For instance to-night when I got the milk, I was in the yard already, and Mr. Winkler went past and he said something about my having worked all day, I could just tell he was smiling even tho I really couldn't see it. Then I can just tell what sort of expressions Stella & Tussy & the rest make when they're talking. This is really too silly to waste so much space on so I'll stop with this.

Wonder if I can come to-morrow, to school, I mean. I guess I'd better go to bed, my writing is getting rather dreamy isn't it?

I'm trying to save up for the time when "Beverly of Graustark" comes. If I can't see that—well, I'd feel just in the mood to cry. Just made a list of all the characteristics of all the high school teachers. Average of 14 characteristics to 1 teacher.

Nov. 5, Friday

We had a program to-day. Our side won. The orchestra played 4 times. Mr. Winkler is the director. The music was splendid, Mr. Winkler looked handsome, everything did, because there was music.

The other morning while I was still in bed, half-dreaming, I thought about the original story I'm to write (for the program). I saw a book and as I was looking at its contents, I saw the words "Gooseberry pie." My story will be about a pie. When I told Miss Lee about the story I said, "Gee whiz." Talk of feeling cheap! I always come in so awkwardly when I oughtn't to.

Nov. 9

Wrote the last part of my original story last night.

Yesterday nothing especially interesting happened until the evening. It was about ten o'clock when a man telephoned asking whether they could come up and look at some oil paintings. I said yes, of course, and they came, Mr. Wald and another man. The other man has been at our house before but I don't know his name. He looked at my drawings too. He is a tall man with gray pressed trousers, that's something which seems very important to me when I think of a well-dressed man. His nose was almost Roman and he had the queerest little whiskers which didn't look like whiskers at all. He knows all about Cleopatra, Rembrandt, McCutcheon, Briggs, Reese and others, and seems to be quite well educated.

I have never had such perfect lessons on the whole, I think, as I did this morning. That means since last September, of course. That's mainly because the orchestra played last Friday, I think.

Nov. 12, Friday

We had a fine dinner to-day. Oysters—oh I almost jumped for joy.
Judy was here and brought "Graustark" for me to read.

Nov. 13, Saturday

Worked in the morning. This afternoon I drew—and read. I'm making Mrs. Fischer's birthday book and I have half of it in ink. During the time I had to wait for the ink to dry—and sometimes I waited a little longer than necessary, I admit—I read "Graustark." It's perfectly grand. Incognito, ideal Americans and all that. It's perfectly delicious to get little bits of such splendid reading in between the times you're drawing. Rain. Dreary & damp, on the whole. Mrs. Fraade paid me for the placecards the other day. Oh, if I could only, only use part of it to go to "Beverly of Graustark." I just know I shall cry if I can't go, especially as I'm reading the story. And I guess it will cost 50 cents in "Nigger's Heaven," just think, and how will I ever be able to scrape that much together?

Nov. 14, Sunday

Quite a nice day on the whole, even tho it was dreary and cold outside. We had a nice warm furnace fire, and that burnishes up matters considerably. I'm thru with "Graustark." Just like Mr. McCutcheon's other books, bright, entertaining, original, just enough adventure and not too much, and just the right amount of sentiment.

I really didn't do much besides reading, and playing little snatches on the piano. It's too queer for anything, as soon as I go to the piano the rest all come in and play their games in the parlor even if it's cold, and of course they jog me and the result is—a discord every once in a while, etc., and so on.

Nov. 15, Monday

We're making sauerkraut. We got some wood to-day.

> "The snow is falling fast,
> The pretty birds are gone——."

It is really, truly snowing, and snowing in earnest, snowing beautifully, grandly, splendidly—you may guess at the other adjectives, if you please. But it's true. It's perfectly grand, that beautiful, hazy sparkling mist in the sky, and that soft solemn, "Christmasy" whiteness on the ground. As far as appearances go, it looks exactly like a Xmas night, but—of course, the Christmas spirit is lacking, and isn't that just about the most important part of a "Christmasy" feeling? I think so—quite much anyway, don't you?

Oh I do wish time wouldn't fly so fast, I am always afraid it will be too short a time before school closes again.

I haven't my algebra all done, but what's the dif? A person has to enjoy the sweeter parts of life when they come, isn't that so? There are times when you have to look for them, and search for them good and hard, aren't there?

I guess I had better stop—I am getting a little bit sentimental. The snow, and the beauty of the snow makes me feel that way. Perhaps I won't feel so sentimental, tho, when I see the kitchen floor all marked up with muddy spots. Anyway I won't let that trouble me now, would you? I have piles to do, neither will I trouble myself about that now. I shall slip into bed directly, so goodnight, and good cheer.

Nov. 16, Tuesday. Snow still.

Asta and those have brought out the sled already. I was awake very late last night, contemplating and planning, against my will however.

Ancient History is very interesting just now, we're studying about Socrates, Demosthenes, Aeschylus, Aristophanes and all the rest. I would compare myself with Socrates as far as looks are concerned—I mean the degree of handsomeness—but I dare not—he was too good and wise for that.

It looks clean and nice outside but oh—my prophecy of last night has come true—the kitchen floor verifies that. I haven't got any shoes yet and have to wade thru that snow with my slippers.

Later:—It snowed until late last night. I got myself a pair of new shoes. Am awfully glad I've got some. Every time I get new shoes, I have to go to the piano and play a little, I don't know why it is but it always seems that belongs to it.

Tests are raining thick and hard. I hope I pass in all.

Stella dressed up (in a sheet) as Kris Kringle & knocked at the door, and gave the baby a bag. The baby runs around with the bag, telling us over and over again that she's got "chocolet candy." Poor thing, it's only a cracker.

Nov. 20, Saturday

I painted part of Mrs. Fischer's birthday book but was not entirely excused from the Saturday work. I have a cold, speaking of colds, our piano needs a tuning because it sounds exactly as if it had a bad cold. I have heaps and heaps to do but I won't get excited. I've had enough experience to know that it doesn't pay to be too hasty.

Nov. 26, Friday

The orchestra played and the Glee Club sang at the program. I read my story and got the point. Some of those Freshmen have more nerve than they ought to have. During the program one of the Freshman boys sat in my seat and when I went back to my seat he said, "That's a fine diary." I said, "Diary?" and then I caught on; they had been reading *you,* Diary! Wish you could speak so I'd know what parts they read. There is one advantage—I guess a person who isn't used to my writing can't read half of this stuff.

Yesterday was Thanksgiving and I had a great many things to be thankful for. We got one hundred lbs. flour as a present from Ritschl's grandmother. We had a duck for Thanksgiving, and mince pie and other things, and I ate just as much as you're generally supposed to eat on Thanksgiving—consequently I'm not at all very hungry to-day. I sent Thanksgiving cards to Ritschl's and Harrington's and Elise Martin. Aunt Mary came in the afternoon and brought some mittens for the girls.

Guess I'll rip the hem in my sailor dress, it's getting too short—no it isn't either. I'm getting taller, that's the reason why all my dresses are too short.

My cold isn't gone yet. I wish it would kindly take leave. Oh hum,* here's Christmas coming in jumps and I haven't started a single Christ-

---

* I used this exclamation to express various emotions, usually excitement or joy but never boredom.

mas present. Counted up all the people for whom I'm intending to make Xmas presents,* and there are about 25 not counting members of our family or relatives.

Nov. 29, Monday

Went over to Fern's last night and read in some magazines, and saw some of the cutest pictures by Jessie Wilcox Smith. Rose O'Neil—whoever that is—seems to be getting awfully popular. There is an illustrated poem of hers in the Ladies' Home Journal, called the Kewpies. Oh hum! don't I wish I could have those magazines and fine pictures? Really, some people don't realize how lucky they are.

I'm determined to work like everything to-night, get at each task and do that thoroughly before I undertake something else, just like a goody-goody girl. This is the easiest and pleasantest task so I went at this first. Algebra next, Oh my stars! It's ever so hard to-night.

Nov. 30. Tuesday

Stella and Tussy went up to Turner Hall to see the little boys turn.** Oh how I wish I could go to Turning School. But there are—well, the turning suit for one thing, and the time for another thing; altho I really think the time isn't wasted one bit.

I had a tooth-ache like anything yesterday. Oh, don't I wish somebody'd say to me, "Go down to the dentist and have your teeth filled. I'll pay the bill!"

Dec. 5, Saturday

Friday Stella and I and Fern went up to Turner Hall to see the big girls and ladies turn. Oh hum, don't I wish I could go to Turning School? I wish somebody'd give me some bloomers that would fit exactly.

I drew & drew & drew and drew *and* drew & painted, ditto [place cards]. I made some rules regarding painting and reading. As I've said before, I generally read while I'm waiting for the paint to dry. Now the rule is:—When I've finished one picture I may read two pages, with exceptions in case the drawing is not dry by that time, and get this book out of the way when somebody's coming up the steps, (sometimes you're in danger of getting a lecture, especially when Stella or Tussy come with their "fire-and-flames"!) But I don't care, I didn't really read much to-day.

---

* Pictures which I made for people who had been kind to us.

** *To turn*, as used here, meant *to perform gymnastic exercises,* and *turning suit* meant *gymnasium suit.*

Top: The Gág Home at 226 N. Washington Street, New Ulm

Bottom: left to right, standing: Stella, Dehli, Wanda; sitting: Howard, Asta, Tussy

Elisabeth Biebl Gág

Anton Gág

I worked pretty hard and had a little cry after supper, don't care if I do say it, because it's true. Snow outdoors, whiteness, brilliancy, anything you please; inside—well, scrubbing doesn't help much unless you scrub about 2 times.

Dehli's birthday was yesterday, and she got, besides 5 cts. worth of candy, (which she had to share with us all) a paper-doll set, some cloth and a drawing book.

Miss Lee gave me a check for $1.50 for the birthday book. They have Hudson-and-Fulton-Expedition-2-cent-stamps now. (What a long word.) Oh hum! I wish my red dress were sewed. Those glad rags I'm wearing at present are tearing up, all snip-snap.

Dec. 11, Sunday

It's snowing, snowing—and snowing beautifully, too. Christmas is jumping awfully fast it seems, and the Christmas spirit is here already, at our house at least, raging full force. Oh glory! They're laundering doll-dresses downstairs, I'm painting to beat the Dutch upstairs, and things are quite humdrum, generally. How will I ever get all those Christmas presents done? I'm asking myself over and over, but I suppose I'll get them done some way, as usual.

I ought to write dear old Santa a letter but I'm scared; there are so awfully many. Here:—

A sweater, (no that's wrong. Stella and I have one together, and altho it isn't new I think we can fix it up nicely). Well—a tam-o'shanter, a new dress, a hat pin, gloves, (I need some badly) skates, hairribbons, (mine's tearing all up, and it's pink, and I prefer black or dark red.) A bottle of India ink, (Asta spilled nearly all of mine) drawing paper, one book at least, about 50 cents to go to "Beverly of Graustark" when it comes. (Oh dear, I just know I'll cry like everything if I can't go.) A tablet, pencils & pens, and stockings. I guess there are more only I can't think of them all at one time.

Oh dear, I wish we had apples. I haven't tasted fruit for ever so long.

I feel as if I had Santa's pack on my shoulders, only the toys unfinished, you know, and as if I had to finish them. Still I love to make Christmas presents; it's fine fun if you like to do a thing, and I put a generous measure of love into every present, even tho there are so many that it would seem my supply of it were quite exhausted by the time I got thru. But it won't. I shall have plenty left, I'm sure.

Got "Life, Letters & Journals of Louisa M. Alcott" last Friday. It's just grand. She really deserved the fame she got. They were poor and she worked hard and was so much like other people that you can't help thinking you knew her ever so well.

We had sauerkraut for dinner, consequently I didn't eat much and am getting hungry. I wish we had butter. We haven't had any for ever and ever so long.

Dec. 12, Sunday

The snow is falling, or it did anyway, if it doesn't now.

TRIED RECIPES

Drowsy Pop-overs

Put One pound drowsiness in a cozy dish "Feather bed Brand." Add one pound of delicious dreams and a generous pinch of delightful stretches, and a very little bit of time, and fill with the following cream:—

Filling:—One ounce of delicious plans, the most splendid kind of ideas you can find, (Bright, Clever & Co. sell the best) $1\frac{1}{2}$ oz. Thoughts (mixed). Mix thoroughly. Flavor with a few "It's time to get up's," and serve hot.

Doesn't that beat the Dutch? But it's a tried recipe, isn't it? Awfully good too, especially if you can only get a few delicious snatches of sleep after the first "Get up."

Dec. 15, Wednesday

Poor diary, how did you feel being left up here at school two nights and a day? I needed you badly last Monday, I was so cross and exasperated I nearly cried, and it would have done me good to write my troubles in here and drop them from my mind after that.

Yesterday was Tuesday and I stayed home from school because—well, I may as well say the reason—I didn't have a decent dress to wear. Those happy rags of mine!

Stella and I went down town yesterday evening and played Santa Claus. Got myself a hairribbon, 15 cts. a yard, black and white. I'm so tickled I'm sure if I had a hundred legs like a centipede I'd jump them 3 times around, one by one. Then I got a little book for Tussy, Asta & Dehli to-gether—and 3 tablets. Oh yes! and a penny doll for Asta.

It has struck me that I write next to no stories now. I haven't written any at all since vacation I guess.

Oh glory! What fine books they have down there. I'm head-over-heels in love with half of them. It isn't very easy to buy Xmas things with so very little money. I feel as dejected as the bluest thing you can find. Stella has turned a pessimist and says, "It isn't nice if you haven't any money," with a very tragic effect. It's true tho, it isn't nice to go shopping with about 3 dimes and four pennies. I feel as if I could cry quarts of tears only I shan't. If I were a thing with a hundred & one ears, I believe I should box them 3 times all around for sheer vexation. It feels as if my castles-in-the-air were tumbling 'round my ears on all sides. I wish I'd get as many cents as the numbers my test marks represent. That would make $.89 $.98 $.96 for this month or $2.83. I'd jump for joy but——, let that dash run on ever and ever so long, for that's what it stands for. I can't help it if I'm writing rubbish to-night. Everything is so silly. I think I shall be going to bed pretty soon to sleep my troubles away. Oh I do hope I'll feel brighter tomorrow and I *do* hope Santa will be good to us. Oh dear, I'm entirely out of sorts with myself and other things—I'm especially dissatisfied with myself. Goodnight.

Dec. 16

I did feel better to-day, and perhaps our little money will reach to some extent. We didn't have much of an Ancient Lesson to-day. Miss Dillon lectured. She said exactly the same thing which I've been thinking of ever & ever so often: That some children don't realize what an advantage it is to go to school. I'll confess I dream away some of the time sometimes, but then I'm generally dreaming useful things.

> Oh hum-te-dum
> Time's going some.

Program to-morrow. Vacation after that. Heigh-ho.

Dec. 18, Saturday

To-day I felt like April, happy part of the day and tearful the other part.

These are some of my favorite artists—Harrison Fisher, Jessie Wilcox Smith, Rose O'Neill, Philip Biouleau, Mary True Ayer, Howard Chandler Christy, Charles Dana Gibson.

That 10 cents I got from Mrs. Pfeffer—I can't decide whether I prefer a diary book to stamps, or stamps to the diary book. Ritschl's grandmother bought all of us girls each a pair of stockings and a handkerchief. I'm ever so glad.

Dec. 19, Sunday

This morning I went down to Harrington's. They were ever so nice to me, and I brought a calendar which I made for them and a Christmas present for them too. I returned with a Christmas present of 8 glasses jelly for all and a dollar all for my owny self! Oh I'm tickled.

I drew most of the afternoon and read a little. Oh that India ink of mine *is* the limit! There are only a few drops left and it's all thick and horrid; and I'm supposed to make neat-looking pictures with it.

Dec. 20, Monday

Oh hum! Oh joy! I have new India ink. Allow me to dance an imaginary jig. Bought myself 2 nickel diaries. Oh Ho! What joy! Also some candy, nuts, and some blocks for the baby. Oh dear I'm madly and sadly in love with those lovely lovely books they have at Eggen's, but I love in vain, ah me!

It is snowing again, and I am happy again. I sent presents to Diel's and Prenzel's to-day. Also to Joliffe's and Dr. Haftel.

Dec. 21, Tuesday

Oh glory! I'm as discouraged and dejected to-day as I was happy and light-hearted yesterday. I think I could cry quarts of tears if I had a wish to do so, but I haven't the least bit of time.

I had a horrid dream last night. It was so much as it really might be that I cried in bed. I had a nice dream too tho. I dreamt I got a pair of finger gloves from Karl Ritschl's grandmother and in each mitten was some money, $1.60 in all, I guess. On top of each mitten was a sprig of real holly. Now that's a very sensible dream for I need gloves badly. I am wearing, at present, a pair of black ones the right one of which is hopelessly torn; torn beyond my art of mending, and every time I go into a store or house I take off the right glove so as to escape criticism or anything else equally disagreeable.

Stella and Tussy are in ecstacies over the fact that they have bought me a Christmas present of which I don't know anything. They told me it cost 13 cts. and I couldn't imagine what it was, but yesterday I was

over in the clothes closet where we keep most of the things and I saw—
5 cents worth of drawing paper and a 5-cent note book! I suppose the
note book was meant for a diary book, and I've bought *two!* At first
I was disappointed—because it isn't very nice to know what you'll get
for Christmas—but up jumped the funny side and I took advantage of
it! I sat down and laughed. Those girls don't think any farther than
the end of the town, it seems, for the things lay there all unwrapped
and everything. I can't imagine what they bought for the 3 cents. Possibly it's a pencil, 2 for a nickel, you know, and when they bought one
they had to pay 3 cents. You can't tell however, and I'll gladly bide my
time.

Have another present nearly done, only it looks awful; the painting
anyway. The only decent color in my box is prussian blue, and all the
borders I've made lately are blue, and I haven't enough baby ribbon to
match them all so I'm in a quandary again; for who would think of
tying red or pink baby ribbon to a present in which the *very noticeable*
color is blue? I can't help it, I only hope people will not think it's my
bad taste in colors if the painting is a little queer.

It is snowing again. Oh dear, I feel as blue as my old threadbare
sailor dress, and that's saying a good deal for it's a very dingy-looking
blue by this time. I wish somebody'd give me money to go down to the
dentist's with to fill my tooth—for a Christmas present.

Oh hum! I have to work. I guess I had better not dwell on my disappointments any longer.

Dec. 22, Wednesday

Better to-day on the whole. In the first place I went around town
with Aunt Mary to help her choose our presents. Then I went home
and sat down to draw like a goody-girl. Mama baked cookies to-day and
we got some from Birnbaum's too. Miss Brexel sent up a present which
we aren't to open until Christmas, and we've been nearly cracking our
heads trying to make out what it is. Supper's ready.

Dec. 24, Friday

Oh hum! All manner of things have happened. We got a swell magic
lantern from Ritschl's, and in the afternoon we got the bundle of Christmas presents Aunt Mary bought for us. It consisted of—a pair of gloves
for me (I'm still in ecstacies over them), a hair-ribbon for Stella, a
sweater each for Tussy, Asta, Dehli and Howard, and dress-goods for

Baby. Tussy and the rest are so delighted with their sweaters that they want to wear them all the time. Mama got lace curtains from Aunt Mary and Nora.

After supper I dressed baby's doll, fixed baby's Teddy Bear, went to bed, was awake with miserable thoughts until eleven, and then I guess I fell asleep.

This morning I did housework, and then went to see if I had any mail. Did I? Here:—A postal from Daisy, a dollar from Prenzel's, and a check from the J.J. for 2 accepted articles. Talk of being tickled! Went down town and got mama a Christmas present (from my own money) cloth for a waist. To-night! Oh ho! Behold Santa in a blue skirt all out of press and a nonentical waist, stout shoes and an "ear to ear" grin. You will recognize me readily, I am sure, especially if I would have mentioned a silly nose.

Now diary, a word with you. Now don't be shocked, but I'll be heartily glad when I'm done with you for I'm ever so anxious to write in those dear little notebooks; and anyway, I shall make another special effort to get that neat.

Oh I wish and I wish that I could get some cloth for bloomers, and a tam-o'shanter. This ink is simply awful. Ta-ta.

December 25

A Merry Christmas and a happy New Year! Christmas is here at last. This is about 6 a.m., dark as night outside, everything wide-awake indoors.

Yesterday we went up to the library but the door wasn't open, so we went home where we found a surprise waiting for us. Four big bags cookies, 1 bag of nuts, one of candy, another of oranges from Martin's and Elise Martin's grandmother! I was so glad I jumped right in to the piano and played Christmas songs with all my might. Oh yes, yesterday we got 100 lbs flour from Dr. Haftel. Oh hum! Yesterday evening we opened the package from Miss Brexel and there were 5 German books—nice ones too.

We didn't eat much at all for supper because we weren't hungry. After supper we opened the presents which we made among ourselves. I got a pretty blue bag from Tussy, 2 pieces candy from Stella, and a blotter from Dehli. After that we sang and played piano until about 7 o'clock. Then the little ones went to bed and we mustered the Christmas Tree Brigade which consisted mainly of Thusnelda and me, for Stella didn't feel very well.

We fixed the famous tree, mostly with apples, cookies, candy and candles, because we haven't hardly any of those tinsel and picture things. Then we put most of the presents in their places, sent Tussy to bed, and put her presents there. Oh, my legs were tired! This morning we were awake at about four—not I, just exactly, I was still rather drowsy, but the rest—when the bell rang.* This morning I am the proud possessor of

1 ink tablet
1 pencil tablet
2 diary books
3 pens
5 cents drawing paper
1 note book
1 box "Oh My!"
1 German story book, which I share with Stella.

So here's Christmas in all its glory and sweetness and goodness, and here am I—without skates, without a tam, without goods for bloomers, without the book I longed for, without the hat pin, without the tie, and without the 50 cents to go to Beverly of Graustark with, *and* without the money to go down to the dentist's with. But still I have a great many things too, considering—well, considering the circumstances. I am quite satisfied, so——

Peace on earth
Good will to men.

Dec. 26, Sunday

"Sieht nur so fällt der weise Schnee
Über die Felder weit und breit."

Oh how I wish I had a tam. That old cap I have always pulls my hair all awry, and it's so heavy. Got the J.J. and I had a heading and an illustrated story in it. Have an idea for a Christmas story. Perhaps I'll write it while the Christmas spirit lasts.

Uncle Frank came this afternoon and played guitar. Oh nice music. I just love to read while I'm listening to music, it makes the intense parts intenser, the beautiful parts more beautiful, the gay parts gayer, and if there are pathetic parts it brings them out clearer and makes everything

---

* The tinkling of a bell on Christmas morning showed that Santa had finished arranging the tree and presents, and was the signal for us to come downstairs.

more real. Just when Uncle Frank was playing I had to go out to grind the coffee, and I wanted to spoil the music as little as possible by the noise so I ground in time with the music. Isn't that a queer idea? Uncle Frank stayed for supper, and after that our grand orchestra, which consists of the astounding number of 2, played some grand duets,

> And crowds of people did over here dart
> And gazed and listened with lips apart.

Only, of course, they didn't. That was only an inappropriate verse. I'm writing everything I can think of, just so I get this book filled. In the other diary I intend to write plainer, a little more "bookish" with less slang (if possible. You see I sometimes use it to express my feelings with as much "snap" as I can.) Excuse the parenthesis.

Dec. 27, Monday

Oh dear, we have to clean up so often. Those children can't leave anything in order and it gets me awfully cross, and I'm afraid I scold away like a regular vixen.

With our goose it's rather funny. It seems as if it were an everlasting goose. We had it for dinner and supper on Christmas day, breakfast, dinner and supper yesterday, and breakfast this morning, not counting the times it was dished up between meals for lunch—and there's still some left. I asked mama whether I could buy a tam for $.50. She did not refuse, neither did she promise, so I'm in suspense, doncher know. Wish I had a good book to read.

Oh hum! I could laugh myself sick. I got a letter from a boy in Madison, Minn., asking me to be his friend, and answer. (I think he saw me at the basket ball game.) I haven't seen him, and don't know the first thing about him. Answer? Oh glory! Drop it here.

Stella's got a cold and says she doesn't enjoy this Christmas very much. I think last Christmas it *was* nicer in a way.

Aunt Magdalene is here.

I'm not so sorry to leave you, diary, because I have two others, and you had to play second fiddle to-day. I like you nevertheless.

Good bye.

*   *   *

December 28, Tuesday

I have dared to give myself the allmost impossible task of writing as neatly and legibly as possible. Inasmuch that I have a decided scrawl, and an illegible hand on the whole, it will be almost as hard for me to fulfill said task faithfully as doing myriads of other things—no excuse me, I don't mean that—as writing a rival to "Beverly of Graustark."

I am at grandma's. Aunt Magdalene came up to our house yesterday afternoon. This morning after breakfast I decided to go with her down to grandma's. I asked mama whether I could buy myself a tam and she said "yes." Oh I was glad! Aunt Magdalene and I bought some cloth for a waist for myself. It is black and white checked. It's quite far to grandma's house but I wasn't very cold when I came down, indeed I felt quite lively and fresh, with my blood all a-tingle from the sharp wind and cold air.

In the December American there is a picture of James Montgomery Flagg. He is described as the most versatile illustrator of the day. I don't like some of his pictures so *very* well. There's one picture of a girl who arches her eyebrows too much to look as well as she might otherwise. The coloring is good and is laid on deftly. The strokes are accurate and well-placed and none are wasted.

I have seen at least about 50 pictures by Harrison Fisher and I guess they were all perfect; in my opinion, at least. It sometimes seems as if he made them in pastel, and not only sometimes—very often. The people in his pictures look fresh and young and life-like, and the coloring is splendid. The faces are always well worked out and you cannot see each stroke as plainly as those of Mr. Flagg's.

I've seen a picture of Howard Chandler Christy and I know that he recovered from a severe illness not long ago, *and* I know that he can draw awfully pretty pictures too. (Excuse the "awfully", please.)

I saw a picture of Jessie Wilcox Smith and she doesn't look at all as I imagined her. She draws the sweetest children.

I saw a picture of Charles Dana Gibson, and I know he is a pen-and-ink artist, and draws things true to life. I also know that he went to Europe to study painting.

About Rose O'Neil I know nothing at all except that she's getting more popular all the time, and that she has a very pretty and original style of drawing. Also that she can write the loveliest "snappy" and "fetching" poetry.

Of Mary True Ayer I know only that she draws pretty pictures of children.

So much for artists. Grandma baked mince-pie today. Oh hum!

Dec. 29, Wednesday

My waist is done. Oh it's cold outside to-day; 20 below zero (If the thermometer goes right.)

Have read 2 "Adventures in Contentment." They are perfectly lovely, with such deep feeling and yet so simple. You find yourself thinking why you haven't thought these same thoughts before. Perhaps I shall go home tomorrow if it isn't too cold. I shall simply have to go home for New Year, and if it rains cats and dogs. I suppose it wouldn't rain in zero weather but it might *snow* cats and dogs.

Dec. 30, Thursday

The river looks like an improved drive-way, all white and smooth, covered with snow all over. I fell asleep last night thinking about those at home and wondering how all the High School teachers were enjoying their vacation. I guess to-day is butter-making day but I'm afraid I won't stay long enough to help. I like to make butter because afterwards when it's done I can have unsalted butter on my bread, which is perfectly delicious.

Later:—I am home now. I didn't get any unsalted butter because I went before they had started. It *was* a splendid day, and *is* a splendid night, only I don't feel very splendid.

Aunt Magdalene and I started about three, and grandma, dear old grandma, gave a bag of apples along. We went up to Nora's first. Her sister was there too—she said I looked good in red, which is the first compliment I've received for ever so long, but I think I don't look very good in anything, I'm too homely.

Last night Aunt Magdalene and I played Parcheesi on a cardboard game which I had made in a few minutes. We used a dice cut from pumpkin, which, you may be sure, didn't go very well. We didn't have any spinner so we took buttons, which wasn't very good either. Once Aunt Magdalene won and once I won.

When I came home I went to the piano and played with the baby on my lap. And then I helped make supper and then—oh everything went crooked. I cried, and I don't care if I do say it. Louisa Alcott cried too sometimes, and *she* wrote it in her journal. I long for school— and lessons—and true happiness. I am sorry that I have to write such things, you may think I'm a pessimist, but I'm not. I really think I'm an optimist; I intend to be one anyway, but you can't be happy when things go up-side-down. Oh I do hope I can go to school next year too.

It is getting cold in here. I guess I had better go to bed and sleep off *some* of my troubles. Not all—I can't, *all*. But I have a new waist and I may buy a tam! I am sad, and I am glad. Goodnight.

Dec. 31, Friday

The last day of 1909! A year, and what did it do? All kinds of things, pleasant and—some not so very pleasant. I went to school, and I am—oh, so glad! I only, only hope that I may go thru High School, and I hope our good teachers will stay longer.

Uncle Frank is playing on the guitar, such sweet, clear, free music. I love to read or draw or write while I'm listening to music, so I take advantage of it now—and—write.

It is after eleven now, going pretty near to next year. School won't start until next year, which would be a deplorable fact if next year wouldn't be so very near! I shall try to make the next year a brighter one, a more interesting one, and one—that is, if it's possible—in which I have done something worthy of myself.

Oh dear, what *have* I done? Next to nothing. Compare my drawings to those of Jessie W. Smith, J. M. Flagg, H. C. Christy and all the rest. What *are* they? Why, they're noughts, zeros, nothing, against them. I've often thought of this but never wrote it down. I wonder whether I'm making any progress at all, and whether I'll be clever enough to earn much money, at least enough to make us all comfortable. I wish I could see and talk with such artists as Jessie Wilcox Smith, and Mr. Fisher, and Mr. Flagg and the rest of my favorite artists.

About 10 minutes to next year.

1910

Jan. 1

A Happy New Year! The bells are still ringing. I threw my shoe over my head but I don't remember whether I'm going east or west, I was so excited. 1909 has gone forever! They're shooting the cannons, or something, now.

Fern was over here, and while Uncle Frank played guitar and I played piano, the others stepped the light fantastic toe—which really was only a two-step, and then Uncle Frank played guitar alone and I tried it. I'm glad I can dance a little yet; I haven't danced for ever so long.

Oh yes, we had for 10 cents oysters among us nine, and some nuts.

Why, I haven't eaten any cookies since last year, would you believe it?

RESOLUTIONS

1. Resolved that I shall try to make the next year brighter and pleasanter.
2. That I shall try to do neater and better work at school.
3. Resolved that I shall try to keep my things properly mended.
4. Resolved that I shall earn some money and try to let mama buy myself a gymnasium suit.
5. Resolved that I shall try to have more patience with my sisters and especially my brother.
6. Resolved that I shall clean up the attic so that people will not begin to feel faint when they look at it.
7. Resolved that I shall try not to worry any more than is necessary and to skip over troubles as lightly as possible.
8. Resolved that I shall try to practice more on the piano, and not such easy 1,2,3,4 ones either. Good ones I mean.
9. Resolved that I shall have to keep my clothes in their places, and not have them hanging all over the house.
10. Resolved that I must try and not forget to clean my teeth *every* day.
11. Resolved that I *must* try and not talk so awkwardly as I sometimes do.
12. Resolved that I must remember that I have to do my work before I can draw or read or play piano.

Jan. 3, Monday

School started to-day, and oh, how glad I am. I got up quite early, and had the worst time getting that unmanageable hair of mine to look as if I were really civilized and not a barbarian or Zulu chief. Went to school feeling as bright as a button.

Jan. 5, Wednesday

I am positively in love with Ancient History now. In a way I'm awfully sorry when I'm thru with it. I've found out a new way for studying and it works beautifully. It may seem queer, but perhaps I'll not love it so much some other time. Perhaps it's just because of circumstances too that I like it so well to-night. I should think girls who can study in nice comfortable rooms (in which you don't freeze as stiff as a poker if you sit quietly for 30 minutes) and who have no things to bother them, ought to fall in love with all their lessons.

Jan. 8, Saturday

I'll admit I didn't work much to-day. Aside from making beds, cleaning upstairs, washing the dishes, cleaning the dining-room and taking care of the baby, I had a pretty easy time of it. Of course I had to make the supper with Stella and saw wood—oh *that's* hard work—and there are piles of little things which all count something.

I've been trying to get an idea for a story all day but I couldn't think of a single thing until to-night, while I was drying dishes, it struck me that I might use this:—"Calico Trousers." Perhaps I shall write it to-night. Oh hum! I wish I had a whole lot of stamps, and I'd send things to 76 places. (Of course I really don't mean quite so many places. That's in there just to excite the imagination.)

Read over some of the stories I wrote last year in English Comp. There's one sentimental one about a flower which is simply awful, and another one about a dog which is awfully simple. I guess nearly all of my stories belong to either of those two classes.

Dehli keeps a diary now too. So does Tussy. I wonder how long they'll keep them up. I feel as if I couldn't get along without a diary.

Yesterday evening Miss Allen phoned about some programmes I'm to illustrate. Made 4 yesterday evening. I don't know whether I can take bookkeeping. I don't see where under the sun I'll get the money for the Bookkeeping books. I had better stop, my hand feels so scribbly.

Jan. 18

I feel quite happy to-night. I had a joke in the J.J. Got the check to-day. I'm mighty glad I got it, because now mama let me use a quarter for the Bookkeeping books. To-gether with the dollar I had put aside for a rainy day I brought it to Mr. Jolliffe and he gave me the books. Oh, a pile! Final Ancient exam. Farewell Ancient History, interesting study thou hast been!

Had such vague and dreamy feelings and thoughts to-day. Saw Halley's comet last night. It's too cloudy to see it to-night.

Bookkeeping is interesting and easy, except that you're apt to make mistakes. I've made 2 already but I think I can fix them allright. Got 65 in the algebra test. Have an order to make 5 Valentines. Started to-night.

Jan. 29, Saturday

Worked to-day. Swept, cleaned, dusted, and made the beds upstairs; and mended. Saturday is scrubbing day—Stella and I had that to do, and I'll have to iron yet, too. We got butter the other day from grandma's.

Talk of being Delighted. (Draw the *e* long for the desired effect.) I haven't had butter for a perfect age before this. Judy came in the evening and we acted. Am thru with "The Love of Azalea" and "A Cathedral Courtship."

About a week ago Mrs. Martin brought some nuts and apples. Also a lot of dress-goods. Oh a nice gingham for me!—and I'm in the highest stage of delight over it, too.

Feb. 1, Tuesday

When I came home from school I got a lecture. I'll confess I deserved it too; you just ought to have seen our attic the way it looked. It looked almost tragic (when you considered the person whose task it was to clean it up [which was me, as you'd see at first sight{ for it consisted—the things lying around, not the attic—of my papers & things, and magazines }]). If you got thru that safely, I congratulate you.

Attics are awfully queer things, I think. I dread to clean them up, still I don't want anybody else to clean it up, because they might throw away some of my things. And then it's ever so queer—every time I clean up I carry down armfuls of paper, and I never remember putting anything up which I didn't think valuable.

Ethel Kraft is coming next Saturday. She wants to take drawing lessons. Behold the drawing teacher, the famous world-known talented Vάνδα °Αζελ Γάγ (Sarcasm here.) I will try and see whether I can do it, anyway.

Miss Dillon gave me a basket ball ticket. Talk of being glad; I could have hugged her. Miss Lee wants a dozen Valentines. Stella and Tussy were at a sleighing party.

Buoyant feelings to-night. Goodnight. Sweet dreams.

Feb. 5, Saturday

Do you see this caricature? That's Miss Wanda Gag, Drawing Teacher, doncher know? I know the chin ought to recede a little more, but—a striking resemblance, isn't it? I got a compliment last night which nearly staggered me. Still, I think I'm still as indescribably homely as I ever was. My lovely big feet ought to be there to complete the beauty of the picture, *nicht wahr?*

Worked this morning, cleaned upstairs, and other things. The kids are criticizing my caricature, and say it doesn't look like me at all. Anyway, it doesn't make any difference as long as it shows correctly the degree of my homliness. She agrees (Stella, I mean) that my bow looks like that, "so little and squeezed to-gether." Don't care a snap.

Do you see this caricature? That's Miss Wanda Gay, Drawing Teacher, don cher know?) I know the chin ought to recede a little more, but — a striking resemblance, isn't it? I got a compliment last night which nearly staggered me. Still, I think I'm still as indescribably homely as I ever was. My lovely big feet ought to be there to complete the beauty of the picture, mi'st wahr?

Later:—It's all over, the drawing lessons, I mean. Elsie Myers came too. If they are as well satisfied with my work as I am with theirs, everything's allright as far as drawing lessons are concerned. Two hours they lasted, and I haven't the slightest idea of what I'll charge. They each made 3 Valentines besides a great many separate hands, faces, feet, and flowers. Am as happy as a lark. I got another ticket for the basket ball game and Stella's going along.

Later:—Our *girls* and *boys* won to-night. Did we cheer? I just think we did! Oh but those girls were pretty. Especially one who wore a red sweater and had light, fluffy hair. She looked for all the world like a Harrison Fisher girl. And cute! I wish I could have sketched her. She was a perfect picture.

I had visions—just as I was dropping off to sleep—of basket balls and basket ball players. I remember distinctly the New Ulm H.S. players at the very tip top of a sort of tree, and the Mankato players being trampled on unmercifully as our players were ascending to victory. (Rather flowery, isn't it?) Prenzel Bros. gave us a chicken.

February 7

Nearly done with the jobbing business in B'k-k'p'g. Had chicken to-day. Am nearly done with "Anne of Green Gables." L. M. Montgomery, the author, certainly has a great many original phrases and descriptions, I think.

I guess Fern and I will learn a new duet. Talking of music, our piano needs a tuning as badly as just about any other piano under the sun. The way it creaks and moans and sighs and squeals and hums is positively heart-rending. Still it's a great deal better than nothing, and it's a great comfort sometimes. Especially when things go crooked and I feel "weepy." Then that dear piano of mine is very sympathetic and its moans and lamentations sooth me ever so much. Then when I am happy I drown the squeaks by playing louder and forgetting them alltogether. If it didn't cost so much and if I weren't saving patiently for other more necessary things, I should save for having the piano tuned. Strange to say, altho I'm constantly saving, there isn't generally much money in my box. It generally goes for *still* more necessary things than those I had intended the money to go for. For instance, when I was saving for "a rainy day" (That certainly ought to be money invested in the right way, or kept), and there the dear, precious old dollar had to go for the book-keeping books.

Anyway I'm awfully apt to raise my aspirations and hopes and ambitions up on too high pinnacles and you can't imagine how very disappointing it is to have your castles in Spain come crashing about your ears like thunderbolts. Still I generally manage to get over the shock, uninjured; I'm used to dwell briefly on such things because I simply have to. I've been saving for a tam for ever and ever so long, and *guess* how much I have. Thirteen cents! And I've saved for anyway about 2 months! Of course I'm earning money right along only I can't keep it. And I'll gladly give it as long as I can go to school, so there's really no way out of it.

So much for pecuniary talk. There was something more I was going to say about that interesting piano of ours. There is an *f* that positively refuses to join in the squeaking and the "Giving-a-musical sound." It's so confusing not to have it sound at all.

I generally play different songs according to my moods. When I'm sad or meditative I generally play "The Johnstown Flood." When I'm dreamy I play "The Böhmerwald," when I'm furiously, recklessly disappointed or dejected, or in the "depths of despair," I play songs packed full of grief and disasters. The best I've found so far is "The Storm." Still it turns out well in the end and I was *so* disappointed. I had hoped there would be a total wreck, I was in such a cheerless, reckless mood at the time. Then when I feel loyal and glad and high spirited I play waltzes or High School songs.

I know this may sound silly and I'm positive I'll laugh at myself when I read this over later, but I have such "sentimental streaks" occasionally and I feel a great deal better when I've put my thoughts down in black & white (blue and white sometimes; colors vary according to the color of the ink, you understand.)

Feb. 8, Tuesday

Am just about as low-spirited this evening as I was high-spirited yesterday. Talk of adapting yourself to extremes. Drew some Valentines tonight. Mama went to Nora's and stayed for supper. We made supper, Stella and I. I didn't eat much tho, because we had sauerkraut and I don't like it at all.

I was in a royal mood last night. When I'm in such a mood I generally make elephants out of mosquitoes—our piano for instance (not that I mean that our piano looks like a mosquito. Not in the least. It's a veritable elephant as far as size is concerned.) The tune I mean.

Daisy and I did our B'k'p'g. I got stuck. Then we snapped apples.* My snaps turned out to be perfectly outrageous—one wasn't so bad because it was "I cast away." Stella keeps a diary now too.

Feb. 13, Sunday

Just piles of things have happened since last night. This morning Professor Koehler came with Mr. Hasenclever. Professor Koehler is a

---

* A method of telling fortunes similar to that of pulling petals off a daisy. The apple, while whole, was flicked with a snap of the thumb and forefinger and named for some boy. After the apple had been eaten, the seeds were carefully counted and one's fate determined by the following rhyme:

One I love,	Five I cast away.	Nine he comes,
Two I love,	Six he loves,	Ten he tarries,
Three I love I say,	Seven she loves,	Eleven he courts,
Four I love with all my heart,	Eight both love.	Twelve he marries.

drawing teacher in Minneapolis. He said I ought to go thru High School. There will be an art exhibition here about April and Mr. Koehler said I should draw something & put it there. He's a very nice man, not so very young, and very agreeable.

Feb. 14, St. Valentine's Day

The baby's drawing and we nearly died laughing over her.

After Glee Club when I came home I had to saw wood. Talk of physical exertion! Especially when you use such an excuse for a saw with a

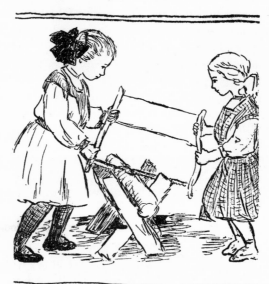

crooked blade. The saw-buck (or whatever you call the contrivance) turns around like a merry-go-round. "Sing merry, sing ho!" It takes my whole weight to keep the wood down on its place so I stood on it. We sawed until supper time and sawed anyway 16 to 18 pieces, which is really a good deal when you come to try it. Then I popped corn, got the milk, ate supper and washed dishes.

That's supposed to be Stella & Thusnelda, sawing wood. I was going to make myself standing on the wood but I'm so tall, & I wouldn't have my height diminished nor my head cut off, on account of that picture. I know a sawbuck doesn't look like that but I didn't want to go down the cellar to see, so it has to do, whether it wants to or not.

Tussy asks such silly questions sometimes. To-day she came down the steps while we were sawing wood and she asked, "What are you sawing?" I told her we were sawing ice cream with a butter knife. Suppose I'll dream about saws and wood and axes.

Am done with the "Crimson Sweater." It's a dandy. Goodnight.

Feb. 15, Tuesday

Can't think of anything to write but I haven't anything to do just now so I'm practicing penmanship and, possibly, orthography. Under the uncertain circumstances, my somewhat conjectural supposition, which happens to be whether or not I am positively sure of my Economics, may turn out to differ widely and greatly from said conjecture, as my weakly founded suppositions and guesses invariably have an odd way of doing.

Later:—I conjectured for nothing—my inferences and suppositions and guesses were for naught. I didn't have to recite in Economics; I only had to read out of the book.

Got my Ledger and Journal back from Mr. Winkler and he had a slip in each (on one he wrote, "Write your *best,*" and on the other, "Write as *neat* as possible"). I don't see how I can do it any neater. I've taken special pains in trying to do so. It's very humiliating to be *doing* your best and then getting slips with "*Do* your best" on them.

Feb. 19, Saturday

I worked. Played the scrub-woman, cleaned upstairs, washed dishes, and gave drawing lessons. Am going to get 2 new pupils next week at 25 cts. per lesson. Talk of being tickled. That makes a dollar a week! 4 dollars a month. The drawing lesson takes from 2 to 2½ hours. My two first pupils are certainly improving. They learned to draw faces from the side and they did well.

I got a compliment. Prof. Robert Koehler said to a lady that I was a "regular artist." I don't believe it goes as far as that, do you? It seems to me I'm not improving in the least. Wish somebody would tell me whether I am or not. They (whoever that is) hope to find all the "mute, inglorious Michelangelo's and Raphaels and Rosa Bonheur's" by that exhibition in April. Would that I were one. I'm inclined to feel "artisty" to-night so I'll let my thoughts have full sway. Am reading "Our Helen" which just suits me now because it's full of artists too. That reminds me, when, about 3 years ago, I was at Mankato a lady said to me, "So this is the paintress." It struck me so funny to be called a pain*tress*.

Fern is here to-night. We played Consequences. Last night Judy was here and we played Consequences too. Oh, we nearly died laughing, (at least my cheek bones felt pretty lame.)

The girls (Tussy, Asta & Dehli) have a drawing fit on. They are drawing from pictures and from life, to say nothing of drawing things out of their heads. They're just wild to take drawing lessons, but I haven't time.

Yesterday we had to sieve ashes. "Yen Yensen, Yanitor, at your service, sir, I bane." Then we made supper. Oh hum! some dandy sausage, don't care if I do say it because it wouldn't have been good if we hadn't taken such pains in making them. Oh glory! I'm tired. Just got thru sawing wood.

Thursday Daisy was up at our house. We told fortunes which were enough to make the sphinx in Egypt laugh.

Feb. 21, Monday

Had a dandy dinner to-day. I think Aunt Magdalene will make me a tam, Oh joy! I feel mighty wicked to-day and it always seems to me I look like the Cheshire cat with a horrible ear-to-ear grin predominating. Stella does beat the Dutch to-night. Rather witty speeches, to do her credit. *"Aber lass sie nur grad gehn, sie werd schon wieder zu sich kommen."* That's the popular expression just now.

Feb. 24, Thursday

Two tests tomorrow and I don't know beans. Lucy and Daisy were up at our house to-night. Gee, talk about laughing! We told fortunes and gave each other some new nick names. Lucy is "Clams," Daisy is "Scissors" and I am "Kettles." We're all mixed up in book-keeping.

Feb. 25, Friday

I'm stuck in Bookkeeping, stuck in the truest, awfulest sense of the word. Chopped and sawed wood until dinner was ready this noon. Our physical exercises are the saw, the ax and the saw buck. Oh Hum! talk of it! But I'm improving, if I *do* say it, I can chop one piece of wood at about 3 strikes.

February 28

Aunt Magdalene was here to-day and brought my dress. It is almost done. Oh, I'm glad. My grey jumper looks so funny already. I mean, not very clean.

Stella and Tussy stayed at Fischer's over night. They and Fern and Kurt were the only ones home. They were having a pillow fight when the bed cracked down! One of those boards at the bottom broke, and the mattress and springs and covers all went down with all four kids on it! Stella had rare presence of mind (she generally has) and asked for a hammer and nails. Then they took out the spring and mattress and everything and Stella nailed the boards together again.

Tomorrow I shall write in my new diary, so goodbye, dear journal. I welcome every new diary, and I welcomed you, so I welcome my new diary too. My motto, likewise the emblem, will convey my ideas for some time, until I have another idea.* I am free to change it if I wish. Motto: *Draw on, draw ever*.

*   *   *

Mar. 10, Thursday

Made an account of all the place cards, postals etc. that I have drawn and painted. There is over $100 clear profit since I have started to draw and paint for money. I started about October or September, 1908. After school I went down to Neeml's Store. I am to make 2 Easter rabbits, each 2 ft. high for the window.

Mar. 12, Saturday

All four girls were here to take drawing lessons. Chopped a whole lot of wood again and one piece fell on my head, too, a great big one. It's nicer to chop wood in the evening because people can't see all your awkward antics. I suppose I wasn't cut out for wood chopping any more than I was for good penmanship, but I'll have to do it anyway even tho I look like a jumping jack.

I had a drawing fit last night and drew Howard twice and Tussy once. When I am in a drawing mood:—

Not all the king's horses
Nor all the king's men
Can get Wanda to do her lessons
Or other things again.

Mar. 16, Wednesday

Yesterday after school I made supper with Stella. I made a cake. I

* A drawing of this emblem faces page 93.

just love to bake things, but it always costs so much. Daisy asked me to come down, so I chopped some wood and went. We got a pile of wood yesterday. Pleasant prospects, aren't there?

Mar. 17, Thursday

We had our new wood sawed. It's fun chopping now, because there are so many easy pieces which you can get thru at one stroke. Mama gave me her ring to wear. Gee it's cute.

Mar. 19, Saturday

To-day is a perfectly splendid day, warm and mild and sunny and cheerful, and oh I feel so happy! And what is more, I feel sentimental. When I am sentimental I am either gloriously happy or grievously, recklessly sad. When I am sentimentally happy I love everything, I feel as if nothing could ever make me sad. When I am sentimentally sad I sit and look pensively at Nature, at books, at pictures, at everything, except people. I scarcely see people then. I play either sad pieces or songs which have disasters or wrecks or accidents in them. When I am happy I play happy, jolly songs on the piano, my heart feels as if it were running over with happiness and I feel perfectly grand altogether.

I am sentimentally happy to-day, oh it is sweet to live and breathe and be happy! The trouble is, I have so little time to dream and think and enjoy nature as much as I want. I have to work, I have to draw, to help do my little share in keeping the wolf from the door. Oh I wish we were rich, just so I could only draw and dream whenever I want to. It is very queer but when I am with the girls or anybody, I hardly ever am sentimental, and half the time I can't express my thoughts, but when I write I generally can. Papa once said I could write better than I could talk. I think I inherited most of my dreamy nature from papa; dear, darling papa. I think I can cry any time when I think of papa, even if I am ever so happy.

It is still lovely outside even tho the sun has set.

Mar. 20, Sunday

Yesterday four drawing pupils came. Another dollar. In the evening the fire whistle blew. It was the Empire Mill and we could see the flames way up here. It was burnt to the ground.

Oh hum! Last night I did have the funniest dream. I dreamt Mr.

Winkler died and we had to make a Journal entry of it in Bookkeeping. I guess that comes of the speech of Brutus I'm always reciting:—

"Had you rather Winkler were living, and die all book-keepers and slaves; than that he were dead, and die all freemen?"

But that dream was nothing compared to the one I had about Mr. Evans. I dreamt he asked me whether I drew, and I said it was almost all I did. And he said, "You do all kinds of drawing, do you? For the Journal Junior, city drug stores and everything? So you are a monopolist." And there was another man there and when he went away, Mr. Evans started to walk across our lawn with me in the moonlight. Oh it was delicious, such a lovely night! Just when we were nearing the front sidewalk, Mr. Evans suddenly turned around and threw his arms around me and said, "I must have one kiss from you!" I just gasped and threw back my head and laughed; so he didn't get a kiss after all. When he had turned around so suddenly, some papers and things flew out of his pocket. I picked one up and found it was a sort of diary and started to read it. Just then we saw the other man putting up a dummy on the other side of the street, evidently to fool Mr. Evans. So we went around to the back yard to await the other man's appearance, while I read the paper. It was something like this:—"Came to this town in 1907. We won at the fair." And then I was just going to read something about myself when I woke up.

I know it is a perfectly ridiculous dream, I don't see how I ever came to dream that, but I thought I'd put it down for the fun of it. Mr. Evans is handsome; he is tall, too, and a little bit lanky. I guess I could know Mr. Evans any time if I'd only see his legs because he walks so funny. I think there isn't anybody who walks worse than I do, tho.

Mama told us about her beaux. There were about five men who were struck on her, and it's so funny to think every one of them wanted her and didn't get her after all.

Oh hum, last Saturday evening Daisy and I were out walking and we went up to Turner Hall and looked in the window. We saw Mr. Winkler and Mr. Evans turning.

Mar. 25, Friday

I'm in the Wholesale Flour Business in Bookkeeping now but oh hum! I'm mixed up. Have orders for 9 painted Easter Eggs.

Today when I went to look how the lilac buds were getting along, I found that the leaves were out already. So I took this diary and drew them in. I guess I shall do this until they have grown to their full size. Oh I'm glad spring is here.

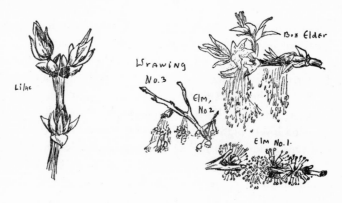

March 27, Sunday

Easter day. I got up at about five this morning and started the fire. Then Stella got up and we hid the Easter eggs all around the yard. The others got up at about 6:30 and then we hunted eggs until about eight.

Just got done drawing these branches again. It's so windy I could scarcely draw, because the twigs blew back and forth all the time.

Stella and I colored our eggs at Fischer's last night. On our way home we saw "Love in a One-seated Carriage." I'd like to croak! He had his arm around Her, and She didn't seem to object in the least. If it didn't come to kissing, it came near it anyway.

March 29, Tuesday

We are starting to clean house, beginning at the attic. Stella and I want to fix up our room properly once more in the third story. We'll have a bed up there, and a Japanese corner I guess, but we've got awfully little furniture.

Nearly bawled in Bookkeeping. Gee I could have smashed the whole books. It isn't fun when you get so mixed up you don't know whether you're going bankrupt or cheating.

Last night I drew Stella "laughing for to beat the band." I mean she was and of course I was, because when I draw, my expressions generally match those of the persons on the picture.

I wonder what makes me feel ready to "go in for it" as far as mischief is concerned. It must be the spring weather. Every day I feel as if I could do anything if it only means fun.

April 1.
Lilac

Drawing
No 7

. Apple
: Tree
. Bud

is hard for to-morrow, I mean Monday. Knew my Economics to-day. I will have to be drawing pretty soon, if I want to have some pictures at the exhibit. The leaves and buds are not growing very fast just now.

April 1, Friday

Got fooled only once. Oh but that Algebra is hard for tomorrow, I mean Monday. Knew my Economics to-day. I will have to be drawing pretty soon, if I want to have some pictures at the exhibit. The leaves and buds are not growing fast now.

April 2, Saturday

It seems to me I'm not improving one mite in drawing and I think I had better do the best I can; I must aspire to higher, more perfect things in the future if I want to attain the height I desire. I dream too, of better times, every bit as much as anybody else; of the time when I can get a new summer hat when I need one, and when I can make floating island and angel's food and other good things, and when I can fix up my room as I should like to.

To-night after supper I went up to our attic room and watched the sky. It was perfectly lovely. Blue fading into golden yellow and the yellow melting into a rosy red. The hills rose dim and grey against the glorious background. The lower part of the landscape was a misty bluish-green.

Towards the left I could see the hospital lights glowing thru the hazy distance. I don't know why it is but I love to see the hospital when the lights are on, and I always think of it as a place where you get well, always; and I think of the time when we went out so often to see papa, and where they made his leg well once more.

April 5, Tuesday

I guess to-night's election or something, anyway the band played the dandiest, danciest tune, so Stella and I went out and danced on the lawn. I just love to dance, only I can't dance very much yet.

I don't know whether or not I shall draw for the Art Exhibit here. Of course I don't expect to win a prize, there is too large a field, but as long as Mr. Koehler asked me I ought to put some there anyway. Perhaps I will have someone pose for me to-night—that is, if somebody wants to. I always have to practice on such little kids and I had rather try older girls, I think, for a change.

April 7

I drew Judy and Dehli last night. I don't see what's the matter with me, I can't draw these last days. I suppose just because Mr. Koehler asked me and I ought to do it, I can't.

I've got some drawings all sealed and addressed for the J.J. but I lost my stamps. The letter is dated Mar. 31, and if I don't get those stamps pretty soon I shall have to get it out and change it, and then make a new envelope again.* I feel nutty. Guess it's spring fever, eh?

April 10, Sunday

"The top of the morning to you!" I feel like a dozen of the grandest June days condensed into one splendid one, and that's saying a good deal. Some of the plum blossoms have opened and they are ever so lovely, so dainty and sweet, and others are just ready to open and look for all the

---

* We made most of our own envelopes out of wrapping paper.

world like little puffs of velvetty cream popping out of green scalloped vases.

April 13, Wednesday

I've got the "drawing fits" now; I could "draw on, draw ever." It's a lovely day; sunshine, flowers, green trees, blossoms and perfumes all in one grand, delicious jumble.

This noon Prof. Robert Koehler of Minneapolis was at our house and picked out some of my drawings to put on the exhibition, also some of papa's paintings. Oh dear, I wish I had somebody like Prof. Koehler to criticise my work. It would be so much easier for me if somebody would show me my mistakes, and a person can never find her own mistakes very well.

April 14, Thursday

Oh glory! if I feel as if I were anywhere I feel as if I were in the seventh heaven of delight! Honestly, I feel as if I had had a grand splendid dream, only it wasn't a dream at all. Lucy and Daisy asked me to go up to the art exhibit. Mr. Koehler speeched. And then Pres. Cyrus Northrop (of the State University) read the list of prizes and of course I didn't get any because I didn't expect any anyway. And when he was done he said something about an extra prize awarded to a young girl of New Ulm, and he meant me, just think of it! Really I had such a queer feeling, I was so awfully surprised. And then all the people turned around and looked at me. And then he said my name and asked if I was there and if I were I should come up and get my prize of $5.00 and Oh hum! I didn't want to go up there until they said, "Go on, Wanda," so I had to go. Gee (excuse this) I wonder how I looked stumbling up there (I suppose I *did* stumble) and then Pres. Northrop shook my hand and talked ever so much. I don't remember half he said because I was quite certain it was only a dream or one of my flights of fancy. And then he pressed the five silver dollars into my hand and said "if it wasn't too heavy." The money, you know. I thanked him and went back to my seat as red as a beet I suppose.

I got about 30 congratulations that evening, and all the while I couldn't see why so many people complimented me on such a few little drawings.* Pres. Northrop asked, "Since when have you been doing this work?" and I told him ever since I remembered. And then he said

* Three of these drawings are shown in the illustrations facing page 93.

that I ought to be sent to drawing school and Mr. Jolliffe and Prof. Koehler said they thought so too. Anyway I think this is about the happiest day of my life, and I'm not sentimentally happy to-day; it's just a pure, real, material happiness and it's grand.

It has snowed and it looks very queer. Green trees and plum trees which were white with blossoms—and snow! I wish it would go away soon. I have just about come to the conclusion that I like summer better than winter.

April 20, Wednesday

Saturday four drawing pupils came. Monday went to the exhibit with mama. Tuesday went to the exhibit with Fern. Mr. Hiller gave a splendid speech about artists. Mr. Winkler looked handsome that night. There is something fetching in slightly hollowed cheeks; it gives rather a firm resolute impression, and makes the lines of the face those decided lines which are rather bewitching, almost alluring.

May 2, Monday

Saturday five drawing pupils came in the morning.

Fischer's took Stella and me to *Shauturn*.* The exercises were fine.

Got my report and got 80 in Bookkeeping. I'm not going to let Mr. Winkler off before I give him a piece of my mind. I'm a little bit sore because I think I deserved more. Still I think it's rather nice to go to the teacher and act as if you were in the eleventh stage of fiery rage when you're really only angry in a mild way. It's a good deal of fun to go stalking up and down steps past your teacher glaring at him (or her) and he or she glaring back. Especially if the teacher makes up *himself*, like Mr. Winkler did last time.

May 9, Monday

I went down to Mr. Winkler Tuesday and gave him a piece of my mind. Saturday all six of my drawing pupils came, and I chased around the table like a race horse. My Trial Balance right at last!

May 22

This is two years since papa is dead. We wanted to go to the cemetary first, but I think we will go later in the week so that we can put some flowers out a few days before Decoration Day.

I found a new motto:—"Draw to live, and live to draw."

* The annual Gymnastic Festival. The correct spelling is *Schauturn*.

Bookkeeping's over. I nearly went bankrupt but the crash was cleverly (?) avoided.

June 4

Fun in school all week except exams. About half the Bookkeeping kids got zero in the state exam, and naturally I was one of the unlucky *"schluckers."* It seems to me bookkeepers were "born and not made" as well as poets. I can never, never hope to be a decent bookkeeper, and I'm mighty glad too.

Monday was Decoration Day. Daisy and I watched the parade. At first I wanted to go on the cemetary but I didn't anyway. I think I had rather go out with two or three others, than to go around, dressed up. Drew Mrs. Pfeffer's place cards, sketched the kids and wrote poetry. Bawled in the evening, I was so discouraged I could have cried quarts of tears, I guess. I wish papa were living so that there would at least be somebody who can understand me. People may think I am queer, I think myself that I am queer, sometimes; but I'm sure I can't help it. One who is an artist, or one who wants to be one (like me) has to dream and think, and that's all there's to it.

I felt blue to-day, I don't know why. People may say I have talent and they may say they wished they had it, but I'm sure if I have any talent at all, I have to pay for it; I do not have it for nothing. But I know I wouldn't want to exchange places with anyone else; there is always the talent (?).

June 9

Saturday all my drawing pupils came. Monday I went up to Turner Hall to practice singing. Paula Hershl was there too and we had ever so much fun.

I wish we had more money so I wouldn't have to draw so many things to sell, because I cannot afford to make the best kind of pictures at such very low prices. I need advice, and the time and means to improve my drawings, to do much better than I have been doing. I mean, work more true to life, with expression and strong, bold lines which I once learned to use and which I am almost forgetting. But what's the use of dreaming and thinking these things when we need the money right now?

June 11, Sat.

School's out and I'm not one bit too glad. Yesterday afternoon Paula,

Lucy and I said goodbye to Mr. Winkler. We stayed until all the others had gone, and played and sang High School songs all we were worth for; we couldn't bear to part with our dear old High. Afterwards I walked on top of the desks and Paula and I made farewell speeches, and finally I drew on the board with green, yellow and white crayons, a girl crying, and wrote beside it, "How can I leave thee," and some more such illustrated things. Then we went home.

June 14

I feel lonesome not going to school. I dream of school or the teachers nearly every night. Stella had an illustrated joke in the J.J. Sunday.

June 25. At grandma's.

Stella does have the funniest notions. The other evening Uncle Josie gave us a ride on the launch, and it was evening and the scenery was too lovely for words and I was sitting there looking at it when Stella said, "Oh, now she wants to look like a Harrison Fisher girl again!" when, in fact, I was only trying to think out a story to send to the J.J. next week! And the idea of comparing myself; turned-up nose, brown skin and straight hair to the Harrison Fisher girls with their perfect noses, roseleaf skin and lovely wavy hair!

If I could only ever learn to draw as well as Harrison Fisher or some of my other favorite artists! When I compare my drawings to theirs they seem so pitifully stiff and childish and unfinished. I'd like to sit down with a dream of a model before me and dash off something worth looking at. That's a great point too, models; models who are willing to pose for you, lovely models—with those, a good drawing pencil and proper drawing paper, I might be able to improve a little.

But there's always that unavoidable, bothersome money question. Of course I'm not anything near to a miser, not even tenth cousin to the great-grandmother of one, but in these days a person can't get along without money; cold hard cash.

> "Here's to good old cash,
> Which Bill Shakespeare called trash!"

But I don't agree with William Shakespeare as to the "trash" part. He wouldn't either I guess, if he were in my shoes. Sort of unlucky shoes too, I should think, with holes & worn heels. But it's not my shoes that bother me so much, there are other things. I think by mixing the proper ingredients I might concoct a very delectable dish, a dish for the spirit and the mind, one to make unhappiness a foreign dish. My recipe would be something like this:—

> Fold together lightly a generous amount of money and time (care must be taken, however, not to use *one* atom too much). Then add slowly one teasp. good cheer, a good pinch of Baking powder (Sunshine kind is the best to elevate hopes and spirits.) Let this stand for a few minutes & add a scant tablesp. each of sentiment & dreaminess & fancy. Beat to a cream and add a flavoring (Work, Fun or Music or Drawing are best, never use Worry or Glumness in making this dish.) From this paste you can either bake Happiness Tarts or Contentment Wafers. They are beneficial to the health even when eaten between meals. (Silly, eh?)

That is *my* idea of happiness. I do not know whether others agree with me. I wish someone else would express opinions as to that, it isn't much fun to express one's opinions without knowing what other people think.

Was up at Paula's yesterday afternoon and had a lovely time. We mostly expressed our thoughts as to various subjects. Paula seems to think a great deal the way I do, and I'm mighty glad there is *someone* who gets "sentimental streaks" as well as I. After supper we went to singing practice at Turner Hall. After that we took a walk and talked of scores of things but mostly the teachers, we never tire of that. Paula always plays pieces on the piano according to her moods as I do, and she always plays piano, too, when she gets new slippers or shoes. That's been a habit of mine for ever so long and it seems so funny to think someone else does that too. I used to think I was the only one.

June 30

Singing Chorus practice again at Turner Hall. Paula and I have the most delightful game that we play between the times we sing. It's making sentences having words which start only with a certain letter. Like this:—Flirty, frivolous, flat-headed Frederick finds fun forming fanatical fancies for Florence's flowery future.

I dreamt I saw Mr. Winkler shaving himself thru the window. (I mean I *saw* him thru the window) and then Mr. Evans came over, tacked up like a regular dudified chap, looking unusually foxy, and wearing at least eight big, imposing rings. I asked him to play piano but his rings were in the way so he tore them off and threw them over to the other side of the room.

July 1

I feel positively nutty. It must be the heat for I feel as if I didn't care for a single thing. I'm beginning to tire of vacation, it's too much the same thing. Of course there's the Turnfest, but I suppose I shall only be there the afternoon we sing because otherwise I'll have to pay a dime to get in, and I simply can't afford it; so what's the use of building diamond-studded gold-pillared castles in the air? Such is life without chink!

Goodbye diary, the time has come to bid you a fond farewell and welcome a new diary (altho I haven't as yet any to welcome). May dear old Sister Fate provide me with a decent book. *Au revoir.*

* * *

Part Two

FRIENDS AND CAVALIERS

1910

July 12, 1910

By every new diary I make up my mind to try to write legibly and keep my book neat; every time I start out with a pretty fair penmanship and a few decorations such as mottoes or tinted illustrations, and every single time my writing gets worse as the days pass by and a great many decorations such as crossed-out words and ink blots fill the pages. I got this book from Stella, via exchange (don't know whether that's right; used it for the silliness of it.)

I started to read "Truxton King;" all McCutcheon's books are dandies, so of course this is.

Last Sunday Lucy came up and in the evening we both went down to the park and *"verblitzt"* a nickel. I saw a couple down there. I thought it was a perfect match. He was tall and very handsome, for he had lovely, kind eyes and a firm mouth which looked "fetching" when he smiled. And he was strong and well-dressed, and his cheeks were somewhat hollowed, which I like. His wife was a sweet little thing with a mass of lovely brown hair, a clear complexion and pretty eyebrows and brown laughing eyes. I fell in love with them both, not each one separately, I just liked to see them to-gether—but—he was a butcher and she was 5 years older than he, and one tower of my lovely thought-castle crumbled and fell.

I made up a game the other night. You name a person's fingers and decide upon what it shall mean, such as, "With whom are you going to go home from the reception next year?" "What teacher will you like best?" "Whose pet will you be?" and ask her to choose one of the fingers, which will answer the question.

Thursday Paula asked Daisy, Gertie and me up to her house. It was a perfect jumble of conundrums, jokes, cakes, fruits, anecdotes and laughter. Gertie always teased me with Mr. Evans.

July 13, Wednesday

Yesterday evening Paula and I walked around for a while. We planned to get up early to-day and take a walk, and eat our breakfast, to some out-side place. This morning at 5.30 we started off over hills and thru valleys until we came to a fence. On the fencepost we set our lunch and started to eat it. Delicious? Talk of it; it was "delicatisch!" We came back at about seven and decided to go tomorrow again, for it's fun.

Stella and I are cleaning house, one room at a time, and by jinks! it's hard! We washed the woodwork and most parts of the walls, and hung up foxy pictures. We have the evenings free tho, that's one good thing.

Gee, but I saw a lovely group of trees and underbrush. Dark gloomy foliage in the background, white-trunked birches standing before this as slender and tall as can be, and a green undergrowth of bushes here and there, while a large golden sheet of barley spread out before it. Splendid? Well, I should guess!

It just strikes me that it's rather "story-bookish" to be poor. I maintain my old view tho:—That it's no *fun* to be poor. (Listen to the wondrous sayings to the world-famed philosopher "Kettles." Ahem!)

July 23, Saturday

Yesterday Paula and I walked out on the prairie. Have been out every morning this week except Monday.

Up at school we were looking at the College Annual and saw a picture of one of our High-School teachers of next year, Mr. Doom. I also found out that Mr. Winkler & Mr. Doom intend to room at Logan's.

Today I drew & painted & painted & drew (place cards). To be sure I worked. Had all the Saturday cleaning done at about ten.

July 24, Sunday

Last night Lucy and I went to the depot to see the 2nd Regiment Band and Co. A come home from camp.

There are a nurse, Miss James, and a handsome man, Mr. Cone, room-ing at Logan's across the street and it seems they have struck up a delight-ful acquaintance, and it looks as if they are already beginning to fall in love. They sit in the swing or on the bench and laugh and talk which are pretty grave symptoms of love-fever. And last night they were at the

depot together and I kept tract of them right along. When they came
near Diel's they made a Dutch crossing and so did I, walking right be-

Cupid where ANT THOU ?
Theres a couple
Across the street
Needs you ! "

fore them. They were walking side by side and he was holding her hand.
I nearly croaked!

Oh yes, I am counting hat-tips. They say the 101st man who tips his hat
will be your better half! I have seven so far. I hope for the cat's sake that
the 101st one will be a decent one (and one who appreciates art!)

July 25

Washday. Got done before dinner. Yesterday evening the Singing
Chorus went out to Kesterbaum's. Had a dandy time, dandy music and
dandy lunch. (I hope I have dandified enough!) But the loveliest part
of the whole evening, for Paula and me at least, was spent the last hour
or so. We were both in the hammock. Comfortable? I should hope so.
There were some lanterns strung up and Paula named them for me and
I named them for her. We agreed that the lantern which went out first
showed that he for whom it was named was the first to prove untrue,
and the last was the truest. Mine came in this order: Mr. Doom, the boy
from Madison, Minn., and last of all, oh horrors! Mr. Evans! Paula's
last one was a conductor in St. Paul, No. 1552. Oh hum!

Last night Lucy and I went to the band concert and whom should we
see but Mr. Cone and two other ladies (not Miss James) and later we
saw Miss James and a man (who was not Mr. Cone)! And I thought
they were head over heels in love with each other. Oh hum!

July 28, Friday

To-day Mr. Diel phoned and asked whether I had a picture of myself; he wants to print it. Did I nearly fall over? For you to say. You see it's this way. In the paper there was an article about an Art contest—once while I was drawing lilacs Mr. Winkler came with the article cut out, and gave it to me and I said I might try. I did try it for the fun of it (it wasn't worth two cents for I didn't feel like drawing those days—I guess I would have gladly exchanged it for an ice cream cone) and with it I sent a slip saying I was sending it mostly for the criticizm because I needed it so badly (that's only too true). It was still early Spring when I sent it and I thought it had gone into the waste basket. It happens that it's *considered* (that isn't saying that it *is*) the second best of Minnesota and I'm to get a medal. Fancy! And the picture, and a picture of myself, is to be published. (Much they'll have to see on either.) Sarcasm, here.

Anyway it happened that I had no picture taken of myself lately, so I stalked down town to Mr. Madl the photographer's and he said he'd get it done by Monday. I suppose I looked like a perfect stiff even tho he said my pose was natural! Jinks! but I'm glad I'm going to get a picture of myself once! Seems to me "Good things never come singly" either. I'm optimistic tonight, don't you think so?

Still I wasn't so awfully surprised when I heard. Splendid things come so often, I'm learning to take them in quite a manner-of-fact way. It seems the Art Exhibit gave me such a shock that I haven't recovered from it yet and am still quite senseless to the succeeding ones.

July 30, Saturday

Got up pretty late—seven; and did the Saturday work.

Went and got my medal. Oh it's cute; I'm simply in love with it. I haven't shown it to anybody except mama yet tho, because nobody is supposed to know about it yet. I read the note they sent along for me—it's an awfully nice one, too—and also a reproduction of my drawing.

Aug. 7, Sunday—At grandma's.

Monday I went down and got my picture. Mr. Madl gave me three and didn't charge anything for taking them, which I thought was awfully nice of him.

Have 10 hat tips now. *Only* 91 more, oh hum!

Friday Aunt Magdalene came up, and in the afternoon Stella, Baby and

I went with her down to grandma's. The grasshoppers are fierce and spoil the tomatoes and cabbage. The corn is not quite ripe but there is a good deal of it. I have read three acts of "Chanticleer." It's perfectly splendid. My arms and face and neck are beginning to tan beautifully (?). I don't give two cents, as long as I feel good and cool.

Gee, I wish I hadn't drawn this pieface on here; so much space wasted.

Perhaps Aunt Mary is going to Rosen's to-day and *perhaps* she will get the *Volksblatt* along so I can see the picture of myself and see what they have written about me. I'm pretty anxious to see it, for this is the first picture of myself that ever was published.

Yesterday evening Aunt Magdalene set the phonograph a-going while we stretched out on the bed and listened. You don't know how delightful it is until you've tried it.

Painted 2 ladies' heads yesterday.

Aug. 10, Wednesday

Sunday afternoon Miss Peters and her nieces came down. I made the phonograph go and then sat down a while and talked. It bores me to talk about people of whose affairs aren't any of my business, so I went out and helped Aunt Mary get supper. I wore Aunt Mary's dark blue dress with the white dots and it fitted allright and Stella gave me two compliments. (Just think, Stella of all people! She's always criticising my clothes and hair and walk.)

Aunt Mary was at Rosen's yesterday and mama phoned and said I should come home to-day because there is a letter there from Prof. Koehler to be answered. I'm on pins and needles to see what he has to say (or write!) so I got up quite early this morning in order to get ready in time.

2:25 p.m.:—Went up to town about nine a.m. When I got home I read what the paper had to say about my medal and saw the picture of my humble self and also the picture I drew, which was printed in the paper.

Read the letter Professor Koehler sent me. He said papa's paintings are worth $50 and more apiece. He advised me to draw from nature as much as I could and addressed me "Dear Wanda" and signed himself "Your Friend, Robert Koehler." I thought that was very nice of him.

I got myself a bottle of India ink. I had an illustrated poem in the J.J. last Sunday.

Aug. 14, Sunday—at grandma's.

Yesterday I ironed. Read "His Wife and His Work" in Hampton's Magazine. It is the story of an artist whose wife didn't want her husband to paint from models because it made her jealous. When I read stories about artists I get to thinking about art more than ever. This morning it was deliciously cozy in bed so I looked over my drawings to see if I couldn't criticise them a little myself. I could; I found some mistakes which I knew how to correct—to some extent, I mean. It strikes me so queer that every one who does any drawing or painting, whether he is an artist, or hopes to be one (as it is in my case) has a style of his own. One would think there weren't enough styles to supply them all! And just think of all the scores of artists still waiting to become famous; where *will* they find enough individuality in their work? I'm sure I don't know, but I suppose they will when the time comes.

It always seems to me that the styles of drawing and painting are divided into several great classes and these great classes are divided into smaller classes. For instance there is the style Jessie Wilcox Smith uses, which is also used by Katharine Wireman, Katharine Shippen Green, and B. Cory Kilvert—to some extent. Of course there is a wide difference but I mean the general "outline" style.

Then there's the pen-and-ink style which is used by Gibson and Flagg. There is a much different touch in both, but so very much depends upon the heaviness and lightness of the lines.

And now I come to what I was thinking of this morning. I don't remember who the artist was, but she uses the kind that depends almost entirely upon the relative denseness of the different parts, and the difference in designs. I mean the way the drawings are filled out causes the contrasts, and not the heavy and light lines.

Aunt Mary baked four cheese cakes, oh hum! Hope we'll have some for dinner, for you can't imagine what good ones she can make.

My Seven Sweet P's
1. Pallete
2. Paint brush
3. Pencil
4. Pen
5. Paper
6. Pastel
7. Paint

* * *

Aug. 29, Monday

The first day of school and I am a Junior. Oh hum! People must think I am a pretty giddy one. Never mind, I shall sober down sooner or later. Honestly, I feel like dancing a jig sometimes to give way to my feelings. I feel as if I had bushels of "delightfulnesses" and ever so many other happy things at my disposal. I know I am very vague, but for the love of soup, do not criticise me to-day—I'm too excited.

This morning when I came to school I was simply bubbling over with joy. Fancy! :—

Plane Geometry—by Mr. Winkler
Modern History—by Mr. Doom
Civics—by Mr. Doom
B. Literature—by Miss Lee

After school Paula and I went down town to get my medal. I had it at the jeweler's to get a ring put on. Now I can wear it with a ribbon (inasmuch that I have no chain). I shall wear it to-morrow. Didn't eat much supper—was too excited.

Mr. Doom doesn't look half bad. He wears glasses, has dark brown eyes and dark brown hair. He looks and acts as if his temper were not easily ruffled—he smokes. Last but not least; he is pretty small, smaller than Mr. Winkler.

Nineteen hat-tips so far.

August 31

Geometry is all right so far. Understand everything. B. Lit. is first rate.

Yesterday evening I went to Turning School with Paula. I intend to go right along now. Oh how I wish I had bloomers.

Sept. 4, Sunday

Aunt Magdalene and Uncle Frank came.

Mr. Doom is a specimen. He laughs half the time and seems to take life as a huge joke. He twists his eye brows so one is much higher than the other; still this is not a great accomplishment. I could do that years ago. He can't keep his hands still, and Daisy and I have the most fun watching him give his row of books their "ten-minutely push."

After he's been in class for a few minutes his cheeks grow pink at his cheek bones which looks rather queer.

Whatever else he may not be able to do, Mr. Doom can talk rather nice. If he would only leave his r's out halfway I would think he were a . Southerner. He has a drawl, and no doubt.

Yesterday morning I worked, naturally. In the evening Paula called for me and we went to turning school. I wore Fern's bloomers. Oh how I wish I had some of my own, and turning slippers too. But what's the use of wishing? We walked around for a while after turning school and went to Hershl's where I got a *"Berliner Pfankuchen."* Um! it was delicatishe! Then we went to our house, when something struck our funny spot and we all laughed until it was positively an impossibility to laugh any more, so we stopped.

This morning I read a chapter in "Anne of Avonlea." It was a perfect dream of one, too, for its characters dream and think just as Paula and I often do. One of the girls thought that if a soul could be seen it ought to look like a flower.

In that case Miss Dillon's soul ought to look like a snowdrop, I think, pure and fair and unpretentious, and still with a graceful dignity.

Miss Lee's would be like a butterfly orchis, gay-looking; and Miss Alden's would look like a dahlia, rather dignified and with somewhat severe lines at places.

Mr. Evans' ought to look like a bashful peony, with reddish streaks to stand for occasional embarrassment; like a camelia would be that of Mr. Winkler, I should say, simple and resolute and amiable.

Mr. Doom's would naturally be like a buttercup, untroubled and somewhat extravagant.

Paula's would be like a pansy, I know, full of lovely thoughts and kindliness, and Gertie's would be like a Purple Columbine, resolved and gracefully reserved.

Sept. 6, Tuesday

Monday morning I got up quite early. Dressed and did housework before school. Oh yes, Sunday afternoon Paula came down and oh, I made up a ridiculous poem—that is I really didn't make it up but the poem simply presented itself to me. It ends:—

> He wraps his nose in curtain-tails
> And hardly ever shaves.

I'm too silly to be awake these days. I guess I had better go to bed at 6:30 and get up at 8:00 so I'm out of eyesight of the people for as long as possible, because else their opinion of me will fall until they've got none left for me at all, at all. It is a good thing that I am serious for days at a time, tho, only at times I am too serious, but of course that can't be helped sometimes.

Sept. 14, Wednesday

Friday evening after school we sawed and chopped wood. We do that nearly every day, for that matter. It's hard, too, and knocks your hands up like everything. Last year I could do it quite well already, tho. I could easily chop up four pieces in half an hour.

Friday evening Paula came down and we practiced duets until Daisy came. After nine Daisy wanted to go home and on the way a queer idea struck us. Paula made off she was Mr. Winkler and started to ask me questions in geometry. She was just asking me to define vertical angles when a man passed. And it was Mr. Winkler. Fancy! And I, to top all, gave the wrong definition while he was still about one or two feet behind us. Oh hum! He must have thought that was the way we learned our lessons. But it wasn't. Then we started asking Modern History questions but we didn't meet Mr. Doom.

Paula takes B. Literature and Modern in the same class with me. Tickled? Oh Glory!

Oh yes! before I forget; Paula and I have counted 7 stars for 7 nights and guess what I dreamt last night! That Mr. Doom was growing a mustache!

The other day I started to draw Mr. Doom and perhaps I could have drawn some more on it to-day, but by the great sizzling sky rockets! he has got his hair cut and I'll have to start right over again.

Sept. 15, Thursday

Yesterday evening Paula and I practiced duets at our house after supper. Then we went to Turning School and later to Paula's. Had some dandy fudge and snapped apples. Paula and I have a code called "Kumilikam." Geometry's fine. Chopped wood after school to-night as usual.

Sept. 18, Sunday

Yesterday when I went down town I met a little boy, and he said, *"Oh du Swellie."* I was wearing my 48-cent dress, mind you! I nearly went up!

Am done with "Anne of Avonlea." It's a perfect dandy, and I hope Mr. Montgomery will write another book about her.

Yesterday evening I was sitting on the swing—it was a lovely evening —and I was dreaming, as usual, when I decided to say over my geometry proposition, and, as I had no paper, imagine the figure. I just happened to glance up, however, and I saw something oddly beautiful (for this instance at least).

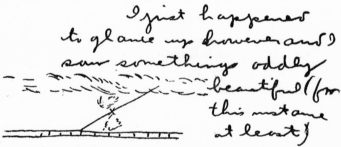

This lower thing is the telephone wire, the top part is a long narrow cloud parallel to the wire, and the slanting line is a wire which serves as the transversal of the parallel lines. The two little clouds served very well for a line perpendicular to the parallel lines, and at the place marked x there were no clouds at all, so that was the middle point of the transversal when it is met by the imaginery perpendicular. As the proposition for Monday is "when two parallel lines are intersected by a transversal their alternate interior angles are equal," this bit of landscape served admirably for a figure. And with it I worked out my geometry proposition easily enough. I will try hereafter to find other figures in the same way.

Sept. 19, Monday

I had an illustrated story and an illustrated joke in the J.J. yesterday. I got first prize at the Fair for my drawings. Dehli and Asta each got a 2nd prize. After supper Paula came down and we studied very little and played piano for a long time. Our duets, of course, again. Every day occurrence.

I wonder how Miss Lee can always tell when I want to ask or answer a question. She always says, "What is it, Wanda?" when I want to say something even if I don't raise my hand.

Sept. 22, Thursday

Mr. Doom has a pair of new button-shoes. To-day during Modern I sketched them and wrote underneath, "Ahem!"

Mr. Winkler has a new motion to denote silence. He will say, "I want *absolute* silence!" and sort of wave his arms back and forth, lower and lower, until he has raised his eyebrows and looked around to see whether his orders have been obeyed. Mr. Doom took a notion to be graceful too it seems, for the other evening when he went out of the assembly room, he spread his arms to the side and twisted his hands up and down beginning at the wrist.

Paula dreamt that Mr. Winkler ate a lily. *Ich sag nichts mehr!*

Yesterday evening I went to Paula's after supper. Played duets, went to turning school, played duets, studied and snapped apples, and played duets again.

I suppose Mr. Doom got himself extra high heels on his shoes to make him several inches taller. Oh hum!

I may be wicked to-night but I can't help it. I feel so bum anyway. When things go crooked you generally grow cross and pessimistic. I will dismiss the subject however; I think it is best to leave out unpleasant things.

Sept. 26, Monday

Friday morning mama, Howard and Baby went down to grandma's. After supper Paula and Gertie came down just as I was finishing a picture of Mr. Doom. I made him short, let me assure you! The girls said I got the sarcastic smile, too. Hope I did.

Sunday we organized a Club. I am President, Paula Secretary, Stella

Vice-president, Fern Treasurer, and Gertie the entertainment committee. We have a yell, a password and a foxy handshake. Also a motto.

Got a letter from a girl (or a boy, who knows?) who signs himself "A Journal Junior Reader." It's a sweet little letter saying that she (or he!) is always disappointed if I have nothing in the J.J. I wish I knew the writer's name so I could answer the letter.

After school I was showing Daisy that picture of Mr. Doom when Harold Hiller looked over our shoulders and saw it. He asked if he could show it to Mr. Doom. I didn't want to at first, it seemed so silly, but finally I said, "I don't give 2 cents" and gave it to Harold. Then Harold and some of the other boys went over to Mr. Doom with it. When they came back they told me that Mr. Doom thought it "pretty good" but that he had remarked on the shape of the head—"It is almost like a cube," he said. Fancy! I suppose he didn't know before that his head looked quite much like a cube also. And he said to the boys he was going to keep it and hang it up in his gallery, whatever that contrivance may be. I hope he knows where to join it—it's in 2 parts, and if he joins it at the wrong place it would make him too tall. Oh but there are some slams in that picture, his hands in his pockets, for instance, and the sarcastic mouth. Anyway he can see that his pupils have noticed his new shoes for I've got them all shiny on the picture.

Sept. 29, Thursday

Life is not always so bright as it seems, and I am seeing my share of the dark side at present. Still I try to keep a shiny outside, and maybe I try too hard at times. I feel as if I had to-day. I hope people will not think I am very silly, because it's really only a sort of re-action of pent-up energy—and trouble too, for that matter. If I only had a great deal of drawing to do, matters would straighten out noticeably. If I could, I should give up wishing for things for which it is quite impossible to come true. For instance, my wish regarding a gymnasium suit and turning slippers:—there is just about as little hope for that wish to be realized as there is for the moon to turn purple.

I know I've been acting pretty silly lately, but I can't help it, it seems to come so natural, altho I never used to cut up like that last year.

October 10, Saturday

We have current topics every Friday in Modern, and last Friday when Mr. Doom called on me I strung off a lot of stuff about Winslow Homer

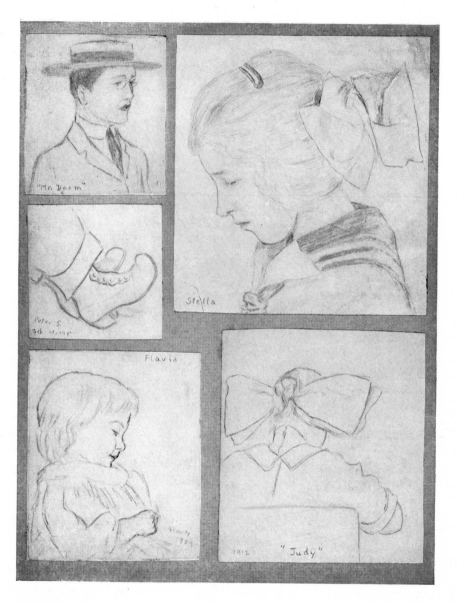

Five Pencil Drawings—Mr. Doom, Feet, Stella, Flavia, Judy, 1909-1912

Emblem and Three Sketches—Asta, Tussy, Dehli

who died last week. I said, "I think Mr. Homer has done more for American art than we realize for he developed National art." Said something too about Mary Cassatt and James McNeill Whistler. I gave a good many opinions of my own. When I got done he actually knew a good deal about art! All about Whistler's having spent most of his time in France and all that sort of thing. But he didn't seem to get the difference between National art and characteristic Art, and when I said, "But I mean *National* art not *characteristic* art," he sort of smiled with an "I-give-it-up" kind of a look and marked me. Wonder what I got.

October 24

Jinks! I'm sore at Mr. Doom! He said—or is supposed to have said, at least—that all, with the exception of one, who go to High School, are kids. Kids indeed! It wouldn't be such a bad idea for him to stand on his manly dignity a little more, *I* think.

And then he said that New Ulm girls have never been in love before, because every time he looks at them they blush. Also that Daisy and Lucy were in love with him for that reason. Did you ever hear the like? I didn't, but he needn't think he's as cute as all that, don't care if I do say it. If we smile, he thinks we're struck on him; if we don't, he thinks we're sore and comes stepping up to see what's the matter. How does he expect us to act anyway? Like some mummiferous idiot who doesn't crack a smile nor frown, just staring around in ignorant bliss, not dreaming of being offended whether they were called a pie face or a stewed oyster? Suppose so; but I shall not do it. Pooh!

Paula and I have certainly got it in for him and all his conceited ideas. We were fully resolved to act sore, and we kept our resolutions. When Mr. Doom called on Paula to recite she said, "I don't know" just as cooly; and right after he had asked me and I said, "I don't know" as cooly as I could, he tried to crack a joke again and said, "That's very serious." Serious indeed! His opinion on the matter isn't worth an oyster to me. Later he called on me again and I shot daggers, let me tell you. I had plenty of wrath in store and didn't try to keep it either. After class I stalked out of the room just as haughtily as I could. He is greatly mistaken, that's a cinch. He really thinks he's the cutest fellow that ever came to New Ulm. Thanks, your graces (?) have no charms for me!

He said we talked German slang. Thanks for your information! Certainly can't blame me for not talking German correctly when I'm not German at all.

Forty-one hat-tips. Last night Uncle Frank and mama developed some of the plates I took last year. One of Paula, Gertie, Baby and me isn't so bad except that the baby moved, and I look like a melancholy, stretched sardine.

Here are my test marks. Modern 99, Civics 80, B. Lit. 93, and Geometry 100. On my test paper Mr. Winkler wrote something I never expected of him. He gave slams! He wrote, "Avoid a medium between shorthand and good writing." I wonder whether he is taking lessons from Mr. Doom.

This diary is almost done. Don't see where I'll get the money for a new one. Mr. Doom may *think* I've patched up, but I've got it in for him!

Oct. 28, Friday

Paula has a new waist. Looks pretty nifty. Oh Glory Hum! I have a new diary. Also a belt-pin. Got 25 cts. from Miss Lee for making a Hallowe'en book so I dared myself to invest a few cents. Farewell, diary, you have often been my friend when I felt blue.—Wanda.

* * *

October 31

To-night's Hallowe'en. Heigh-ho. I notice in looking over my old diary of last October that I was a great deal more dreamy and poetic than I am this year. Miss Allen gave back my birthday book and ordered some for herself.

This morning I saw Mr. Doom across the street. At first I wasn't going to look over but then I thought, "Well, another hat-tip," so I did anyway. Forty-two hat-tips. I wish Mr. Doom would do something to show his real character so I would know how to act. He certainly is a riddle from the top of his square head to his button shoes. Moreover he talks in riddles, acts in riddles and looks in riddles. Who will solve him? I hope to goodness I'm not as "riddly" as all that.

Thusnelda had an illustrated joke in the J.J. Got the check to-day. I hope Miss Alden wants a stack of birthday books so I'll have some money to save up for the time the Junior-Senior Reception comes next spring. I'm sure I don't know what I'll do about it. I suppose I'll just have to stay at home, that's all.

Paula was on the program for an original story and won the point.

November 1

I haven't solved Mr. Doom yet; altho I am trying very hard. You can't imagine how interesting it is to find out the characteristics of a person, comparing them, and then decide on his or her real character.

I actually pity little Felix for all the slams he gets from Mr. Doom. If he doesn't get up to recite Mr. Doom says, "Get up; I can't see you," and some time ago he said, "Felix, you had better take this front seat"; then as an after thought, "For obvious reasons." Obvious reasons, indeed! For what reasons besides *obvious* reasons has he got such high heels, I'd like to know—and for what reasons does he stand on tiptoe against the wall and *try* to look tall, if not for obvious reasons? Pooh!

To-day he called on the class all around except Felix and then he said, "Why Felix, I overlooked you." As if Felix were made of toothpicks and pinheads! Some day, if I get a chance, I shall overlook *him*, just you wait.

Mr. Winkler has a new accomplishment. He can raise his eyebrows in such an appealing way. It makes him look quite handsome. He always looks so dreamy lately. Wonder what makes him so. He has a cold sore. Oh hum!

I felt so sentimental to-day. I don't know what's the matter. When I came home from school I helped with the housework and then played piano in the twilight. When I play piano when I'm sad I don't hear its miserable squeaks and wails, I just play to drown my feelings. I don't see what I'd do without our piano and my diary. It's getting cold in here so I'd better hike off to bed. Goodnight.

Nov. 6, Sunday

Just pasted up all the rest of the pictures, poems, stories and things we've had published in the Journal Junior. In all I have earned $76.75 from the J.J., Stella $3.50 and Thusnelda $3.00. I have had in the J.J.:—36 pictures, 4 stories and 4 poems, besides of course the Robby Bobby set which really consisted of 60 pictures and a story.

I haven't earned much last month, $4.55—sometimes I earned from $8 to $9 or $10 a month. But now in winter I think I will get more to do. There are more parties and things. I hope I'll get stacks of place cards to do. Last night I started a Thanksgiving poem and this morning I finished it. I intend to send it off to the J.J. to-day with an illustration.

Worked yesterday like a beaver—scrubbed, cleaned upstairs and downstairs, washed dishes and did all manner of things. Miserable day on the whole. Bawled because I haven't a thing to wear on my head this winter.

Dreamt of Miss Allen and Mr. Winkler last night, and music.

The other night I felt like drawing and no one whom I wanted to pose, wanted to do so. Get's me sore, when I'm in a drawing mood and have nothing decent to draw.

Life is not an easy proposition. I've been composing some very tragic speeches lately. Indication of the depths to which my spirits have fallen. And the trouble is, when I want to seek consolation in the piano I can't play very long. They'll either call me out to do some kind of work or else my fingers get so stiff that I've simply got to stop playing whether I want to or not. I'd like to slap myself when I think of how fast I fill my diaries but I can't help it, so there!

Nov. 10, Thursday

Yesterday noon my eyes had a fit or something of the sort. About five years ago my eyes were quite weak and every once in a while half of what I looked at was a blur. And yesterday noon I went up to school extra early to study modern, and half the page was a blur and I couldn't study. Just before the bell rang for Modern I could see allright again but my eyes felt so weak that I scarcely dared look around. In Modern, of course, I didn't know my lesson; I only said "I couldn't study." I'll try and take care of my eyes tho. I don't want them to get as weak as they were several years ago.

November 14

Had an illustrated poem in the J.J. yesterday. Drew and painted Sunday. Got a circular or bulletin, or whatever they're called, from the St. Paul Art School. It's ever so interesting. Glory, I hope I can go to an Art School later.

The other night during Glee Club practice Mr. Doom and Mr. Winkler were there. After we were outdoors already we heard Mr. Doom play piano. And what of all things do you suppose he played? A funeral march! Paula and I have come to the conclusion to think just the opposite of what we think of Mr. Doom first, and in nearly all cases it has worked beautifully. I think Mr. Doom really thinks deeper than we think he does.

Dec. 1, Thursday

Was up at Paula's house and had a royal time. Glory, we were philosophical. We decided that New Ulm needed a Renaissance. I got several compliments, so Paula says, but she won't tell me from whom. The truest compliment I've ever received is that I am different from other people. I am beginning to realize it myself but goodness knows I can't help it; I try to act like other people, but whether I succeed or not is something I can't tell. Doubtless people think I'm queer; I have yet to find the person who entirely understands me. Paula understands me better than anyone else so far, and I thank my lucky stars I have her. I feel dreamy to-night altho I don't know why.

I don't remember what I did all the rest of the days I haven't written up but I do know that I felt pretty blue sometimes and thought, with Chaucer,

> "This world nis but a thurghfare ful of woe,
> And we been pilgrimes passing to and froe."

December 2

We are studying the Renaissance in Modern. Glory, that's interesting, but some don't seem to think so. I think I like Raphael's pictures best of all those by the old masters. Even better than Michelangelo's, I believe. Michelangelo's works show action and power, but Raphael's show gentleness and delicacy and a great deal of feeling. Mr. Doom is handing pictures around, Perry pictures, and the one I like best of all is Raphael's "Sistine Madonna." Next best I like "Madonna of the Harpies" by Andrea del Sarto. Nearly all those artists were taught to draw when they were very young, and there seem to be few who worked under difficulties in their youth.

Dec. 3, Saturday

Life is not an easy proposition. I feel like having a good little "weep" but I have no time. There is too much to be done.

At home here we are singing Christmas songs, in the stores they are putting toys in the windows, and the Christmas spirit is gradually creeping in. Sometimes I think I'm glad Christmas is coming and sometimes I could sit down and cry at the mere thought of it. There are so many things I want which I will not get anyway. Last Christmas I didn't get half I needed. Stamps, for instance, and a tam (I have at present not a thing to wear on this button of a head of mine) and a gym suit and turning slippers, oh there were stacks; and to make a list of them all over again just makes me want them all the more. For the last two years I have always been more or less sad around Christmas-time.

People positively don't understand me, that's all there's to it. Here they even tell me to stop drawing and painting altogether. Goodness knows I *couldn't,* and if I could, I shouldn't, I'm too much in love with art for that. I wasn't made to be a book-keeper or a store clerk or anything like that.* If I had been, I would be better off than I am now perhaps. I can't help it that I've got to draw and paint forever; I cannot stop; I cannot, *cannot*, CANNOT! They say it doesn't pay to draw, that it is not appreciated, that I do not get for my work what it is worth. That is only too true but it isn't my fault. Besides, I earn more than some other girls. I wish we were rich, so rich that I could draw and paint for people and not charge anything. I hate to ask people for the money for my work.

I am not as prosaic as some people think I am. I wish I were a little more prosaic sometimes. If I do dream they think I'm posing for effect or am wasting time; when, in truth, I'm dreaming very sensible things. I mostly dream sensible things; I have to. If I could, I would sit and dream, just delicious, idle meditations, but I have too many other things to think about that simply must have thought.

Thank goodness I have this diary, and an old creaky piano—and Paula. She is really the only person who understands me that I know. If anybody else does, let that Anybody come. I need them all.

I must go and chop wood now.

Dec. 6, Tuesday St. Nicholas day.

The Christmas spirit—the mystic, the beautiful, the inevitable—has gotten the better of me. I cannot resist it. The other day it snowed, my heart leaped with joy; unconsciously I am counting the number of Christmas presents to make, and find joy in it, and on the whole I am joyfully, hopefully looking forward to Christmas, the day whose spirit of happiness and love I hope I will *never* be able to resist. At home they are writing letters to Santa Claus. Stella, Asta, Dehli, and Howard have dialogues for Christmas, and when I hear them reciting lines about jingling bells and snow and so forth and so on, way down in my heart of hearts I feel happy. Is there anyone who can resist the Christmas spirit under such glorious circumstances? Not I; No-siree-sir! not by a jugful! I sing and play Christmas songs, plan Christmas stories and poems, and draw Christmas pictures. I know all this sounds silly, but while I am happy I like to make the best of it. I know there will be times before Christmas has arrived when I will not be happy, when my spirits will fall quite beyond my reach and when I have only a handful of hope left to save for seed.

Am in a fierce drawing mood at present; actually *fierce* because "bolts and bars confine not" these moods of mine. Come what will; I shall draw,

* A number of people were urging me to follow one of these courses.

I *will*. Yesterday I drew 4 pictures in civics, two in Geometry, two in B. Lit and one during the modern period. To-day I drew two during Civics and one in Modern, I think.

Dec. 16, Friday

School has closed for the Christmas holidays and the teachers are gone. I shall feel lonesome these next few days without school—I loved school to-day; it was splendid.

A great many things have happened since I wrote last. Last Monday we had Current Topics. I had an idea that Mr. Doom thought we were all suffragettes so I decided to take a subject for woman's suffrage. When he called on me I got up and talked of the English suffragettes, their riots and also about their going to jail with their knitting. Jinks, he thought that was funny but I didn't crack a smile, and when I was done he asked, "Do you approve or disapprove?" I thought for a while and then with a laugh I said, "Disapprove." That seemed rather unexpected, and after looking up rather surprisedly (if that is a word,) he said, "So you are not a suffragette?" and I said, "No sir!" He said, "Good!" and gave me my mark. If I didn't get 100 that time I miss my guess.

He looks so childish and innocent in that new blue suit of his. I'll bet he has that left over from graduation. He had his hair combed down *round* in back, so his head didn't look square, as usual.

Dec. 28, Wednesday

Christmas is over. Had a splendid time on the whole. Went up to Paula's when I felt blue, to divert the mind. That, and going to school, is the best thing I know of at present for diversion of the mind.

To-day the world is a splendor of whiteness and daintiness; a perfect fairyland of hoarfrost. The sere, somber trees are covered with it, telephone wires look like fairy washlines swung from rimy poles, and wire fences are transformed into the sweetest silver fairy network you can imagine. Our rosebushes spread out their spare, slender branches with an easy grace and look like the snowy fingers of some Christmas spirit. And our wild grape vines, why they're simply indescribably beautiful, like silky white garlands and festoons hung up carelessly, and they're artistic all the same; and their blue-black berries, touched up with a wee dash of downy white, hang in most alluring clusters. And cobwebs—for all the world like fairy lace, delicate and silvery.

It's no use trying to describe it, I see; but really, all taken together, the dullness, the duskiness, and the gloominess of the branches, posts and leaves is forgotten in the delicious magnificence of the feathery pureness of the rime; just as a person's troubles are forgotten in a kind act or a good deed. Paula bought a doll for the baby and together we dressed her. We got a sack of flour for a Christmas present from Ritschl's.

Well, of course Christmas Eve Stella and I trimmed the tree and got everything ready for morning. At five o'clock they woke us and we had barely dressed when the bell rang, so we chased down. Usual ohs! and ahs! of course, and hunting for presents.

Here's what I got:—A pencil tablet, an ink tablet, a pencil and pen, hairpins, a toothbrush, a barrette, a box of paints and book for photographs from Uncle Frank, cloth for aprons from Aunt Magdalene, a scarf from Aunt Mary, rubbers from Mrs. Harrington, a coat and the loveliest pink dress goods from Ritschl's. Guess I'll keep that for reception. Then I got the sweetest picture of Baby Stuart from Paula. I also got a book from Daisy's cousin, Philip, and a picture from Mr. Winkler! The kids got lots of presents from Mrs. Harrington, too, and baby got a doll from Fern.

Christmas day I went up to Hershl's. After supper went to Hasenclever's and heard Miss Hasenclever play zither. Beautiful? More beautiful than I could tell, and ever so touching. Paula and I were both on the point of having "weeps." I wish I could play zither; I believe I prefer zither to piano. One can put such a lot of feeling into the music; I remember when papa used to play zither he used to play such sad, plaintive airs, and they could not help going home.

Tuesday I went to the Glee and Mandolin Club concert. It was dandy. I wanted to get the pictures of some of those mandolin players but woe on me! I had no pencil. So I took a pin and pricked three sketches on my program paper. But I have made up my mind to take a pencil along the next time I go to some such place.

Tussy had a story in the J.J.

1911

Jan. 1, Sunday

Happy New Year. It has come! We've just been out to hear the bells ring. Resolutions later.

Jan. 4, Wednesday

Sylvester eve Paula was here. We opened the dictionary and pointed to a word without looking and the word we'd get would be our fortune. I got "chatterbox" which was not inappropriate. Well, a little after twelve Paula and I went up to Hershl's. We played piano duets until after one and then we went upstairs and talked until about three. Oh yes, Paula and I made some resolutions.

RESOLUTIONS 1911

1. Resolved that I will try not to act silly in Modern History.
2. Resolved that I will try to learn some pieces on the piano that are worthwhile.
3. Resolved that I must try once more to write properly (so that Mr. Winkler can't give me any more slams).
4. Resolved that I must keep my clothes neatly mended, and that I must not have them hanging all over the house but up in the attic where they belong.
5. Resolved that I must try and not quote unless they are half-way appropriate. (Quoting is our latest fad, you know; Paula's and mine.)
6. Resolved that I must take care of my eyes.
7. Resolved that I must try and keep up a style of drawing that's worth while.
8. Resolved that I simply must draw more from life.
9. Resolved that I simply must have more patience with my juniors, especially Howard.
10. Resolved that I must not read too much (at least storybooks, I mean.)
11. Resolved that I must try to make as few breaks as possible. (Now, I I think that's one of the most sensible ones I made because I do say the worst things sometimes.)
12. Resolved that I must not dream so much but keep my mind more on material things.
13. Resolved that, since I need an increase of my vocabulary, I must try to learn several new words a week, and look up words if I have doubts as to their meaning and pronunciation. (But also, I must not use words or phrases unless I am sure what they mean.)
14. Resolved, that for the above-mentioned purpose I must listen closely when I hear people talk who have a good vocabulary.
15. Resolved that I must not make so many grimaces while talking. (I know I must look awful doing it.)
16. Resolved that I must go down to the dentist's pretty soon. (Costs so much, that's the trouble.)

Jan. 16, Monday

I had an illustrated poem in the J.J. yesterday.

I'm in love with Modern at present just as I used to fall in love with Ancient.

Mr. Doom has new shoes, laced gun metals, and he wore them until he had his others soled. But one day he came back wearing his button shoes once more, soled; and with some more put on his heels. Now they're high, let me tell you. He wears what used to be his best suit every day now, so we've decided that he got a new suit for Christmas.

Jan. 21, Saturday

Have a terrible cold. I have at present 62 hat-tips. I am just too dreamy for anything these last several days and in a drawing mood into the bargain. This morning I read some of the poems papa wrote. I believe I have never finished one of them without crying; they are so sad.

Got a letter from the Art School to-day saying that the new session was to start and that there would be a reduction of prices for new students. Beyond my aspirations at present. Miss Lee talked to us about aspirations the other day. She said there is a time in almost everybody's life when one suddenly builds high, high air castles, and it struck me that my aspirations were really rather high; most likely I will be an attic artist, an artist way up high out of the interest and noise of the world. I cannot stop to draw, whatever comes between, and so that naturally must be the course, the only course, left for me to take. The life of an aspirant to art is queer, and often sad. Hoping that mine, being that of such an aspirant, will not be any more sad than is needful to make a strong character, I say goodbye to this diary.—W.G.

*   *   *

Jan. 23, Monday

This morning as I went to school I saw such a picturesque bit of landscape that I decided mentally to paint a picture like it, some time in the distant future—if I ever will be able to handle a brush so well as to do it satisfactorily.

There were some evergreens almost covered entirely with snow, and it was the most unique combination of steel-greys and bluish-whites! Then over the whole thing there was a glorious shower of mellow morning sunshine which softened the greys and blues and gave it a most effective warmth of tone. And the prettiest part of it was that it was just such a wee patch of landscape, and as simple in outline as can be. It was prettier than ever I could describe, and most likely I will never be able to paint landscapes well enough for this; because I'll most likely paint more portraits than anything else. I'm in an awful drawing mood, and naturally my seven wits centre about art principally—for the present.

January 26

Mr. Doom thinks he's too smart for anything because he wore a belt. To-day after school he came up to the assembly room and sat down in the seat in front of me. Glory he's got cute hands. I don't know what he wanted to say, but anyway we started talking about geometry. He said, "Oh, Geometry's easy!" and I said, "Yes, but I'm behind there just as well as in my other studies lately. Because when I have to draw I have to neglect everything even my lessons," and I said that when I had the most work to do I felt most like drawing. And he said, "Well that's the true artistic temperament." And I said, "Is it?" and he said, "Sure, it is."

Then he said, "You are one of those people who get so very unmanageable later," and I said, "I am?" and he said, "You *will* be," and I said, "Well, if I will, I can't help it," and he laughed and said, "Of course you can't."

Now, what do you suppose he meant? Hope I'll find out some day. I don't know how he started, but anyway he said that some day I'd belong to the "Bohemian Circle" (I thanked my lucky stars that I knew what that was!) and that I'd have parlors where my friends (he said "we") could come and drink a cup of tea with me, and I said, "Oh no, because I've decided that the best thing for me to do would be to be an attic artist, away from the world—" but he interrupted me and said, "Oh no. Of course you must be alone with your work, but then you must have some coterie" and insisted that some time I'd be one of those "Bohemians."

In geometry I sketched John Hansen's feet. Mama is making a foxy patchwork quilt.

Feb. 5, Sunday

Friday afternoon Mr. Doom went to Tracy with the boys—for basket ball. I can just imagine him chasing around. They say that the girls took him for one of the High School boys, and thought he was a pretty cute fellow. One of them asked him why he didn't play basket ball and he said that he had flunked in his studies that month so he couldn't. He has his hair cut. I wonder why men have their hair cut so often; always makes them look more or less sheepish.

This noon I told Mr. Doom that I wished he'd not hurry us so, at least until we'd caught up in recitations, and he said, "I'll try to do better," and as we went out he went to the window and heaved a deep sigh. He's just about the most insoluble riddle I've struck as yet.

Feel pretty poetical to-night. Learned a new word:—Quintessence.

In B. Lit Miss Lee read Hamlet all the period. I just love it. Paula and I have decided to mark all the good passages in our books at home. Books always look as if they'd been read, then.

Miss Lee wrote in my notebook, "Your characterizations are certainly splendid. They are so appreciative." It's easy as falling off a log. You just sit down and write; the thoughts come flocking in just as fast as anything.

Feb. 17, Friday

Last Tuesday Paula wanted me to stay for supper, and just a little while before suppertime I phoned home to see how Howard was getting along. He had such an earache and mama had called the doctor. Mama said that he was pretty bad and that perhaps he'd have to have an operation. I nearly fell over, and wasn't very hungry at all for supper. After supper I hurried away—very unceremoniously, I confess; but really, I was so worked up about Howard that I couldn't wait any longer. Stayed up until about twelve; we had to tend to Howard. Now he is a little better. The day before yesterday the doctor pierced right into Howard's ear. Howard's awfully brave tho, at such times.

This morning, I painted a Japanese picture (I'm just wild about anything Japanesy, at present). Wish Mr. Doom would wear his belt again; he always acts up so when he does, and it's ever so interesting. I have read "Queen Zixi of Ix." Rather queer for a Junior in H.S. to read such a thing but I am mostly an exception to the rule.

Feb. 25, Sat.

Howard is worse. The doctor was here and said he would advise us to take him to the hospital and have him operated. He is going this afternoon, and Stella and I are going out too. I have paced from one room to another, upstairs and downstairs, and outdoors; the suspense is awful. Howard has asked already when we go; I think he is anxious to have it over and done with. He is ever so brave tho. I can't write any more just now.

Later:—We didn't go yet. Dr. Haftel and Dr. Fraade were here. We are not going until tomorrow afternoon. I don't feel like doing anything.

Mar. 4, Saturday

Sunday afternoon the doctor took Howard out to the hospital, and Stella and I went along. I stayed overnight and slept very little because Howard cried so much. In the morning mama came out and we both stayed until evening. Howard was operated at 9 a.m.,* it lasted over an hour, and he didn't wake up from the chloroform until about 3 p.m. The less said about this the better, too, I think. It's enough to live thru it without dwelling upon it in diaries. He's getting better day by day now tho, and it is a great relief. Some of us were out there nearly all the time. I stayed two nights and mama stayed three. Poor little fellow, he suffered his share.

Aunt Mary was at our house several days.

Yesterday after school I had to chop wood. After a while Mr. Winkler was on his way home, and when he saw us he came over and said, "I see where I come in handy." He chopped a big pile, and said, "Any time you get any pieces that are so hard, just call us up over there and we'll come over in full force."

Mar. 11, Saturday

This morning I was the last to come down to breakfast and when I did come there was a general exchanging of happy knowing glances and funny little smiles. The air was heavy with mystery, and I could feel that either I wasn't "in it" at all or else I was "it" entirely. I looked around, rather blankly I imagine, and wondered what this new scheme might be, and when I was just ready to sit down to eat they started up and *slapped* me! Then I remembered it was my birthday. Eighteen, sensible eighteen—Oh glory, if I'm sensible I misjudge myself entirely. Of course I can't get sensible all at one jump after having been Silly Seventeen for 365 days, but somehow I have a premonition that I shall be endowed with that characteristic for some time to come. However, "We can only hope to get better as we grow older" and I sincerely hope that I will.

Well after breakfast there was some running to and fro, and whispering, and joyful anticipation (on the joy I would find on getting my presents—for they were preparing them). And then I got my presents, a blotter from Asta, and one of those cunning little notebooks from Asta, Dehli and Tussy to-gether. From Aunt Mary I got a handkerchief, a glass pitcher and some summer dress goods. Paula gave me some sealing

* For mastoid abscess, apparently the aftermath of his fall on a stick two years before.

wax—green, red, silver and gold—and such a sealing wax stamper or whatever you call it.

Saturday evening we went to turning school. Sunday Lucy and I went out to the hospital.

April 1

To-day Howard went down to the doctor (he's been going daily since he's back from the hospital). He didn't have any bandage around his ear at all. It's healed far enough now to be without. It was a big hole all-right.*

April 7, Friday

I'm as blue as blue to-day, I could just knock things about, and have been more or less all day. I did so want to have a talk with Paula, and I'm sure I was as uninteresting as a plastic monkey. It's snowing like everything. It looks lovely but I did so want spring to come. In school I was off on flights of fancies all the time as usual, and I could have made sarcastic remarks at almost anything.

Stella and I made supper. We had an awful fuss because the tapioca pudding (Minute pudding, which gets done in about an hour) and it tipped over (the dish, I mean) and part of it spilled over the stove and baked on in a most marvelous manner.

After supper Daisy asked me to come down. Her cousin Philip has come and he brought two dandy pennants. (They have me simply groggy in the knees.) I'm supposed to have my choice, I guess. They're perfect dandies, and as I'm right in the midst of a pennant mania (I'm making a stack of little ones for myself) you can imagine how tickled I am.

April 10, Monday

Saturday we colored eggs. Sunday, of course, was Easter. Paula came up in the morning, and Mr. Winkler came over and talked to us about— Easter bonnets! He said, "One sees many Easter bonnets to-day," and I said, "There is more to Easter than hats, altho some people don't seem to think so," and he agreed and said, "Yes, girls especially." Paula said, "By men it isn't so noticeable." And mind you, what did I do after he

---

* We were never charged for medical attention—three of the local doctors were always very kind to us.

had left, but chase up into the attic, hunt up an old hatshape, a piece of old silk curtain and two straw rosettes—and make myself an Easter bonnet! Honestly, I did it before I knew what I was doing.

Sunday afternoon Paula and I went to Becker's. I got absorbed in a Gibson book. Glory, Gibson has ideas! His pictures are full of expression and action. He is a master of pen and ink.

To-day Mr. Winkler made an announcement. The St. Paul Art School has made an offer to award a prize of $100 and a scholarship for one year, for the best pencil drawing sent before May 10. They want me to try (I don't mean the Art School people, of course) but I haven't decided yet.

Next year all the teachers are going to stay except Mr. Winkler and Mr. Doom. We asked Mr. Winkler if he would come when we graduated and he said he thought so. Then Lucy said something about it being so nice if he would be here next year, and he said, "Oh they don't want me. They'll be glad to see me go." And then he said, half sorrowfully, I thought—"That's why I'm leaving next year."

I ventured—I was bold enough to say, "You haven't a good enough opinion of yourself, it seems," and he looked at me queerly as if he were doubting my words—perhaps he thought I was flattering. He looked me straight in the eyes, but he seemed pretty satisfied afterwards and walked off, smiling the life off himself.

April 25, Tuesday

Saturday evening was Turning School. Jinks, one feels spry in bloomers and turning slippers. Yesterday I got a check for $1.50—had a poem in the J.J. We are reading Sir Roger de Coverly in B. Lit. Queer but interesting. I feel like making poetry to-day. One reason is because I need some to send away, and my old store—which was begun several years ago—is almost exhausted.

I'm in the beginning of a drawing mood—at least I think I am. Let us hope so; I need it. To-day I fell up the school steps right in front of the Superintendent's door, and I had barely time to pick myself up before he came hurrying out to see whether I had hurt myself. Then to-night coming home from the moving picture show I fell flat across some cement steps, and two girls passed just as I was murmuring to myself, "For the love of soup." They thought it was pretty funny. Begorry, I hope I won't keep it up. It might prove rather embarrassing at times.

May 5, Friday

Reception is coming in jumps. My dress has not been begun. I am in the depths of despair. I am on the committee and the expenses are to be about $75. Fancy! about $3.25 for each one. I cannot pay so much— I cannot, I cannot. I have been scraping and scraping to-gether the silver since last fall and I have now $1.30—and I can't afford it, I can't. Besides one can't buy happiness and enjoyment with money. I know I shall have no fun as it is. I can't dance worth two cents, and the boys here don't seem to care with *whom* they dance just as long as their partner dances well. That is what it is to be popular—to be popular *here,* one has to be able to dance well.

I know I shall be awake just about all night worrying about it. And they want $5 worth of crepe paper to decorate with, and $8 of carnations and roses. They will just *overload* that hall, and take away all beauty, let alone "artisticness." I could just bawl. If that's what society is like, I choose a cozy little attic, pencil and paints—one can at least be sure of enjoyment then.

May 14, Sunday

I am at grandma's. My reception dress is almost done, thanks to Aunt Magdalene. Last Wednesday we had another committee meeting and we cut out the $8 worth of cut flowers entirely, and the cost of crepe paper to less than $2. Altogether that makes about $2.85 expense for each Junior but I managed to get off from paying all that. You know for finding partners for supper we are going to have names, such as Jack and Jill, Hans and Gretel, Beauty and the Beast, etc. and then at the tables we're going to have place cards with a name or a picture of that person on each. Those place cards I'm going to make. Of course it really would cost more to have them made otherwise, but I'm perfectly willing to get off that way.

Farewell, old diary—Wanda.

* * *

(NOTE:—The diary covering the period from May 14 to July 1 is lost. It was chiefly concerned with:—

1. The Junior-Senior Reception.

2. Our farewells to our beloved teachers.

3. The first half of Paula's and my visit in St. Paul. The diary which follows covers the last part of this visit.)

* * *

July, 1911, Saturday

I am in New Ulm now, but Paula and I returned from St. Paul Thursday evening. We had a most glorious time. Paula took me along to Governor Eberhart's* where we stayed during the time we were down. In my old diary I have written up all the events through last Sunday.

And now comes the loveliest part. Monday evening we went to see "Macbeth." Well, Paula and I were just going up the steps when somebody tapped me on the shoulder and when I turned around I saw—of all people—Mr. Winkler! If my wits hadn't scattered far and wide at the sight, I might have asked him what happy chance brought him there, but as it was, I only managed to say, "Why, there's Mr. Winkler!" He had a reserved ticket and said, "I wish I had two tickets, but one of you can have this one." I told Paula to take it and Paula told me to take it; but finally by our combined efforts, Mr. Winkler and I persuaded Paula to take it. For us there was standing room only.

The play was simply great. The parts of Macbeth and Lady Macbeth were taken by E. H. Sothern and Julia Marlowe, respectively. (Paula and I think that Sothern and Marlowe sound so lovely together, so round and full and soft, and that there are just the right kind of letters in one name to harmonize beautifully with the other). Between acts we sat down behind the seats on the platform and had nice talks. At these times a most delightfully cool breeze would come swooping thru the back of the hall—oh it was most delicious. Mr. Winkler is going to the summer school at the University and so is Mr. Doom.

After the play he took us to a restaurant and ordered three "Merry Widow Sundaes." (Paula and I looked it up later, and they're 20 cents a dish.) After that we went to wait for our street car. We were still waiting, when a car went past and Mr. Winkler said, "There goes Mr. Doom. See him?" We did see him, and he saw us too, and tipped his hat. And mind you, about five minutes later, here he comes stepping around the corner. Why, I was too amazed for anything. Think of the condescension on his part (to say nothing of the sacrifice—5 cents extra and cars running only every hour). He shook hands most heartily and said, "How did you girls get here?" I told him "on the train"—which was unnecessary information but anyway he needn't ask such questions.

* A. O. Eberhart, who was then Governor of Minnesota. Paula and Mrs. Eberhart were cousins.

He had his hat off for about fifteen minutes. We didn't blame him tho, for—of all things!—he wears his hair pompadour; it was only natural that he should want to show it off. And then to top all, he was forever running his hand through said pompadour and remarking that he had "such a headache." He asked whether everything was quiet in New Ulm—he might have added "as usual"; his tone implied as much. He was awfully nice tho; and Mr. Winkler was too, naturally. When our car came they went along to the car and shook hands, and Doom gave us both a swoop up the steps. They tipped their hats (99 hat-tips) and then waved until we were gone.

Sunday I had had my picture in the St. Paul Daily News with something written about me that I had sketched the Governor and his wife etc.

Now I am going to write about last Tuesday. The day before, a man, the cartoonist of the St. Paul Dispatch, phoned to Eberhart's and said he wanted awfully much to see me. So Tuesday afternoon Mrs. Eberhart, Paula and I went to his office. His name is Tyler McWhorter and he is also the business manager of the St. Paul Art School—the place where I got the medal from. I didn't know this tho; and you can fancy how surprised I was when just about the first thing he said was, "We expected you to win that scholarship this year." He said he had seen my picture in the paper and had read that I was in St. Paul, and that he had been afraid that I'd go off without seeing him. He said that he had been more interested in me than anyone in the state until that boy (Sylvan Lyksett, who got ahead of me in the last contest *) turned up. Mine was second in rank and he said that after my pictures there was a big drop. By that time Mrs. Eberhart had left, and he asked me to draw a picture of Mrs. Eberhart for the next Sunday's paper.

Then he took us over to the Art School and showed us all around. He showed us pictures by Nathaniel Pousette-Dart and some splendid ones by Lee Woodward Zeigler, the chief instructor. I wonder whether he thought I didn't appreciate all those pictures, but so often I can't find words to do them justice, so I remain silent and just *look*. One might say instead of "Rare is the nature-lover who can silently absorb the beauties of nature"—"Rare is the art-lover that can silently absorb the beauties of a picture." Anyway, I had used up all appropriate exclamations and remarks before he had showed me half of the things.

---

* Mentioned in the entry of April 10 (page 107). I got the First and Second Honorable Mentions for my two drawings. See drawing facing page 113.

Once he asked me how I pronounced my last name and I said, "Gaag" but he kept calling me Miss Găg all the time. I wonder, *will* I have to get used to that?

That night Governor Eberhart gave us an auto ride, a most glorious,

1911

Governor
Eberhardt

never-to-be-forgotten ride. I told Paula in fun, "I am waxing poetical," and "wax poetical" I did (altho I had not really expected to). And no wonder. It was a night to make the most prosaic feel thrills of rapture stir their sense of the beautiful. Paula and I thought how queer, how "un-nice" it would be if there were no crooked trees in the world at all; and I remember now distinctly that I was almost constantly talking about "beautiful grouping," "curves in roads" and the like. We talked of forest glooms, how fascinating they were and so sort of awful. And when we went past Minnehaha park I was lifted into the most lofty transports of joy. There were lights you know—common lights; but you cannot imagine how their light enhanced the surrounding trees, and how they set off their forms against the glooms behind. I thought of how lovely the willows looked on concert evenings in the German Park at home and talked to Paula of their "fleeciness" and "laciness." I wonder what all else I said—I only hope I didn't become too emotional—or else what would the Governor think of me?

Well, finally we turned towards home. The ride had made me very dreamy, and in the garage I nearly upset a bicycle. By the time I had set it up straight, they had all gone out except Governor Eberhart, so he followed me. When we were going on the path he put his hands on my shoulders and said, "Such a small fourteen-year old girl." Now I was really feeling pretty big for I was wearing Mrs. Eberhart's long linen coat, so I said, "Don't I look tall in this coat?" and he said I didn't. You see, he always says I don't look as if I were eighteen. He is too nice for the world. He says so little but, to put it in a popular phrase, "Every little action has a meaning all its own," and a good "worthwhile" meaning at that.

He is one of my ideals.

Well when we got into the house, the others wanted to eat something yet, but eating was too material for me so I went into the diningroom and sat down in the dark and listened to Mr. Eberhart playing and singing. He has such a deep lovely voice. He can sing "The Böhmerwald" too. It had been an evening after my own heart and I went to bed perfectly satisfied with the day.

All pleasures must have an end.

On Wednesday I drew nearly all day. After supper Mr. Eberhart went away and we went along down to the depot in the auto. That was the last time I saw him because he didn't come home until several days after and by that time we had left. I don't know how it happened, but somehow I felt terribly blue. We went into the den, Paula and I, and Paula played sad pieces on the phonograph, and I just bawled—in spite of all my efforts to stop.

The next day we packed our suitcases. In the afternoon I drew that pencil portrait of Mrs. Eberhart and then came the goodbyes. I could have bawled again—I was so sorry to leave—but I managed to control myself comparatively well. On the way down to the depot we stopped and went up to Mr. McWhorter, and I gave him the picture. He asked whether he could keep it, and I almost flew over because I had been scared stiff that perhaps he wouldn't accept the picture at all. Then he shook hands most heartily and said, "—and any time you are ready

Two Pencil Sketches—*Top:* Howard Asleep; *Bottom:* Flavia

Honorable Mention

Pencil Portrait, 1911

to come to art school, just write to me and we'll find some way for you to go. Minnesota needs you."

Then we started off on our train. On the way Paula amused herself—and others—by making people laugh by beaming upon them amiably—you know what a genial-looking countenance she has!

Home again. The next Sunday the picture of Mrs. Eberhart was in the St. Paul Dispatch, and several days after it was in all the New Ulm papers.

July 4, Tuesday

We went down to the park where we saw Mr. Bredford—our future teacher in B. Lit—on the grass, and I drew his leg. I also drew the feet of the man who made the speech. One is not safe when I am around with paper and pencil.

Soon after we had come back from St. Paul I got my 101st hat-tip, and who do you suppose it was? Mr. Knispl *—and it is a wonder I wasn't lying in the gutter, pale and wan, right after the incident. Just think of counting hat-tips for so long for such a miserable, disappointing and unwelcome end. Fiddlesticks!

Last Sunday I had an illustrated story in the J.J. I got $1.75 for it. I ought to make up some poetry pretty soon—the poems in my poetry book have nearly all been sent away. If I would only get a drawing fit, a poetical streak, or be in a sentimental mood, I might accomplish something—but the trouble is, one cannot call such things at will.

I met a girl the other day who undoubtedly thought it her duty to inform me of the wrong path I was taking. She broke it to me gently and considerately—she told me she thought art didn't pay. I told her I didn't care if it didn't; and that I intended to be an attic artist any-way—also that it was immaterial to me whether I were rich or not, just as long as I earned enough to support myself comfortably. I told her that, of course, *now* I did have to earn money, and that it did pay in larger cities altho it doesn't very much here. How some people worry unnecessarily. I am sure I worry exactly enough to cover all the "worry-able situations" well.

July 17, Monday

Yesterday evening Paula, Lucy and I went to the park concert. I showed Paula those "lacy fleecy" willows but she wasn't so enthusiastic

* A silly local character.

about them as I—she likes oaks better. We differ on *some* subjects, after all. But still on the majority and on the most important subjects we agree. Anyway, Paula and I have come to the conclusion that it would not be nice if we were both exactly alike in everything.

I made mama a black dress and am making baby a blue chambray now.

July 21, Friday. At Grandma's

Tuesday I sewed. Wednesday ditto. Today I sewed too, and to-night I went rowing.

I think it was yesterday that I discovered such a beautiful bit of landscape across the river. It's too lovely for the world. First the river and then the trees on the other side of the bank, and then fields with oats and barley stacked up in the most picturesque little heaps, and beyond that clusters of green trees, with the yellow fields beyond, a hill and a lonely tree. Great.

Last night I dreamt of school and caves too. I dreamt that Mr. Cheevers * had not only a mustache but also a beard. I dreamt that he was married. Now just supposing he really is. That would certainly be the limit.

Aug. 3, Thursday

The day before yesterday we were out at Kesterbaum's, and there we got some wedding cake. Paula and I have slept upon ours for two nights. To-night's the third. But honestly if such things would happen as I have been dreaming for the last two nights I'll eat my hat. Guess I had better go to bed. I hope I'll dream something worthwhile and something nice to-night. I am up in our darling attic room. Nothing grand about it, but it feels so one's *own*.

August 4, Friday

This morning Paula left for Echo. She won't be back for one whole week. Just fancy poor me.

Well about the dreams that the wedding cake brought us. The first night I dreamt all manner of silly things but most important was this: —Gertie and I were at the seashore. We were running toward the beach and my hair, which I had in one braid down the back, opened and flew all around. There were two men on the shore further back

* Our next year's science teacher.

whom we did not know, and one cried, "Say Wanda, you look pretty with your hair that way." (Save the mark! But dreams, as you know, go contrary—so it's anything but a compliment for me.) Gertie and I turned around and I flared up fiercely. "Oh yes," I said, "Just as beautiful as a Harrison Fisher girl, or one by James Montgomery Flagg, or Rose O'Neill, or Howard Chandler Christy" and so I rattled off a string of artist's names with lots of sarcasm. Just at that moment the other man, who had taken a fancy to Gertie, raised his umbrella and lowered it playfully at Gertie, and Gertie gave the umbrella a whack which sent it flying back into her admirer's face. Then she took me by the hand and pulled me away. I was sorry that we went because the man who had talked to me seemed to have been an artist and looked as I fancy Mr. McWhorter might have looked some years ago.

The second night I dreamt that I came out of Gertie's house and as I went past their lawn, Mr. Groos (who quite miraculously sat on a bench there, with a young man) said, "Miss Gág let me introduce you to the Honorable Mr. ———" (I forget the name). The man being such an "honorable" individual, I did not know whether it would be proper to take the liberty of shaking hands, so I hesitated a while. Then I held out my hand and he took it limply, and I knew I had made a blunder again. He was a handsome man and always lowered his head and regarded you from under his eyebrows when he talked. He had dark hair and eyes and a good complexion. Then he got up and said something about my going east to study art. I noticed then, that as soon as one looked at him from below instead of from the top of his head, he looked entirely different. He had light hair and blue eyes and a different shape of a head. His complexion however, remained fair—but it got a little shiny. Well he talked some more about art and then asked whether Fairfax * had done anything for me and I told him "no" and chased off—just like those "Daffydillies" in the paper after they have said something witty or flat.

The third night I dreamt we painted all three rooms downstairs in oil, and Paula and I didn't like it at all. I don't believe in wedding cake dreams.

Aug. 27, Sunday

It is exactly time that I started to write in here once more; for to-

* A nearby town.

morrow school starts again, and I had intended to finish this before school began. So here goes. Tuesday Paula came home, and I of course was in my highest bliss. There is, after all, no one who can come up to Paula. I was at Paula's Saturday, Sunday, Monday and Tuesday night. I can assure you that we had fun—raving about school half the times. We have been counting the days with the most joyful anticipation. Let us hope that our hopes will not be shattered.

I have a drawing mood at last, thank goodness. I knew I would get a fierce one when school started, when I should have my mind on other things. Nice impression the teachers will get of me. But I honestly cannot let the opportunity slip by—drawing moods are so rare of late. I only hope I will not have to buy any new books.

September 6

Upon Aug. 28 I set out bright and early to meet Paula, and together we went to school. When we came up we were greeted with a hearty handshake from Miss Lee, and Miss Lee introduced us to Mr. Bredford. He is nice. At first he used to pronounce my name Găg but he has learned better since then.

Sept. 18, Monday

I have neglected my diary shamefully, but somehow I feel very much like writing to-night—at least I think I do. At present I don't seem to be able to know my own feelings at all, at all—I couldn't analyze them to save my life. I wish I could, so I could see what measures to take to get rid of that mixture of sadness and joy, and of the inexpressibly jumbly atmosphere about me. For one thing school is far from what it used to be, and almost any time I wished I could flop down on the bed and have a good weep.

Mr. Haywood * does not greet us in the morning with a smile as Mr. Winkler did, and I yearn to see Mr. Doom's smiling face at the door. Empty, in a vague sense, seems to explain it. Must save the rest of this space for some other time as I have no new diary.

October

We have now a Glee Club of which I am the president (Save the mark!) Mr. Bredford is a great leader. He is queer but doesn't know it, which in itself is queer.

* Our new Principal.

The new Assembly Room Desk is a dandy. It is open in the center so one can see people's feet—such a good chance to enlarge my collection. Miss Lee says, tho, that they intend to put a curtain on later.

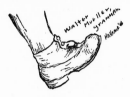

To-day Mr. Haywood asked to look at my sketch book and kept it a long while. It is just about full. Among some of the most important things are Mr. Haywood's feet sitting pidgeon-toed, his and Miss King's feet together, and Felix's new high-heeled shoes.

Mr. Haywood seems to be pretty much interested in drawing. One day he sketched—actually sketched, during school hours. He saw me watching him, and finally crumpled them up and threw them in the waste basket. During the fourth period he came and we had a long talk about many subjects. I said that I had noticed that he sketched and wished that I could have seen them. He said it had always been his ambition to take drawing lessons when he was a mite but that he had never had any.

This entry has no "unity, mass, and coherence" but these things have happened so long ago that they don't interest me much.

December 25, 1911. Christmas morning.

I am far behind in my diary and have a great deal to write up. I will therefore start at the beginning of affairs and write them up to the present time so that I can continue as time goes on for, it seems to me, none of them are over yet. Some are rather silly but I think I will write about them all, if only for the fun of it.

Last year [1910] during the Christmas holidays, Daisy's cousin Philip came to visit them. (He is studying Engineering in Minneapolis.) I didn't notice him much at first, except when we played games I noticed he was awfully funny. When I went down to Daisy's the day after Christmas (it happened he was not there that afternoon) and he had left for me a book as a Christmas gift, I almost bowled over with astonishment, I scarcely expected it from such a bashful-looking fellow as he. I didn't give him a present, tho—I was too bashful for one thing, and for another thing, I was not acquainted enough with the laws of etiquette and form to be able to decide whether it would be proper or not. We had a grand time that Christmas tho.

Daisy had made some "chocolate wurst." One day Philip wanted me to take some but I refused. Why, I do not know, but as Burns says, "We cannot account for our whims." He tried with all his might and main to make me take some but to no avail. Several minutes later when he offered it again, I took a piece without any urging. This he thought was very queer, and seemed pretty puzzled at the nature of my character. I told him I was versatile (a pretty new word in my vocabulary at the time).

When he left he promised to write once in a while, which he did—three postals. The last one he sent just before the Easter vacation, and wrote that he had a pennant for me if I wanted it. Of course I wanted it and it was a dandy. We had enjoyable times (during that vacation) and sometimes he took me home. Once he said that India ink would look white against my hair and I told him I thought he must be color blind. He did not come to New Ulm this Christmas, but I sent him a sketch.

In the beginning of November I was asked by Mr. V. M. Logan to sing in the Women's Chorus at the *Turner Stiftungs Fest*. Paula and Daisy went too. Before supper I didn't dance at all, neither did Paula. We girls decided to stay together for the supper march, but some one got Daisy, and Otto Felz (save the mark!) asked to walk with Paula and me. Well, it happened that Daisy and her partner sat opposite me. We had a swell time. But honestly, during the whole time almost, I felt that Walter Gennert (that's his name) was looking at me all the time. Finally I got so embarrassed that I didn't know where to look and several times I caught him looking square at me. I could see his feet under the table—button shoes, and wished—as I always do—that I had pencil and paper to draw them. In my mind I put him down as tame, but somewhat fascinating.

After supper Otto asked me for the first dance, and when I was back in my seat who should come stepping along but Daisy and Walter Gennert. I was so dumbfounded that I'm sure I must have looked like a Mutt, and right then and there he asked me for the next dance. I still marvel at the fact that I had enough sense to say "certainly." Fancy! I danced the dance with him, but we didn't talk much, for altho I had known his name long ago, I had never met him. Two more times Otto asked me and once more this quiet-looking Gennert asked me for a dance. Then when we had our wraps on and were just ready to go, he stood out there near the hall again, gazing at us like anything. We barely escaped being taken home by Otto. He's the funniest fellow—told me all about how their family could shoot so well.

The next day when I came to school Daisy said, "Weren't you surprised when I introduced Walter Gennert to you? He nudged me at the table and asked me who the girl was with the black hair and the pink dress and said, 'I'm just crazy to get an introduction to her.'" That's really the best compliment I've had in years—that anyone should like me at all, before they knew I drew. He is really pretty handsome and has dark hair and a pretty fair skin. To-night I saw him in turning school and he looked pretty jolly and cute.

Then came the Thanksgiving dance. I went with Stella, Fern and Judy. Afterwards we went out into the Club room and sat down, when all at once Walter stood before me and asked me for the next dance. Of course I went. It was Casey Jones that they were playing. The other two times we had both been too sort of strange to talk much but this time we managed to say a few things of interest—about ragtime music and about it's being pretty near the end. After he danced with me he danced only with Mrs. Hiller.

I honestly wonder what he thinks of me. Sometimes I think his infatuations last only one or two evenings. He has taken Ellen Hennel to several dances—which is a point in his favor for there he certainly chose well.

Harvey
Wellner

1912

Mar. 14, Thursday

Gee, in the Class Play Sam Dinzler has to take me by the hands and oh it makes one feel so silly.*

I'm glad already for *Shauturn*. I only wish I had a decent dress to wear. I've worn my pink dress to every social function, dance and entertainment since last spring and I'll bet people will always know just

* Sheridan's "The Rivals." He was Faulkland and I was Julia Melville. Paula was Mrs. Malaprop.

how to look for me. "The same pink dress" would be sufficient description. Aunt Mary, I believe, will buy me my graduation dress.

April 9

Yesterday afternoon Paula and I went down to buy our graduation slippers. We went to Binz's. Paula was fitting on slippers, but I was not, when two people came to the door. One was Walter Gennert. To tell the truth, a most delightful thrill went thru me. I wonder whether he felt something like that too. I imagine our meetings don't mean so much to him, and possibly he cares for some one else now. Well at any rate we looked at each other several times in silence, real genially I imagine—at least he did. Then he asked the clerk, "Is Mr. Binz here?" He was told that he wasn't so they closed the door again and went. We went to several other places. In vain I looked to see him again, but I was miserably disappointed. Paula, on the other hand, was looking for Eugene. Well, she saw him. We went to Hershl's. I was terribly lovesick—real pleasant in a way—played sentimental songs on the piano and quoted class play. Stella and Judy were up. They all noticed that I was pretty far gone. I do hope I'll see him again soon. Perhaps I'm stuck on him, perhaps I am not, I do not know.

April 14, Sunday—at Grandma's

Friday Stella, Flavia and I went down to grandma's. Aunt Magdalene is making my reception dress. To-day I went into the front room, drew myself, and then practiced my whole part of the play in front of the mirror. Talk about being melodramatic.

Gee the other night I had a silly dream—most impossible and highly improbable. Well, I dreamt we were practicing for *Shauturn* and during the intermission Walter Haus whispered to me whether he could take me to supper at *Shauturn*. "Or," he added, "has Walter (meaning Walter Gennert) asked you already?" Positively senseless. I scarcely look at Walter Haus, nor does he look much at me.

I got a compliment the other evening which I certainly do not deserve. Paula said that Judy said Ione Dekker said that she (Ione) thought I was the prettiest girl she had ever seen.

To be frank in expressing my thoughts, I am longing to see Walter again. I hope he will be at *Shauturn* and I hope he will ask me for one dance. I borrowed Aunt Magdalene's tan dress to wear. Am glad that I won't have to wear that everlasting pink reception dress of last year.

May 6, Monday

At *Shauturn* I saw nothing of Walter until the last number—when the *Activen* performed. I can't deny that he was the chief object of my attention then. But that was as far as I enjoyed it. Had a perfectly miserable time. No one but that pie-faced "swell-shooter" Otto asked me to dance. Walter took Ellen, that much I know, and he danced with scarcely any one else except her. Paula said consolingly that he only wanted to make me jealous (which I don't believe) and that Ellen was mean to flirt with him like that. Only she didn't seem to be flirting. Well I was quite undecided that evening and the next day or so what to think of him. If I would have had lots of other offers for dances it might have been borne, but this way it seemed as if I stood no show whatever among even high school boys (who by the way were terribly poky).

Then on May 3 came the class play. The scenes between Faulkland and me (all three love scenes) were certainly the limit. I felt mighty silly at first, acting so lovesick when you aren't, but there's nothing like getting used to a thing. I had two dresses, a red one—in which I looked like a gypsy. (At least I must have.) Then I had a white dress and a love of a black velvet cape. The play went swell and we had a full house. Oh yes, before the play had started I looked thru a peep hole in the curtain and almost the first person I noticed was Walter Gennert. On one side of him was a Bauer girl—I imagine he came with her. Then and there behind the curtain I tossed my head in indignation and fiercely renounced him. If he can't find anyone better than that—! I tossed my head many a time that way to myself, and I guess the very thought helped me to act my part better.

To-night after Glee Club some of us girls went down to Pritzl's ice cream parlor and as we were returning I saw Walter coming towards us. At the corner we would have met. I switched around the corner without a look at him and—cut him dead! Gee I could have cut capers the next moment. It did feel good to ignore him *thus*. If he does not care for me, very well. I am getting along nicely without him. That he is fascinating, I will admit still—but that is all. He is not my ideal anyway, altho he has dark hair and blue eyes. I might say with Faulkland, "Love! Tormentor! Fiend!" only it isn't love. It was only a crush at the most, and crushes are very common and undependable things. Meanwhile I will act enjoyably indifferent to him. I will also have to jilt Otto again. He does "give me the hydrostatics to such a degree."

May 12, Sunday

Yesterday evening they had a "social hop" at the May Festival. Walter had taken no one there, it seems, which was to his credit—his taste is so ridiculous some times. I never looked at him (except when he wasn't looking) and he was mighty near sometimes. Just looked past him and was enjoying myself immensely without him. He didn't look very cute to me last night either, and not half as fascinating as at other times.

Well, for the first dance he asked the girl next to me. The next dance he asked me. I feigned surprise and said something like "Why—yes." When we arrived at the dancing floor we talked of this and that, and somehow I couldn't help throwing off the cold reserve I had intended to use, and acted naturally.

I danced, too, with that abominable idiotic Otto. Wish he'd join the army or navy. For all I care he can exhibit his shooting powers there to his heart's content. Then I danced with Harold Hiller and then once more with Walter. I don't believe he danced with any one else that evening, and went home by himself before the last dance or so.

And now I haven't the slightest idea how I ought to act towards him. It would seem silly for me to act cool just because he didn't dance with me at *Shauturn* when he had always asked me on previous occasions. I imagine it would be best for me to act natural, with not much eagerness and no indifference either. Last night I dreamt that he took me to Pritzl's and Eugene took Paula. He wore knickerbockers (Walter, I mean) and was awfully nice. Dreams go contrary.

June

Paula is going to Chicago all summer and perhaps all next year,* and "What will poor Wanda do then, poor thing?" I don't see how I'll ever stand it, but I must.

June 16, Sunday

Tomorrow Paula is going, consequently I am feeling sad. Last night I cried, this morning I cried, and since then I have been mighty near it every few minutes. Everybody, everybody is going. Judy has left for the country, Gertie for Minneapolis, tomorrow afternoon Paula and her Mother. And now Phil Becker (who by the way came last Monday) is going away too—tomorrow evening. Depressing? Hm.

As I said Phil came Monday. It didn't take him as long as usual to

* To attend the University of Chicago.

get re-acquainted. Yesterday he got a telegram calling him to Colorado where he has secured a position. He immediately started packing, and dropping his jolly mood, and becoming very serious. All day he was serious. Hope I'll get a chance to say goodbye to him, because now that I come to think of it, I really like him awfully well—as a friend. He ranks first now because he has sense and Walter has none that I can see at present. I am not in love with Phil, neither am I struck on him. He is a good friend, that's all. He has a resolution of manner and a fine character which is to be admired. As to looks, I object to his pompadour but he has cute feet.

* * *

(NOTE:—At the close of my high-school term I decided, if possible, to teach country school the following year. During the summer my time was so taken up with teachers' examinations, art jobs, and my long installment letters to Paula that my diary was neglected for months. As these letters cover this period I am using extracts from them, in lieu of diary entries, beginning with the following entry of July 1 and ending with October 10.)

July 1, Wednesday, 4.25 p.m. At Home.

I ought to be drawing, I want to send something to the Journal Junior, but this is far more interesting. I am not in the attic room now. It's too hot up there in the daytime.

Right here beside the window the roses are blooming. I wish I could be as patient and persevering in bringing joy to my fellow-beings. Do you believe that on one bush of roses there is only *one* perfect flower at one time? Perhaps in our lives there is *one* time when we are entirely perfect. I like to think so, anyway.

The kids are playing Indian. The rule is that whenever you're shot at with a cap revolver (minus caps) you're wounded. Asta, Dehli and Flavia are generally the captive maids because the boys are forever insisting that they haven't been wounded. Asta has just announced that she is the Chief.

All last night I dreamt that I was eating ice cream Sundaes and sodas. Five in succession and some more at short intervals.

I am nearly always wearing my hair without a ribbon and *with* the little comb. More comfortable. What's the latest style in hair dressing? I feel like experimenting if there are any new styles.

I feel like an indefinite quantity, and look like a cannibal, these days.

July 3, Friday 9:30 p.m.

Just think, yesterday I suddenly discovered that I was in a fierce drawing mood. I sat up in my room and *drew* for all I was worth. In ink. I suddenly got so *bold* in making strokes, and made several sketches in ink without drawing in pencil first. After a walk with Judy I went up again and drew some more, with myself as a model. I did not try for likenesses tho, merely the lines and shades and so forth. I had shade over the *whole face,* that is something I've never dared to do before. It looks fierce from near but "distance lends enchantment to the view." I made some such weird pictures tho that I actually got scared of them myself. One girl had such a *"höhnish"* smile on her that I had to scratch out her face before I got hydrostatics or something like that. One was a gypsy girl, and one happened to get real dreamy-looking.

Later:—Oh say, I'm so afraid I've lost my drawing mood again because to-day I drew Asta and Dehli and they got so silly. I was up until after eleven last night, drawing. I should probably have stayed up longer but it is a wee bit uncanny all alone on the 3rd story.

Judy and I were up at your house last Sunday. I was discussing (did you ever hear of *one* person discussing?) the sad and sudden departure of my drawing mood, and Jenny * just sat and gazed, and then she could contain herself no longer and said, *"Na was ist denn das? Eine Krankheit?"*

I am still wearing my hair with a comb. How are you wearing yours, with or without a bow?

You will wonder how I change so abruptly from one topic to another so entirely different. I just stop writing for a little while in between sometimes, and during that time my thoughts travel on. See?

July 5, Sunday.

The night before last I dreamt that there was a swell social function at grandma's, and stacks of Persian sheiks and their wives came—just by wagonloads-full. I suddenly noticed that this letter—almost nine sides of it—was gone. Finally I found it in the hands of two young men, one a tall dark-haired fellow and the other a light-haired fellow and not so tall. I said to the one who had light hair (his name, by the way, was Chesterfield), "Are you sure there was nothing *very* confidential in it?" and he said, "Oh no, for once it is a love-letter." The tall fellow's last name was Wicherskipresident, and was a very melodious name in my dream.

Perhaps I'm having a drawing mood, a poetical mood and a musical

* Paula's older sister.

mood in a wild jumble. It is so vague as yet tho, that I can't tell for sure.

I am wearing my hair with a ribbon—a bow at the side, you know. Made Howard a waist this morning. Am going to grandma's soon. You ought to have heard me sing this morning. Had *such* a singing streak. Wrote a poem yesterday. "A Dream" it's called.

July 8

Do you know where I am? Down at grandma's under the big, big cottonwood trees, with the wild, free breeze fanning my face and lifting my hair as gently, as gently. Asta and I came down here yesterday afternoon. After cooling off we played croquet—oh yes, I must tell you about this croquet. When Stella and Tussy came down here they must have yearned for croquet and manufactured themselves some mallets— little weak, shriveled-looking affairs. For lack of balls they used potatoes, but it happened that Jack (that's the dog) used to eat them up. Uncle Josie, not being able to look upon this, I imagine, with calm nerves, made them 4 fine mallets and 6 balls—also arches; and now he has learned the game himself and is getting to be quite a shot.

I've had some sort of *relapse* of my drawing fit or perhaps the "Drawing fit proper."

"Swell," you will say, but let me tell you something. Perhaps I told you I was to decorate clay pipes for Mr. Minne as souvenirs for the Home Coming Festival.* At 5 cents a piece I agreed to do them. Then I managed to get up enough nerve to go into Annen's Drug Store and ask if they'd undertake selling some hand-painted souvenirs for the Home Coming Festival. I was scared stiff, I believe I looked wild, and I *know* that I stammered. And fancy, he was *enthusiastic* about it! And then he saw my bag—you know my Indian bag with the blue and white beads,** and he said that would be dandy, especially if I'd paint an Indian head on one side.

Saturday I went to the County Superintendent of Schools. He gave me the address of a school clerk and told me that Teachers' Examinations came the 29 and 30 of—July, mind you! And now—along comes a drawing mood. You can't expect me to study Civics, can you? And when

---

* The New Ulm Home Coming Festival is celebrated at five- or ten-year intervals on the anniversary of the Indian massacre of 1862, in which the Sioux Indians were finally defeated and driven off by the New Ulm settlers.

** I had made this bag out of the remnants of some real Indian clothes which I found in our attic. My father had used these costumes in painting murals which depicted scenes from the Indian massacre. One of these murals now hangs in the Minnesota State Historical Library.

will I ever get all those clay pipes painted? I can just hear your mother say, *"Ja, die Wanda, die ist halt so ein kind!"* with that smile of hers which verges so often on the Doomesque kind.

Nevertheless the Drawing Mood carries all before it. Sketched Asta twice with the most elaborate shadings I could produce—and Stella twice to-day. I learned several new things, among them how to paint blonde hair, a grain to my very few grains of shading knowledge, a little new method of drawing hair so as to make them look fluffy, a little stroke in the upper lip and a stroke in the chin. When I have once mastered the mouth I ought to have a celebration. I have the *worst* time with mouths.

Just sketched myself before. I was disgusted with my countenance so I changed it (or the picture) to my heart's content. If my face were less a circle and more oval, if my nose instead of having that turn-uppy tilt were more straight, if my chin were more decided, and if my mouth were smaller either way, I shouldn't be so bad looking after all!

I guess I'll write a sonnet or something to that dandy little paint brush I lost. I bought myself a new one and it isn't worth two cents. I almost despair of getting one quite like it. It takes so long to get them trained too—about a year at least.

When you write, write stacks, will you? Let this take the place of our chats. I miss them already.

July 15

Today I went home. "Any mail?" was my first request. And when it was a letter from you, my heart gave a bound way up into my head, quite upsetting my brains and putting my associational fibres entirely out of kilter. That was a very cute letter, and the darling little porcupine—I nearly felt like crying over it. It seemed so much a part of you. Now don't laugh for I don't mean looks—I mean drawing porcupines is one of your own owny characteristics.

The reason I left such a gap (of silence) between the 8th and the 15th is because I had so "unmenschlich" much to do. Have finished 18 badges, 3 bags, 3 bookmarks and 3 penwipers and 4 blotters.

Aside from that my drawing mood continued fiercely. One day I drew myself and when I had finished I had "great joy" (as our cousin from Austria expresses himself) for my arm "came out" from the rest of my body, I mean it didn't look flattened against the rest as all my arms had done up to that time. The next day I drew myself again and of all the shadows I didn't put in! Learned some swell points about drawing

Four Self Portraits in Pencil, 1909-1913

Top: The Biebl Place—"Down at Grandma's"
Bottom: left: Wanda at Graduation; right: Flavia, about 1917

noses and some very helpful points about the mouth. Right here I will say, you can skip those parts where I rave about drawing. I only do it because I don't *dare* tell it to people. I simply can't stand that half-bewildered, half-pitying, half-scared gaze (there now, that's a gaze-and-a-half already, but you ought to *see* it) they give me at such times. I know you'll understand, and anyway it's a great comfort to only put it on paper.

Well, to go on, I drew myself again after that. And then again. Well, I was quite wild by that time and would have gone without supper if I hadn't missed lunch already. I don't stick to that theory any more that artificial light is *the only* light. The daytime light in grandma's bedroom is just swell and doubtless I'll find lots of other desirable places.

Asta's doing some stunt at the piano that sounds like "chop sticks" only more so. One of her own creations with a whistling accompaniment. Soul-inspiring.

July 16—6.30 a.m.

Good morning. Am I not up early? Guess I'll make myself a shirt waist today, because perhaps if I have to visit the clerk of some school I'll have one to wear. Gertie said that that made a fine impression—if you dressed rather severely and business-like.

Yesterday I got a mirror and fixed my hair all kinds of ways. Spinster curls, big bow in back with a curl hanging down, one-sided effect, and Indian style. You should have seen me!

Sketched myself twice but they both got fierce. My drawing mood is going. Isn't it sad? My spirits took a tremendous drop when I discovered the alarming fact. However I might have expected it. All joys must have an end. Might make a poem out of that:—

> All joys, all joys, all joys, all joys must surely have an end
> And so must every drawing mood, my friend, my friend, my friend.

Doesn't that sound as if I had been inspired—moved by the Divine Afflatus? The repetition is for emphasis, and you'll have to admit that it makes it very effective and brings out the main thought so well!

You're going to miss something at Homecoming because Governor Eberhart is going to be here and make a speech. I'm just wild to see him. When I heard he was coming I just yelled, *"Oh, der liebe Governor!"* before I knew what I was saying. I wish he'd know me yet but I suppose he won't have time to notice anyone in particular.

P.S. The other night I dreamt there were a whole lot of porcupines in town and one held all his quills in his front paw. Inspired by what?

July 24. At home

Is it so hot down there too? I have been *so* busy; honestly my head seemed to be going round and round like a weathervane with my poor neck as a pivot. I have finished 13 bags and 6 tobacco pouches. They are now on sale. The last time I was down all the bookmarks were gone with orders for more. Nine of the bags are gone. Mr. Annen says I could sell 100. Yesterday evening I decorated 11 pipes, and this morning before breakfast I decorated 19. It's real dandy work if you have time.

How do you like this writing? I've just finished writing my applications and the effect is still upon me. I believe I told you I applied for a school. Well, they never answered, so this morning I stepped up to the County Superintendent and informed him of my "unsuccess." He gave me 2 other schools to write to. I told him I'd like very much to have a school because I wished to send my sisters thru High School. Somehow that *utterance* had a very pathetic effect on me and I believe my eyes became misty. They *felt* very appealing as I looked at him. I hope they looked it. He certainly is nice. I do wonder what I'll do if I don't get a school. I don't know of a single way to earn money, and Stella and Tussy are going to High School if I can help it. Am wearing my new shirt waist to-day because I wanted to look somewhat "severe" up at the superintendent's.

July 25

Yesterday I went to get my State certificates and fancy, I didn't get a pass plus in either History or Civics. So here I am with 3 examinations staring me in the face (there is also Composition) and only *3 days* between me and them!

Then I went to bring some of my pipes down (did I tell you that I had 34 done?) and to get some donkey oil at Stein's. There they interviewed me for a while and gave me 170 buttons (for more badges). They are left from 1902 but have no printing matter on.* Yesterday I finished 3 match scratchers and 5 blotters.

I must go at my entertaining (?) Civics again. I've been trying to ab-

---

* On the 1902 button was an Indian picture which my father had painted for the Home Coming Festival of that year.

sorb Local Government and my head is a perfect jumble. I could just shrivel up when I think of examinations.

Have you seen the new Ladies Home Journal with the H. Fisher girls out camping? It is just about inspiring.

Do you cut up a lot down there or are you a demure maiden? Keep up your diary. I'm neglecting mine for this, but that doesn't matter. I enjoy this more.

July 27

Yesterday I tried putting up my hair in the Psyche knot and failed as far as my object was concerned. I got it up in a very unique way tho, a style of my very own. Psyche knots are all the go here now.

Joke:—This is the *psyche*-logical moment.

Made 3 more bookmarks and 18 badges, and two bags.

The night before last I drew an idealized picture of Stella. Then I drew another one of Stella on the window seat (we have one now just below the skylight, Stella manufactured it) it got to be a perfectly *hideous* picture, but I gained my end which was to make the head "stand out" from the wall. I'm just about tickled stiff every time I succeed in that.

I must study the subject in which I got such encouraging marks— History.

July 29

At 2:45 p.m. I take the exam in Composition, tomorrow at 8 a.m. History, and at 2:45 p.m. Civics. I must get at my History again. My brain fairly swims in dates and wars and treaties. I'll try to keep them arranged until after the History test. Then I'll clear my brain for Civics. Ah Civics!

July 31

Do send me an imaginary pat on my shoulder for having written to you in spite of exams and all else that kept me in the highest degree of suspense, excitement and fear. The exams are all over, but of course something had to interfere with my little plan. I have been planning that plan for the last several months. You know it—I was to teach school and give the money to those at home so that Stella wouldn't have to stay out of school to earn money. Oh no, it isn't that I didn't pass those 3 exams. I think I managed to slip thru. It's this—you see, I got 70 in the penmanship and arithmetic tests when I took them last year, and now

I should have taken them this year again because 70 lasts only one year.*
I found that out when it was too late. Isn't it provoking?

I haven't heard from the two places I applied to, either, in spite of the
neatly addressed envelope I put in each. I quite despair of getting a school
this year.

This is the ink I used in writing exams. I'm sick and tired of them.
I do my double, double best to forget all that I have crammed into my
poor confused little pate (You can fancy what a confusion it must have
been up there with about 30 dates scooting around trying to find the
little pigeon-hole labeled "Dates" when I never have had, or never will
have, a space reserved for them. Why I haven't even a department named
"Numbers." As it was, the dates just crammed into any little crannies or
crevices that weren't full of Civics, and things pertaining to U.S. History
such as wars, treaties, compromises and so forth) but I still find myself
reciting the preamble to the Constitution, and rattling off:—

Alaska, acquired 1869 by Purchase, Grant's Administration.
Louisiana, 1803, Purchase, $15,000,000, Jefferson Administration.
Florida, 1809—But what's the use?

This morning I went thru all the papers on my table up here (Attic
Room) and eliminated from an alarming chaos all examination questions, all History and Civics books, in fact anything that reminded me of
those exams. I want my mind to be free. I don't want to look at a History book for about 1000 days—unless I get a school. And as I've said
before, I don't think I'll get one. I'm already looking around for something else to turn my hands, heart and mind to. Life is a grind just now,
and is going to be for several years, or I miss my guess.

August 5

Mr. Peffer asked me if I wanted him to sell some souvenirs for me too.
He won't even charge a commission, isn't that nice of him? I accepted
with thanks and a grateful look.

The Superintendent said I ought to see those school clerks in person,
but it's too far to walk and you can't get there by railway, and I have too
little courage to ask someone to take me in their auto. A livery team, of
course, is out of the question—too expensive. Fine kettle of fish, isn't it?

* This meant I could get only a Third Grade Certificate, which lessened my chances of
obtaining a school.

I don't give two cents now any more how I write, since I'm not going to be a school teacher anyway. I have given up my hopes. I am just going to let things take their course. I have worried *exactly* enough. If I get a chance to go out with some one's auto I'll go, if not, then not. I never was cut to plan such *big* projects all by myself, never.

August 7

This morning we went to the Cottonwood River for a picnic. I took out some bookmarks to draw. By the way, yesterday I had completed 76 in all. The day before yesterday I had a terrible painting fit and painted three heads—all blondes, of course. The next addition to our room (besides the Indian corner) will probably be a "Love corner" and an "Artist's corner." We have a picture (cut out of a magazine) of a man hugging a young girl, and the man looks a lot like Mr. Doom, and Judy is just wild about it. His coat looks just like Mr. Doom's grey suit.

I am getting to admire blondes so—I think fluffy blondes look positively captivating in dark blue. And men with light hair look real handsome to me now too. It just struck me that I had *never* thought of falling in love with a light-haired man. In those wild flights of fancy of mine I had always imagined The One to be dark and of a striking appearance, but since then I just looked—merely for an experiment, you understand— to see if there wouldn't be light-haired ones that would be equally lovable. Don't look so shocked, you know you have ideas like that in your head sometimes, and I'm only human.

Monday night at singing practice Mr. Logan introduced me to a Frenchy-looking (but very nice) man. He immediately started complimenting me on my drawings (really wish I could have remembered all the adjectives he employed, merely as a sort of curio collection). I didn't know which drawings he referred to and felt rather weak when I finally realized that he meant my bookmarks & blotters etc. You know one can't show the least bit of inspiration on those things and I can't say that I'm the least bit proud of them. Must finish my ten bags that are left to make. That will make 33 that I've made.

August 17, Saturday

I've seen Walter lots of times lately, the last time was the day before yesterday when he returned with the militia. I must say he looked rather handsome in uniform, but of course everybody does. He looked awfully tall. Hm.

Aug. 19, Monday

Here is Homecoming. I wonder whether I'll enjoy myself. Rain is predicted for every day except one.

Last night was Park Concert again. I saw Walter too, but not one greeting did he get from me, altho I met him a number of times. I ignored him neatly and completely. Later in the evening he was sitting alone on a bench, listening to the music in a most docile and amusing manner. For that he goes up one peg in my estimation, but *one* only. His face haunted me all evening.

Tomorrow night we sing. Mr. Logan [the conductor of the Women's Chorus] has told us that we would either be greeted by "frost" or "vociferous applause." Puzzle:—which? He has promised to omit "antics" from his part of the performance, but has decided to smile at us once in a while. I've gotten entirely used to his "antics" altho I still am awfully afraid at times that he'll jump off his platform and cause a panic. And his smiles, why Paula, they're enough to make that black-haired-girl-at-Pritzl's smile. And when we come to some sentimental part such as, "I feel the kiss that was in youth so dear," or a place where there is an exquisitely blended chord, a look of almost divine joy or feeling steals into his eyes, and he raises his pupils and a smile plays about his lips. He looks ever so much like Don Quixote. He has an exceedingly nice ear for music (notice correct use of "nice") and I like him too, but he is so funny.

Before we sing, Stella and I have to wait table for the banquet. Gee, I have to finish a dress yet for Stella. Have about 50 badges yet to make.

August 21

Well, last night we sang. It went all right and Mr. Logan behaved most beautifully.

Glory there are a lot of strange soldiers here. And flirty! I usually ignore them entirely, and sometimes I deign to shoot them a dagger or two. Once when Stella & Judy & I were walking on Main Street, one said, "I like the chicken with the black eyes." Hm. They look almost irresistible from a distance tho, with their uniforms and when you can't see the eyes they are forever making. I've sketched a few, but I haven't a bit of a drawing mood, not a bit and it's so provoking.

This morning we went to see the parade. They had some dandy floats. I saw the beloved Mr. Eberhart riding in a coach down to the park where they had the speeches. Dr. Haftel first, and all during his speech I feasted my eyes on Mr. and Mrs. Eberhart. Bliss, unalloyed.

And then our Darling Executive made a speech. It was just dandy (needless to say) and took awfully well with the people. At the dance in the evening Mrs. Eberhart gave me such a hearty lingering handshake. The Governor was so occupied that he didn't see me at all I guess. How I do wish I would have had a chance to speak to the Governor.

August 26

Homecoming is finally over. By the time I get all that is due me, I expect to have made over $45 or $50 dollars during the summer.

I am sitting up in my attic room. I have on the light but the sky still looks blue thru the skylight. You know how one sees one's reflection in it, and now it looks like a blue-print photograph of myself.

Just think, if I'd have a pass-plus in algebra and had had sense enough to take the exams in Writing and Arithmetic I'd have a first grade certificate. But that *if* is so very irrevocable!

How I wish I were once safely launched on an art career, however small, because then I'd be in my sphere and feel *at home*. I sometimes think I'm a failure right thru, and that people have brighter hopes for me than they will ever realize. If I ever have desires for distinguishing myself it is because I do not want to destroy these people's faith. I *should* love to repay them by doing my best.

Judy took a picture of me standing at a little fence. The road and the fence are on the picture but there is just a gap where I ought to be. She took another of me, and the film is flashed so that my head is invisible. The other one she took of me is perfectly blank. Makes me seem pretty unsubstantial, doesn't it?

My ideal is still a blonde, but *not* an artist. I think two artists would get along just horribly, don't you? I want a man who appreciates art and who is willing to let me draw when I have a drawing mood—he'd have to let me anyway whether he'd want to or not, and if he'd have to throw me out of the house.

My ideals all have to have an *r* in their names.

I am at present wild about reading and sewing. Nothing else. I read "Thelma" and am almost done with "The Bishop's Emeralds" and "The Circular Staircase." I don't like "The Lure of the Mask" as well as some others of Mr. McGrath's books—anyway the heroine smokes cigarettes and that always sort of dampens my ardour.

August 28

The weather is distinctly autumnal, hazes, breezes (and, who knows?

sneezes). But weather isn't what's on my mind. It's *schools*. I didn't have nerve enough to ask anyone to take me to either of the schools because they are about 20 miles from here and I didn't know what to do. I went up to your house and poured out my troubles there. Your mother sympathized beautifully with me and telephoned Mr. Harrington whether he couldn't take me, and he seemed very willing. I always hesitated about asking him about taking me to a school because I felt it was asking too much—they have done such a lot for me already. He was awfully nice and said he'd take me just wherever I liked. I must confess I shed a few tears, his kindness was so greatly overwhelming.

September 4

This letter is not going to be a wail so prepare yourself with an indulgent smile. I think I have a school. Yesterday I went out to Springfield with Mr. and Mrs. Harrington. We rode 66 miles in all. We went to one school. They had hired a teacher. We went to another. They had not hired any yet. The way Mr. Harrington praised me to those people was nothing slow tho; and the fact that I drew pictures was no mean factor in convincing them of my brilliance (?). "Why it's pure luck," said Mr. Harrington, "that you get a teacher like this. You don't often get one as good as she," etc. I sat meekly by.

I do hope I'll get it. To-day I'm going over to the School Supt. to see about the contract.

Do you know what I'm going to do? Learn to play the guitar, so that I'll have some music when I get out into the country.

Sept. 11

I have sent the contract down to Springfield for them to fill out and they haven't answered, and I am considerably dashed in spirits this fine morning. If I ever marry—next to marrying for love—I shall marry so that I won't have to bother myself with financial matters. At least I think so now.

I went to turning school and decided that "Turning school without Paula is like potatoes without salt."

If only the old school business were settled one way or the other—I could stand defeat better, I guess, than this misery of suspense and uncertainty. If I do not have some diversion my nerves will rise to the same pitch of excitement and unrest as they did before the teachers' examinations.

September 18

What do you think is Mr. Doom's latest enterprise? Superintendent of Schools at Blue Falls. In the wildest flights of my imagination I cannot think of him as such. John Dekker was up there and saw him. He told John he had given up a number of things, among them—*smoking*. Do you believe it? I cannot help wondering whether he *could* ever give up sarcasm. I can't think of anything else that he might give up, except his high heels and that adorable (?) pompadour.

Yesterday I got a letter from the School Clerk. He said that there would not be more than 20 scholars in their school, and that one member of the School Board was unwilling to give $45 a month but if I wanted the school for $40 I should write him. I sat right down and wrote a letter of acceptance. I don't think tho, that I have the school for sure. Not until I have the contract would I think that.

I had the funniest dream last night. A band was playing here in town and it played such "dancy" music that everyone, regardless of dignity or custom (or grace!) danced wherever they went. I did too. I was barefooted.

Do you have any nice dreams? I always snap my own apples now. Do you ever snap any?

The other day I got a blue envelope addressed to Miss Wanda Gag, Artist. Now this isn't going to be the revelation of some grand new hope or possibility. It was a very kind little missive tho, sent by Mr. Charles Weschcke of St. Paul regarding my art career (?). He said that I could probably get a position at Brown and Biglow's and go to the St. Paul Art School at the same time. He said that if he could give me advice in anything, I should please "command" him. Nice of him, wasn't it? He knew papa very well.

September 22

Did I tell you I sent a letter to Mr. McWhorter asking him to explain what he meant by saying, "Whenever you're ready to go to Art School, just let me know and I'll find a way"? Well, I did and the other day I got an answer, and he said that if I were able to pay my living expenses they would find a way for me to enter this fall. Which is certainly dandy, but the school experiment goes first, so Mr. McWhorter—a great deal of thanks and a pile of regrets to you.

How wild I am to see you! The night before last I dreamt that you were here. Then last night I dreamt that the dream of the night before was only a dream but it had really come true, and glory I was tickled. I have your picture in my locket (the locket's fixed now).

Your letters are getting so Chicago-i-fied. Keep some of your characteristics tho, won't you? I like the You-ness of You. I imagine I, due to the absence of such edifying influences as Chicago, become too much *I*. I philosophize so much, against my will and by myself (probably with my Other Self) that my mind is a veritable Chaos. I need you to clean it up. I need Diversion. I am wearing the old rut (in which I am at present sliding along) so *very* smooth that it simply shines from pure monotony. Ah, that metaphor was a masterpiece, wasn't it?

I am working with great zeal for the school I am hoping to get. I am of course deeply interested in my "Primary Plans" which I get every month.

October 10

How are you? I couldn't tell you how I was if I tried, I feel so "nothingy." I got that school and now that the time for my going draws nearer I get more & more scared. Supposing I only get big kids (I am preparing mostly for primary work) or supposing I wouldn't be able to teach the little ones how to *begin* to study. Oh it's quite a solemn enterprise when you look at it in the proper light—quite like a wedding. I feel that getting ready to marry couldn't be any worse.

I gathered some leaves today & pressed them. I went to take them along to use as busy-work in my school. I shall soon start packing. I'm planning on taking Shakespeare with me, so I'll have something cultured to read while I'm out in the wilds.

(Note:—This is the end of the period covered by my letters to Paula—the Diary entries are now resumed.)

* * *

Nov. 14, Thursday. Springfield

My I haven't written for a long time.

Well, I got a school and have taught 9 days. I came out here Nov. 4—that is, I came to Springfield first. It was a little after 9 a.m. when I arrived at the depot where I whiled away three happy (?) hours, the reason being that no one cared enough for me to get me. Well, it was getting rather tiresome. When it was nearly twelve I grabbed my umbrella, suitcase, and papa's guitar (I admit I can't play a note on it but I was scared I'd come to a place where I'd have no music and one can always learn) and stepped along Main Street. I tried to look as composed and "un-lost" as I could but whether I succeeded is another matter. I finally came to the conclusion that I'd better hire an auto out.* It cost me $1.50 but it had to be. Anyway the livery man was nice and gave me some advice. But think of it, no one wanted to board me. I wished with all my heart that I were so fascinating that they couldn't help but say, "Certainly, come in, we'll make room for you." Only I wasn't. I was on the verge of tears (the genuine kind too, not the coaxing variety) when I prevailed on Klinger's to keep me at least for a day or two. I have been here since, and even tho it is a mile to my school house, I'll stay here if they'll let me.

I like these people awfully well. There is one girl who is about 23, another who is 15. Besides the two boys who go to my school there are 4 other boys at home. Every evening after school I write or read about half an hour and then I play piano for about a half hour, or dream, compose poetry or plan things (for school).

Last Sunday there was a dance out at a farm about 4 miles from here. We went, of course. I got introduced to about 30 people I guess, and danced nearly every dance. We slipped on wax until about 2 a.m. Now what do you think of that?

1913
Jan. 7

I just got a letter from Phil. It was such a serious one, and I do feel so queer. All I can do is to say "Goodness" at irregular and short intervals. I knew, ever since he gave me a book for Christmas two years ago, that he didn't exactly hate me, and I could see by his latest letters that he was getting to like me better right along, but who ever would have thought that it was as serious as this. He says I'm not confidential enough, and asks me to be frank and honest in my next letter—that if I don't care for him and his actions he will be willing to listen to me. Goodness. Frankly, here, I like him as well as, and perhaps better than, any other young man of my acquaintance. But goodness, I'm not in love with anyone yet—at least not to my knowledge.

I only hope he isn't terribly serious. I am too young to play seriously with love and—well, I'm so frivolous yet. Perhaps it's only a case of "Distance lends enchantment to the view," only he is a man who generally knows how to read his own heart. That is an accomplishment which I lack.

* My school was ten miles out of town.

5:45 p.m. Well here I am again, with my affections as unsettled as ever. I don't suppose I can sleep much to-night, I do keep revolving all my most serious problems around in my head before I go to sleep, and as a consequence I generally don't succeed in falling asleep for two hours or so. I used to say that I wished someone were struck on me. I didn't think then that it came so near being a calamity as it is. Perhaps it isn't so calamitous as it seems to me now, but it's exciting enough.

7:05 p.m.—I must resort once more to my diary. A great deal has happened since I am out here in the country. I have been, so far, to two dances and one party out here. I generally make about two hits at every dance, but it isn't bragging or conceit for me to say so. I hope it isn't anyway. They only last one night anyway and the school teacher is always a novelty. I have learned how to dance the polka and the "barn dance" which is something like the "Come to me kid" dance.

I enjoyed the first dance the most. It was in a barn and I was introduced to just stacks of people. Met a graduate of the Springfield High School too. He wore a Mackinaw coat, and I do think those Mackinaw coats are so irresistible. His name (that boy's, I mean) is Sven Peterson and he does waltz splendidly.

The second dance was in a machine shed. My catch of the evening was a young man from Springfield, his head conspiciously adorned with a checked cap. It seems he couldn't dance much else besides a waltz and how he *did* dance! Honestly one felt that his life depended upon it, he danced so vigorously and earnestly. I felt as if I had mowed a whole lawn after every waltz with him.

I went home for the Christmas holidays of course, and it was just time that I got home then, because I should surely have gotten homesick if I would have had to stay longer. Paula came home from Chicago and of course we were just wild to be together once more. I had two weeks vacation.

Jan. 19

We are having a pretty fierce snow storm. There is nothing new out here except dances and the fact that I have carried a whip to school but have not used it. I have been having trouble with my discipline. Once I was ready to whip one of my hopefuls but at the last minute my sympathy (for *I* used to misbehave too) went out to him, my courage forsook me, and the boy got off with nothing but a lecture which was *supposed* to have sunk in his heart. I don't know whether it did. They always look so repent when I talk to them but when they get out of the door they smile complacently again.

I have now what may turn out to be a drawing mood if properly encouraged. My Divine Afflatus of the Art Department hasn't moved me since last August. My latest fad is drawing from photographs—I copied a picture of a 19-year old girl who earns $10,000 a year in the moving pictures [Mary Pickford], and I've copied four of Billie Burke and one of a Swedish actress, Martha Hedman.

I am reading Shakespeare again. I've read "Romeo and Juliet" and today I read "Much Ado About Nothing." If I keep on I shall become a little philosophical. It would do me good. If I feel pleasantly dreamy, sentimental or poetic, I try to hide it. It is not style here.

I hear that Mr. Doom and Mr. Winkler are married. Don't I feel bad about it tho? At present I have absolutely no crush on anyone, nor has anyone a crush on me that I know of.

February 22, Saturday

If he isn't the limit—Phil Becker. After that "serious" letter he sent me, I sent him one equally serious, showing my side of the question and giving my arguments. There came another letter from him in answer to that one and he seemed satisfied with it. After that I wrote again, of school and other events—just like I write to anyone else, and if he doesn't go to work and let his temper fly entirely away with him! And for nothing at all. He wrote that he was positively *disgusted* with my letter, and I feel mighty insulted because it was a sensible one and a long one, and not uninteresting either, if I do say it myself. It actually seems as if he wanted me to write mushy letters, and if that's what he's after he can wait until the end of the chapter for them—I never have and never write mushy letters. I can't stand them.

He wrote that I continually treat him like a mere acquaintance and that he absolutely refuses to do so any longer or he'll know the reason why. I'm sure I treat him as civilly and politely as any of my best friends, and that is all the nearer my treatment will go. I am certainly not going to be tyrannized over by anyone. I'd rather be an old maid—in fact that course seems a very sensible one to follow. I don't suppose anyone will ever want to marry me—I'm sure I wouldn't want to marry anyone like myself. Even tho I am not as frivolous as I seem, I shall certainly not give up drawing (my drawing moods are the only things I ever wish to be ruled by) and no one wants a dabbler in art for a wife. Nor

do I care—at present at least. And even tho I got a fortune once that
ended thusly:—

> "Until the right man comes your way,
> Then 'Welcome love' and 'Art good-day'",

that does not bid fair to become true.

As to what kind of an answer I shall give him is beyond my powers
of tact, originality and invention. If I cross the bounds and become
defiant and angry, it will be all over between us; and altho I do not
want him to have a crush on me, I do want him for a friend.

I am thinking seriously of becoming an old maid—with a singleness of
purpose and a purpose of singleness.

And what vindictive lines there were in his signature!

March 1, Saturday

Now I have finally answered that letter, and it wasn't gentle, either.
I told him that his letter had an equally ruffling effect on me as mine
did on him. Also, that if he expects soft, mushy letters from me he will
never get them. Also that I saw no reason why we should forget each
other just because I refuse to write the above-mentioned slush, also that
I never have written such letters and never will as long as the tip of
my nose points upward, which means always.

I got a letter from a man in Minneapolis. The Journal Junior has
changed editors, and now a man by the name of A.J. Russell has taken
charge. He wrote me:—

1. that he had found some of my drawings in the office
2. that he had published one and would soon publish the others
3. that he had taken the liberty of mentioning me and my work in an
   editorial, and
4. that he would like to see me if I ever came to Minneapolis.

He put something in (his editorial) about Stella and Tussy too. He
said that he thought that they could illustrate books when they got older.
He asked if he could send me some good books if he'd come across them
cheap in a second-hand store, and offered to lend me one of his own
books. He asked if my father or mother had talent for drawing—or
what first drew me to it. He is married, and I am mighty glad of it
because I feel more free to talk to a married man.

I guess if I would not have to teach school, I would get a drawing
mood. It cannot be properly encouraged here, and there is absolutely

no time to draw at school. Goodness knows, I have trouble enough keeping them moderately settled even when I am constantly on the alert. The whole trouble of the matter is that I am too absolutely good to them. How I wish I could be hopping mad once, so angry that I could wallop every single one soundly. Nearly every night I think, "Now to-morrow I'm going to be strict. I'll give it to them good and proper" but it's the old story over and over again—and if I ever was near crying, it was yesterday.

If I teach school next year I'll know better. How well I remember when Mr. Harrington advised me to "put my foot down." And there were bits of advice of a similar nature from other people. I smiled complacently and planned out a brilliant system of "no whipping and no scolding" rules. It was to be almost ideal, the children were to be educated in morals, in politeness, and the main feature (Ye gods and little fishes!) was to be discipline by kindness. It is now nondiscipline by kindness. My pupils can absolutely twirl me around their little fingers—anyway the seven big ones. Why wasn't I stern in the beginning—inspiring them with awe and respect, why didn't I give them a smack once in a while?

Of course I know I was never cut out to be a school teacher but I *did* think I could do it better than I am. As far as lessons go, I like it very much. My pupils are bright and I like the studies myself—having been able to conjure up a liking for arithmetic, which I used to hate so of yore.

The reason why I hate to slap or whip my pupils is because it is not style any more. They don't do it at home anymore. I don't like it, that's all. It isn't right, and one ought to do right before anything else. And besides, schools are not the cut-and-dried, prim, stiff and formal affairs they used to be. They strive to bring out individual characteristics, tendencies and talents. I think I know the characters of all of my pupils pretty well, and a couple of weeks ago things went just fine. We all had a good time to-gether, but *Now*. One Riot, one Rebellion, one Revolution.

And my system sounds so plausible too, when recited orally. I could give my system, giving only truthful facts, and I could make anyone believe that mine was a model school—as long as they didn't see it. Once more I have resolved to be strict next Monday—I shall probably do so until school is out. Well I wish myself all kinds

March 11

—of luck, I was going to say, but forgot to finish. Well, today I am

20 years old. Out of my teens. It is time I began doing something worth while.

Mar. 12

I am so blue to-day. School is not such a farce. One has to work for one's pay everywhere, I guess. Most of the people here think one should whip children systematically as part of the daily routine, and that the whole school should sit with meek propriety as if it had not an individual thought of its own.

One I have whipped—it is hardly to be believed but it is so—I was somewhat surprised to see the sun shining as brightly as ever, and the clouds sailing along as peacefully as if nothing had happened, and it didn't make me feel so much as if I had done something violent.

I dreamt last night I whipped another of my scholars.

April 7

There is such a high snow out here that sleighs have come into use again.

Well the honorable Philip has not yet written. Nor did I expect him to. The only thing that bothers me is how we'll have to act "when we meet again." I suppose Daisy and the rest of the family will be pretty shocked when they see those icy looks and fiery daggers which will pass between us, he furnishing the former while I supply the latter. I'm just wondering whether I ought not to give Daisy a hint as to what she is to expect.

I answered that nice Mr. Russell's letter too, and believe me, some nerve I had too. I introduced just a little suggestive sentence about drawing moods. Well anyway he wrote again, and I sent him a letter in which I raved about my cherished drawing moods to my heart's content, for I knew he would understand. At first I thought perhaps I had gone too far but I don't think I did, for in his third letter he also raved somewhat and talked—oh so deep. He also sent me a book on Cosmic Consciousness, called "Illumination of Whitman, Tennyson and others." Glory, I felt like having illuminations and things myself, but you get that kind only when you're about thirty years old already. It's a mighty interesting book anyway, and I guess I'd better write him again.

I started a new story, "The Violet Mouse." I am composing it with great deliberation, turning out only a few lines a day, but I suppose one might attribute it to slowness of originality in my intellectual dome.

April 15

It is a lovely day. I am writing this in school during recess. I have been having only six pupils during the bad weather [a blizzard] but to-day I have a round dozen again.

I know a few new songs again. They are:—"Silver Threads among the Gold," "Jungle Moon," and "Cubanola Glide." The first is a perfect beauty.

April 28, Monday

Only one more week of school. I am beginning to long for home. As a result of this emotion I have been packing my trunk for the past week. I was at a dance last night and I had a glorious time. I guess I was on the floor every time except once. I don't go a-wall-flowering out here.

May 5, Monday. New Ulm.

My school closed Friday, and Saturday I drove to town with all my worldly goods and chattels. Then I went to the home of Flora Davis who lives at Springfield and had asked me to spend a few days with her.*

There was a dance that evening in the cutest little hall. I didn't know a soul when I came up there, but I was knocked down to nearly all and they were a nice little bunch. The orchestra played all the popular pieces with the most charming variations—and so "dancy"! Some of the pieces they played were "Pink Lady," "I'd love to Live in Loveland," "Let me Call you Sweetheart," "Will you love me all the time?" and some more like that. We usually sang along and it was just great. I never used to think that singing while dancing was nice at all, but it is—especially if your partner can sing well. And Donald Reeves can. Donald Reeves is a cute little laddie and a fine little dancer. He knows the greatest number of pretty songs—he certainly has a song to suit every one of his moods. There were some other nice young men there too, and they showed me all kinds of a good time. Flora and I had agreed to go home together so Donald took us home.

The next morning I went to church with Flora. After dinner we took down my suit case, guitar etc., and had my suit case checked. Donald is a telegraph operator there, and just a little while before I left he came and talked with us. He told me to be sure and look at the suit case well when I got home and *do* what it said on there. Paula, Stella, Tussi and Judy were at the depot to meet me and they just about smothered me.

* A new friend. I had met her at a dance.

To-day I wrote a letter to Flora Davis. Oh yes, I forgot to say what was to be seen on the suit-case. On the back of the name-tag was "Donald Reeves," and five other boy's names. And below that was "write."

May 19, Monday

Over a week ago Flora answered my letter. In my first letter I told her I had a comp. for her but that I would have it as a trade-last. In her last letter she wrote something to this effect:—

> "How can you be so cruel as to make me wait for the comp. when I have more for you than I can remember. The fact is that you have all the boys in town so dipped that they can't talk of anything else since you're gone."

Of course that is more than I deserve (and it's so *modest* of me to put it in here, isn't it?) but it's encouraging after having a feeling akin to wall-flowerism for a number of years. I have followed part of the advice which I found on the suit case tag. That is, I wrote a card to Donald Reeves. I got his answer the other day. He wants me to come down again *soon* and said they'd try to show me a rollicking time.

Miss Wayne asked me to write a poem and illustrate it for a special edition of the New Ulm Review. Of course I haven't a hint of an inspiration in my intellectual dome. I don't know what's the matter with me, I can't buckle down to anything lately—I haven't patience for sewing, writing and even drawing. I guess I've got sort of a prosaic streak for just now dancing and jolly things like that are just in my line. I haven't had a drawing mood since last August—isn't that awful? But of course this was mostly due to the fact that I could not encourage the drawing moods that were struggling for mastery over me while I was teaching school.

June 7, Saturday

It began this way, my latest adventure, I mean. We have been having University Week here, and as they are both highly instructive and exceedingly interesting, I attended them every day. As usual I had my pencil and paper along and did quite a lot of sketching. I have a drawing mood. Yesterday afternoon I was sketching again. On my left sat Tussy, and on her left sat a young University student whom they called Mr. Emraad. He watched me draw but I did not notice it at first. Then finally he said, "Pardon me, but may I see those drawings?" I assured him that they were not worth looking at but showed them anyway. Then he asked Tussy whether he couldn't change seats with her so he could watch me sketch.

This accomplished, I drew a picture of a girl who was sitting in one of the boxes. When I had finished he asked to my great surprise whether I would sign my name and give it to him. He wanted it for a University publication, he explained. I did so but said I did not like to give it away—it wasn't a very good sketch and I told him I had made better sketches the day before. He asked almost eagerly where I had them. I told him at home. Then he said, "I wonder how I could get to see them." Of course I *had* to take the hint, so I said, "Well you could come to the house some day or else I could bring them along tomorrow." I tried to explain where he could find me but he doesn't know the streets very well yet. And then fancy what he said! "Supposing we sneak out now and go there!"

Of course I could do nothing but to comply, to be polite—and on the other hand I didn't mind doing so either. So we went thru the back stage entrance and down Washington St. We were out of step first, and I, with my usual habit of trying to keep in step with people, gave that little sliding hop—but at the same time he was doing the same thing. And when one gets started it's pretty funny, so we laughed, and I told him that I had formed that habit two years ago and that it had stuck by me ever since, whereupon he informed me that that was the "artist" in me; sense of rhythm, you know. We kept up a lively conversation and found to our immense satisfaction that we had the same ideas on many things. For instance, we both like Browning awfully well, and like also Carlyle. We both love music (and I gathered that he plays the classics) we both love art, we both hate conventionality (rather) and both like children awfully well.

When we came to the house I told him most informally to sit down while I chased up for an armful of drawings. Well, then we looked at the drawings. He certainly knows something about drawing, there's no doubt about that. When he came to the picture which I have lately been considering as my best so far, he asked if he could have it. I had posed for it (which I did not tell him, however) and I worked conscientiously at my beloved "lights and shadows" while I drew it. Well, I gave it to him anyway, because I didn't want him to think that I thought so much of my pictures.

He had to be back by five o'clock so we went up again. He asked how I liked Scott. I said I liked him and he asked for *what* I liked him, and I answered that I liked him mostly for picturesqueness, whereupon he remarked more to himself than anything else, "The artist again." Then we got to talking about nationalities; and he said, "Do you mean to tell me that you are all German?" I told him that altho mama was born in America she was Bohemian, and that papa had been born in Austria. Then he said, *"O, ich sehe—Wien. Wien scheint Ihnen auch aus den Augen."*

He certainly did not hesitate in asking me every question that entered his head. I distinctly remember that he asked me how old I was (upon 15 minutes acquaintance, mind you) and when I told him I was twenty he seemed mightily surprised, altho which way he meant it I do not know. But I guess he didn't think I was as old as I am. The funniest part of it was that we never were introduced to each other. He said, "We've never met each other but I guess we know each other by now," and every few minutes he would remark upon the unconventionality of our friendship.

When we came back to the Hall, we sat on the steps at the back stage entrance where we had a most delightful chat. He asked me, *"Sind sie auch ein Philosoph?"* and I answered that I sometimes did a little philosophizing. Then he asked me what my philosophy of life was and I said that I thought it was a perfectly good world, which seemed to coincide with his opinion too.

He said, as we were sitting there on the steps, "You are observant, aren't you?" I told him one had to be.

June 13, 1913. Friday

Look at that combination, will you? Friday the thirteenth, year 1913. No wonder I feel so blue. And do I? I could sell myself for wash bluing (almost).

Glory it's fierce to be poor. It's all right to talk about the fine character moulding and some more of this song and dance, but oh glory it's hard lines all the same. We're having a thunderstorm—sort of pathetic fallacy, isn't it? If I only had a thousand dollars—but as you know, one half of life is *if*. L/if/e

It's raining like everything. Good night.

June 14, Saturday

Please regard this last day's entry as a parenthetical insertion. I'll have to finish the sentence of the entry before that:——if you wanted to draw things correctly. Then he asked whether I tried to see and draw the things beneath the exterior—to get the character and characteristics of my subject into the picture. I told him that was what I *tried* to do and hoped to be able to do later. I said that I had noticed the characteristics of all the speakers so far and gave a few of them, which seemed to match with his observance too. Then he asked me the startling question, "What are my characteristics?" I hesitated there a little, because my first impression had been that he was mighty conceited and a regular poser. He said then, "Down at the University we learn to be perfectly frank, so don't be afraid to say what you think." "Well," I said, "This" and I raised and lowered my eyebrows the way he does sometimes.

His approving look gave me courage and I said further that he liked children awfully well and that he said things gently. "When I want them to hit?" he said, and I said "Yes." Then I was going to describe his walk which is very characteristic and *not* very graceful, but found that I had not words in my vocabulary to express it so I said I could just see him *go* but I didn't know how to describe it. He told me to try but I spared his feelings.

His favorite authors just now seem to be Meredith and Ibsen. I've not read much of either so I switched gracefully off to the poets. "Then there is Browning," I said at a hazard, "I like Browning." "Ah you like Browning," he said, and right here is the link between this and our next meeting. He had, before this, asked me whether I were going to the lecture that evening. "I haven't decided yet," I answered (the fact was, I had definitely decided *not* to, because it was a lecture on the Gyroscope, and how I do hate scientific things like that.) "Well, supposing I invite you, will you decide then?" What could I do? I accepted. He said I should try to get as near to the door as I could so that we could slip out unawares and read Browning.

Well, I came. I sat pretty near to the door but not very, and he came and sat beside me. I know the people who were there were properly ruffled about this, for I could feel their gazes upon me.

"Have you your pencil and paper along?" said Mr. Emraad. I answered in the affirmative and he told me to start drawing. I sketched a man—and then—we scooted. Out into the Green Room, then out on the street and down to Pritzl's where he ordered us a whipped cream chocolate Sundae. It was "delicatishe" but I was not at all hungry. I do hope the people that were in there got an eyefull. They certainly did their best.

We talked about Cubists and all manner of interesting things and then I asked him what he thought of our Modern American artists. He thought Harrison Fisher, Gibson and Flagg had the talent but that they did not use it in the right way because they tried to satisfy the public. He said, "I wouldn't want to marry a Harrison Fisher girl for anything," so I suppose he thinks beauty is only skin deep. It is true that the Harrison Fisher girls are charming but they do not, as a rule, look as if they did much deep thinking. As to Gibson's "stroke" (which I have always, and still *do* admire) he said one got tired of it. There is something in that, but I suppose Gibson can't help he's got such a touch that will crop out all the time.

I said (for I thought it was time that I should make some original remark too) "I'll tell you what I don't like about Flagg. His characters always looked so affected, and raise their eyebrows too much." I remember I suited the action to the words but I don't know whether I looked the way I wanted to. Anyway, he greeted that opinion with an encouraging remark. After that we went back to the Hall again and on the way up he made plans for the morrow. In the afternoon, he said, we might have a little picnic somewhere, the place was to be of my choosing. I suggested Herman's Heights.

Oh yes, at this time he said boldly, "Let's make an agreement. You call me Armand and I'll call you Wanda." I was quite astonished at the matter-of-fact way he said it, but said "allright." I turned the name "Armand" about in my brain a few times (it was the first time I had heard his first name) and decided it was a rather nice name to say—but I haven't ever called him that when speaking to him. He said he liked the name Wanda and said something in that polished German of his about its being *"ein guter alter Name."* When he talks that classy German I always hasten back to English unless I can answer in monosyllables. This New Ulm German *will* always get the better of me.

When we parted he said, "Wasn't that gyroscope lecture fine?"

Saturday right after dinner he called me up and we agreed that I would meet him in the Green Room. I did, and we went out in the park where we sat on the grass and talked poetry to our heart's content.

He asked me to sketch him, which I tried to do but it got very bad. He took it and after looking at it said that I had one characteristic of his in the picture. "I guess I'll keep it," he said, "so I can take it out once in a while and say, 'You haven't gotten over it yet, old boy'." Of course I wanted to know what the characteristic was which seemed to cause so much compunction on his part. "It's selfishness," he said. "I'm very selfish. Oh you don't know how selfish I am, but I am." I had never noticed that and I don't see now where it would come in, but he insists that he is, so I had to let it go at that.

"I have a copy of Browning that I'd like to give you," he said. Also he said, as he was reclining on the grass (I might also say, to give the thing a more picturesque atmosphere, that he brushed back the blonde curls of his pompadour and looked musingly at the grass) "I'm noted for my laziness with the pen but I guess I'll write to you if I may."

Once he said that he thought that Browning had had a very romantic courtship and that Browning and his wife were an "ideal" match. That is so, I think.

We rhapsodized like that during the whole hour, and then we went in because Armand was going to introduce me to one of the girls of the Dramatic Club. Her name is Marjorie Moss and she has dark, dark eyes and black hair. She is awfully nice. Armand had asked me whether I have any objections if Miss Moss would join us in our picnic. I was glad to have her with us and so we started out for Hermann's Heights with a big basket of lunch which he had ordered.

Once after we got there Armand said to Marjorie, "Why don't girls in Minneapolis wear dresses like that?" (meaning mine). Marjorie said, "Well, don't they?" and he said, "No, I haven't seen a plaid dress on a girl for a long time." My dress is a red plaid. I was so struck on the cloth when I saw it in Springfield that I bought it even tho it isn't style. I told them that I had taken quite a risk in wearing it because no one else had one here, and he said, "Well, that's original—you can't help being original can you?"

After we had completed our lunch we sat and talked. Suddenly Armand said, "For Heaven's sake, Wanda, get your pencil and paper. You look so unnatural without it," and he got them for me. I was pretty thankful for this, for I don't feel at my ease if I haven't them. Then Armand suggested that I sketch Marjorie, and he offered to talk to her while I did so. I learned a good deal from that talk, they discussed books and things like that.

It was about at this time that these two people got it into their heads that I ought to go to the University for one year before I took up art. I gave a decided "no" at first, but really those two days I had spent under University influences had almost completely revolutionized my ideas on art, music, literature and things in general. Well, not exactly revolutionized either, but they set a higher standard in all these things. When I went to High School, I had learned, and *did* appreciate the highest of these things, but after my half year in the country, my mind had adapted itself to life out there in such a way that I was not so discriminating in my tastes as I had been. And the worst of it was, I had rather liked the idea of being flighty—and I confess that there was a time when I thought dancing ranked next to drawing as far as interesting amusement was concerned. Oh I like dancing still—am wild about it, in fact, but I see there are other things that will give you a good time besides dancing, and drawing of course.

I'll say right here that all the six months that I was teaching school, I had only *one* original idea, being this:—that it takes all kinds of experiences to make a life, in the same way as it takes all kinds of people to make a world. It's pretty flat too, now that I think it over. But during that University week I had all kinds of original ideas that absolutely had to get out of my system, and since then I have acquired my former taste for poetry and I once more revel in the higher things of life. There you are.

This was an awful digression, but it will probably show why I am really so wild to go to the University. I feel now that it is the only thing that will satisfy me, that I really will be at home when I can study the poets and authors and things, and above all, I feel that I need the broadening influence for my art that such an institution offers. So it happened that before long I was admitting that I should like very much indeed to attend the "U" but that I couldn't afford it. But they declared that I could earn enough money by drawing to pay all my expenses and to send home $25 a month so that the kids can go thru school.

Armand told me to get near to the door that evening. We were not going to scoot that night tho—it was the night of the play, and of course we didn't want to miss that. I couldn't very well sit near the door without attracting the attention of the ever-watchful public, so I didn't. It happened that there were six or seven seats between the door and myself, and these were soon taken. Then there was a row of seats behind, so it seemed as if the Honorable Mr. Emraad would not get a chance to talk to me about our plans until after the play. But he was undaunted. While racing around trying to get some one to play piano between acts he told one of the girls in the row behind me to tap me. Then he asked whether I wouldn't play (and called me Miss Gág so formally). Of course I told him I couldn't play, and he asked me whether he could speak to me at the end of the second act. But before the second act started he squeezed thru my aisle half-ways and asked if I could come right then. So I, taking my coat and paper and pencil, went with him to one of the rows further in front where we could sit to-gether. Such a sensation.

I had with me a book in which I keep all kinds of notes. I have in there a list of all the books I have read (that is, all that I can remember) and ideas for stories and poems. He looked over the list of books and checked all those he had read. Then he looked at my ideas for stories and poems, and asked whether I had written any stories after those outlines. I told him I had, and he told me to send some to him and he would criticize them for me—which was very nice of him. He took my address and gave me four of his.

After the play, which was splendid, we went up to the stage where Marjorie and I talked together, and Armand played piano. After saying goodbye to Marjorie, Armand took me home. He had a copy of Browning along, and while we were going thru State Street, he wrote something on the fly-leaf. We talked a good while before I went in. He told me to keep right on drawing children, and then compared children to roses or something—I forget the metaphor. Before he left, he told me to be sure and write him "sketchy" letters, not "business" letters.

When I came home I looked on the fly-leaf of Browning and this was what I found:—

"To my 32-hour friend; no less a friend thru brevity of time.
Wanda from Armand"

June 20

Two weeks have passed since then—and the influence, the raising of my standards in art, music, and literature, and enjoyments in general, has remained. I have had more philosophical thoughts and original ideas since then than I have had for many a day.

Tomorrow Mr. Weschcke of St. Paul will call here to discuss my coming to Art School next fall. I'm so afraid I'll give in to him. The martyr-like act for me to play would be to teach school and deny myself everything until I had the family properly settled. Then I could begin upon my career in life, however small it might be. But oh, I'm only human and I do want to go to the University or to Art School.

June 21, Sat. 3.22 p.m.

Well, it's over. Mr. Weschcke's visit, I mean, and I'm to go to Art School. And such charming arrangements! I don't even have to work for my board. I shall probably stay at the Y.W.C.A. and be independent. Have a definite amount of money put in the bank by someone or a number of someones * and not do anything but "Do the things I was meant to do" as he expresses it. He impressed it fully upon us that his was no charity work but that he was predestined—so to speak—to do what he was doing. He is doing it for art's sake and for humanity's sake. He thinks (oh, how can he) that I will repay humanity a thousandfold for what is being done for me. He knows just how I feel about things, simply taking words out of my mouth.

He advised me to take good care of myself until I come, and take a good rest. It was Mr. McWhorter's wish that I should not do any other work at all in order that I might put my whole self into the thing I love best. Some class to their reasoning, I don't see how they can just see thru me like that. A crash will have to come—such joy can't last.

Mr. Weschcke showed me a letter in which were voiced the opinions of Mr. McWhorter and Mr. Lee Woodward Zeigler. And oh the nice things they said about me. It quite unbalanced me. Mr. McWhorter said that the Art School *wants* me—that I'm under no obligation to them for offering me the one year's tuition free. Isn't it bombastic? Only I'm so afraid I won't come up to their expectations, and I should so hate to disappoint people who take such a kind interest in my work.

Mr. Weschcke said to me whether I didn't sometimes feel way down in the bottom of my heart that I was meant to be famous and that I was here to give something great and grand to humanity. I told him that I had given up all ideas of fame long ago. I said I used to think when I was younger that fame would be a nice thing but that I had lost that ambition.

"Why?" said he. "Was it because of adverse circumstances?" And I told him that I thought wishing to be famous was not the noble thing to do. I told him that I couldn't help drawing, that was all. And it is, it is—I can't any more help it than I can help eating and sleeping and thinking. I must confess, or rather I can frankly say, that I never had that idea of doing something grand and great for humanity that I know

* Mr. Weschcke and his brother.

of, but there is always the feeling that there is something bottled up within me that has simply got to come out sometime. Not all at one grand sweep, but little by little—for instance when I haven't drawn anything but weak things for a long time I feel as if I were not doing my duty toward the world. That probably explains why I am so happy during my drawing moods.

Oh I am so afraid of the times when I have no drawing mood down at the art school. I do hope that my work during inspired days will make up for the miserable things I will necessarily have to turn out during the times when my whimsical Divine Afflatus forsakes me. Oh I hope things will go smoothly so that I *can* go next fall.

Neither Armand nor Marjorie have written. I wonder what is the matter. I do not remember whether I was to write as soon as my decision was made or whether I was to wait, as is proper, until one of them should write first. It is bothering me considerably that Armand and Marjorie do not know of my decision. Still, I don't know Marjorie's address, and it would be just a little bit too "unconventional" if I were to write Armand before he ever wrote.

July 7

I have written to Armand—not a letter, but a sort of note to announce that I was not coming to the "U." I told him to forgive the unconventional act of writing to him first, and that I would have written to Marjorie had I known her address. I told him my purpose in writing was to keep them from using precious time in looking for something to keep me busy next fall.

He has not answered yet. I don't care either, as long as I know that Marjorie and he know of my decision. Marjorie has written tho—a sweet little letter in which she told me about the philosophy of life her teacher had taught them. He thinks that all of us isn't here, but that some parts of us are somewhere else, in trees or flowers, in people's faces; and that the aim, or at least one of the greatest aims in life, should be the finding of the rest of yourself. Marjorie wrote something like this:—

"and some find it in the soul-faces of their fellow beings. And see, I have found part of me in you, and probably you will at sometime find part of yourself in the best of me."

I like the idea awfully, and I think I believe the same thing.

July 8, Tuesday

I've been to Springfield. Donald Reeves and Flora and I went to a dance. I met all the boys whose names were on the suitcase, and they all seem to be nice fellows. I learned a couple of new ways to dance. Flora and I originated a new waltz, one man danced a two-step in a unique way, and another man showed me a new way to schottische and do the Rye Waltz. Of course I danced with Donald most of the time. He took us home, and we sat down on the steps at Davis's house for quite a while and talked and sang. I told them about how I had intended to make a list of kitchen utensils when I was a kid, so that I'd be sure not to forget anything when I'd get married. It struck Donnie awfully funny. It certainly was a silly notion.

The next evening Flora, her cousin, Donnie and I went out for a walk, and Donnie and I in some way (Flora's way, I guess) got separated from Flora and her cousin. We had agreeable rambling chats, interspersed with songs and nice, unembarrassing silences, and most of the time he had his hand on my arm, the way they do when they return you from a dance. And I must confess I liked it, which is a shocking thing; but it's true nevertheless. Oh I was recklessly happy; and happily reckless, too, for that matter. Donnie has such a charmingly chivalrous way of managing to keep you on the inside of the sidewalk. If there is anything that makes me disconcerted it's when I have to walk on the outside with a boy.

After a while we didn't see Flora and her cousin any more, and as it was getting late we decided to wend our steps homeward. When we came to Davis's we sat on the steps and talked for a good while, mostly reminiscences of our childhood days. He told me that whenever he looked at the stars and thought, it made him blue. "I'm a dreamer, anyway," he said, and I agree with him there. He said too, that when he read a book like St. Elmo it made him blue for a week. Isn't that queer and nice of him? He isn't a pessimist at all, tho.

While we were talking, Donnie's arm stole round my shoulder. Now I have always had about half a dozen remarks in readiness for the boy who would ever put his arm around me—and I never said a single one. I don't know why I didn't, but I didn't, that's all. In the first place, I was so surprised that I was mute for a while; in the second place, it was done in such a nice comradely way that I didn't have the heart to say anything; and in the third place, I liked it. I repeat it—I liked it. I'm shocked at myself but—well I hope no one will criticize until they've gone thru the same thing themselves. And Donald had never acted soft anyway.

After a delicious silence which, in my memory, was filled with stars, he said suddenly, "Wanda, are your eyes as black as your hair? I never noticed." It wasn't so much what he said as the way he said it that thrilled me. I managed to say that I didn't know but I didn't think they were quite as dark. It was immaterial, anyway, what I answered. I know it because I felt it.

It was twelve when we parted (glory that sounds as if we had done so with a kiss and a hug, which of course we didn't). When I came upstairs Flora was still up reading. I slipped into bed and turned my adventure round and round in my brain, and into my mind there stole this line from dear old Browning:

> "How sad and bad and mad it was—
> But then, how it was sweet!"

The next day was Sunday, and Flora and I went to the depot and sat in the waiting room until the train came in. Their depot is not such a disreputable place to be as it is in most towns. It is a sort of gathering place for people.

After dinner Donald came and sat on the lawn by the side of the house. I was drawing Flora when he came. Next I sketched his head. Glory they couldn't make him crack a smile—he's a swell poser. His head was lowered a little and his eyes had that dreamy, half-sad, half-wistful look and his mouth was set with his characteristic determination. When I was done with this there wasn't much time left. We went down to the depot, and then came the final goodbyes. I was very dreamy all the way home. Occasionally I would take out the sketch of Donnie and put on some finishing touches. So sentimental.

I like Donald. I like him for his dreaminess, his chivalry, his consideration for older people, and for his protectiveness, but most of all I admire him for his high moral standard. I am not in love with Donald. At least I don't think so. I like him better than any boy I know just now, tho. There's no doubt, however, about the fact that he's got a crush on me. That goes against my theory of "opposites attract" because he has dark hair and brown eyes. So be it then.

Oh yes, we decided (or rather it was Donnie who did the deciding. I did the permitting only) that he was to come down to New Ulm for the band concert Sunday, July 20.

Gee, I have a homely streak. I could knock myself flat every time I catch a glimpse of my *mug* in the mirror. It has lasted a couple of weeks already. I hope I won't get homely streaks (*extra* homely, I mean) in my array of streaks, such as:

> sentimental streaks
> piano   "
> drawing   "
> letter writing "
> poetry & story "
> reading   "

July 23, Wednesday

Well, Donnie has "came and went."

We drove around in his car for a while and then went to our house. After supper we walked down to the park. He said music always made him feel blue, and that he got the blues about once a week. He likes the weeping willows by the fountains too, and said he did not blame me for going wild about them at all. I *do* wish I could return some of Donnie's deep affection. I like him awfully well but I simply can't get myself to get a crush on him. And when he looks at me with that nice (and what Stella calls his "I-adore-you") look in his eyes I feel so guilty, knowing that I'll have to turn him down sometime. I do so like to have him for a friend—a nice comrade to go with and confide in, but Donnie's attitude towards me seems so different.

It was about 10:30 when we went home. We sat down on the bench in the moonlight. It was a perfectly divine night—the moonlight flooded our lawn and fell full upon us, and it cast enchanting shadows among the trees. Donnie sang part of the time, part of the time we talked, and the rest of the time we were just silent, and we enjoyed it. Of course the moonlight had a sentimentalizing effect on Donnie. He took my handkerchief and put it round my neck and put his cap on my head. And then he declared he'd like a flashlight picture of me. I can fancy how I looked, especially the handkerchief.

He did not put his arm around me that night but he did put his arm on the back of the bench and his hand rested on my shoulder. I had firmly decided that I would not permit it again, but I did. I absolutely do not see why I don't say anything, but I don't and that's all. It all sounds so simple when you think it out beforehand. I had planned to say real gently, "Donnie, you mustn't," and I know if I would say something he would do as I wish, but it isn't as easy to do as one might think. I know it's not right for me to let him go on like that, but it doesn't seem one bit "soft" when Donnie does it. I cannot stand *softness* but Donnie has such a comradely way of acting. And then—I may as well throw the bomb and be done with it—he rested his head in my lap. He said, "Have I got too much nerve, Wanda?" Now here was an excellent opportunity, but I didn't know how to meet it so I was silent. I finally thought of saying, "You ought to know how far you can go" but the psychological moment had passed so I didn't say it. But he had sense enough to get up and sit in a nice approved fashion after my silence.

Well anyway, we always *talk* sensibly, and I'll use all my determination and virtue and every other quality that you need, to prevent a repetition of the actions. The worst of it is, I wouldn't *mind* it at all, weren't it for the fact that it is wrong. When I think over these things I am more and more determined to be an old maid. I'm always afraid I'll marry some one out of pity and that I'll meet my real affinity (I *do* believe in affinities) after that, and then of course my life would be a sad one. Stella, who has more strength of will in that way (or at least she thinks she has—she's never had the experience, so there's no telling) says that in that case one must entirely disregard the affinity. Which is all very fine, but is it possible?

Our farewells and meetings are always so tame. I haven't shaken hands with Donnie once.

July 28, Monday

I got a letter from Mr. Weschcke and I guess I am really going to Art School. At any rate they are flaunting it all over in the newspapers and people always greet me so amiably (they always do that right after there's been something in the paper about me, and it amuses me immensely). Poor Donnie—he's been wishing all the time that I'd get a school near Springfield.

Armand hasn't answered my note. I wonder whether he is angry that I am not coming to the "U." If he is, he is narrow-minded, I think.

I guess I'm going to begin working with an easel—I want to get a little used to it before I go to Art School. Isn't Mr. Weschcke the darlingest ever?

August 13, Wednesday

Am down at grandma's sewing. I got a new black silk petticoat from

Aunt Mary. It's called "Made-rite" only it isn't for I had to fix it all over.

I got a letter from Donnie and he informed me that if he had different hours to work in, he would be surprising me every week. It's rather fortunate, therefore, that he has his present hours because New Ulm wouldn't have time to recover from one shock before it got another.

Saturday evening Stella made me help rake up the front lawn, saying that it was for my benefit anyway. Which was as much as to say that Donnie and I would want the lawn, the bench and the moon the following night. So I went and raked until I got a blister.

Sunday dawned with a dreary sky and unmistakable signs of rain. At 3 o'clock there was a knock at the front door and there was Donnie. We talked for a while and then he said, "Play some hymns, Wanda, and I'll try to sing them." Wasn't that quaint and nice of him? In this age of turkey-trotting, ragging and spooning youths it is a surprise, and a pleasant one, to find someone who would suggest singing hymns in preference to "Billy Billy Bounce your Baby Doll" or "In My Harem." Of course I played the hymns and he sang them, and it was short of sublime. He sang alone once too, and chorded on the piano, and it was at about this time that it started to rain. By supper time it was absolutely pouring. Perhaps we weren't disappointed! We vibrated like pendulums from window to door, and door to window, hoping against hope that it would stop so that they could have the band concert. But there were no signs of clearing up, so we tried to resign ourselves to our fates and talked about other things.

In some way we got to talking about Eternity. It was plain that Donnie had done some deep, serious thinking about the matter, and he said thinking about such things always made him blue. (Of all the things that make him blue.) We finally got down so deep that we got stuck and gave up.

I told him that everyone who knew me got to hate me after a few month's acquaintance, but he said, "I know one exception." I ignored the remark and he, thinking perhaps that I had not heard, repeated it with such a "feelingful" look that I thought it wise to change the subject.

After a while I called Stella and Judy in to sing and we sang just about everything we knew. I told Donnie to sing along but he said he'd rather listen, and as I noticed the dreamy look he had when he said so, I decided not to urge him. He has the most captivating droop to his eyelids, and once during the evening he looked so handsome that I had all I could do to keep from running for a pencil and paper to sketch him with. By the way he talks, he surely intends to see me Christmas. I do hope Paula can meet him then. I wish those two would get a crush on each other, then I could have Donnie for company and still not have him struck on me.

I had no occasion to say the little speech I had planned to murmur (notice, *murmur*) if he should let his feelings run away with him, and I was glad I didn't have to say it, but it was a pretty tame farewell and I know I should have liked it if we would have made it a little more touching. But we didn't, and I guess we were both surprised that we didn't. Then we said goodbye once more, and as he was walking down the street, I closed the screen door and at the same time a yelpy screech rang out, for Nuggie the cat had got her tail between the door. I cried, "For the Love of Soup!" and Donnie called back, "Did you kill her?" Such an effective denouement to the night's romance.

I am down at grandma's sewing like fury. We go boat-riding once in a while and it's usually moonlight and oh it's great. Of course I think of Donnie, one can't help thinking of such attentive youths even if one is not struck on them.

August 28

Sent the Donnie-boy a letter today. Also one to Paula. Paula, by the way, is probably coming to the Minnesota "U" after all. That surely would be splendid.

September 17

Since I have my new trunk, I am deep in the joy of packing. I verily believe I shall write a poem to that beloved pastime if I *ever* write poetry again. I have sort of decided to give up poetry writing and also story-writing and stick to drawing. Only if I don't write poetry I don't see what I'll ever do with the sentiments and thoughts which overflow once in a while.

I don't see what under the canopy I'm going to wear all next week— I want to wash all that is not already packed. It is so cold here lately that I have already put "em" on.

Oh, I am getting to be such a cynic about love. My beloved theory of Affinities is even becoming alarmingly infirm. Sometimes I go so far even as to doubt that there is such a love at all. Of course, I believe in sisterly, brotherly, motherly and fatherly love and also love for your friends, but I mean *The* Love. I have yet to find a boy who is satisfied with a Platonic friendship. They are always allright as long as they think one has a crush on them, but if they find out that one's affection is not *The* kind, they feel badly about it.

Sept. 23

I got a letter from Donnie today. Tomorrow I am going away and will start a new diary. So long—Wanda.

* * *

Florence

Part Three

ART SCHOOL—ST. PAUL

1913

September 27, Saturday, 9:05 p.m.

I am finally at St. Paul, and in my room at the Y.W.C.A.—its number is 412. It's the darlingest little room—it has cream-tinted walls and the woodwork is plain and stained brown. The furniture matches the woodwork, being in Mission style and stained brown too—except the bed which is white iron. I am tickled stiff that I have a good mirror in my dresser so that when I have a drawing streak I can at least draw myself.

The Y.W.C.A. is right across the street from the Auditorium * and there is a library just a couple of blocks away. One can have use of the laundry at 5c an hour and one can have gentlemen callers in the parlor until 10 p.m. One can stay out until 10:30, and longer if one has a card.

September 30, Tuesday

I have been to Art School two days. My drawing was the first one to be criticized in our class, because I was nearest the door. Glory, I fairly quaked in my shoes when Mr. Zeigler stood there and gazed at it. But it wasn't so bad. I like him awfully well. He explains things in such a masterly way that you can tell just what he means.

I am taking the regular course, which consists of Antique by Mr. Lee Woodward Zeigler, Design and Water Color by Miss Elizabeth Bonta, and sketching by Mr. Nathaniel Pousette-Dart. The girls in my class are:—Doris Evans who is tall and pretty and has lots of wavy golden hair, Hortense Dickman, Aline Swanwick, Peggy Hare who has pretty hair and appreciates jokes; Grace Brownell, Theresa Willink who is tall and blond; and I, who have black hair and didn't get the high lights in my sketch of the ear to-day.

* The Art School was in the Auditorium.

To-night some one knocked at my door. It was Mrs. Weschcke and her friend Mrs. Nelson, and they asked me whether I wanted to go for a drive. I jumped into my jacket, jammed on my hat, pulled on my gloves and raced down. They were in the auto, and also Mrs. Nelson's son David. They set me in front with him and we soon got started in a lively conversation. We started in about art, and he thought he'd like better to be able to draw people than landscapes or anything like that because of their character interest. He said he liked scientific things, and believe me, when he gets started talking science he's almost as bad as when I get started on drawing moods, autumn or Zona Gale, and that's saying a good deal.

We agree on a great many things—we both like autumn best of all the seasons for its bracing air, we both like music and, he didn't tell me so, but from his conversation I should judge that he plays pretty well. He knows some of the Springfield boys I know. (Talking of Springfield just reminds me that I haven't written to Donnie for about a week).

It was after nine by the time we got back home again and I told them I thought I'd sleep like a top, and they said they'd take me again some time, for which time, Hurrah! Oh yes, I asked him what he liked to read best, and he said with an apologetical little sort of laugh, "Just now I like sentimental stuff."

Oct. 2, Thursday

Yesterday we went to the design class, and in the afternoon we sketched a light-haired girl in a blue suit, who had a fine profile and lips that formed themselves in curved, clean-cut shadows. I sketched her from the side but got her head a little too big for the rest of her body. One of the older students prophesied that it would be the best in the class, only it wasn't, which is most likely a good thing for me because it will simply mean more effort on my part next time. I know one of my faults—I draw too light, and so it looks weak from a distance. I need my shadows blacker and I have neglected to make dark material dark enough—I'm deficient in tone values. Believe me, at the next sketching class, which is not until Wednesday and comes only once a week (to my great sorrow because I like that best of all so far.)

Mr. Zeigler is nice, awfully nice. He has a charmingly characteristic way of saying, "I feel this, and I feel that," just as if artists felt instead of seeing, which perhaps is not so far wrong, taking into consideration, however, that one has to learn to *see* before one can feel instinctively.

Oct. 3, Friday 8:25 a.m.

Yesterday morning we had Design. We had to draw outlines of flowers and leaves, etc., and then we had to draw six-inch squares and break them up into smaller parts so as to produce a symmetrical design.

In the afternoon we "Antiqued" again. I drew a hand clutching a scroll, and it was mighty hard. In antique, as also in sketching, I make the mistake of being too fussy. I put on little lights and shadows and in this way I lose sight of the larger values; and it is the larger values, of course, that give a drawing strength.

Peggy Hare is my rival. I know it, and I guess she knows it too. Especially in Antique. She has taken charcoal work before and is therefore so much ahead of the rest of our class. And we are jealous of each other. There is absolutely no use denying it, altho it sounds as if we were both mean and narrow-minded. Perhaps we are. I think she has been used to a good deal of praise, and she deserves it too because she draws remarkably well, but she goes at her work with such a confident air.

One of the girls at school thought I was French and not more than 16 or 17 years old.

October 6, Monday

Saturday Paula came and we discussed love, humanity, justice, and similar things. We disagree on a good many points lately; I suppose it is because we have been apart more and have become used to thinking in our own particular lines of thought. But that makes it only the more interesting. Paula is emotional; I am almost cold in comparison to her.

Well Paula went home soon after supper; and Theresa Willink (who has a room near mine) and I discussed the same subjects plus religion. We agree on a great many subjects. We discussed boys too, and we are both in about the same boat I guess, because a boy has a case on her too, and she likes him awfully but not in the way that he likes (or rather loves) her.

Oct. 13, Monday

Thursday I had a fierce drawing streak.

The day before, I had had such a fierce streak too. I went to chapel with Theresa and afterwards she wanted me to go to one of the classes at the Y.W. on "First Lessons in Nursing," but I was then already absolutely wild to finish the picture I had started before supper so I didn't go. I locked myself up in my room and just drew. Three of the girls came and wanted me to go to the movies with them but I asked to be excused and I drew until about eleven when we have to turn our lights out.

Well to go on with Thursday. There was a Geneva party that Theresa wanted me to attend. I told her I couldn't stop drawing but she begged me to come all the time. I told her, "Theresa, you don't *know* what it is to have a drawing streak." She came in my room and sat down beside me on my bed where I was drawing away for dear life. She said, "Oh, I think you're a little too much that way," and I said, "Perhaps I am. Not thru any fault of mine, however." And she said, *"I* think so," and oh it hurt my feelings so much that I could have wept right then and there—and I *don't* cry *easily*. She inferred that I was just doing that to show off or as an excuse for not attending the Geneva party. If people who have never had drawing moods would get one once they would see that showing off was the last thing they would think of.

I can see easily enough how it would be hard for people to understand drawing moods. They are a grand and beautiful mystery to me. I am glad that I have been able to analyze them as much as I have. It comes very unexpectedly (the drawing fit) and still you don't know it's there at first. All at once you find yourself drawing with that gratifying fervor that always distinguishes a drawing streak. Now I think there is scarcely a time (if any at all) that I don't look at things without thinking of how it would look drawn, or trying to figure out how I would get to work at it if I were to draw it. I really wonder how people who don't draw, look at things. But when I have a drawing streak things seem much more beautiful than they do at other times, and I see something all the time which I'm wild to draw.

Well, after Theresa left I sat down on my bed (or rather knelt on it so I could see my reflection in the mirror) to draw myself full-length. I've noticed, since I've taken sketch class, that I have been paying too much attention to the head alone, so now I'm trying to get the right proportions and good action into my sketches. I had my shoes off because I was on the bed with my feet. I was right in the middle of a sketch when someone knocked at the door.

It was Mrs. Weschcke and Mrs. Nelson, and they asked whether I cared to go out for a ride. Now it was a grand, mild, moonlight night, and anything as romantic as that appealed strongly to me notwithstanding the fact that I had a fierce drawing mood. I jumped into my slippers and into my coat, and jammed on my hat, and before I knew it we were skimming along in the free fresh air. I sat in the front seat with David Nelson.

We talked about a good many things. He asked me whether I had ever noticed anything in him that was different from other people and I said, "Oh all people are different," and he said he didn't mean looks but whether I hadn't noticed something *wrong* about him, but I couldn't think of anything so I asked him to tell me, which he didn't do because he was afraid I'd laugh at him.

In turn I asked him if he had noticed anything individual or characteristic about me, and he said I always said things all at once—sort of in jerks (a thing which I never knew before). He said it sounded as if I never knew what I was going to say until I had said it and asked me if I didn't say things I was sorry for afterwards. I told him that I made it a practice to think before I spoke, which is true.

By our conversation I could see that he sometimes felt sentimental, and played the piano on such occasions. He said too that he liked sad music, and soft music. Later we were talking about romance and I said, "You're strong on romance, aren't you?" and he said with an absolutely indescribable look (it was sort of eager and very sincere) "Oh *am* I!" He said that was the fault that he had referred to before. I said, "Do you think yourself too romantic, then?" and he said it was that, but that still he liked to let himself get too romantic. I told him it was a good feeling to play piano by, to which he agreed. I told him he'd get over his romantic inclinations but I doubt whether he believes it. The funny part is he thinks it's so queer and unusual for him to be sentimental, and goodness knows, they all get that way between 18 and 24 years. Take it from me, I've seen them in various stages (ahem!).

He asked me whether I sometimes felt romantic and I said "Sure," but I told him I wasn't as bad as I used to be.

He said he always wore a mask to hide his real self (this was only in fun, I'm sure) and I told him I always wore a mask too. I said, "You know, I'm naturally very pretty, but as it is I wear a mask," to which he said, "Oh you haven't anything to kick about," and I told him I certainly had because I had a turned-up nose, but he didn't seem to think a turned-up nose was so bad.

We saw a man with crutches on the street and I said, "Gee, sometimes I wish I had blue eyes and brown hair, but when I see people like that I think I oughtn't to wish for things like that"; and he said, "Do you like brown hair and blue eyes?" I said I did. He probably expected me to ask him what he liked, but I didn't so he told me. "I like dark brown or black hair," he said, "and black eyes."

That night when I jumped out of the car Mrs. Weschcke said, "Good night Honey bunch."

Gee it made me feel good. She certainly is a dear.

When I got back they told me down at the office that there had been a telephone call for me, and that I should call up the number. I called up and after I had said my name, the Person said, "Well this is Armand Emraad." Gee I was surprised. I thought I had gone entirely out of his life, not to any great regret of mine however, altho I like him allright.

He told me that Marjorie Moss had told him that I was going to Art School here, and he asked if he could come and see me the next night. I told him that we had a meeting at Art School that night so he said he'd probably come and see me sometime the next week.

He said, "I said I'd write, didn't I?" I said yes, and he said, "Well I didn't." I said, "So I noticed." He said that he had been so terribly busy all summer that he didn't have time, which I didn't believe but I was polite enough not to tell him so. The voice didn't sound like his at all. I've forgotten how he looks except that he has blue eyes, light curly hair and a funny walk, and a queer rather interesting way of raising his eyebrows.

Sunday evening David Nelson called for me and we went for a walk. I asked him how he and romance were getting along and he said, "Pretty badly." I said there were three reasons for being sentimental: (1) You either have a crush on someone, (2) or you want to have a crush on someone and haven't anyone to have it on, (3) or someone has a crush on you and you haven't any on them. He didn't say exactly which applied to his case but it was either the first or the second.

All at once he said, "Why do you always look at me like that?" I said, "Why, can't I look at you? You look at me too, don't you?" and he said, "Yes, but my looks don't affect you as yours do me." It was said so sincerely that I was too surprised to say anything, so I didn't, but I tried to look at him no more than was necessary.

Once he said, "Let me put my hand in your pocket." My hand happened to be in there at the time, but I said, "Oh no," and he said, "Why not," but I just said "no" and laughed, and we talked about other things.

Paula always thinks one can pick out a number of individuals (boys, of course) who are absolutely perfect and who would not get sentimental even if you'd let them. Theresa agrees with me that any boy, however respectable and good he may be, is tempted to put his arm around you or put his hand in your pocket or something like that. If you don't resist they'll do it, too, even tho they hate themselves for it later. And if you don't let them, they feel sort of bad about it just then but like you the better for it in the end.

He didn't try to put his hand into my pocket, he only asked. One peg up, sir, in my estimation for asking permission first. He asked me whether I'd like to go to the Symphony Orchestra Concerts this winter. That was what I had been wishing for all the time, and I felt like jumping a couple of feet into the air and giving a whoop, but I said just as matter-of-course-ly as you please, "Sure."

At about this place I was beginning to think that he was getting a crush on me, but I wasn't sure. He said, "I think you and I would never get along to-gether." I felt like saying that there was no occasion for doing so, but he looked so lovesick that I decided to spare his feelings and said instead, "What makes you think so?" He said because he likes scientific things and I like art. I told him I thought it wasn't any fun when people agreed on everything because there wouldn't be any chance for argument or discussion. That sort of satisfied him.

He suggested walking to the Wabasha bridge and looking at the river, and since it was only about 3 blocks away, I agreed. We walked down and looked down across the city spread out below us in a smoky, misty haze with the lights shining thru it. Glory it was great, and I just stood and gazed at the scene almost forgetting that someone was with me.

When we were standing there he said, "I guess you'd better put your hand in my pocket" (*his* hands were in *his* pockets at the time) but I refused again. He said he thought my pockets were too small (which I might have taken for an insult because they were monstrous) but I said pointedly that they were just the right size for *my* hands.

Well he got over that, at least I hope so. Afterwards I said innocently, "Oh isn't the moon grand?" And he said with such an earnest look, "Don't talk about it" that I replied, "No I won't" and I tried hard not to say things that would make him more romantic (if such a thing were possible—he was absolutely *steeped* in it that night). But I could see that he was making a tremendous effort to behave, and gee it must be hard for them.

The scenery was so soul inspiring that I just stood and looked and thought, and finally I noticed that David hadn't been looking at the scenery at all, but at me all the time. Suddenly he said, "Gee, but you're a pretty girl." It was a good thing that there was a railing there, because I guess I would have plunked right into the river. I knew it was only the atmosphere that made him think so, so I laughed and said, "Oh it's only the moonlight that makes you think so." But he declared it wasn't and I said, "Oh yes it is. I'll bet you never thought so before, did you?" and he said "Yes, I did. The first time I saw you, I thought you were a pretty good-looking kid."

I told him I didn't see how he could think so with my pug nose and no chin to speak of. He told me that after I'd been in the city a while I'd find that what he said was true, and said that other fellows would tell me the same thing. I said, "Well next time I'll dress myself in rags, you won't think I'm pretty then," and he said I'd be even prettier then. Oh Jimps. Gee it makes me laugh now to think what sentimental stuff we talked with utter seriousness, but believe me, it didn't sound silly then. It never does when it just happens. That's why one does act silly anyway—you never know how silly it is until you think it over later.

Just before I went into the door at the Y.W. I warned him not to get too romantic.

I've had a drawing streak for the last two days and some of the kids at Art School bawl me out, but Doris Evans is nice about it and reproves the others for teasing me. Theresa thinks it's silly to have drawing streaks. She doesn't just say so, but I think she thinks it anyway. Mr. Weschcke thinks drawing moods are perfectly allright, and he told me not to mind it if people didn't understand. He said also that he thought I ought to sit up and draw until the "wee sma' hours" if I felt like it, providing I was dressed warm so I couldn't catch a cold. It felt awfully good to have him say that because there are very few who really do understand.

October 17, Friday

Mr. McWhorter was at the Art School the other day. He told me he'd be watching me during the term (or rather my work, not me) and he said, "Well we're depending on you and Mr. Hendrickson to distinguish the school this year." Mr. Hendrickson is the fellow who won the scholarship last year for the best Antique Drawing.

I take Lettering now too, by Mr. McWhorter. He is awfully nice, and has a scar on his right cheek. He has a good nose, black hair and brown eyes and his right eyebrow is more curved upward than his left. He told me I shouldn't neglect getting plenty of fresh air and exercise, and invited me to come and see "us" which probably means him and his wife.

Last Wednesday in Sketch Class we sketched one of the art school girls, Phyllis Saxby. She was dressed as a Spanish girl. I had no intentions of making more than one sketch but I saw the new Chicago fellow turning some out, one after the other in quick succession, and I decided I wasn't exactly going to be outdone by him so I dashed off three.

Mr. Pousette-Dart always marks the best one and the marked ones are hung up and stay up all week for the others to look at. Last time mine was marked, and this time all three of mine were marked and hung up, but glory, I'll not be satisfied until he says mine's the best.

He said to one of my last ones that it had a freedom of line that he liked but that it was almost too free, and that it was cleverly done but that it was almost too clever. I don't exactly understand what he means by this last, and I guess I'll ask him next Wednesday just what he means by "*too* clever." Of one of my others he said that there was something individual about the way of handling it, that it was different from anything else made by anyone in the class (merely different, you understand) and that it was a little bit insincere, and I can't imagine what he means by it.

Paula had supper with me last night here. She has met a boy (his name is Larry Morse) who seems to have quite a crush on her—they have long talks to-gether, but Paula says she won't let herself get a crush on him.

Last night we had a Victrola concert downstairs in the blue rooms. It was just swell, only sometimes some people forgot that other people might like the music better than their voices and it sort of got on my nerves.

November 2, Sunday

Last Tuesday Armand called me up and told me to be ready to go out at eight. Well, I got ready and waited downstairs for him. We shook hands and asked each other how we were, and silently sized each other up (I am sure of that). I put on my coat and Armand suggested that we go to the Shubert Theater. We talked as fast as we always did at New Ulm, and on practically the same subjects. He said I had changed and I wanted him to tell me how I had changed, and he said he'd tell me later.

We got a good seat near the front. After the first act another University fellow, Timmie Frendel, came and sat in the seat in front of us. Armand wanted me to sketch him so I did. Once while I was doing so Armand said, "Get that cynical droop to the mouth." That tickled me awfully because about five minutes after I was introduced to the young man I decided that he was somewhat cynical. The little Cynic took the picture home with him.

After the play Armand and I went and had some ice cream. (I chose a Pineapple Happy Thought). We didn't eat much of the stuff tho because we talked so much. Armand said he had been able to see a number of things about my character in the letter I sent him. I asked what they were, and he said one of the things was that I was making discoveries (about myself) at about the time I wrote the letter. And glory it's true. I probably never found out so much about myself, and other things too, as I did then. He is quite a reader of character, and I don't dare be anything but my true self when I am with him because I always have the feeling that he'd see right thru my mask anyway. I told him that I wore a mask (so to speak) a great part of the time and he said it wasn't a good thing to do so, and I told him I was afraid people would think me somewhat off if I showed my true self all the time. I told him there were only a few to whom I did show my true self.

He said he'd run up unexpectedly some time.

Friday evening I went to the Orpheum with David Nelson and after the show we went for a walk up on the hill. Once I couldn't exactly see my way and David asked if he could take hold of my arm to help me across. You see I've got him nicely trained. Usually they don't ask in such a case.

We talked about dreams, and he's had many of the same dreams I've had, for instance, being able to fly and walking in the air about a foot above the ground. We got to the subject of painting and powdering once, and I said that I couldn't respect a girl who painted. He said, "Can't you?" and I said, "Well, do you like them?" And he said, "Yes, I like a girl who paints—pictures."

I asked him what he admired most in girls. He said, "What they haven't got." I asked, "What haven't they got?" and he said, "What you've got." He rather took me by surprise there but I asked, "Well what have *I* got?" and he said evasively, "What they haven't got," which was pretty clever I thot. I wanted him to ask me what I admired most in men to which I should have replied "Good morals," but he never asked me.

Saturday evening was the Hallowe'en dance given by the art school. I wanted to go but was scared to ask for a permit so soon after the other one—and when Paula came and begged me to stay with her that night, I gave in to her after a mighty combat with my inner thoughts (or whatever you combat with, when there's the Whole of You fighting with a part of you).

November 9, Sunday

Last Wednesday Armand called up and asked if I wanted to go to the Symphony concert that evening. He arrived about ten minutes later and we sat in one of the parlors for a while and talked. I had hastily grabbed some paper before I left my room, and it happened that I got some with a couple of pictures on it. Of course Armand spied them right away, and after looking at them, tore off one which he said he wanted to put with the rest of my drawings. He said, "I think I'll take one every so often, and then later you can see just how you've progressed." As if I weren't doing that myself.

He asked if I knew Jack Alden, and told me that he would have him come up to meet me some time. Jack Alden is an architect, and Armand said if he (Armand) would be rich enough (some time) to build a house he'd talk it over with Jack and say, "Jack, build me a house." Then when it was done he (Armand) would say to the Girl, "Here is the House. Will you have me?" and if she didn't like the house she couldn't have him—which is some more of his Modesty (?). I felt like suggesting the possibility of the Girl's wanting the house and *not* him, but I didn't do it anyway.

Well we went over to the Auditorium. We sat in the balcony, and both on one seat, and glory it was close quarters. Timmie Frendel was there too, and sat in the seat in front of us. He didn't look so cynical but was, in fact, exceedingly agreeable. He is like Armand in that he is analytical and does not like pomp and ceremony. I think, however, that he is more emotional than Armand.

The question that I am just wild to ask Armand is, "Have you ever been, or are you ever, emotional?" It would be a somewhat startling thing to ask but I want to know if I've judged him correctly. I think, at present, that he is decidedly unemotional. Another thing I'd like to ask him is, "What is my worst or noticeable fault?" I'd like awfully to tell him, too, that his worst fault is not Selfishness (as he seems to think) but *Self*.

Glory I wish David would get the notion to take me to the Symphony Concert this afternoon, but it's after twelve and no telephone call. Boo-hoo.

November 19, Wednesday

Today I was out in the hall waiting for Sketch Class and two second-year students, Dave Hendrickson and Bob Brown, came along and stopped to look at my sketches. Bob Brown declared that my technique was very good (technique is Greek to me) and he said that I did not work in *lines* and that was a good thing. They think it's so funny that I sit up nights and draw, and they think it's funny too that I sketch myself. I thought all people who aspired to be artists drew as much as I do but it seems they don't. I thought too that all, or at least a good many, of the art school students would be *queer,* but they aren't; and it sometimes makes me wish that I weren't so different. For I am—there is absolutely no getting around it. And a whole lot of my new acquaintances are in that stage now where they misunderstand me. I will stick to my old theory which is this:—That I usually make a fairly good impression (I don't mean to compliment myself by saying this, but it's true and it only serves to make it so much harder afterwards) but that after they know me for a while they are disappointed in me. Then, if they have the faith to stick by me thru this second stage, they will find my true nature—at least as much of it as I ever show. Roughly speaking, at first they think I'm jolly, then they think I'm frivolous, and finally they find out that, after all, I am more serious than anything else.

Paula has been the only one that I know of who has not come to the second stage after a year of my acquaintance. She stood by me for four years but even *she* is beginning to doubt me. Larry Morse said that I was "giddy" and altho Paula does not agree there, the remark has served to make her think—to think that perhaps he was not so far wrong.

I am frivolous sometimes—giddy too, *and* silly—I can't deny it. But often I act that way only to hide my real feelings. Besides (and I told this to Paula) if I were not frivolous once in a while, I am afraid I'd go mad or something like that, because I'd think too much.

No one can know what it is to be I.

Nov. 30, Sunday

I must have felt pretty unappreciated when I made my last entry.

November 13 we had an Oriental supper here at the Y.W. Some of the Y.W. girls turned out in Oriental costume and I selected a bright red kimono with lovely white sprigs of flowers over it, and wide flowing sleeves.* The supper was mostly Oriental, so much so, in fact, that our appetite was about as big at the end of it as it was in the beginning.

After supper I went to my room, jumped into the Japanese gown, stuck some chopsticks into my hair, painted my lips and eyebrows to make me look more Japanesy, and sketched myself, letting my hands do what they had been yearning to do from the time I set eyes on that dream of a kimono with its tempting, adorable folds. I didn't realize how late it was

* These costumes were lent to us for the night.

getting to be when the matron, Mrs. McQuaide (after knocking and receiving no response from me) entered. It must have been quite a shock for her to be confronted by a be-painted, brightly-gowned, and dream be-sifted damsel. I was so absorbed in drawing that I said nothing, I believe. I remember I glanced up at her somewhat smilingly and then went on with my sketch. She told me gently that it was bed time (it was almost twelve and lights are supposed to be out at eleven) but I told her I couldn't stop, and went on drawing. She went out soon after that but I didn't go to bed until I had made another sketch. All the indescribable joy of a delicious drawing streak was gone tho, and in order not to be outdone, I determined to get up early the next morning. I got up at five, jumped into the kimono, and sketched with glee, yes with glee, until almost eight.*

On November 15, the Y.M.'s gave a program at their building. I did not want to go because I felt too much like drawing. But Mrs. Fordham (one of the secretaries) begged me so to go that I finally consented under the condition that I might be allowed to sketch. So I got ready and rolled up some paper and took my pencil and eraser. A young man, Mr. Glenn Edgerley, was sent over to escort us over to their building. Afterwards while we were waiting for every one to get ready Miss Dean, who was talking with Mr. Edgerley, called me over and explained to him that I was the girl who had consented to go to their program only on the condition that I might draw. Then he asked me whether he could watch me, to which I replied that he might. Well, right after we had disposed of our wraps at the Y.M. Mr. Edgerley had spied me, and asked me whether I'd rather sit in the balcony or downstairs. We finally decided that the balcony afforded better opportunities for sketching than the other so he led me up there. After the program he showed a number of other girls and me all around the building and proved himself to be a considerate, gentlemanly young man.

Afterwards when we were standing down in the lobby Mrs. McQuaide saw my paper and pencil, and asked me if I couldn't stop drawing long enough even at the program and I said that I couldn't. She said, "I think you can," which hurt me very much. I think she thinks I did it only to attract attention or something like that, but I knew she wouldn't understand if I'd try to explain that attracting attention is the last thing you think of when you have a drawing fit, so I didn't say anything.

Mr. Edgerley got my wraps for me and walked home with me. He

* One of these sketches faces page 264.

asked if he could come to the Y.W. some time to see my drawings and I said he might, and also invited him to come to art school some time.

November 28, Friday

The day after I had met Mr. Edgerley, he telephoned to me and asked whether I was too busy drawing to take a walk. I learned that he came from New York and that he had seen Sleepy Hollow and had attended Art School for a couple of months.

At about this time I discovered the space method of drawing. In this method you draw the outlines of the spaces which you would be least likely to draw otherwise. For instance in this picture; instead of drawing the head and shoulders you try to get the exact shape of the space which I have marked A. It's awfully interesting but I have only tried it once.

Mrs. Fordham came to me one evening and said, "Do you know what we've decided to call you?" Of course I wanted to know, and she told me, "Baby Doll." Now that was supposed to be a compliment, be it known, but honestly I don't consider it as such, way down in my heart. Just at about this time one of the Y.W. girls told me that so many people had told her I looked "just like a doll" and honestly for a while I was really scared I had an expressionless face like a doll. I'd really rather look like Simple Simon than like a doll, I guess—Simple Simon's face at least looked characteristic.

December 3, Wednesday

On November 30 I went to Christian Endeavor with Glenn Edgerley.

Then we returned to the Y.W. where we talked of Browning, psychology, and religion. I promised, at his request, to bring my Browning down the next time he called, so we could read it together. Miss Fordham said to Theresa that evening, "Miss Gág is in there with Mr. Edgerley. Don't they make the cutest couple? He's so light and she's so dark." Tra la.

Today after sketch class I showed Mr. Pousette-Dart a bunch of my sketches. There was one picture of myself on which I am sitting and have my hands clasped about my knees. He said, "How could you draw that?" and I had to confess that I didn't know. I didn't really. All I remember is that I saw the pose in my mirror and that it interested me. The next thing I remember is that I had drawn it, but how I did it (with my hands about my knees) I don't know. He looked them all thru and at the end he said, "I guess I'll mark some of these if you have no objections." I thought that was rather a queer thing to say for of course I had no objections to his marking my drawings. He marked about 9 or 10 of them and then walked off with them. I hadn't expected him to do that, and then I understood why he had asked about objections. But the girls said I ought to be glad that he had taken them, seeing who had taken them.

Dec. 13, Saturday

Last Saturday Phoebe Ames called for me and we went to the Mechanics Arts H.S. Gym, where we were to take Morris dancing.* I like the dances awfully well and after our lesson was over we danced; waltzes and schottisches, etc. I danced a couple of times with Raymon Bowers, and when we finally stopped he asked me if I wouldn't have supper with him. So we went to a restaurant where we talked a lot and ate little. After that we went to a movie (not because we were wild about movies but because we wanted some place to sit in until it was time to go to Composition class). We didn't notice the movies; we were too busy talking. I think Mr. Bowers must be good at writing. He gave me a couple of pointers too, about drawing. Then we went to Composition class, each minus a Composition.

One night I went with Mr. Edgerley to see Pavlowa in the Russian Ballet. We had perfectly grand seats down in the parquet and the program was simply grand. Of course the costumes appealed strongly to me —they always do, when they're good.

* Free to art students.

That night I started a pastel sketch of myself, but before I could get very far the night lady knocked at my door. I put out my light and listened at the door until I heard her patter away again, and then I put on the light once more and sketched on. Pretty soon the night lady came again, and I had to put out the light again. Wasn't that nerve racking? I tried to sketch by the light of the moon, but finding that somewhat inconvenient, I seriously contemplated sitting there until about 2 o'clock (I thought the night lady would be asleep by then) but then I thought it wouldn't be worth while, so I went to bed feeling quite unappreciated.

Dec. 12 saw Glenn Edgerley and me at the Auditorium listening to Paderewski. I made a rough sketch of the musician but everything was so dimly lighted that I couldn't see very well. He sat on a chair which had a good portion of each leg sawed off. He was, of course, absolutely grand.

Dec. 18, Thursday

Saturday afternoon Armand called for me and we went forth on a little romp. It was a beautiful day—bright and sunny and not cold at all for December. We took the street car to the outskirts of town and, of course, started as usual on good sound talk.

On one occasion I mentioned how badly I had felt when some one told me I looked just like a doll. I said I'd rather look like Simple Simon any day. Armand sat and laughed at this, and then he asked whether I believed it. I said, "Well, I don't know. I don't *think*—at least I *hope* I haven't—a perfectly expressionless face, but *I* can't tell whether I have or not." Alas that I should have made that statement for I didn't hear the last of it the whole afternoon. Armand said that my face did not look like a doll's and insisted that I knew perfectly well, and had known right along, that it wasn't.

Afterwards we talked about whether we had changed, and of what kind of impressions we made on people, etc. I asked him whether he wanted to know what his chief fault was, and of course he did, so I asked him whether he remembered the time he had told me that he was very selfish, and then I said I didn't think it was selfishness that was his fault but Self with a capital S. At that he laughed.

He said once, "You are too popular." I said, "How do you know I'm popular?" He said, "Look at me." I did, and smiled as I did so (involuntarily) and he seemed to be sure that he was right.

I cannot remember all the things we said, but I know that I came out wiser in the end than I had been. When we got back to town we went to a bookstore where Armand bought me a copy of Whistler. He went with me to the Y.W. where he wrote all kinds of remarks in the book and then bid me goodbye.

On December 14 I went to Christian Endeavor with Glenn Edgerley and he came to the Y.W. after that, where we talked on Platonic Friendship.

December 17 I went to Nelson's in the afternoon. David's cousin Janet was over there too, and we sang and played piano and I taught Janet how to dance. The rest of my time I spent in trying to turn David down gently but firmly, but he wouldn't be turned.

1914

Jan. 7, Wednesday

December 19 Glenn Edgerley came to see me again and asked whether he could see Paula and me to the depot the next day. He gave me a book as he left us. It was a nice soft leather-bound copy of "The Pickwick Papers." Well we got home that evening and saw all the dear folks again. Of course Stella and I stayed awake a long time, discussing things.

We had some fine discussions up at Paula's, too, during the holidays. I am the only one left of our bunch that wants to be an old maid. That is, I don't *want* so much to be one, but I think I had best be one, because I told the girls that I didn't want to marry unless my husband-to-be would promise to get someone to do the scrubbing for me (I have been denied all talent for that art) and to run the house when I had a drawing streak. Paula thought that would not work very well and told me I had better let Love conquer Art. Indeed she said it *would*. I don't believe that —I don't think I can give up art and my beloved, delicious, tyrannical drawing moods, even for the man I love.

December 30 I had my adenoids removed. They gave me gas and it's the grandest feeling. You just slip off so peacefully. I stayed in bed over New Year's and stayed indoors for a number of days after that.

On Jan. 5 Paula and I returned to St. Paul. I came to the Y.W. at about 9 p.m. I tried on my costume (which I had made at home). We were to have a Twelfth Night Robin Hood party the next evening and I had decided to dress as Maid Marion. Of course after I had gone to the trouble of putting on the costume I thought I might as well sketch it, so I did—a full length pastel.

Last night the Art School gave its party. I had intended to go over with the girls. Each girl was supposed to furnish a man if she could, but I thought Armand and Glenn Edgerley wouldn't want to dance, and I didn't want to ask David (and fan the fires of his emotion anew) so I didn't ask anyone. The last time I had seen Armand he had said that he'd like to go to the Robin Hood party too, and added that he supposed I'd be going with some one else so he'd probably go up with Jack Alden. I would just as soon have gone with Armand but I did not want to seem too eager so I said nothing to that.

Well, last night right after six, Armand telephoned. He said, "Wanda, I believe I have an engagement with you to-night." I was somewhat dumbfounded at this startling announcement, and said at a hazard, "Well what is it?" He said, "Well don't you know?" And I said, "The Robin Hood Party?" Then he remembered that it was a costume affair—and he had none. I told him he would not necessarily have to come in costume, and he asked, "Supposing I come in full dress?" "Full dress" is always a sort of appalling phrase to me so I said, "Oh I don't think it will be as formal as all that." Then he said, "Well how would a Tuxedo do?" Now I hadn't the slightest idea how a Tuxedo differed from any other suit but I said bravely, "I should think that would be all right," so Armand decided he would come in the full glory of a Tuxedo.

He asked whether I didn't want to come to dinner with him and I said with a sort of gasp, "No, thank you." I always have steered shy of "dinners" and consequently wouldn't know how to act if I ran into one. I told him I had had supper (as we call it here) anyway, and besides I had to fix my costume yet.

I got into my costume and had Theresa sew me into it, and then I went downstairs to wait for my cavalier. He came at 8:50 (or so) and we went to the hall which is only a little distance from here (otherwise Armand would have ordered a taxi. Thank goodness he didn't—I wouldn't have the slightest idea of how to act). We got over allright and when I had rigged up in my cape and wreath I met Armand upstairs. Armand declared (the day we took our romp) that he had given up dancing because it was "not aesthetic for those who looked on." I don't see what makes him think he can't dance (or at least *say* so) because he can. He showed me a number of new dances too.

To my great surprise I found Glenn Edgerley there. He came up to Armand and me and talked with us, and afterwards he asked whether he might have a dance with me later. I said he could. I was introduced to Armand's (so to speak) Jack Alden and danced with him a number of times. I danced with Raymon Bowers too. Then I danced a couple of times with Glenn Edgerley (and he's a nice little dancer) and practically the rest of the time I spent with Armand.

Armand said there was a time when he was wild about dancing, and I said there was a time when I had considered dancing as ranking next to drawing. He raised his eyebrows sort of amusedly and said, "I can well believe it." I wanted to know why and he said, "Because you dance well." I said in all seriousness, "No flattery, I won't take it." He insisted that he had not been flattering. I said that to outward appearances flattery might sink in, but that it didn't really.

After the dance was over (it lasted until a few minutes to one) we took a "walk around the block." Armand said that it was almost an insult to him for me to say he flattered, and asked whether he looked as if he were a flatterer. I said, "Sometimes," and he declared that that was another insult. Good for him.

He asked me to do him a favor (for purely disinterested reasons, he assured me) and when I asked what it was, he asked whether I would go to bed right after I got in, and not sketch first. I told him I'd see about it. As a matter of fact I would have gone to bed directly that night, I think, if he hadn't said so, but with the perverseness of woman I made three four-minute sketches just *because* I didn't want Armand to think I had to do what he wanted me to do. On the whole tho, Armand acted very satisfactorily that night.

This afternoon Paula and I went to Eberharts. They are all just as nice as ever.

Jan. 9, Friday

Armand said he wanted to see my sketches sometime, so to-day he blew in here at the Y.W. at about 4:30 or so.

A lot of them were sketches I had made while I was still at home. These I showed him first, and showed him the rest in about the same order in which I made them. Nearly at the beginning he said, "Wanda, if you get me enthusiastic over your drawings you will be doing what no one has done for a long time" or words to that effect. I asked him what he would do and he said he'd go around and toot my horn etc. And he really did seem to get more interested in them as he went on. There was one picture of myself laughing (and I'm really laughing, too, not only stretching my mouth) and he asked me if he could have it and I said, "I don't know yet," and he said, "You better decide" and finally I said, "Well you can have it, but remember a part of me goes with it" (it *is* sort of hard to part with things in which you have put a whole lot of yourself into). By the time he was thru he was pretty enthusiastic.

On January 10 I went to the Morris dances again and we learned the Shepherd's Hay which is an awfully cute dance. That day Paula came to see me too and we discussed art and love etc. again. Also I insisted that Armand was allright—I do think so—and besides he isn't as conceited as he looks. I know Paula was disappointed in me again—she still misjudges me once in a while and it was rather unfortunate that she should strike me just as I was steeped in art, the Robin Hood Party and things like that.

I sometimes don't know whether I envy or pity people who have no drawing streaks. I envy them for having more peace of mind and for being able to eat when they should and go to bed when they want; and then again, especially at the beginning of each new drawing fit, I can't help pitying them for not being able to *know* even what fierce joy there is in being tyrannized by one's Muse.

Just lately I have found out that at the beginning of a drawing streak I can just turn myself over to the demands of my Divine Afflatus, and draw and draw and draw with a pleasure which is too fierce to be called a pleasure—rather one might call it a wild sort of ecstasy or exultation—a hilarity of the Soul, so to speak. But as the drawing mood keeps on and begins to take hold of me (almost cruelly sometimes, for it will make me sit up nights and draw, and miss meals because I have to draw, and make me forget to be polite to people because I am so enraptured by the things I see) I become what I call "done to a frazzle," and I draw not so much for the joy of it but because I have allowed my drawing mood to put me completely under its power.

Right in the midst of a drawing fit I do not know what I am learning or how I am learning it—I only know I *am* learning—but towards the end of each particular drawing mood I begin to analyze it.

I have forgotten myself entirely and raved about my cherished drawing moods in this book whereas I should have done it in the book which I have reserved especially for my "drawingisms," but one does not know one is raving until one is well started, and then one might as well finish. I have just now decided that I will not keep a separate Art Diary as I had intended. I can't keep my adventures pertaining to art separate from the other things in my life, and I was sort of a fool to think that I ever could.

January 8

Yesterday I showed Mr. Pousette-Dart the new sketches I had made and the next day I showed Mr. McWhorter the same batch of sketches. They differed so interestingly that I am anxious to have Mr. Zeigler criticize the same group of drawings to see which he will like.

Mr. Pousette-Dart said he liked my pictures for their spirit, and said he admired me for my patience. I said, "Do you mean in posing for them?" and when he said "Yes," I told him that I didn't have much to say in the matter—that when the mood came upon me I simply had to draw, and if I hadn't anyone else around I'd have to pose myself. So often those pictures which get in by accident, or which I don't care for, he likes better than the others.

There is one of myself in black and white Conté pencil on gray paper that he liked. I did not pay so much attention to the face because I was mainly interested in the draperies. He said that I showed a nice appreciation of the shoulders and the "form underneath" in general. This statement inspired in me a queer kind of a drawing mood. I have noticed lately that I am very much interested in draperies and how they hang on the figure, but I was never so wild about it as last night and this morning.

Last night I made six sketches of myself, paying little or no attention to the face and simply reveling in the folds. I am afraid some of the Y.W. people would be just a trifle shocked if they saw them because I "appreciated the form underneath" (and I even let my imagination run riot) but art is art, and as my drawing moods are very tyrannical I can do nothing but comply with their demands.

This morning when I got up I turned on the light, pulled down the shade and began drawing again. I became so interested in my new method of drawing that I did not even go to school this morning. I simply couldn't stop and I am glad I didn't for I learned more this morning than I have in a long time. By noon I had turned out four sketches, three of them in pastel. I finished the last one just before dinner and it is, in my estimation, the best thing I have turned out since I am down here. Of course my instructors may think differently. So much of me went into it that I simply can't help liking it, however un-modest that may seem. Moreover, if much of me went into it, not much of me was left. I was too excited (I always am more or less excited when I have a drawing streak) that I did not feel like eating, but I got myself a piece of cream pie and a glass of milk and ate it in my room so I could see and criticize my pictures which I had set up on the commode.

How I wished I could be in the life class today! It seemed to me that the human figure was the most beautiful thing in the world. To me, at present, it is most beautiful when draped with thin material.

Jan. 11, Sunday

Friday I went to art school with really good intentions of sticking to my beloved (?) Antique all day, but before the morning was over Mr. McWhorter telephoned and asked me to go to Keljick's Art Gallery with him, where there is an exhibition of original drawings by American illustrators.

The main criticism that Mr. McWhorter gave me was that I should feel around more before I put down a definite line—not to let my first guess be my last guess. He told me I was trying to do what even a master couldn't do, because Gibson and other great artists do all kinds of erasing and changing in their pictures.

Well we went to the exhibition. The main reason why he wanted me to come there was because he wanted to show me how even our greatest artists *felt around* for the right lines. He said it was not so much that they had more talent than other people that these people have become famous, but because they worked harder. He told me that Gibson sometimes stayed up all night to finish pictures, that he erased a lot, and that he always drew from models.

He told me that Frost would go around in country stores and post-offices, and when he found some farmer in particularly picturesque clothing, he would take the farmer to the store, buy him an entirely new suit of clothing, and take his old clothes in return for them. These old things he'd take to his studio and drape his models up in them. Some class.

He told me Rose O'Neill had been married and divorced two times. Artists seem to have a little way of getting divorced without much compunction. Guess I'll never marry for fear the same thing will happen to me.

Mr. McWhorter told me that in a short time there would be a play in Minneapolis in which a former New Ulm girl would play, and he wants me to go over and sketch the girl. (I wonder who she is). In preparation for this he told me to not do Antique that afternoon but use the rest of the day and the 2 following days in drawing heads and part of the figure (to the waist about) almost life size. I am so afraid I won't be able to draw the girl well, because drawing so large is so hard and new to me.

I made four that day I guess, 5 yesterday, and six today—and all are more or less punk. I find, in trying to take Mr. McWhorter's advice, that I don't know when a second or third or fourth guess is necessary—I am not in that stage where I can tell when I have made the perfect mark. Also I find that in many of my pictures I make more lines than are necessary instead of making each and every line tell a story.

Another thing I have discovered is that whenever I am terribly enthusiastic about some part of drawing, people can be sure it's new to me, because I can take calmly the things I have learned before. Here's hoping that later on I will have learned so many things that I won't have to have such terrible drawing streaks any more.

Jan. 12, Monday

Last night I had such a fierce drawing streak that I felt I simply could not go to bed at eleven as good girls should. I put my dark blue serge skirt over the transom (so they couldn't see I had a light) and sketched until about one o'clock, feeling very wicked, especially because I was continually singing, "Holy, holy, holy." I simply couldn't get the tune out of my head.

I saw the picture they took the evening of the party. I guess I'll buy one because some of the people like Dobie and Hendrickson and those might become famous and it would be nice to have a picture of them.

To-day I went down to Mr. McWhorter's office to show him some pictures. He said I should try to get my proportions better, not to make my eyes "button holey," look out for perspective in the human face and figure, not to exaggerate little characteristics (he said I had the mouth too big in one of my sketches, but glory he doesn't know what an expanse of grin I have when I get started), that I should not go too far in detail, and that I should be about 3 times the length of my study away to draw. He said my work had a characteristic which was not exactly an advantage to me—it had the appearance of being better than it was. That is, it appealed to people who do not know so very much about art, but that people like he and Mr. Zeigler etc. could see the mistakes.

Next Wednesday I am to go over to Minneapolis with some newspaper man to the matinee of "The Bird of Paradise." That is, I'll be behind the scenes and Lenore Ulrich * (the former New Ulm girl I mentioned) is to pose for me and I am to sketch her in black and white Conté on brown wrapping paper (the last article being of my own choosing). I am absolutely scared stiff, because what if I can't turn out

* This was the spelling Lenore Ulric used at that time.

a half-ways decent sketch and usually at such times I can't. It will be sort of nice tho, I should think, to be behind the scenes of a real play in action.

Jan. 19, Monday

On January 14 I went down to Mr. McWhorter's office to wait for Mr. Farrell, the newspaper man. At about half-past one Mr. Farrell and I took the street car to Minneapolis. We talked about Macbeth, Hamlet, Kubelik, Melba, Paderewski, and things like that on the way down— which was interesting enough but was not making much headway according to my ideas. I've gotten so that when I meet someone I always want to know directly what their greatest likes and dislikes are, their attitude towards Browning, Carlyle, and David Grayson, how they look at things (I look at everything as if I were drawing it in a picture, and I like to see how other people see things) and whether they are practical or not, etc.

Well, when we got to the theater—Mr. Farrell, my portfolio and I— I was introduced to the manager who was very nice to us, giving us box seats and introducing us to the leading lady, Lenore Ulrich. She was awfully nice to us too, and said she would have all kinds of time to pose for us after the matinee so we went to our seats. We were the only ones in box seats so we were generously stared at, especially since I would sketch from time to time (as Mr. McWhorter had told me to).

The play was absolutely grand and the Hawaiian music simply took me "by storm." After the play we went to "Luana's" dressing room again and I sketched her, first from the side and then from the front. She put me quite at my ease. She is German and was born in New Ulm altho she only lived there the first two or three years of her life so we did not remember each other. We must be about the same age. She said she did not see how anyone could draw, and I said I didn't see how anyone could act like that. She declared that acting wasn't hard, you just acted natural.

On the way home we got deeply interested in talking. On one occasion Mr. Farrell said, "You are rather unconventional, aren't you?" I said "Rather? I'm very much so." He asked me just what I meant by convention or rather what it meant to me. I told him that of course I thought convention was necessary but that I hated undue ceremony of any kind, and told him how I hated dress suits, dinners, and the idea of wearing certain dresses for certain occasions. I said that of course I liked to be dressed properly but I didn't see any sense in being so fastidious about it.

He said that there was only one person in St. Paul with a personality and that was Jim Hill. I said, "Well, he can afford to have a personality." He asked whether I meant because he was rich and had a position that he could do what he pleased, and I said yes. I told him if I were entirely independent and would not have to consider our family or relations I'd be perfectly natural and not wear a mask as much as I do, and that I wore a mask now only to spare the feelings of my people—because of course people would think I were sort of off if I were perfectly natural.— Nor would I blame them.

We got started on my cherished subject of Platonic Friendship. I said I believed in it and he said he did too, but that he thought it was very rare. I agreed to that and said that often it started as Platonic Friendship but did not stay that. I believe I mentioned that I had been looking for it for the last two years. "I am on a quest for Platonic Friendship," I said.

"A quest for Platonic Friendship?" said he with a queer look.

I'm sure I don't see anything queer about that.

Then he said, leaning his head forward on his hands, "Do you know what I want you to do?"

I said, "What?" and he said, "I wish you would telephone to Tyler as soon as you get home, and ask him if it will be allright for me to take you out to dinner."

I said, "All right, I'll be conventional enough to do that," so I did.

Mr. McWhorter's approval being secured, Mr. Farrell called for me at about 7:30 and we went off. He was going to take me to Carling's but I asked him not to because I hated to be so formal, so we decided on the Frederick which is classy enough, goodness knows. We got a private dining room. It was the first time I had ever been out to dinner with anyone and, believe me, I didn't enjoy the dinner part of it (except the ice cream and hashed brown potatoes—I was used to eating those). Why even bread is eaten differently there, and glory I hate to have to think of eating certain things in a certain way. When it comes second nature to a person it may be allright, but I don't believe it will ever become even third nature to me, or fourth, or fifth. The other part of the dinner was allright tho—the talking, I mean. He has read very much and gives quotations from almost any author you may name.

Saturday I went to the Morris dances and learned part of "How-do-you-do-sir" and all of "Shepherd's Hay" dance. Besides those, I know the "Princess Royal" and the "Bag-o-pipe" dance. That evening I went to Paula's and the next morning we went to a store down the road and got a paper. My sketch was in it and a rather cute little write-up about Miss Ulrich and me. Mr. Farrell referred to us as the "Great Actress" from New Ulm and "The Little Artist" from New Ulm and put me down as a very timid creature and called me "Little Artist" all thru the thing. At Mr. McWhorter's suggestion, I made a smaller copy of one of the drawings I had made of her and sent it to her. I wrote on the back, "From the little artist from New Ulm."

Armand telephoned and asked how I'd like to go to the Symphony concert last night and I said, "I'd like to" so we went. We did not get much chance to talk but I had time to tell Armand that the director looked so much like him from the back (and Armand did not feel flattered by it) and Armand had time to tell me that my work was inclined to be clever, and I said that it was sort of a disadvantage and he said, "Worse than that. It's a crime."

After the concert we went to get a sundae. We told each other a number of German anecdotes (it's such a relief to find someone here who can talk German) and when someone at the table next to ours said, "She's engaged to be married," I told him that one of the Art School girls was engaged to be married. She's about as old as I. Armand thought she was a little fool. Then I said that I had pretty firmly decided to be a spinster. He said, "Do you think that you have control of the whole thing?" (about falling in love or not) and I told him that was not exactly it, but that I was mighty particular and if I could not find the "right man" I would not take anyone just for the sake of escaping Spinsterhood. I told him if I could get Love and Art together, allright, otherwise I wanted Art. Well, Armand agreed with me, for which he goes up one peg in my estimation. He said, "You are aiming for a high goal; don't let anything come in your way."

Now all this talk about my work being so clever as to make it look good when it wasn't, had dampened my ardor just a little bit, so I said that it was going to be a hard fight if I wanted to get there. I added, "If I were sure I could do it I'd gladly fight, but if I can't—" Armand wanted to know "What then?" and I said recklessly—"I'll go and be a superficial artist like Harrison Fisher." It had the desired effect on Armand for he got excited and demanded that I look him in the eyes and repeat it, which I didn't. Instead I asked, "What would you do to me if I'd do that?" and he declared he'd drag me four blocks to the nearest river.

I said I hoped it wouldn't keep on all my life like this (my drawing fits) because I didn't see how I could stand it, and he became excited and said very seriously, "Now Wanda don't make me get serious because when I do I'm almost bearish," and he was quite concerned (about my not taking care of myself) all the rest of the evening.

January 20

This noon at dinner we were discussing Love, Art & Marriage again. Miss Dean declared that she didn't think there was any real love in the world. She believed in mother love, sister love, brother love and the rest, but not in *The* Love. I told her I had had that bee in my bonnet once too. She said, "Oh I know why you got over it," and when I wanted to know why, she said, "Since you met Mr. Edgerley." I told her I did not love Mr. Edgerley nor any other boy.

I reeled off the old story about taking Love & Art together etc. She thought I ought to sacrifice my art for my love. Theresa declared that I couldn't take care of my children if I wouldn't give up art, and I said if I *would* get married I'd drape my babies up in chiffon and sketch them, and that my husband would have to pose as king or beggar (according to what my latest fit would be like). To this Miss Dean said, "I pity your poor family!" and we ended up with a good all-around laugh.

Jan. 24, Saturday

Wednesday I did a sketch of Etta Bergmeier's head in pastel, almost life-size. I was quite sure Mr. Pousette-Dart would not like it at all because all the kids liked it, and usually what appeals to the kids doesn't appeal to him very much. Well I put it up anyway, shaking merrily (?) in my boots. To my great surprise he hauled out my sketch the first thing and said it was the best in the class as far as the character was concerned. And none of the others were exceptionally good (mine included, of course) so mine was about the best. See, I said I'd not rest until my sketch was the best in the class. All the same I'm not satisfied—I want to have the best when a lot of the others are good—*ding* good.

He criticized the color in my sketch—that is, the color of the shadows. I did the shadows in black Conté pencil which I should not have done. Guess I'd better not use black for the shadows any more.

After class I showed him the sketches I had done during the last two weeks, and there was a perfect stack of course. If I don't have them criticized every single week they accumulate like fury (which of course is an excellent and very original simile). Among this set of sketches were all of my "drapery fit" sketches—about ten or so. For once he liked what I expected him to. He said I was good at draperies.

He said my work was queer, and that some of my sketches he liked and some he did not like in the least (pictures of ladies' heads etc. that I make for presents) and I said I didn't either because they were superficial, but that I only did them because they appealed to people. He told me I ought to "fix" * some of my drawings, and I told him I didn't like to take the time to do it in because I'd rather be using it to draw new pictures in. But he said that I really shouldn't let them spoil because it would be interesting later on to see the different stages I had passed thru. He marked nine of them, I believe.

Jan. 26, Monday

Last night Mr. Farrell telephoned and asked if I wanted to sketch Leo Slezak for him the next day, and I said I would so he said he'd make an appointment with him.

Oh yes, I got a picture of Flora Davis and also a letter. She wrote in the post-script, "Saw Donnie and he is pretty nearly heartbroken. You are very cruel to him, I think." I felt sort of badly about it because I do feel sorry for the people I turn down even if I don't seem to. Here I thought I was doing Donnie a favor in dropping his acquaintance before he got too serious, and this is what I get for it.

Jan. 30, Friday

On Monday the telephone on our floor rang. I had a caller downstairs they told me, so I went down. It was Armand. We sat down in one of the parlors and began talking. Armand asked what news I had. I said I was beginning to like Antique and that I had discarded The Mask during most of the week. He asked how it had worked, and I said I couldn't tell yet.

I was wearing my red waist which is minus the fourth button from the top. Armand called my attention to the fact, and I said I knew it was off but that the design of the buttons down the waist was more agreeable to me with the button off than with it on. He insisted that I had better put one on, because he thought it was necessary if I wanted to make a favorable impression. I said that if people didn't like me

---

* Spray them with Fixatif to keep them from getting rubbed.

that way they didn't have to like me at all, which Armand dubbed a childish argument. The discussion lasted fully 15 minutes, but since neither of us would give in to the other we changed the subject.

I don't know how we came to talk of personal power but in some way we did. I said that as soon as I had people under my power I got tired of them even tho they were very interesting and nice and good.

He said, "Do you think you have ever had me in your power?" and I said, pointing my finger emphatically at him, "Do you know why I like you? Because I haven't you under my power."

He asked what I would do if he should allow himself to come under my power and I said I supposed he would have to follow in the paths of the others whom I had turned down for that reason.

Then he said, "Well, do you know why I like you?" Of course I wanted to know so he said, "When I first saw you I thought, 'There's a girl who has imagination and brains which she knows how to use." (So you see we were not mushy or anything like that.)

We were talking of illustrating. I know well enough that Armand does not consider magazine illustrating as a very high aim, and that is, you know, what I am aiming for at present. I said that if I should become a magazine illustrator of some note, some people would say, "Well, Wanda has turned out to be something," but I gave him to understand that I did not propose to stop there. He said that when I had gotten to that point I had gone only 1/50 (or so) of the way and I said, "I know it."

Armand told me that if there was anything he knew and I did not, he would be glad to tell me. He said too, that if ever I were in hot water I should call him up and he'd try to help me out if he could—which I think was very nice of him.

I asked him what he thought of my racing around so unconventionally while he was at New Ulm, and he seemed to think it was all-right. I explained that I had not seen anyone for a long time to whom I could talk freely, that I was awfully glad to be able to relieve my mind. He said, "When I first saw you I thought, 'Here is someone who is just what I was five years ago.'"

He said that right after he had met me he didn't exactly know whether to race around with me or not, because he said there were two things to think of. He couldn't exactly decide whether it would be best not to and so spare me from any remarks, or to walk and talk with me and give me the chance to unburden my brain which obviously was crammed with the thoughts of a number of years. As it was, he decided on the latter. "And," he said, "I think I did the right thing" to which I agreed, for goodness knows I was so tickled that I had found someone who could really understand me that I didn't care what ten New Ulms would say. Besides we talked only of art, poetry, human nature and things like that, and did not have a crush on each other as people supposed. Queer how people can't understand that there can be such a thing as a friendship between a girl and a boy without a crush on any side. At the same time it's the kind of friendship I like best at present.

Armand said that at the time of University week I was obviously a girl who was purely herself—that is, I had not the influence of things around me to mix me up, so to speak. Just at present I am decidedly mixed up with all the things about me, and am doing my best to extricate myself from the chaos so that I can look at myself and know what I am. I am beginning to find myself gradually too, and Armand told me this too.

Well, that evening Mr. Farrell called for me and we went to the St. Paul Hotel to sketch Slezak. We went up to their room and knocked. They said, "Come in" and we did, and glory you should have seen the confusion. They expected only me, and Mr. Slezak's wife was in her kimono, and Slezak himself was hastily putting on his vest. It was somewhat embarrassing, especially for Mr. Farrell, and he excused himself. But Mrs. Slezak said, "Oh well, now zat you have seen me anyway, you might as well come in." So he did.

Mr. Slezak seated himself and while I began adjusting my drawing materials and myself, he said to his wife, "*Lissi, das ist aber ein schwarzes kleines Käferchen.*" I smiled at him and said, "I understood that," and he laughed and asked me what nationality I was. I told him that my father came from Austria and that my mother's folks were from near Prague.

Once he said, circling around his eyes with his fingers, "*Sind sie immer so schwarz? Von Morgens bis Abends? Die ganze zeit?*" He meant my eyes.

I said, "*Ja, das kann ich nicht helfen.*"

He told his wife that I was "*ein Geschicktchen,*" and talked German to me most of the time. He doesn't seem very much at home with English, and his wife would have to interpret it for him. I felt sort of sorry for Mr. Farrell because he can't understand German. Then to cap all, a locksmith came to fix their suit-cases and he was German too.

The telephone kept ringing all the time and once it was a man who was going to arrange about trains with them, and after his wife had answered the call, Slezak began to sing, "The train-man is coming, the train-man is coming!" He is the nicest, jolliest, homey-est man you can imagine, and has a sort of babyish mouth and twinkling eyes and is Austrian to the core in manners.

He told me that I shouldn't make him a double chin because he wanted to look young. I told him that he was hard to draw, and that that was a compliment because good-looking people were always hard to draw, and he twisted up his face in the funniest and most Slezakesque way and said, *"Ja, ich bin ein schöner Mann!"* It was very hard to draw him tho because he was tired and moved nearly all the time. For a while I almost despaired of turning out anything available but I tried not to show it.

That same Monday evening Mr. Farrell took me to see Gaby Deslys in "The Little Parisienne." He was thoroughly disgusted with it but I rather enjoyed it. I like to see, once in a while, what fools people will make of themselves if you just let them go.

Wednesday we had sketch class. I was not interested in the model and as a consequence turned out a very punk sketch. "Inclined to be mushy," Mr. Pousette-Dart said. I didn't finish it at all, but went down in the Design room and sketched Rags and Phoebe instead.

That day I got a letter and a box from home. Stella had written me to send my measurements because she knew of a "Fortune of Measurements" and I sent them, and what do you suppose she used them for? To have an evening dress made for me! That was what was in the box. The dress is pale yellow and is trimmed with ruffles of delicate lace, and has narrow bands of brown velvet ribbon around the sleeves and belt. It's awfully cute, and the skirt is made in two tiers. I thought that was a pretty clever idea of Stella's. She was brilliant enough to ask me for the length of my fingers—little unimportant things like that—so I never suspected a thing. Pretty cute.

Feb. 1, Sunday

Armand had told me that if he could manage it he would take me to see "Disraeli" but he said he probably would have to call up the last minute. Thursday night Mr. Farrell called me up and asked if I didn't want to go with him to see Disraeli so I accepted. I telephoned to Armand and told him about it and he said it was allright. That's where it's an advantage to have boy-friends who haven't a crush on you and on whom you haven't a crush—they don't get jealous.

I am going to try to get sketches of as many noted people as I can. So far I have one of Governor Eberhart, two of Lenore Ulrich, two of Slezak, three of Gaby Deslys, one of Paderewski, and one of George Arliss.

Saturday afternoon I went with Armand to the Symphony Concert. I had during nearly all of that week felt very serious, and somehow every one thought I was either blue or grumpy or something like that. Even Armand asked me what was the matter. I declared there was nothing the matter, but he was so persistent about asking me all the time that finally I said, "Oh it's those ding cavaliers." (I don't know to this day whether that really was the reason or whether I imagined a reason because he kept asking all the time.)

Armand said, "Ding cavaliers?" and I explained that they were bothering me too much etc. He smiled a superior sort of smile as if he thought I were imagining most of it. I could not make him understand either that it was not such an easy problem as he seemed to think it was. I told him I wished I could put him into my place for two days. He doesn't know what it's like—how can he when he isn't a girl?

Once right in the midst of a perfectly grand piece of music he said, "Listen to that. How can you talk about such things (meaning "unimportant things") in the face of anything like that?" I didn't say anything. In one way he was right—my troubles seemed a bit small compared to a grand thing like that, but on the other hand, it is the small things that make and cause the grand things to be.

Some day I may make clear to Armand that, altho the crushes that people have on me may be petty, it does not necessarily mean that it is a petty matter. I said, "Not that I blame them—it's only part of their education," at which Armand laughed long and heartily, tho for what reason it struck him so funny is more than I can see.

He told me about a crush he had (many years ago) on a young damsel with china blue eyes. "I thought she was the whole show," he said, "and thought that the sun rose and set on that female." I told him about the crush I had on a druggist when I was about 8 years old, mainly for the reason that he smelled like the drug store and played violin.

Feb. 2, Monday

Today I started portrait class and turned out a very bad sketch, for

I had no drawing mood. It is now a whole week since my drawing mood has forsaken me and I feel so forlorn, so very much lost.

I had an idea that I was making fine progress in my quest for Myself, but this week I am so different again from what I have ever been before, that I have done a lot of groping and very little finding. When this mood first came upon me people thought I was grumpy or blue but they are getting sort of used to it. I wonder how I act—I haven't the slightest idea for just at present I am not in the least self-conscious. All the same I am not unhappy. I feel sort of incomplete without my drawing-mood, it is true, but I have so much to think about that I can almost forget the drawing for a while. I am turning out fierce work at school. I am quite ashamed of it, but there is no use hoping for anything better until my Divine Afflatus sees fit to move me again.

Feb. 9, Monday

I did not show Mr. Pousette-Dart my sketches after class last Wednesday because I had drawn only a very few that week. That evening I went with Hazel Bergen where I had been invited to dinner. They were not very formal so I got along allright and remembered to use the right silver etc. I slept there, and the room that I slept in has a full length mirror in it and I discovered the next morning that I am very lanky.

Paula stayed with me Saturday night and we had a very heart-to-heart talk.

Read some more Browning—"Saul." I can cry almost any time if I choose to let myself go, without having the slightest idea why I do it.

Feb. 11, Wednesday

Yesterday Armand called up and said he would be over directly. He brought with him a Mr. Wing, who is a "U" man and one of Armand's best friends. He is dark, handsome and sensible. Armand told me he could not go to the concert that night but that he had found that Fred Wing was going, and that as Mr. Wing had been wanting to meet me anyway, I was to go with him.

I told them that my drawing mood had disappeared and I said, "I don't know when I feel more miserable, with a drawing mood or without one. When I have one I just have to draw and draw, and when I haven't one—"

"You just think and think," finished Armand, which was just what I had intended to say.

Armand and I, as usual, got to the subject of my staying up late and drawing. He said that I could say what I wished but that he knew positively that if I kept on as I had been, I would break down and after that my work might not be so vigorous any more.

Well I went to the symphony with Fred Wing. Saw Timmie Frendel up there too and he sat beside me for quite a while and talked. He asked how I was getting along—I told him about the loss of my drawing streak. I told him that my friends were rather happy over the fact because it forced me to take a rest. He said he had begun to worry about me too, because he thought I would narrow myself to drawing, but I told him I didn't think there was much danger of that because I used drawing as an instrument to study life.

When we came back to the Y.W., Mr. Wing said he hoped my drawing streak would come back soon. He seems to be very nice.

Today I did nothing worth while at school. It's terrible not to feel like drawing, when you *want* to, so badly, so badly. I made a charcoal sketch and it was very bad. Everything I have made during the past week is so bad that I am ashamed to show it to anyone. The girls say, "Why Wanda, what is the matter with you? That doesn't look like your work," and they laugh at the things I turn out, and I laugh and we laugh together—they look so ridiculously weak and uninspired and bad, bad, bad.

I don't feel like myself without my beloved drawing mood—I feel so incomplete, as if part of me were gone—and part of me *is* gone.

I don't care, people can say what they want about hard pegging bringing one to the goal rather than inspiration. Hard plugging will bring you there but not without the inspiration. I was talking with Raymon Bowers tonight. He said, "—as Edison said, 1/10 of great things is inspiration and 9/10 perspiration." I said that the 9/10 of perspiration wouldn't bring you anywhere unless you had the 1/10 inspiration to start on. I grant that one does have to work. I work when I draw—I work hard, altho most people say, "Oh well, it's perfectly natural for you to turn out so many drawings—it comes easy to you." Some of it does, but the things that really count, the sketches that he picks out and marks, do not come so easy. I toil over them as much as anyone else.

No one, not even Armand, quite understands how much I am ruled by my drawing moods, or rather in what way. Armand thinks I am ruled too much and thinks I should turn around and rule my Divine Afflatus but he does not seem to be able to understand how utterly impossible and disastrous that would be.

Even tho Armand and I differ on such subjects as being ruled by drawing moods, walking around with red shirt-waists minus a button, and going to bed late, I must give Armand credit for being the person who, more than anyone else, has taught me how to live, and who has pointed out to me, and is constantly doing so lest I lose sight of it, the goal for which I must strive.

I got a nice fat letter from home the other day. Thusnelda asked wildly what had become of Mr. Edgerley (which indeed I am not qualified to answer). Stella declared vehemently that I shouldn't turn Mr. Edgerly down. "You with your old Armand," she wrote, "—the nice ones you always turn down and with the others you go." She raved on thusly for about half a page and I nearly exploded while I read it. It seems that Stella, Judy & Tussy are feeling very sorry for poor Donnie and think I was a cruel fool to turn him down, but of course they cannot understand. I still maintain that I did the right thing, altho on the outside it may sound heartless.

Feb. 15, Sunday

Life without a drawing mood is miserable, miserable, miserable. I am trying to entice, to lure, and to re-capture it, but of course it's all in vain. Drawing moods, delicious tyrants as they are when they let me draw, are cruelly tyrannical when they don't let me see things so that I want to draw them, and they cannot be brought by human aid.

I moved the furniture in my room to-day, hoping that by so doing I would discover such inviting light effects that I couldn't help but draw, but it's absolutely no use. I carry my paper and pencil about with me as of old but the veil is never drawn back for me to see. I am beginning to understand how other people look at objects—I mean people who do not see them always as a picture. Oh they do not know what they are missing!

I wonder how in the world people can get along who do not draw, write, or play piano, especially those who do not draw. Paula may say what she wants about giving up art for love but I think she's very much mistaken. If anything, my art will only serve to make my love more true and ardent.

In Sketch Class I had four sketches up but none of them were marked, which is quite a calamity. Not that I felt badly about it, tho. I know "myself-without-a-drawing-mood" too well to expect ever to distinguish myself when I am that self. Mr. Pousette-Dart said that my work was in danger of becoming superficial, because I was too careless again and that I was becoming lazy.

Dear Sir, I beg to differ with you. Goodness knows, I don't turn out anything (having made only about 25 sketches during the week, and all very punk) but Goodness is also aware of the fact that it is not laziness, but something much more mysterious and complicated and powerful, that is the cause of the scarcity of my sketches.

I guess I'll go to bed. Good night.

Feb. 21, Friday

Wednesday night I stayed up and sketched until 3:30 a.m. I wasn't tired then yet, but it was rather uncanny to be awake all alone at so late (or rather so early) an hour. I turned out about 5 or 6 sketches.

Thursday for once I worked hard in design. Oh I hate design, I hate it, I hate it.

Today at one o'clock Armand came and we went to the Orpheum. After that we went to a restaurant and had a Happy Thought, and then we went to the Y.W. where we talked for about fifteen minutes. That is, I did most of the talking. I characterized (to a small extent) papa, and told Armand that I thought he had not had anyone to understand him. I have always thought it very unfortunate and sad that, while papa lived, I was not old enough to understand him, and now that I am old enough to understand and old enough to need to be understood myself, papa is not here.

I told Armand that papa's father had been a wood carver. Armand said, marking on the wall with his finger, "They" (my ancestors) "went this way" (indicating to X) "and you'll have to go like this" (with a sweep upward).

Saturday evening we had Composition Class. The subject was a design for a stained glass window. I dashed off a landscape five minutes or so before going over. A very crude sketch in charcoal on wrapping paper. And fancy, Mr. Zeigler pronounced it the most successful that was handed in! I nearly fell off the Christmas tree. He asked for it at the end of the class—I don't believe he's ever kept any of mine before, and now that I attempted a landscape he chose it. It's a joke.

Feb. 28, Saturday

Monday I showed Mr. Zeigler some of my sketches so he could choose the best (which is to be sent to the State Art Exhibit). He said, "You are just on the border-line now, Miss Gág. You have it in you to become either a clever illustrator or a good draughtsman." He said what I needed was a lot of severe study, namely Antique.

Tuesday night I went to a dance with Raymon Bowers. I danced only with him because we knew no one else, and we had very interesting talks on various subjects—mostly art. He told me about one student of the St. Paul Art School—Teddy Van Solen, if I'm not mistaken—to whom one of the instructors said one day, "See here, young man, you can't draw. You've been here three years and can't do anything. You might as well stop coming here." And that night, I believe, Van Solen turned out the best picture he has ever made, I guess—and later won the Crescent Scholarship. He named a number of similar instances so I guess I'd better do my double, double, double best lest some of the seemingly untalented scholars get ahead of me.

I saw Mr. McWhorter the other day and he told me that he was expecting me to win the scholarship for Antique that year.* But I can't, I can't—for I'm not very good at Antique. I told Mr. McWhorter so too. I wish they wouldn't expect me to win it—it will make it so much harder for them to bear it afterward—the disappointment I mean.

Wednesday after class I showed Mr. Pousette-Dart the few sketches I have succeeded (or rather unsucceeded) in turning out. There were only about a dozen and very punk, very punk. He looked at them, and I explained that I had not been having a drawing streak which accounted for the very poor pictures I was making. I said that of course I did not waste my time in such cases, but that I studied people around me and things like that. He said, "Yes I think that in this art school they draw too much and don't think enough." I am inclined to agree with him.

He said also that he thought each pupil should be studied and his work criticized accordingly—some would have to be encouraged, he said, and some needed to be "sat upon." I said it didn't matter much to me how I was criticized—if I was encouraged I felt happy and drew, and if I were treated otherwise I would draw and try to turn out something good

* The Antique Scholarship was the only one for which First Year students were eligible.

in spite of the criticism. He said, "Frankly, I think you need to be sat upon." I told him if that were the case I wanted to be "sat upon." He said he thought I would resent it, but I told him in the long run I'd be thankful for it. Every one seems to be so afraid that I'll topple over the "border-line" and be a clever illustrator, which of course they do not want me to do. I told Mr. Pousette-Dart that I knew I made superficial things sometimes but that I hated them, and that I thought there was no danger of my getting in the habit because I was too interested in life.

That evening I sat in my room, mentally bemoaning and bewailing the non-appearance of my drawing streak. I was fast going down in the dumps and was on the point of having a good, vigorous weep as I had had some two weeks before, when I decided to call up Armand. I told him I was in "hot water" and he said, "Well, what's the matter?" I said "That's just it—nothing *is* the matter." One reason I called him up was that I wanted to see what remedy he would prescribe. "See Robert Mantell, and don't worry." Easy talking.

The next morning he called up and said that he thought the matter should be seen to, and that he would call on me at 4:45 p.m. that day. He came and told me to spill it out, which was a very tactless way of beginning, I thought. He should have started on some subject and led me unexpectedly to questions in which I, by answering them, would reveal to him the state of my turbulent mind. Well we finally got started in spite of his unclever beginning, and I said that I was floundering. I said that I had thought I was getting on famously in the search for myself but that it seemed I was more lost than ever—which certainly seems to be the case.

He asked how far I was in Barnaby Rudge and told me to tell him when I got thru with it because he wanted to start me on plays after that. He also said again that I ought to go to college. I told him that I intended to some time, whereupon he said, "and I suppose in the meantime it's up to your friends to hand over as much of the University as they can" and I said "Yes" ("Ya," to be more correct) and then he said, "and that means me?" to which I again answered in the affirmative, and he said he'd play the role, which is rather nice of him.

I don't know exactly how we got to talking about friendship. Armand asked me whether I had ever thought what had caused our friendship to be and to remain, but I told him I hadn't tried or even thought of analyzing it, and that I thought it was almost impossible to analyze friendships entirely, to which he agreed. He said he supposed it was because there was some one thing or force or something way down within us that was the same. Then he went on in a little soliloquy (for I must confess I was so occupied with my own thoughts that I did not listen) about the queerness of friendship and suddenly, probably because he was getting in rather deep, he ended up in the midst of his little ponderment, inserted a dash and said, suddenly coming to himself as it were, *"Well, anyway,"* and changed the subject. Funny.

Well, he told me not to worry about the floundering, because it was natural to do so, and that he had been expecting me to get into the dumps anyway. I told him that it wasn't the fact that I was floundering that had bothered me, but that I had been afraid that I was floundering in the wrong direction. He assured me that I was floundering in the right direction, and told me to take a day off once, take a long walk in the country and forget myself, and then he left.

I can't help wondering what he would have said if he had not put in the "well, anyway."

Thus endeth this diary. I do wish I could write legibly.—Wanda.

* * *

March 4, 1914. Wednesday

This morning I went to two of Marjorie Moss's classes with her— "Study of the Drama" and "Aesthetics." After lunch I went to her German class where I almost bawled once when I thought of how badly I wanted and needed the University. I thought too, how crude I must be to Armand and Marjorie and those, after they had been associating with brilliant University people as they do. And then on the other hand, when I think of how much I learned in just a day I have to think, "No wonder they know so much."

I saw Glenn Edgerley in the street car to-night. I nodded and smiled, and he did too. I'm awfully sorry about Mr. Edgerley's not going anywhere with me any more and coming to see me because I like him (altho I don't think I could ever love him) and I have a feeling that he considers me faithless and fickle. After he's been so nice to me too.

March 11

To-day I saw Madge Peterson. She knows some of the "U" people so I said, "Do you know Armand Emraad?" and she said, "Oh yes, he goes with a girl-friend of mine." It sort of gave me a jolt somewhere inside of me and glory, altho ours is a Platonic friendship, I can't help wishing he weren't going with anyone—which is silly. Of course Madge may not have been certain of what she said—it might be that this is only a Platonic Friendship.

March 12

It rather bothers me—that news. I wonder whether I like Armand more than I know—my feelings at present might very well indicate that. It really isn't so much that I want Armand to "go" with me as that I don't want him to "go" with another girl. And I really can't be indignant or angry with Armand for he has not been pretending to go with me. To think that I—who has had a good many people fall for me without falling for them—should (in my own eyes) fall for someone else. I say "in my own eyes" because I do not intend to show it. Of course I may be mistaken. I have been mistaken a number of times about my affections.

I was over at the Auditorium to-night—reception night for the State Art Exhibit. I got Second Honorable Mention for illustration I guess— I wasn't interested enough to notice. Everybody seems to think it quite an achievement to win an honor after five months of art school but, ridiculous as it may seem, my mind is more taken up with Armand than with that. I—who has continually been setting Art before Love. Wanda, Wanda, what are you coming to?

I imagine it is rather good for me in a way. I have been made so much of that a couple of come-downs are perhaps what I need.

Raymon Bowers took me home from the exhibition to-night and we went down town and had a Happy Thought. He wants me to go to a dance Tuesday too. I don't care much about dancing any more.

March 15

To-night I had a call. It was Armand. He said he'd call on me and at eight o'clock he came. He asked me how I was and I told him "rather queer." Of course he wanted an explanation. I said, "Well you know how when grass grows in spring, you can almost see it grow?" He said, "Yes?" I said, "Well, in just that way I can feel myself change."

I told him that I was slipping backward towards the old school-teaching days, which of course made him very serious and put a growlish look on his face. He said, "So you like dancing and all that kind of thing?" and I said, "No I hate dancing." Which is as much of a surprise to me as it was to him. He said, "Good," and asked me just how I was slipping. I said that I was in danger of becoming superficial again, in my work etc.

He asked what the outward signs were but I said there were no outward signs—I only felt it. I said too that it didn't even show in my work as yet, and explained that I was slipping because I had nothing to hold on to. Armand declared in that case I needed a mule to deliberately pull me back, and added that at times he made a pretty good looking mule.

He said he would bring me a book to read, and quoted Tennyson, saying, "We have to sail beyond the sunset" or something like that.

I showed him some of my latest pictures. Once I held one up and I said, "Pousette-Dart liked that one," and Armand said he had just intended to ask me for it. I think I rather surprised him by telling him he could have it, but I explained that I had changed in regard to my pictures—that I didn't care for them very much after they were done, and that it really was only whether I could learn something in drawing them that made me draw them.

March 16

It is queer that I almost forgot about my "rival" when Armand was here last night. At any rate Armand seems to be sincere in his Platonic Friendship-ness.

Last Monday afternoon I went with Raymon to Minnehaha Park, where he made some sketches which he needs for his illustration. After supper he called for me and we went to the Shubert to see "Brewster's Millions." He is paying a good deal of attention to me so I suppose I'll have to turn him down. Too bad one has to turn them down just when they get to the stage where they take you to plays and things.

Mr. Pousette-Dart showed us some pictures of different paintings and sculptures, and explained them as he went along. He said that it was better for a person to have a thought and express it badly than to have a perfect piece of work and not have any feeling in it.

Yesterday noon Paula came up and had dinner with Theresa and me. Etta and Pilchie were at our table too. We discussed each other's characters and picked each other to pieces. Etta thought one of my faults was having moods. She said she thought I could control them but Paula and Theresa agreed with me inasmuch as they thought my moods could not be entirely controlled. One of them thought my worst fault was being a little bit vain. I did not deny it. At times I have been a little bit vain, altho I am getting away from it rather fast.

Mar. 21, Saturday

Armand came at five and we went over to the exhibition for over an hour, and I had the most splendid time. Armand is certainly a very severe critic of art—Theresa thinks he is almost too severe. I must look out—he is in a fair way of getting me under his power and I don't want that. I want him to have to tug, and I want me to have to pull, but I don't want either of us ever to get the other over the border line—to win the tug-of-war so to speak.

Tonight Theresa and I went to look at the Exhibit again. I spied Mr. and Mrs. Weschcke so we went over and stayed with them all the rest of the evening. Mr. Weschcke thought it would be nice for me to stay here all summer if I could find some work. Of course he thinks it would be best for me not to do any commercial work but either rest or keep on with my regular work, but he thought people would not be able to see that in the right light and would perhaps think, "Well, she might be doing something to help herself along," when I would *apparently* be doing nothing. He said he would consult Mr. Zeigler about the matter and ask him what I had best do, and whether commercializing my art would do any harm. Mr. Weschcke is certainly a splendid man—and really knows things about art that very few people can comprehend.

Lately I have been thinking that perhaps I do not like Armand as much as I imagined I did for a while.

Mar. 25, Wednesday

Yesterday evening, after getting characteristically (only more so) mixed up with the street cars, I arrived at Marjorie's house. I slept at Marjorie's, but before we went to sleep we sat on my bed and discussed many things.

Marjorie insists that the more individual a person is the better does he represent the people. I simply can't see that—I need a very definite explanation of that before I'll believe it.

I said that "cleverness" had become almost synonymous with "curse" for me, and I insisted that as soon as cleverness became so clever that it really did some good, it became art. I didn't seem to quite convince Marjorie of this tho.

On one thing we agreed however. "Why do we have to have bodies?" we said—"and if we *must* have bodies (as a sort of receptacle for our souls and minds and hearts) why have them so unstable?" I said, "Why can't they be like a pail, for instance, where you can put your soul and heart and mind, as you would a rock?"

We decided that in eating one used entirely too much time, energy and money, especially when you consider the manufacturing and preparing of the food and the washing of dishes etc. I thought that if we had food done up in tablets—each tablet containing a certain amount of proteins, starch, fat etc. for one meal—we could just eat one or two of those tablets for a meal and thereby save lots of time and money. Why, you could be reading Shakespeare all the time you were munching your tablet. Some class.

I get absolutely no enjoyment out of my meals at all. I take eating as a matter of course, a thing which has to be done however unpleasant it may be—just like sweeping a floor or washing dishes.

The next morning I went with Marjorie to her Drama class which is given by Dr. Burton.* He is a perfectly grand man—he is not afraid of being emotional and is very good all around. This morning he lectured on Bernard Shaw's "Candida." He has read all of Shaw's works. I just *love* the way he steps off the bottom step of his platform. In discussing one of Shaw's plays he said that it was so cleverly done that it appealed to the masses and at the same time to the more intellectual people. I told Marjorie here was a case where cleverness had become an art and she had to agree.

Marjorie and I discussed Armand for a very short while too. Marjorie said she thought he was a romanticist altho he wouldn't admit it.

Mar. 28, Saturday

Last Thursday Marjorie came over after supper and we had a grand talk. Marjorie has succeeded in doing what Armand and Timmie have been trying to do for such a long time: impress upon me the importance of the right amount of rest, food and exercise. She reminded me of the fact that in order to let my *soul* do its work properly I must take care of my *body*. She said, "Inasmuch as we *must* have bodies, let us take care of them so that they will be as little in the way as possible"—which made such an impression on me that I decided I had better do that.

She looked thru my drawings and said that in some of them she noticed what she thought was a "calm wonder" in the eyes, and in others what she thought was a sort of dramatic tendency.

I tried to explain to her that the academic side of art was very im-

* The late Dr. Richard Burton, Professor of Literature, writer, lecturer and critic.

portant. Marjorie has rather a tendency towards thinking that one's inspiration will see to the fact that the form, color and workmanship of a sketch or even great painting will be perfect. I have now gotten her to the point where she admits that one has to *learn* to draw, as well as one must learn to do anything else. She says that in a picture, as far as she, Marjorie Moss, is concerned, the form, color and workmanship should be so blended with the main idea that one does not notice them, which is of course a sensible view to take but I do like to study pictures and see just *why* they are good, or bad, or indifferent.

Yesterday evening Armand came down. I told him of how Mr. Pousette-Dart had agreed with Marjorie on the "Individuality represents people in general" question, and here Armand goes and agrees heartily! I told him I had a feeling that I would believe it some time, but that I simply couldn't see it. He asked me what I thought my individuality expressed. I said that as yet it didn't express much but that I hoped in time it would express a concentration of all I had learned from the world. That is, I didn't answer all that right away, but he managed by successive clever (they were clever, ding it) questions to make me say that. I remember I inserted a number of statements something like "I know just what you want me to say," and "I know just where you're leading me," and I must confess that he succeeded in making me see what three other people had tried to make me see—but I wouldn't tell him of his success tho, believe me.

I told him I had showed Mr. Pousette-Dart some sketches of children that I had made about five years ago, and that he had said that some of those things were every bit as good as things I did now. And I said, "Well there is certainly something in them which I am losing sight of—" (and, when I caught the expression on his face) "—for a while."

Armand showed extreme signs of irritation and ended up with a sort of smile and this remark:— "Do you know, Wanda, you are about the only person who can irritate me without suffering any consequences?" I wanted to have this explained so he said that for instance the fact that I told him almost half-complacently that I was losing sight of the Thing, irritated him, but since I was not exactly to blame for it myself, and seeing there was no third person on whom he could vent his feelings, he had to let it pass. Hm.

If I irritate Armand, he has nothing on me, because he certainly does irritate me and mighty often too. And the worst of it is that he irritates me in such a—shall I say "subtle"?—way that I can't hold up a remark or action of his and say, "Here, look at this. Bing!" The Bing at the end stands for the slap or whack I'd feel like giving him. I believe I've felt like whacking Armand more than anyone else I know of.

He said that perhaps he'd call, or call me up, Saturday but that I was not to stay at home on purpose. He neither came nor called me up which made me feel somewhat dejected, and as a consequence I turned out a picture of myself on which, it seems to me, I am on the verge of crying. And that's just where I was too. I don't see why I should act that way except perhaps that I like people who don't dance to every tune I play.

Paula has just been here and we had a very interesting talk.

When I look in the mirror I feel that I have changed so much lately. My face is very serious and even somewhat stern, and when I am in a crowd I find myself looking almost severely at people—except when I see children, on whom I cannot help but beam, I love them so.

That is one reason why I have rather given up the idea of becoming an old maid. Of course I could adopt a few children but it would be so much nicer to have some with your own characteristics and with the characteristics of The Man You Loved. I am hoping too that one, at least, would be artistically inclined, and perhaps being an old maid and keeping my art all to myself would be rather selfish. But perhaps I am not a lovable person, and perhaps, altho people are rather glad to have me for a Platonic friend or someone to get a crush on, they wouldn't care to make me their wife.

Guess I'll go and sing for a while.

April 4, Saturday, 4 p.m.

Armand has just been here. I showed him my latest drawings. He said I was improving a good deal. He said he was waiting for the time when I would combine all the good qualities of my pictures in one picture. He wanted me to combine these things:— volume, *luft* (that is, atmosphere), spirit, idea; and I believe the other was a frank rendition of light and shade.

Afterwards I read him extracts from my diary which I had written about University Week in New Ulm last year. Some of the parts struck him pretty funny. He seemed rather surprised at how he had acted and what he had said. He said, "I'm glad you read that to me. That shows me in a light in which I do not know myself."

He told me that after he had received my letter last summer he fairly swore, and then he couldn't help laughing either—it was so conventional.

He said he telephoned to Marjorie and said, "I got a letter from New Ulm." She said, "Well?" and he said, "It's no use," and went on to tell her that he would either have to write me a good scoldy letter or none at all; and Marjorie said he mustn't do that so he didn't write at all.

I said, "Last fall after I had just come down, you said that you hadn't written because you didn't have time. I *knew* that wasn't the reason. I knew just as well as anything!"

He sort of smiled and was just going to say something, I believe, but I hadn't finished. "You often do that anyway—" I went on, not angrily but rather "eye-flashingly" I imagine, "—several times you haven't told me the truth and several times you have agreed with me when you really didn't agree. I knew it every time too!"

After this burst of accusation Armand looked somewhat guilty and said the reason he had done that was because I hadn't arrived at the stage where I could understand. I said that might be true, but he might tell me that I couldn't understand. He said if he said that, I'd be curious to know what it was, but I assured him that I had sense enough not to be curious if I wouldn't be able to understand at the time. As I was giving this explanation of my convenient lack of curiosity, he was far away somewhere with thoughts of his own, and I doubt whether he heard what I said. We were always doing that this afternoon anyway, wandering off and forgetting to listen to what the other was saying.

April 6

Sunday I had a fierce drawing streak. Paula came over at about twelve or after. She found me in front of the mirror in a very queer and difficult pose, of which she made fun. Not that she was aware of it (far be it from her loving nature to do such a thing) but it certainly did hurt. Then she said that one of the sketches I had made the night before looked exactly like the picture of an immigrant, which hurt me too; not because it didn't look like an immigrant or that I objected to having it look like one (for it did look rather like one) but because she didn't see what I had really worked for in drawing the picture.

Paula wanted to talk because she had a lot about Larry to tell me, and I didn't want to talk just then because I couldn't stop drawing, and I have reached the stage in drawing where I must put my whole being into the drawing of my pictures and cannot afford to divide my thoughts. So (altho it hurt me to treat her like that) I was very uncommunicative & drew & drew & drew.

Flavia Asleep—Conté Crayon Drawing

Three Conté Crayon Sketches—Mr. Zeigler, Paula, Marjorie

I absolutely refused to go up to dinner—I wouldn't stop long enough for that—so, after Paula had coaxed and coaxed in vain, she and Theresa went up to dinner. They brought down a dishful of ice cream and I dined on ice cream and doughnuts. I couldn't draw while I was eating so we talked. It seems that Paula wanted to establish a Platonic Friendship between Larry Morse and herself, but that he had said that it were absolutely impossible in their case because there was sentiment between them.

I drew again for a while and then sat down on the bed to look thru some fashion sheets. I want to make myself a nice new drapey skirt (and I told Paula I'd get myself five new skirts all draped differently, if I had the money, so I could draw them). Every once in a while, just as Paula was at some interesting point in her "sentiment-talk" I would pop in with a very earnest, "Say did you notice that lately they are draping skirts *around* the figure in a sort of spiral effect?" or "Oh they make such pretty folds when they're laid in two plaits across the front," or "Oh how pretty that would look if it were draped on a real person" at which she and Theresa would exchange good-natured winks. I wasn't sore at them for doing that, but it hurt me nevertheless, for they did not understand how much those things meant to me, for to me a gown is pretty or not according to how pretty it will look drawn.

Then Paula said she liked me better when Love got the better of the Art in me, and said that I was more womanly then. I said that I was no less womanly when art got the better of Love in me than I was otherwise. She said that when I had a drawing fit all my other qualities were submerged, which I denied. I tried to explain this by telling them that my pictures would not have the spirit they have, if all my other qualities and feelings were submerged, but I guess I didn't make myself clear enough because the tears started rolling down my cheeks and I just let them. I doubt whether Theresa and Paula know why I had been so lachrymose.

Later:—My other qualities are not *submerged*. They are concentrated and this concentration *is* the drawing mood. Glory, that definition for a drawing mood never struck me before.

April 10, Friday

It was either last Monday or Tuesday that Armand called on me and brought me a volume of four of Shaw's plays, among them "Candida." We talked about my writing that letter last summer. Armand had been saying that after he had left New Ulm he swore because he had to leave me alone with my stirred-up thoughts. I said I had had very many "thoughts" after that and told him he had missed something by not having written because I thought it would have been rather interesting to see me unfold. He said, "Yes I was a fool not to have written."

That was certainly a case where Armand's judgement was on the blink. Here he found me bottled up (rather quietly bottled up) with the thoughts and feelings and ideas of some fifteen years or so. He gave the cork a gentle pull—just enough to let *in* something which made things inside of me become deliciously jumbled—a sort of effervescence don't you know—and biff! on went the cork again and I had to spend the next four months with things—(many of them I did not understand, and could therefore not assign them a pigeon hole in my mind—so they raced all around trying to get settled somewhere, and upsetting, often, some of my older and supposedly firmly established thoughts) inside of me that wanted to be understood and analyzed and—oh everything. And Armand thought that I was too conventional!—I cannot see how he failed to see thru the *conventional* part of my letter.

The day before yesterday I posed as a Japanese girl for sketch class. I have been kicking against the poses we have been having at sketch class —they are always so stiff and so much alike so I thought I'd set them an example. My pose was very difficult, I was slightly bending back with both hands clasped behind my head, with my weight resting almost entirely on one foot. My knee soon became almost out of joint and my back seemed ready to crack and my hands became numb after the first five minutes of every pose but (Behold the martyr to the cause of Art) I stuck it out till the end. Even Harry Dobie—that shining star of our school—did an oil sketch of me.

When sketch class was over I posed for the students' sketch class in the same costume, in about seven different positions, each pose lasting about 10 or 15 minutes. Then I went home to supper and posed six times for myself before I went to bed, in the same costume. The next evening I posed once more *in the same costume* for Students' Sketch class.

To-day is Good Friday. We have no school. It is raining and once in a while I hear a few strains of some orchestra and somehow it makes me feel sad. I have felt rather depressed lately anyway, a depression that verges almost on morbidity. I think if I want to be truly happy, I must be with some one to whom I can spill over all the time.

I have been trying to get part of Me out by playing piano and singing but I only succeeded three times—once while I was playing "Dear Little Hut" and once in playing about 3 bars of "Until the end of time," and once *almost* in about 2 bars of "The Melody of Love."

April 11, Saturday

This afternoon Armand came over.

He told me about a little girl whom he had seen on the car. After he had talked to her for a while she said, "You are different from other grown-ups, aren't you?"

He told me also that someone had remarked that he was becoming so taciturn. He also said that when people talked about things of which they knew nothing, he remained silent. "And that makes them think you're stupid," he added. I said, "Proud," and he said, "By Jove, you've hit it! Now I know why people think I'm conceited." I thought it was funny he never thought of that before.

He talked about the New Woman too, and said that some people thought that thru this movement men would cease to respect women. "I think that I respect women as much and more, as those fellows did," referring to the Age of Chivalry I believe.

When he saw my new flowered waist he remarked, "That's a good-looking waist. A darn good-looking waist. Where did you get it?" I informed him that I had made it and that I made most of my clothes. "Is that so?" said he. Said she, "You didn't expect it of me, did you?" whereupon he remarked, "No, I didn't expect it!"

He also said, "For once you have a combination I like." He hates the red waist and said that it looked "dead." No wonder, after I had worn it in this sooty city for a whole winter.

As Armand looked at my latest drawings he said that pretty soon I would become so "un-clever" that I would go to the other extreme, which is logical, possible, and very probable.

I asked him if he would give me a list of books that would be best for me to read during the summer and he said he would. He said too that I could take some of his books along, inasmuch as we have no public library at New Ulm. He asked me whether I were coming back next year and I said I hoped I would be able to. He said, "Oh you've got to come back. We'll have to arrange it somehow." Oh yes, he brought me Ibsen's "Emperor and Galilean" too.

I declared that I had been forced to agree with him about the button-argument; with the result that Armand threw back his head and laughed.

I said, "Laugh! Laugh!" but he said that he wasn't laughing because he had won me over to his side of the argument (he never did that!) but because I seemed so angry over the fact that I had to give in. I confess I did not exactly relish the idea of giving in after I had stuck so valiantly to my side during our 15 minutes' discussion of the matter. Well anyway, his arguments were not the cause of my change in this thing—altho I must give him credit for having called my attention to it so that I became interested enough to observe thereafter. Good-by, long-cherished principle—in abandoning you I have lost a rather convenient justification of myself.

Armand saw a reflection of me in the mirror and said, "You *do* look different in a mirror." A few days before, it had just entered my mind that no wonder my pictures looked different to other people than to me because they see me the way I am, and I only see my reflection which of course turns me wrong side right. I told Armand that if he'd go out on the street after the right side of his face had been made to exchange with the left, people would surely notice a difference.

Armand said, "For once I like both your hat and your waist." He rarely talks about clothes, and he did it so much that day that I am afraid he did it just as an experiment.

April 12, Easter Sunday

It has been a lovely day—a sunny day, a "springy" day, a happy happy day.

I went to church with some of the girls. It seems to me that if I were a minister I should make my sermon short, concentrated, and therefore forceful. And I would not be rhetorical and dramatic—altho, of course, I suppose I would not appeal strongly to most people because I think they rather like flourishes both of speech and gesture.

After dinner I was just fitting on my new skirt and waist when Armand called up and asked if I would like to take a walk. I said I'd love to so we went. We took the car out to the river, both of us taking great delight in criticizing people's Easter toggery.

When we got to the river we walked around until we were good and hot, and then we sat down and talked. Armand said that he was in a Schumann's *"Träumerei"* attitude. He said, "It is, after all, the great power behind things that makes nature so great and wonderful," and later on, "Shall we sail in a purple boat along the rim of that river? And shall we have oars of scalloped silver or shall they be gold?"

Armand said that if I should ever follow art for art's sake, our friendship would terminate directly. He also said that anyone who could pass over Ibsen with a smile was a fool, and that Ibsen was a good example of a person who gave up art for art's sake and turned it over to Life. He said something to this effect: Ibsen was by nature a poet, but his later years are as a pine-tree stripped bare. "But they loom up—precipices of truth."

On the way home Armand said, "Tell me, do I swear too much?"

"Yes, I think it would be more effective if you used it less." We decided that each of us would make it a point to criticise, when necessary, the other's vocabulary, dress, manners and the like.

April 17, Friday

We had school on Easter Monday. We had water color, but the weather was so glorious that I wanted to go out and walk, and sing and see, and smell, and think, and breathe and *live*. As a consequence my water color painting suffered somewhat.

Tuesday—ditto.

Wednesday evening everyone was getting ready for the Y.W. Bazaar here. I had been asked, and begged, and finally persuaded, to sketch people in one of the booths. I didn't like it. I felt "thinky."

I sketched people for 10 cents apiece, and our booth was rather popular. It was hard work—people seeing me dash off one picture after another with scarcely any intermission (making each one in about 10 minutes) undoubtedly thought that it was pretty easy, but it certainly was not. In ten minutes I had to roughly size up the character of my subject, pick out the bad points and put them down so that they didn't look so bad and still contribute towards a resemblance; pick out all their good points and make the best of them; *and* draw all the while.

If I got any good out of these two evenings (for the next evening I sketched again) it was that I got:—

1. Practice in sizing up these things in a short time,
2. Practice in proportions (especially of the face to the rest of the head, and of the distance from the chin to the ear, ear to the back of the head, the lower part of the jaw to the temple, and from the temple to the back of the head) and
3. Practice in determining the depth and size of big shadows, and the size of lighter portions.

I really did not expect to get any benefit out of it but it seems I did. Of course I may have been harming my art too, for the *working out* of these drawings was superficial. By this I mean, all or nearly all the work I did after I had the character and proportion was more or less clever and, worse than that, bad, bad, bad. If I were called upon to justify this I should say that I hadn't enough time to do the thing well *and* satisfy the majority of people, and that very seldom is a pretty-pretty picture a good picture, and you know the public likes to be humbugged. They'd rather have a pretty picture of themselves and imagine that they look like that, than to have a homely picture of themselves and try to imagine that they don't look like that.

There are a few, I admit, who would rather see themselves as they are, but I have even noticed that some very intellectual and broad-minded people (after I have nailed down facts—intellectual, moral or physical) will mildly fuss about them. "Of course I have a big nose" or, "I know that my chin is somewhat double" (Somewhat!) they will say, but I know that they think, "She exaggerated that a little bit" (or "a great deal" as the case may be. It usually depends upon how frank the individual is with himself).

Well, I was afraid that under these circumstances (people standing around, etc.) I might let myself go and either wear a mask, or let myself become clever in actions. Not that I intended to do so. I was prepared to fight against it but I had no need to. I don't think I have ever acted clever, really knowing that I was clever. (I see myself getting into deep water again. I see my way out well enough, too, but it's going to be hard to explain it.) I have said before that I can do clever things (I wish there were more synonyms for the word "clever"—it is completely unbalancing my sentences) and know they're clever and yet make people think I don't know. Which would seem to contradict the sentence just before that, but I—oh, ding it all—I can't make myself clear, but at any rate, I think I am always more or less unconscious of being clever. Dump it, Wanda, until you can explain it without seeming to contradict yourself at every turn. This was myself talking. "Allright." That was me. Myself, you see, stands for my better judgement, for my permanent self, and *Me* is my unstable self, the part that is continually changing. Myself is the part of me that sees its way out of my "self-to-me" arguments, as for instance the one above about cleverness; and Me is that part that writes things in diaries in angular words, angular phrases and angular thoughts.

Like this:—Myself is inside, and *Me* is trying to sort of fit around the outside only it can't very well because it's so angular, you see, and can do no more than touch *myself* and feel that myself is there.

Myself laughs, sometimes mockingly and sometimes indulgently but encouragingly withal, at my poor attempts to express Myself. I do not mind its laughing, for some day *I* hope to become one with Myself.

What in the world makes me write these things to-night? (and that, by the way, was *Me* again. Myself knows perfectly well that I can't help it.)

Well anyway, I have been writing that I had no need to fight against being clever or anything equally despicable. For two reasons. In the first place I had no time to do so—I had to draw and think. In the second place I was so interested in the people I was drawing that I forgot to do so, and in the third place (and I think this is the greatest triumph of all) I had absolutely no desire to do so at all. There, My dear Self, I'm touching you again.

Peggy Hare helped me, and Theresa made three sketches too, but they *worked them out* more conscientiously, and the people (see how they like to be humbugged) preferred to have me do them. I could not fill all the orders.

Peggy and Doris stayed over night with Theresa and me after the Bazaar was over. It was supposed to have lasted until 10:30, and Theresa & Peggy & Doris had left a long time ago, but I was kept busy sketching until almost twelve. I was a fool to do it for I was very tired, but *I* (that is, *Me,* you know) am often a fool. Myself made only feeble remonstrances for at times *I* am stronger than it, and besides It seems at times to believe in letting Me do as I please so that I can learn by actual experience.

In a way I am rather glad I discovered this Me and Myself business because it seems to explain so many things, but on the other hand I don't like it at all for I can just see where it will jump into my thoughts and conversation all the time.

Well when I finally stopped sketching I went to Theresa's room where Doris and Theresa were sitting on the bed surrounded by eats, and where Peggy was parading up and down with some ruffles on her head for a cap, and some shawls and other queer articles of dress floating about her. Peggy is the funniest creature when she gets started, and she kept us all in gales of laughter.

We made up limericks too about each other:—

> There was a young maiden named Peggy
> Who had an appearance quite leggy
>   She was not very tall
>   Nor yet very small
> Her complexion, oh gosh, it was eggy.

> There was a young maiden named Doris
> Who wore a lace waist that was porous
>   At the neck it was low
>   And her face oh, oh, oh,
> It made her look fit for a chorus.

> There was a tall lily named Theresa
> Who was a most wonderful dressa
>   She went out with Bill
>   Who is haunting her still
> Only awaiting her "Yessah."

They hauled my mattress and bed clothes over into Theresa's room and we all slept over there. We didn't get to sleep until about two.

I have a fierce cold, am cutting a wisdom tooth, and am still suffering from the effects of the two nights of sketching.

Last Tuesday the telephone rang and they told me I had a caller. And it was Timmie Frendel. He wanted me to go to the concert with him but I had promised Miss Bonta to pose that night. He told me he'd call for me at four o'clock sometime so we could take a ramble in the woods. He is so different from Armand, and it will be interesting to see what an effect his character has on Armand's and vice versa.

I got a letter from home the other day. Stella, Tussy, & Asta had written. Each wrote about the same things but in different ways. It was mostly about dancing. All three of them are passing thru the same stages that I have, and it will be interesting to watch them.

So endeth this journal.—Wanda

* * *

April 25, Saturday

Last Tuesday afternoon The Chicago Grand Opera Co. gave its first performance of the year here. It was "Manon."

It was a lovely day and I didn't feel like doing flowers in Water Color Class, so I said I was going down and try to get some sketches of some of the singers, who came out to the front of the building every few minutes to be "kodaked." A couple of the girls said they'd go with me so we went. We mustered up enough courage to look in at the door behind the scenes, and in a little while we were within the door, sketching the Grand Opera people who were sitting around on their trunks. When these people noticed that we were sketching them they came up and posed for us, but just as we were in a perfect whirlpool of joy (at least I was) Miss Bonta came and told us we all had to come to Water Color right away. I said, "Oh please, Miss Bonta!" and some of the Grand Opera people said, "Let her stay five minutes" for I had promised to sketch a number of them. Miss Bonta hauled all the rest back to Water Color and told me to come after I had finished the lady whom I had already promised. Before I left I had to promise the people that I'd return after school was out.

I went back and leaned against a sort of shelf, hat and coat in hand, half-sullenly and half-sorrowfully. I refused absolutely to do water color. Miss Bonta said, "Wanda, I wish you would work on your book covers, please?" Book covers! Make book covers when across the street there were live, queer, and interesting people. I said mournfully, "I can't, Miss Bonta" which was very true. She said, "What *are* you going to do?" and I said, "I don't know, but I know what I'm going to do at four o'clock." Miss Bonta is such a dear little lady that I am usually very mild towards her, but I can be obstinate and determined when I am crossed in a thing like this so I continued to stand there, not knowing whether to sulk or to weep or *to act*. The "weepy" inclination must have been the most visible to the outsider (altho it was the weakest of the three, *with me*) for Miss Bonta drew me kindly and gently out into the hall and told me she was very sorry that she had been obliged to call me back with the rest, for she knew that I really derived much benefit from it whereas the others did not, but that the rules of the school strictly forbade any students watching any of the performances whatsoever.

I asked her if I might go and sketch if I got special permission. She said that she thought that would be allright, so with triumph in my eyes, a smile on my face, and a song in my heart I went down once more. When they saw me they came crowding around, each wanting to be drawn first. I asked if I really weren't getting myself or anyone else into trouble, and Campanini's secretary told me I could come any time I wanted. I sketched until almost six, and they made me promise I'd come back that evening.

I didn't want to go alone so I got the idea of calling up Armand. I said,

"You don't by some rare chance happen to have this evening free, do you? Because if you had, I'd like to have you go with me behind the scenes tonight. I've been asked to sketch some of the Grand Opera people." He asked, "What time?" and I said, "Any time during the evening," and he said he'd be there at eight o'clock. He told me afterwards that he had broken two engagements so that he might come, which was surely nice of him.

He said, "What made you call up anyway?" and I said, "Well I didn't want to go over there alone," upon which he remarked something about my being selfish. I said hastily, "No wait, I'm not done yet. I thought, too, that you might enjoy it." "But *primarily,*" he said, "you simply wanted somebody to take you over there." I could not deny this, so I said "Yes," and he said "You beggar!"

They spied me as soon as we got over there and had me drawing the second leading lady before I knew what I was doing. Then I went into the leading lady's dressing room, (Rosa Raisa) where I sketched her. It seems she could talk no English at all so we couldn't say much. Then I drew another man whose knowledge of the English language was also very limited. When the picture was done he handed me his card on which he had written: "Compliments to Giorgini." You know he meant "of" instead of "to." It sounds this way as if he were giving compliments to himself. (Which perhaps is not so far wrong. These people all consider themselves so important.)

It was awfully interesting—nearly all the European countries were represented. Armand said he could just see the cleverness oozing out of my pencil. No doubt he could, but I told him that one had to be a little clever in order to do it in such a short time.

When I came out of the dressing room I looked all around for Armand but wasn't able to see him anywhere. While I was looking for him, a young man who had watched me sketching in the leading lady's dressing room, came up to me and said, "Pardon me, but do you go to school here at the Art School?" I told him I did and he said, pointing to a trunk, "Sit down here. I want to talk to you." So I sat down and before I knew it I had told all about my experiences of the afternoon. He asked me what my name is and then said, "Pretty soon I'll tell you who I am— then you'll be scared." I said, "Don't be too sure about that. I'm not afraid of anybody." He said, "Not even newspaper men?" and I said, "Oh no—I have some friends who are newspaper men." (One—namely, Mr. Farrell.)

At about this point Armand appeared on the scene, so we went off to one side and sat on some trunks until the beginning of the next act when we stood behind the scenes and watched the performance. That was where Armand had been too, at the time when I was looking for him.

After that act Armand and I left. We went to Smith's. He ordered our Sundaes and straightway fell into a reverie. I ditto. Then he asked me if I had a pencil. I had one so he took it and a piece of the brown wrapping paper I always carry with me, propped his head on his hand and said, "You can draw me if you like—I won't talk," and proceeded to write. I went to the next table in order to get a better view and started to sketch him. But I got a poor sketch and would have given up before long if Armand hadn't finished writing. He showed me the poem and said, "I don't understand it yet, do you?" Of course I didn't. He seemed to understand it later tho.

Once during the evening he looked at me long and long, and I, for the first time in my life, could not meet his gaze to the end. To the End.

Wednesday morning one of the girls at school said, "Did you see the write-up in the paper about you?" I hadn't seen it, of course. I had no idea that there was to be one. It was that ding reporter, of course. Oh they are clever creatures, these reporters. Here he had drawn a conversation from unsuspecting little Wanda the night before, and after he had had enough material, he had introduced himself.

Thursday evening was the art school dance. I had asked Fred Wing. I had rather a good time. Learned the Castle Walk, and Mr. Wing and I tried to compose new dances. He asked me to go to a "U" dance with him on the first of May and I said I would.

May 3, Sunday

Thursday Armand called for a few minutes. He informed me that my hands were dirty (it was paint) and that I was going to skip school the next day. He said he'd call for me at 7:30 a.m. We talked of many things which I don't remember.

Armand said that perhaps some day I would become superficial for a while, thru necessity probably. He said in that case he'd probably come around and lecture me, or I believe I advised him to do so. He said I might refuse to listen to him and simply say "Goodbye Mr. Emraad" and in this way end our friendship forever. I told him I didn't think I'd be very likely to do that, but I told him also that if I *should* refuse to listen he should just come around again and whack me. I thought I would be thankful to him for it in the long run. But I am pretty sure I wouldn't terminate a friendship for any such reasons. As I told Armand, it takes a good deal for me to put my faith in a person, but once I put it there it will take a lot for me to remove it.

Armand asked what would make me lose faith in a person, and while I was trying to think of some reasons he said, "Well, for instance, if I should become, as I am rapidly becoming, a second Ibsen as regards looking at things." He meant preferring truth to beauty—being bald. But of course that wouldn't be enough and I told him so. I said that about the only thing that would make me withdraw my faith in a person would be their becoming bad, really bad. Then of course I would have to say goodbye. But even then I wouldn't say goodbye, I think, until I had tried to see if they couldn't be made better.

We talked of Harrison Fisher too, and Robert W. Chambers, and a number of other people who had sacrificed The Better Art for The Art That the Public Demands. I said that if I, like one of these, had made a good start, had gone on the wrong path (that of Cleverness and Superficiality) and had then found that I couldn't get back to Good Stuff——

Armand said, "I'd come and choke you."

I said, "There would be no need of it. I would have killed myself before that." I didn't mean strangling or poisoning or drowning myself —I meant in the other sense.

I went to bed early that night with the most virtuous intentions of dropping off to sleep directly, so that I might wake up bright and early the next morning. But they had a dance in the dance hall next door and I couldn't go to sleep until late on account of their ding tinpan jumpy, nerve-racking music. And besides that, I thought and thought and *thought* and thought.

The next day was Friday, the first of May, and a sunny sunny day. Armand came, as usual, a little after the appointed time. But it didn't matter, for it was morning and the sun was shining and there was a song in my heart.

We took the car to the Fair grounds where we got off, walked for a little while, and then sat down on a hillside. Armand would point out things to me, parts of the landscape. He had told me once that some time I would see not only color and things like that in landscapes and other things, but that they would mean things to me—mainly life. I called his attention to this while we were sitting there, and told him that they had meant things to me for a long time but that I had not been able to understand what I saw, nor did I even realize the fact that they did mean something to me. I verily believe Armand sometimes thinks I don't see as much of my surroundings as I do, simply because I don't say anything about them. I usually pack them up silently and store them away within me. There are a number of scenes that I saw that day, that I disposed of that way and sometime, perhaps in a few weeks, perhaps in a few months, I will use them—or maybe it will take a few years until they will really go thru Myself so that they will have their fullest effect on me.

Armand told me that he was going to give me a lecture. I told him to begin right then, but he said he was going to stave it off until all the green of the world had soaked into him.

When we came to the big house that belongs to the caretaker of the Fair grounds we sat down by the roadside. Armand said, "Shall we go in and pay them a visit? We don't know them but I'll introduce us. I'll say, 'This is Girl-Wanda and myself.'" He called me Girl-Wanda a number of times. I like the name. It makes me feel like part of a poem. Perhaps I ought to be satisfied that I am part of Life—which is more than a poem.

We watched the people who passed us. They were mostly farmers on hayricks or other vehicles equally rustic. All about us things were fresh and green. In the distance we could see people at work in the fields. The sky had just the right amount of clouds to make one appreciate the blue, and in the trees above us a bird was singing a song that had been in my heart all morning. I didn't know what the song meant however.

Once a sturdy young country lad passed us. He looked at us curiously. Armand said, "I suppose he thinks, 'What are they doing here at 10 o'clock in the morning?' but some day he'll fall in love—and then he'll understand."

And a meadow lark agreed.

"And this brings me to my lecture," said Armand. It was the queerest kind of a lecture. He told me to remember that the thing that counts in a picture is not so much the color or excellent draughtsmanship, but Life. He explained farther that the understanding of life was Love—so that in order to have a really good picture you must feel a great love for the people about you, so that you can make it part of yourself and yourself part of it. This great Thing will make a picture; and even tho only a fractional part of what you feel goes into the picture, and even tho people will understand only a small part of what is *in* the picture, you will have done something worth while. This will make people feel that you understand them.

He said much more than I have written but it wasn't lost on me, for I felt it and feel it still. I did not understand the lecture right away and my first impulse was to say, "But what has all this got to do with me?" But I didn't ask it. I don't know why. The birds verified it all. Armand said, "Do you hear that bird? He knows." He surely did. It sang the things I had not been able to understand. Perhaps the bird had just learned to understand, for it is spring you know.

Perhaps I ought to stop writing—I am letting my fancy run riot. Is it Me or Myself that is making me write like this? I am so bewildered with it all that I do not know.

Finally we got up and walked to the carline. We had lunch and then went over to the "U" to listen to a lecture on "Light." Fred Wing was at the lecture too. He came over and shook hands with me and said, "Don't forget tonight."

Armand said, "What's to-night?" and Fred told him. It seems Armand had made plans for the evening. When Fred asked where we had been that morning, Armand said that we had listened to a lecture in Physiology on the heart. The wretch.

After the lecture Armand said, "You were changed this morning."
I said, "Was I?"

He said, "Yes and I would have been disappointed if you hadn't changed. As it is you came up to all my expectations."

He asked if he ever touched "Myself" in me. I said, "Yes, sometimes."
"Well, if I ever touched 'Yourself' I did it this morning."
"Yes."

Once he said, "When I can't stand it any more I'll come down and read you a batch of verse . . . . . . I feel sorry for you!"

Then we went on the street car. He asked me what the state of my thoughts and emotions was just then. I showed him in the palm of my hand with my pencil. Like this:— He said his was just like that too.

Once he said, "I have mounted the horse of my Imagination, and I am afraid it will lead me a wild ride." I had been thinking something to that effect.

He had a rather imaginative plan for the evening. He said, "I'd like to have you on a bank to-night, with the waters seething and plunging below. I would want it a dark night with torn clouds hurrying across the sky; and I would want to see your hair streaming like black snaky banners behind you. And I would want you to *feel* the seething and the roaring of the elements."

Armand had to go to a Fraternity meeting and I had to change my dress for the dance. Armand said, *"Also, des Morgens klare Stimme muss man behalten!"*

I went on the car, took out a sheet of paper and started making a few notes of the things that had happened that day. As I thought over these things I became more and more bewildered, and whenever I came to a place where a period belonged I made about a dozen very emphatic ones. I had to work off my energy some way and that was the only way I could think of that would be proper on a street car.

May 6th

The next day was Saturday and Armand called that afternoon. I won't start writing about that conversation because there isn't room for it in this diary.

I did not go to Composition class that evening. I don't remember what I did—thought, I suppose. As I begin to understand the lecture more and more, I seem to be getting more sure of myself—as to whether or not I love Armand, I mean. All the time I have been down here I have lived, like a plant, thru the effect of his sunshine; and plantlike too, I have always, perhaps unconsciously, turned my head toward the sun—much oftener than he realizes I suppose, for I don't remember ever having admitted it to him.

Theresa says I have changed so much since Friday. I know that too.

* * *

(NOTE:—The diary covering events from May 3 to May 25 is missing. Art School closed and I did not win the Antique Scholarship. In spite of this I was determined to return to St. Paul in the fall and was thinking of conducting a Summer Sketch Class in order to earn the necessary funds.

The following entry concerns a long talk which Armand and I had had on the previous Saturday. We had discussed the new situation which was developing between us and agreed to keep our relationship on a Platonic basis.)

* * *

May 25, 1914, Monday

Much of my bewilderment has disappeared, and as a consequence my heart is lighter and my brain clearer than it has been for a long time. Yesterday at about four o'clock the humor of the situation dawned upon me, and by six I was able to smile about it. Perhaps I am deceiving myself but just at present I feel as if my happiness were really genuine. By this noon I had become mischievous and now I feel deliciously wicked.

Catch me talking enigmatically after this, or allowing anyone to do so! Glory we were a pair of periphrastic fools. I have spent the last two days in writing verse, drinking water (for it is very hot) and trying to think of names to call Armand. Not for what he said Saturday, but for saying what he did during the three weeks before that. Why did the ding fool say he had mounted the horse of his imagination? Perhaps he's in love. If so, why for the love of soup, doesn't he go to her with his sighs and blank verse? Or if he wants to work it off on me instead of on her, why doesn't he tell me all about it? I tell him about my cavaliers.

I was a fool to be so lax in our game of tug-of-war. Why, he has been having me over on his side for almost a month and I've made practically no attempts to get back on my side, which is very bad. I think I'm back on my own side now, and believe me I'm going to pull for a while.

What my attitude is just now, I really don't know. Certain it is that I am almost satisfied and that I feel more like myself than I have for a long time. Perhaps I don't care for him as much as I thought I did. Armand was right—I am too young to judge.

10 p.m.:—It is queer—I have gone thru so many stages during the last three days. Saturday morning I was bewildered, at about noon I was happy, by evening I was wretched. By Sunday noon I could smile, in the afternoon I was happy and could laugh. This morning I was mischievous, this afternoon deliciously wicked, right after supper reckless, and right after that wretchedly serious. And now I have come back to the beginning and am bewildered again.

I am wondering how I will act when he comes next. I suppose I will keep right on changing moods for a while, and it will depend almost entirely upon which stage I happen to be in when he comes. I am hoping I will be cold and happy.

Armand is supposed to come to-morrow to look at a letter—a business letter—that I am to send to New Ulm. It's important too, about starting a sketch class this summer.

Armand said last Saturday that he was afraid that if I should fall in love with someone who did not appreciate art, Myself would be obliterated forever. He thought to me, being an artist, love when it did come would be so intense that I would not be able to withstand it. He may be right, but oh, I hope it will never have to be that way.

Perhaps Armand thinks it's Gratitude that makes me think I love him. Just this minute I almost hate him because perhaps I love him, and on the other hand, I almost love him because I almost hate him.

Oh Myself, Myself, where are you? I am surrounded by Me's and Me's—bewildered Me's, wicked Me's, frivolous Me's and vindictive Me's—and I cannot feel you at all.

May 27, Wednesday

Armand ran over yesterday morning to look at a rough draft of that business letter. He said, "While I'm reading this letter you had better go and get your coat and hat—it'll do you more good to be outdoors than in here."

I raced upstairs to do so and when I came down Armand said, "Do you know you have some good lines here?"

I said, "Oh you weren't supposed to read the poems" (There were two poems at the end of it). He said he was sorry but that he had already done so. The lines he referred to were these:—

> The world has shown
> Its heart to me and will not clasp
> Me to its bosom till I grasp
> The secret of the Great Unknown.

He told me the reason why the world did not clasp me to its bosom was because I gave the world's heart a bat every chance I got. I did not know that at all.

We took a car to Como Park where we sat on the grass and talked. I rather imagined myself to be happy at first for I could laugh. Later on as I became more serious, Armand said, "Now you are getting more like yourself again. This morning your laugh sounded like broken glass."

Of course I had to tell him that I supposed I didn't care for him as much as I had supposed. I think I know just what Armand's attitude is towards me. Of my attitude towards him I am sure—there is no use lying to myself, altho I suppose I must lie to him about it seeing we are to be only friends. I think Armand thinks I am so young and inexperienced that I cannot know whether I really love him or not. He wants me to get out into the world and meet other people to see whether I am not mistaken. Of course it is best as it is, I suppose. A test cannot be for the worse.

At one time (for a little light was dawning on my hitherto gloomy horizon) I said, "Well I'm just about satisfied."

He said, "So you are quite satisfied?"

I said, "I think I am."

He said, "Did you get that little difference?" (it seems he put some emphasis on the "you") and said that he wasn't saying whether he were satisfied or not.

He said once, "Did you ever suffer?" meaning emotionally. "For instance, did you suffer Saturday?"

I said, "Yes I did." I told him, tho, that it might have been either Me or Myself who suffered. He said, "If I could solve that——"

I know he thinks it was Me or the Child in me which talked last Saturday.

I said, "What do you say to my forgetting Myself and Me entirely for a while?"

He said, "That's what I've been telling you right along. I told you to stop thinking."

I think I am not equal at present to wrestle with Myself and Me. I said, "It's this way. Myself and the Me's are like strings which ought to, and will, guide me when I can understand them, but just now they are tangling up my feet, keeping me from going on."

Armand said, "That's a good figure."

I said that instead of trying to obliterate my Me's entirely I ought perhaps set them to some use. Just like electricity or steam. I mean these things can work havoc when they are not properly controlled but can do much good when they are managed in the right way. Armand agreed, saying that I would have to catch them (the Me's) and put them in prison for a while. Then when I had tamed them I could use them to some good purpose. He said that they would serve as buffers for society. He said that the bare truth was usually too dazzling, and that my Me's could be used effectively to sort of veil Myself. Myself, you know, is Truth in me.

May 29, Friday

Paula and I spent nearly all of yesterday afternoon in discussing reason *versus* feeling. Paula maintains that if you let your feelings lead you,

you will do what is best and come out right in the end. I insist that you *cannot* always let your feelings lead you. One has to remember that the people one deals with might be following, not their feelings, but their reason. And reason on one side and feelings on the other will not work. Armand is letting Reason rule him, and forcing Reason to rule me. He is using a System—for the better, perhaps, but it hurts. But perhaps in this case his Reason and feelings coincide.

Armand and Marjorie came to-day so that the three of us could go to the art exhibit. Armand told jokes most of the time. Some of them were funny, too, and I laughed. But why did Armand tell jokes, and let his Me's jump all around and jam their fingers into the flesh of Myself? Marjorie asked me a number of times whether I wasn't feeling well or whether I was unhappy.

When I came home I went to supper with Nina and Mary, two new House-girls. After supper Mary played piano and I did a muscle dance which seemed to amuse them immensely. It did me some good tho. I had felt the floor-stamping feeling coming on—and it is rather effective, now that I come to think of it, to do away with part of the writhing of Yourself by bodily twistings. I couldn't have done it if there had been anyone around who knew how false it was. But no one knew.

I have been gadding about on the University campus for the last two days. With Paula. I went to Sewing Class with her. They have a triple mirror in that room and a number of times I caught glimpses of myself accidentally—took myself unawares, so to speak. I look so much like a Child. No wonder Armand is afraid the Woman in me hasn't spoken. But this I know: I look more childish than I am. My soul and heart and mind feel sedate but my body doesn't. My body is only twenty-one years young—my heart and soul and mind are older than that. And hearts, they say, are stable while bodies are not.

I try so hard not to show Armand that I have not been able to accept him as a Platonic friend, but somehow I always feel that I am not succeeding at all. Last Tuesday morning for instance. I tried hard to make him think I was happy—and he said my laughter sounded like broken glass. It is not the pleasantest thing in the world to feel that a man who does not love you knows that you love him.

Last Saturday I told Armand a few things about Phil Becker. I said that after our spat we had shaken hands and were now Platonic friends. He said, "Are you sure?" I told him that I knew that *I* could be nothing but a Platonic friend, but Armand seemed to have doubts as to

Phil's side of the matter. I wonder how Phil *is* feeling about it. I hope he is satisfied with being a friend.

I think I have a pretty sensible record as far as love affairs is concerned. Nearly every girl of about my age that I have met lately has been engaged once or twice or even thrice. Nina for instance, has been engaged three times, and Mary is engaged for the third time at present. I think, without much trouble I might have been engaged twice. In fact it was more trouble to prevent it from happening than otherwise, I think.

May 30, Decoration Day

I am absolutely beset by social duties, and have the most irritating chance of being popular. I do not feel any more like being popular and whirling in the social swirl than I do like laying a cement sidewalk in a tunnel. I don't see why I should choose this comparison, but I did and that's all.

Nina and Mary would gladly take me to shows and to the parks etc. if I would go. I am very moody—I mean I'm in such a condition that I don't like to promise anyone to do a certain thing at a certain time. Except Armand and Timmie or some such person. I'd gladly reserve days for them.

Paula and I had a discussion the other day as to how much liberty one should allow a boy to take. This sounds quite alarming, I know; and if someone had asked my opinion on the matter a year ago I should have said with the utmost conviction, "None whatsoever." I have always been very severe in that respect too, but I have found since that there may be exceptions.

I do not think it is fair to the man whom you eventually marry (if you marry at all) to let any man touch you any more than is necessary, and I always avoid touching any boy friends for this reason. Of course I am not entirely guiltless. Donnie has had his arm about my shoulder, and David has held my hand for a few moments at times. And Armand has had his hand on my arm. I justify myself in these ways:

The first one (Donnie) was my initiation and I was too surprised to be able to say anything. (I have found since that it is not very often that a girl has reached the age of twenty before she has had a boy's arm about her, so my record is comparatively good.) In the second instance (David) I made him stop—he was so young that I can almost forgive him. In the third case—I was crying (about my fall plans).

Besides I always think that a man like Armand ought to know how far he can go. One of the things I have always liked about Armand is that he does not take liberties.

Yesterday Stella graduated.

To-day is Decoration Day. Dear papa and all the rest, a tender, tender thought for you. Dear papa, I will not let you die. I think when I feel myself slipping I will think this.

I think people always consider me such a child because I have done my *living* in silence.

Nina, Mary, and I went down town for dinner to-night and on the way home we looked at furniture, dishes, gowns, hats and suit cases. We saw a bedroom set of some grayish, brownish, dove-colored wood which was dull in a way but still had a suggestion of a satiny gloss. It was the most beautiful wood I have ever seen, and so nice and restful a shade.

$$\cdot / \cdot / \cdot / \cdot / \cdot / \cdot / \cdot / \cdot /$$

Sometimes all I hear and feel, the whole universe, seems to swing to the above rhythm. I mean concrete things too, like the ticking of a clock or the rumbling of street cars, and people's conversation. I remember the first time I noticed this I must have been about eight years old. I was down at grandmama's and the rustling of the trees, and the whirring of insects, and the very vibration of the air swayed with that same rhythm. It is always the same metre too.

Another queer feeling that I have had since I was a child and about which I have told no one I guess, is a queer *pregnant* feeling in my *mouth*. It (the feeling, not my mouth) feels round and big and heavily light, and I have always had an idea that some time I will find out what it means. It feels as if I were holding all that which I do not understand as yet but which will, some day, be made clear to me. That is why it is heavily light. It is light because at present I know so little about it that it cannot feel heavy, but it is *heavily* light because what I am holding is so much, so much.

I have, somehow, a dramatical streak. To-night I did a Flower dance to the tune of "Goodnight everybody." They are ridiculously melodramatic. I wish I knew some terribly "acty" soliloquy that I could utter with illustrative exaggerations.

I guess I will imagine that I own the dove-colored bedroom set and hop to bed. Think of awakening to a room like that. The color of the furniture would blend so beautifully, in the morning, with any colors of the dawn that would filter thru the opalescent curtains. Now that sounds rather flowery but I should absolutely insist on opalescent curtains. Let me see, I had just awakened to the inside of the dove-cote. Well I would watch things become more distinct, then I would take a few delicious stretches, and then I would jump out of bed and slide back the opalescent curtains and give myself over to the sunshine of the day. And if it were raining—think how beautifully the dove-cote would harmonize with the colors of the day.

Oh yes, I forgot to add that my morning gown would be a *fragant* shell pink with fluty, sea-foamy lace popping and spilling out from unexpected places, and rippling and rolling all over itself in billow-lets. And this is the way the rippling lace would sound:—*Teh-rudel-dudeldoot*—only fifty times softer.

I wonder how far my fancy would lead me to-night if I should let it keep on like this. I should probably get to the point where I could find words to express another old obsession of mine. As yet I have never been able to express it.

I simply must go to bed.

May 31, Sunday

Nina likes to skip and run, and I am so glad. That girl has good ideas but she ought to weed out her thoughts so the good ones wouldn't be choked by the hackneyed ones. She seems not to be afraid of anything. She has given herself entirely over to God, she says, and therefore need have no fear. She thinks she is psychic. I think she ought to get that idea out of her head. It is common sense plus an imagination that is the cause of her guessing people's characters. Besides, she (like many other people who profess to be psychic or something like that) forgets to remember the times when it hasn't worked.

She doesn't consider me foolish in thinking I care for Armand but she does think I'm mistaken and that I will get over it. She says she is better qualified to judge because she has had more experience. I said to know—to really know—one did not need experience. She thinks that Armand's attitude towards me is purely Platonic and she accounts for any misleading remarks of his by saying that they were said by his erring Me's on the impulse of the moment. She thinks the whole matter is the cause of the disappearance of my drawing mood.

She advises me to forget Armand for a while and hinted that I was to sort of let Armand think that I really didn't care much for him to see how he would act. I had to explain to her that I was absolutely frank to Armand, not only in what I said but also in my actions. We finally agreed that time would finally have to decide the matter.

She has as yet not changed my views as regards Armand and me. If I feel that I care for him, I mean to say so in this diary,—if it turns out that I am mistaken in fancying myself in love with him there will be plenty of time to say so when the time comes. If it is true that Armand does not care for me except as a friend and that I will continue caring for him, it will not make me feel any better by *not* writing it down. Here, if nowhere else, I mean to give my feelings a fair chance.

Nina thinks my principles (in never leading a man to think I cared for him when I didn't) are very good. She thinks that a man's love is not as great and refined as a woman's, because with a man passion enters into the matter more than with a woman. I maintain that a man's love can be as pure and great as a woman's.

June 1st
"And what is so rare as a day in June?" The day a month ago.

I am beginning to see that Armand's method is a good one. Of course I hope that he won't stick too rigidly to his System, but I *am* so young. Not that my "youngness" has anything to do with being sure of myself.

June 3, Wednesday
Nina told me to-day that she had just re-discovered Herself. Just think, she has been controlled by Me's for a number of years. She says she owes the re-discovery to me, which is really quite true. When I first met her she was very frivolous but I knew there was more to her than she showed. Her case was so much like mine of last spring that it wasn't hard for me to show her what she had unconsciously been yearning for for many years. In this way my relation to her is about the same as Armand's relation to me. Somehow I can see how Armand has felt in different instances towards me, because I feel that way towards Nina. It makes me feel so happy to think that I have had the chance to show one human being Herself. And what am I doing now but talking "Neatness in dress" to her! Wouldn't that make your hair curl?

The first evening that Nina and I had a talk we discussed the sex question. Nina thought that the greatest cause for conditions as they are to-day was the rapid change of styles. I put up my two arguments which are indecent dressing, and allowing men to take liberties—small liberties that are not considered worth mentioning by most people. She had never seen it in that way before. She said that she had always thought she knew a good deal on the subject but that I had gone her one better.

She thinks also that she knows more about love than I do. Of course she has been engaged three times and has seen more of the world than I have. But most of the time Herself was obliterated, and you cannot depend upon the judgement of Me's. Just about all that I know about the subject, I have learned since I have discovered Myself, so I insist that even tho I don't know as *much* as she does, I know *better*.

I think now I can see more clearly how Armand knew what to do next in teaching me how to live—somehow it comes rather naturally. Of course I can see that it was much harder for him to teach me than for me to teach Nina, because I had gone thru the same thing that she had and besides, I had Armand's method to copy from. Ding good method Armand, ding good method. I wonder if it couldn't be changed a little tho, just a little—so one's heart wouldn't have to suffer so much.

June 4, Thursday

I stayed at Paula's over night. She thought that there was more of the Woman in her than in me. I don't think so. It is true that there is more of the Child in me than in her, but I will not grant that there is more of the Woman in her than in me.

I said that my soul and heart and mind were older than my body. She said she didn't think my soul was. "Because if it were," she said, "It would show in your eyes," which was a stab. I seem to be getting more sensitive than I have been. I wonder if my eyes really show only the Child in me. I always knew that my nose and mouth and my face in general made me look much younger than I am, but I had always supposed my eyes to be true to Myself.

We discussed drawing moods again too. Paula said she agreed with Nina in thinking that circumstances kept away a drawing mood, or made it come, or made it go, and that my experiences and feelings and emotions cause drawing moods. I insist that they do not, because they come whenever they please whether I am happy, sad or indifferent; or whether I am serious, frivolous or indifferent. She said that she didn't think my drawing moods came when I was indifferent. I said they did. "Of course," I explained, "I cease being indifferent as soon as the drawing mood appears." I said also that as soon as the drawing mood was there all my thoughts and experiences, especially those that I had had since the last drawing mood, become part of my work.

She said she was inclined to think I did not really love Armand because I had no drawing mood at this interesting stage. She thought if I were in love I ought to feel so inspired that I would have a fierce drawing mood. I tried to explain that the fact that I was unable to draw at present wasn't a sign that I did not *feel*. I told her that it wasn't that I lacked inspiration either. I told her that I always had more or less inspiration but that I couldn't make use of it until the veil would be drawn for me. I repeat that it isn't that your hand doesn't know what to do when you haven't a drawing streak, but that your eyes do not see it in the right way.

I just telephoned to Armand and asked whether he was terribly busy, because if he weren't I'd want him to come down. I have so many prosaic things to ask him. He said he was swamped with work so I told him to go ahead and do it. He said he'd call up at 7:45 to-morrow morning.

June 5, Friday

Armand called this morning—in person. He said he was going to have his last exam this morning, and that he would come and see me this afternoon. I mentioned inadvertently that I had felt rather indifferent lately, and he said he had noticed it and that he would stir me up this afternoon.

He said he supposed I'd be tickled stiff that I'd be rid of him this summer. I said I supposed he'd be glad to be rid of such a bewildered girl for a while.

Armand said he wished the New Ulm Sketch Class business were settled, and of course I did too. I said, "You don't understand—well, I suppose you can *understand* what it would mean to me not to be able to go back to school in the fall, but you won't *feel* it."

He glanced away and said, "There are two stories to that. That is another dog with two tails."

I said, "Why, how so?" (feeling deliciously wicked all the while) and he said, "Well, you must remember that you aren't exactly a negative quantity. There are some things you do that I like," and went on to say that aside from that, there was myself, personally.

He wants me to stay over to Thursday because Marjorie * and he wanted me to go along on a boat trip up the river. I don't know whether I'll do so or not.

June 6, Saturday

Well, he called yesterday afternoon. I read him extracts from the diaries I wrote when I first came down here. I read those parts which showed the development of my drawing streaks, and of my quest for Myself, and also some little remarks about my cavaliers. Mr. Farrell seems to irritate him very much.

Shortly after he had come he stared into space and sometimes he would regard me in a preoccupied way. It was such a queer look that I dared not look up very often. I wonder how much he heard of what I read. When I would come to a funny part he would smile as if it were very painful for him to do so. It was like it is when there is someone dead in the house, and a little child who cannot comprehend Death, says some funny, happy little thing. One does not feel like laughing but one does not want to lessen the child's joy by not smiling.

When I stopped reading he got up and said something about *"Die Mensch-heit in dem Mensch."* He sat down again and said, "I've either got to talk or play piano. I guess I'd better not talk," so we went into the other parlor where he played. It was a funny thing and was so uneasy and harrowingly sad that it made me quiver all over. I was on the point of asking him to play something soothing but I doubt whether he could have done it that day. He didn't look it certainly.

Then he got up and paced around, sat down beside me on the "curler" for about half a minute, got up again and paced, and finally sat down and played another piece. This one didn't jerk one so much as the other had done, but it ended up with a hopeless, hopeless note—so hopeless that it gave me a funny feeling right below my throat.. Because he *ended up* that way you know. Why should he *end up* that way? He got up and while he was pacing again, he said, "I suppose you know what I mean." I said, "No I don't." He said he thought we'd better go back to the Lounge because he was afraid he'd wear a hole thru the rug. It would have been sort of a *groove,* I think.

We went back to the Lounge where we sat down. He said that he was in a basket that was going down deeper all the time. I asked him how he accounted for this. "Lack of sleep, for one thing," he said. Lack of sleep indeed. Lack of sleep doesn't usually make him act like that. He

* Marjorie graduated that spring and is not mentioned in the diary again.

said later that he had become so used to seeing me here in St. Paul that
—(I don't remember what.)

Then we played the half-dollar game* in which I got my hand
scratched and two nails broken but it was fun. We had a dollar this
time tho, and it was rather clumsy. He also told one joke after another—anything to take him away from Himself. *Himself* struggled
pretty bravely tho. So you are running yourself on a System too, are you?

He said he was doing his best to drown X [our name for his Myself]
and that he was succeeding. How funny that he should want to.

4.20 p.m. I have now known Armand for a year and some minutes.

June 7, Sunday

I must finish where I ended up June 6. He asked me what the prosaic things were that I had wanted to ask him the day before. It was about
New Ulm and what I was to do. Armand told me that when I came
there, I was to investigate immediately about the Sketch Class. I told
him that I couldn't be so business-like, and as we went on talking I
found myself becoming tearful. Talking about next fall usually makes
me cry. I looked hard and long at the furniture in the room, and set my
teeth, and did my best to think of something that would not make me
cry, but in spite of all my efforts my mouth began to quiver and the
tears fell. I did not cry much, but it was as bad as crying much because
I would have done so if it had been proper. But one couldn't, right
down there at the Y.W.

Armand gripped my wrist and said, "Where is the *Woman* in you,
Wanda?" It was the *Woman* that was weeping. Children do not cry
about the things I did.

He said, "Brace up. Show them that you are a Woman."

I didn't say anything. I slid around on the chair (I was kneeling on
it in a very Un-Womanesque manner) and flopped down on it with my
hands grasping the back of the chair. I said, "If I were only more of a
business woman."

Armand said, "You'd like to bite me, wouldn't you?" I said, "No, I
don't want to bite you," and he said, "Well, you'd like to have a good
cry, wouldn't you? I wish you could have a good cry, and I wish I
could cry with you." Sort of duet effect. By this time I had stopped

* A game in which he flipped a coin from the back of his hand to the palm of the same
hand, and I had to try to snatch it in transit, also using only one hand.

crying but I wasn't done—I wept the last chapters after I got to my room.

Well, then we raced over to school where I gave him my stencilled table-runner and a sketch which was on exhibition. Somehow as soon

Stencil Design for Table Runner

as Armand asks me for one of my pictures it immediately becomes more valuable to me than it has been before.

He said, "You're always wearing your hair up now, aren't you?" and I said very emphatically, "You bet I am!" He laughed and asked me why I was doing it, and I explained it was because people refused to consider the Woman in me on account of the Child being so obvious. The Woman-Child thing is certainly my latest pendulum-idea.

We walked to the corner of the park where we shook hands. Armand said, "Well this has been a splendid year and you've been a brick, you've come along fine." He told me to be sure and do a good deal of *"scribbling"* and I told him he might be sorry he said that because when I got started I absolutely pestered people with letters. We said goodbye and he went to catch the train for Lake Minnetonka and I went home. He gave me a copy of Stevenson's Poems. He wrote on the fly leaf:

"To a lover of kids from the same."

He is to call me up Tuesday to see whether I have decided to go on the canoe trip. As I entered my room my eyes were filled with tears but I did not feel badly enough to cry. Somehow I didn't feel as tho we had parted.

June 9, Tuesday. 7:30 a.m.

Oh it is such a lovely day that I want badly to stay over for the canoe trip, but I think I had better go. It will be nice to see the home-folks tho, and plenty of kids. I have an idea that my next drawing streak will be all for children.

I found much in "Aprile's Song" from "Paracelsus" that applies pretty well to me. It's about slipping backward.

Part Four

MYSELF AND MANY ME'S

1914

June 15, New Ulm

It was good to see the homefolks. The first two or three days Flavia followed me all over, philosophizing on anything that entered her mind. Howard straightens his ties and combs his hair down neatly whenever he goes away because there are a number of girls in their bunch now. Dehli is getting prettier all the time. She writes stories, is continually worried about their plots, and always asks Tussy's advice. *"Hat das auch richtig a plot?"* she asks. She is becoming more self confident and is not as afraid of human beings as she used to be, having gathered about her what Stella teasingly calls her "crew." The "crew" consists of two girls.

I see in Asta a promising disciple. She is not afraid to tell her thoughts. Stella is really very sensible and sees so clearly sometimes that I have to marvel at her. Tussy is, as ever, characteristically broad-minded and has not lost her "This is business" air. She is so wild about having the house absolutely neat and clean that she would work herself to a frazzle if we wouldn't scold her once in a while. Fancy getting a scolding for working *too much!* She writes rather well.

June 16. At Grandma's

Te-rutel-dutel-doot! That's how I feel to-day. My spirits are down in the *Heu-land* and are capering and darting around among the tall grasses and flowers. Oh but everything is free and happy and optimistic down here!

12:30 p.m.—Myself and X have just had a romp in grandma's hay meadows. Myself seems to be very strong since coming back. I have not worn a mask and have no desire at all to let my Me's come to the front. In fact, it seems that I could not obliterate Myself just now if I tried. The

235

whole thing is making me rather laconical, I am afraid. Armand suffers
in consequence—thru my Installment letters.

Stella and Tussy consider me as altogether too deep. They told me this
morning that I was so "melancholy" that I had a depressing effect on
their spirits. I don't think I'm melancholy. Once in a while I become
somewhat lachrymose, but it's usually because I want badly to go back
to school in the fall, and that all the kiddies are growing up and I want
so much that they should have the education they need.

I think I shall write a story, or send away magazine covers under an
assumed name, or write a moving picture scenario. I really think I would
be justified in prostituting my art for a while. That would be unselfish,
I should think, because we need the money. It is very selfish of me to
protect and fuss over my art as I do. But of course in a way it isn't. I
mean, in the long run it isn't. Sometimes I have to be selfish now so
that I will be unselfish in the long run.

June 18, Thursday

Just came home from grandma's.

When I walk around to-day, I feel as if I were just a soul walking
around—my face and body being invisible. Well, it feels as if only the
expression on my face were visible. Sort of as if Myself were going out
for walks without any of my Me's.

Flavia is a peach of a kid. She is reading nursery rhymes to me and
every once in a while she'll insert a bit of child philosophy. Just a minute
ago, while she was unravelling something, she looked at me with such a
splendid look on her face that I could not take my eyes off her at all.
Her eyes seemed to grow larger and larger as the thing became clearer
to her.

June 21, Sunday

Yesterday evening Jack Alden (who is here for several weeks working
on the new school) called on me. We went canoeing. I was really very
happy—an untroubled happiness. I wrote to Armand about last night:—

> "I was not *silly*, you understand: simply irresponsibly happy. The
> whole sky seemed to be punched with thousands of star-shaped holes
> so that some happy light could shine thru upon us."

By the time we had paddled home again the stars had disappeared,
but as their happy light had *soaked* right into the water, one didn't miss
them. The reflections of occasional lights dipped into the water like

golden needles. The sky to the right of us was drenched with city lights, and to the left it was veiled with many wonderful things which I do not understand at all, as yet. I found much of Myself in the groups of trees that were cloaked with the evening mists, or in the long sweep of dull silver water. But it was a part of Myself which I have never met before. You see I have been so used to finding parts of Myself when I was either alone, or with Armand or Mr. Weschcke or Paula, and it seemed so different to be finding Myself with someone else. I found a happy part of Myself. I wrote also to Armand:—

> "There was one group of trees that I have made my own. Two days from now I will probably have forgotten what they looked like but I will not have lost them. I have rather an interesting collection of little bits of landscapes that I don't remember definitely at all; but they have had their effect on me, and some time I will put them in the face of a child or something like that. One can do that, can't one? I mean, put a *landscape* in a person's face—well not the landscape itself, but that part of it 'which is not' to so many people.* Perhaps one might say that it is the Myself of a landscape, not the Me part, that I want to paint into a child's face. I'm sure it is just as much possible to find the Beauty of Nature in people as it is to find the better part of people in Nature."

Jack Alden called me "Wanda" most matter-of-factly. I was glad of that because I do not like to be called "Miss Gág." It's too formal for such an unconventional creature as I am, and fits on me about as well as a high-necked, long-sleeved, cuff-buttoned shirt waist does. When I told Jack that I had had a good time he said, "We'll have another."

I feel myself going somewhere, altho I don't quite know where. On a real vacation I think. Armand told me that he wanted me to go home and "kick" and "forget," and I did it last night for the first time since I have returned to New Ulm. I like boys so well that I can't enjoy myself very long without them. They divert one's mind beautifully; that is, most of them. Some divert it too much, but Jack Alden is so quietly jolly that he diverts neither too much nor too little.

In my last letter to Armand I have written the truth and nothing but the truth, but I have not written *all* the truth. I have to let my reason rule, I cannot let my heart do what it wants to. It's all on account of your system, Armand. You are forgetting that a heart which has been taught always to be absolutely true is above a System. However much my Me's

* "That which is, is not; and that which is not, is."—From Ibsen's *Emperor and Galilean.*

have reigned, I am sure my heart has never been affected. I may often have worn a mask but I have always considered my heart too serious a thing to be included in the mask. A sure proof of this is that I have never let a boy think I was in love with him when I wasn't.

June 24, Wednesday

Yesterday we had a picnic out at the river and when I came home I found a letter from Armand. I raced up to the attic, brushed back my hair and seated myself in front of the mirror. I always do that when I get letters from people who interest me, because I always catch myself unawares and I can tell so well how I am taking the letter. Then I opened the letter and read it. He said that I should work hard at being lazy this summer because one could not tell what would come next summer or the next. This made me weep rather violently.

He writes:—"You speak about Stevenson's remaining part child thruout life," and said that there was very little difference between a child and a genius, and explained that the child sees the truth but the genius sees the truth and *realizes* it. He says also, "Of course you will be part child always, it is your heritage, Wanda." He has not found any work for me to do this summer that would pay, and said that I was to take a good long vacation, and work next fall and take as much school work along with it as I can carry.

I have written to him:—"To-day I received your letter. I don't like very well how you write letters. I like *what* you write but I don't like the way you write it. Somehow I feel that I am getting a *theme*." When Armand reads my letters he can just see what moods I am going thru and what I am doing day after day. But in his letter one cannot see that.

Mrs. Hershl asked last night when Armand was coming. I told her he wasn't coming and that I didn't want him to come. She asked why not and I said that people would only talk anyway. She said that they had done that last summer anyway. I said, "Yes I know it," and told her that I hadn't cared for him in the way they meant. Mrs. Hershl said that she had told the people, "Wanda has just as much right as any other girl," which was a perfectly darling thing to say. It hurt me much tho, because it showed so well the attitude of people towards me. Just because we are poor they think we have no right to—to—to *do anything*.

I always have a feeling—I may be mistaken of course—that some people think that I am just a common heart breaker—or else a girl who is serious about her art, but one with everyday feelings about love and life and her fellow beings. They do not know that art to me means *life*. It may sound egotistical for me to say so but I know that I have seen, and see every day, a beautiful part of life which the majority of them never have and never will see. It isn't egotistical when you think it over— I deserve no credit for that. It is my heritage. My father had that power before me, but because he was unselfish it could not be developed as much as Himself wanted it to be. So he handed it to me, and it's my *duty* to develop it. If I ever turn out anything worth while I will not feel like saying that "I did this," but "My father and I did this." Aside from that, I will have to include all Humanity to a greater or lesser extent too; and the Great Power that makes the Myselves in things will be the most important thing, of course.

Yesterday I made three sketches in pastel. I learned how to make white things in shadow.

I felt so much like having a good hard weep yesterday but I have no place to have a good weep in. At home I can't. The family always gets so melancholy when I cry—because they think that when a person cries it must necessarily follow that that person is very unhappy. Mama has so much to think about as it is that I don't want to bother her with my affairs, and the rest are all younger than I and cannot understand. I don't see why in the world I did feel so much like crying, but usually when I cry the hardest I have no idea why I'm doing it.

Tussy told me joyfully yesterday that she hadn't been blue once, ever since I wasn't with her at grandma's. I must be a regular hoodoo. She thinks she is happier than I, I suppose, because sometimes I cry and am what she calls "melancholy." She does not know that I am not melancholy but gloriously thoughtful—and she has yet to find out how much satisfaction there is in being riotously lachrymose.

Tussy, like I, is a person that has to *pass* the glass door.* May I be there to see her pass! Because it will be so interesting to see myself thru her. Stella is a person, I think, who has always been beyond the glass door. Of course she will look thru different glasses when she falls in love, but I think she really has always loved and been able to demonstrate that she did love humanity. Paula surely can demonstrate her love for people. I think I have always loved humanity, but somehow I have never been able to show it. Armand is pretty much in the same boat— I know he has it, but as he himself has said, they do not know how much he loves them.

* My symbol for the realization and manifestation of one's love for humanity.

This morning I washed up three rooms, three halls and the stairs. I don't suppose I made what you'd call a magnificent job of it altho it looked allright to me.

June 27, Saturday

Judy and Stella and I have just been telling our fortunes with cards. Things came out most beautifully.

Judy just put my hair up in a psyche—Stella says my face doesn't look any older. Psyche's are supposed to make you look older. She said my face looked just like it did when I was a baby.

July 6, Monday

I feel so uneasy to-day. And many things make me want to cry. I wish that my sorrow were but the froth upon my heart so that I could blow it off and be happy.

Armand sent me nine of his books. I have read three of them, "The Land of Heart's Desire," "Peer Gynt," and "Cyrano de Bergerac."

On the 28th of June I went canoeing with Jack Alden again. The water was *be-drenched* with the sunset. Jack told me all kinds of things about Armand and his friends. He seems to think very much of Armand. For much of the time I simply *sat*. I believe that I didn't even think. I do that rather often lately. I just sit and let my mind *and* body take a vacation. If one could only do it whenever one wished.

Monday Stella came home from grandma's and in the evening Stella, Judy, and I went up to Paula's where we read "Gems." *Gems* are very melodramatic stories in a "Twenty-five-cent-a-year" Magazine that we found at Hershl's. Only the most sensational ones are given the honor of the title "Gem"—we are very discriminating. Each Gem is read aloud for the benefit of the whole company with all the elocutionary powers within us.

July 9, Thursday. At Grandma's

Tuesday morning Stella and I went down to grandma's. As soon as we came down I jumped into my old art school apron and my gymnasium slippers. That was fun. I spent half the afternoon in skipping around, kicking up my heels and flinging around my arms like a mad windmill. Oh but that was fun. And I whistled, making up the tune as I went along to fit my actions. I thought my melodies were quite unique when

Stella informed me that it sounded like a merry-go-round. And after she had said that, I noticed the resemblance myself so I stopped.

At about four o'clock I suddenly found myself drawing. And such a position! One of my favorite "happy" positions. I am standing on one leg (very characteristic) and have my head thrown back and my arms flung up above my head. I was sorry I couldn't get the fingers on the picture because they showed much of the joy that was in me. I call the picture "Hloopsie."

I wrote to Armand:—

> "By the way, I will give titles like that to all, or most, of my sketches that I send you. So that I will be able to remember which you are referring to when you criticise them, you know. . . . It will be fun naming them anyway. I shall probably find very queer names for them—sound names, much of the time."

I sketched Stella twice that afternoon, and myself 3 times more. They are called:—

"Elbow"
"Stella-down"
"Grin-cat"
"Esel"
"A Step"

Then we went boatriding and I sketched two bits of landscape. One of bending trees is called "The Jilted One," and the other "Moon, blood orange." Yesterday I sketched myself once more, "Draped Chair." Another one of myself is called "Left foot." Yesterday evening we went boatriding again and I did 3 landscapes. They are called:—

"Colored Waters"
"Meadows and Blue"
"Purple Top"

After that I did a pencil sketch of Grandma.

July 10, Friday

Yesterday I got a card from *Donnie*. It quite upset me. He began with "Dear Friend—Almost a Stranger." He is coming to New Ulm Sunday and asked if he might see me. It gave me such a funny feeling because——. Oh well, perhaps he will be a Platonic friend now. Maybe if I'd dress myself real homely——.

Last night I made another river-scape called "Pale Evening." This morning we got up at 5:30 a.m. and went rowing until 7:00 a.m. I made a sketch called "This morning." After that I went in the big rope swing that is behind the house. When one swings very high, it makes *hloopsies* go thru one's chest and throat. Hloopsies are delicious, breezy, half-gaspy feelings.

It's ding hot to-day. I am wearing the minimum of clothing (three pieces) and still I'm hot. I got a letter from Armand—a nice one.

July 13, Monday

Yesterday I made two sketches of Flavia. Their names are "Knuckles" and "Cream on White Slipper." Stella and I returned from grandma's Friday, and Saturday evening I went canoeing with Jack Alden again. We went upstream to meet the sunset. The reflection of the sunset between the *storied* trees was dancy and bronzy and beautifully metallic.

Donnie did not come. I do not know why. Perhaps because I wrote on the card I sent him, "I will be glad to see you, for I have no engagement for Sunday until seven p.m." I said that because I considered it for his own good. In order that I should not have lied I made a date with Stella and Judy—a *sunset walk*. Paula says I lied when I wrote that to Donnie. I suppose I did, but I did not realize it at the time. I told Paula that the reason I said it was because I did not want Donnie to see so much of me. The space between the lines of his postal seemed to indicate that his hopes were not yet dead. I know that Paula and Judy both thought that I was taking things for granted and that I was conceited to think that Donnie's ardor would be fanned anew—but Larry Morse himself has said that a man will not give up until the girl is actually married to someone else. Granting of course that he is really serious about it. And Donald is not one to take things lightly.

I sent Armand about a dozen pictures for criticism.

July 19. Sunday morning

The letter which Armand sent me last was 14 sides long and was an improvement on the fore-going ones. I could see him in at least one third of it, possibly more. In speaking of two drawings, he said they were utterly bad and empty. He said, "You say you have been reading Chambers" * and warned me not to let Chambers get into my pencil. Which made me quite furious. I sat down immediately and wrote four sides or so of opinions.

His letter is almost saturated with his philosophy. Perhaps I know

* Our "gems."

what he means by *"des Mensch-gottes Herrshung"* but I hope I am mistaken. He talks of a great "maelstrom" within him which he has not yet under control, and by the way he talks of it one would almost think that he intended to make himself an absolute monarch over the maelstrom. And there, you see, is the place where *"des Mensch-gottes Herrshung"* might come in. If that is what he means, I'd like to have a little tiff with him over the matter.

I, too, have a *maelstrom* within me (glad I found a word for the feeling) but I do not want ever to be able to control it absolutely. That's what puts spirit and so forth into my drawings, that's what makes me draw the things *I don't know how to draw*—in short, it is that which gives me drawing moods. Of course people might say that if I were master over this power I would also be able to control my drawing moods—make them come and go at will—but I don't want to be able to do that entirely. The joy of the thing is that I am under its power.

July 21, Tuesday

I am a most hateful creature to-day. I hate mys—no I don't hate myself, for I don't hate anybody—but I do make myself sick.

Friday Paula told me that I ought to try drawing for magazine covers. Some of my things were better than some things they have on magazine covers now, she said. It would be the most unselfish thing to do, she said. I owed it to my family to be unselfish, she said. Besides it wouldn't harm my work, she said.

She said that.

In the last statement she is absolutely mistaken. I told her that my work *would* suffer, I was sure of that. "But you can remedy that later on," she argued, which is also a mistake. For every bit of cleverness I let into my work now, I must fight a regular little battle later on. My cleverness is like weeds. It grows fast, *fast,* as soon as I let it take root at all. Goodness knows it leads me a hot enough race as it is. (What I like is the way I tangle up my metaphors.) I mean it's bothersome and bewildering enough when it's only unconscious, to say nothing of my deliberately opening the gate and saying graciously, *"Herein!"*

Paula said, "You can just send some that you have already made," but I explained that they had to be drawn on decent paper with a margin etc. She said, "Well, but you don't have to make them clever or superficial." I told her that as yet there were so many things about magazine illustration that I did not know, and I would have to patch up my ignorance with cleverness. It is not so easy as one might think to sit down and make a *big* picture for publication. When I attempt a big drawing I always feel as if I could possibly manage the *skeleton* and even part of the *idea,* but I always feel that I'm not sure about the filling-up part. (Another charming metaphor. They just roll off my finger tips to-day.)

The worst of it is that people are justified in bringing up the topic (of earning money) to me. Goodness knows we need it badly enough. Especially with a bunch of kidlets who have Myselves that will unfold presently and clamor for educations. As a matter of fact, I had been seriously contemplating cover-illustration but I did not tell Paula so. I would necessarily have to be disappointed again and again. I can bear disappointment, but I would not like to have the family join it. I can take it more lightly than they.

Yesterday I made a few ventures, jokes and some poems. Also in the evening I drew three rather large sketches of myself—these as practice to magazine cover illustration. Rotten all three. Clever, superficial, empty— I have done much damage already. But to bewail that would be selfish again. I am so *selfish,* I am so selfish—I do not want to harm my art. Oh why wasn't *this,* which makes me rejoice and weep and think and *live,* folded into someone who would not have to abuse it, someone who had more to nourish it with?

Last week Armand sent me six booklets, each book containing all the authentic pictures of some great artist. There are Rubens, Van Dyke, Michelangelo, Correggio, Andrea Del Sarto, and the Flemish Painters. Ah, but it made me happy to get them. I did a hloopsie-hop all around the dining room table when I got them, and always put them where I would see them unexpectedly, at which times I always felt like hugging them with joy.

Last Sunday I went to the park concert and did not enjoy myself. The pieces they had did not appeal to me. And Mediocrity stared at me, and bored holes thru me so that Myself was touched. And of course Myself writhed.

But Saturday night I suffered even more. I was at my attic window which faces the west and sketched the sunset. When it became too dark to draw, I sat and simply watched it. It told me so much—much more than I could well hold in silence. And I could not find words to express myself—which was painful. Myself is so far ahead of the rest of me. Myself went right out and touched the sunset and I had to sit there and watch and feel and see, without being able to *say*. I felt again,

> "The world has shown
> Its heart to me, but will not clasp
> Me to its bosom till I grasp
> The secret of the Great Unknown."

I wonder what my present attitude towards Armand is. For a while I was almost willing to accept the friend attitude. Then for a while I scarcely thought of such a thing as an attitude, I felt that it would come out allright—one way or another. And now—I don't know how I feel about it. Perhaps Armand has not been using a system on me at all. Perhaps it was all in the natural order of things.

July 24, Friday

I find I care very little for what the majority of people think of me. I find I care much for what *the people who know* think of me. Only yesterday Judy told me of how people are getting the idea into their heads that, for the most part, I ran around with numerous *beaux* and was having a good time while I was in St. Paul. I am fully prepared to hear it from different quarters.

I know of course, my family knows of course, and my friends know of course, that I have never done anything that I would have reason to be ashamed of. It is true that I raced around a good deal and with a good many people, but I need action and besides, the places I raced to (concerts, good plays and to nice homes of nice people) gave me that which I need, as much as papers and erasers and such, for my drawing. I know that I have done the right thing and that's all that counts. Reputation doesn't bother me much—it's my character that I will take care of so that I may be happy.

July 27, Monday

No one responds to Myself. It isn't so much that I care whether or not people consider me foolish or insane, but that it makes me feel lonely to be saying things alone and in vain.

I wrote to Armand:—

> "What's the use of showing any part of yourself when no one brings out a Self to keep Myself company? It isn't that they show much of their Me's either. They seem absolutely sincere, but there is no one who realizes that it is as necessary for me to draw and

think as it is for me to eat and sleep. They have no ill-feelings towards me but neither has a fence-post. And a fence-post, with a splash of the gold of sunset upon its top and with the purple of an evening upon its shadowy side, can at least make me feel things. It gives me *itself* and does not try to tell me things that it knows nothing about. That's the beautiful part of Nature. It tends so beautifully to its own business.

It ought to teach me a lesson too, oughtn't it? for it shows its purples and greens and golds each day whether people appreciate it or not, and whether or not someone brings a *bared* soul to keep their souls company, they show their Selves because that is what they believe in."

There followed a ridiculous and fantastic metaphor in which I compared myself to a pitcherful of milk. I said that since the cream and the skim milk were still so much *one* in me, I had to spill much milk in order that I might spill some cream.

My letter to Armand is progressing very slowly. And it's such an uninteresting, *waily* letter, too. Paula is away, and Myself has to slip deeper and deeper inside of me. As I refuse to let my Me's take the place of Myself, I am having a rather hard time of it. Oh I want badly to have a good long talk with Armand so that my mind will get a good thorough house-cleaning.

July 28, Tuesday

I am down at grandma's and therefore happy.

On the way down, oh on the way down, I drank in greedily all the sunset-saturated landscape. By the time I came down to grandma's I was practically mad with the joy of life. When I am so essentially Myself I can hardly understand how my Me's have *any chance at all* to bother me. But this much I know, one hour of real joy makes up for an entire week of dumps and mediocrity-slashings and me-troubles.

I have written to Armand:—

"And I have been in the swing just as Evening, which has been calm and dignified up to now, dashed in a rosy flash across the sky. I swang high, and the Evening and I laughed deep into each others eyes for one minute. For one minute.

"And then, when there was nothing but purple and green and a slender moon, I danced all by myself (you may laugh here if you wish) out upon the lawn. To the music of a phonograph. That is, it was the music of a phonograph when it started out, but after it had gone thru purple hazes and things it was something much sweeter. I don't like much to dance *regular* dances. I like to invent all the movements as I go on. They are less graceful, I suppose, but they are so satisfying."

I started an evening poem to-night.

July 29, Wednesday

This morning I raced around and had a simply glorious time. I made two pastel sketches, "Sloping Shadows" which is bad, and one of Tussy picking flowers, "Nasturtiums and Sunshine."

When I was a child I used to be afraid to go off by myself among just trees and meadows and hills and clouds because I used to think such funny things. But now I am not afraid—just that of which I used to be afraid, I like now.

I wrote to Armand:—

"You often write about realizing Eternity in one moment or something to that effect. I know now that when I was about 8 years old I saw, even tho I was too young to *realize* it, Eternity for one moment. And the wonder and bigness of the thing would over-awe me to such an extent that I used to think I had better not go out on hills alone, but with someone who would keep me from feeling things I could not in the least understand.

I read you a diary extract once. I wonder if you remember it. About the entire world seeming to throb to some pattern of sound and about a heavily-light feeling in my mouth? I mentioned the third of my childish 'inexplicables' and wrote that it was beyond my power to ever begin to express it. This last was a repetition of a thought which, altho no words or new thoughts were added to it, became larger and more wonderful and incomprehensible (and strangely enough, comprehensible at the same time) until finally I would find myself so deep *Somewhere* that I became alarmed over the fact that I, little I, should be part of some great and wonderful *All*. It was still more appalling to think that such a young mind as mine should dare to have such thoughts. The whole thing is closely connected with realizing or *feeling* Eternity in one moment, but I don't quite see where it comes in. The words that repeated themselves with such alarming results were simple enough:— 'I am really alive.' "

I remember I used to consider myself in a pretty decent state of mind if I hadn't had the feeling for some time. I was always afraid that it was more or less insane to have such a thought.

I wrote also about some of the things we used to do when we were kids. I believe I shall copy that part too, because I want to remember those times:—

> "Boys were always beneath our notice. I remember distinctly that we would never deign to draw any boys in our pictures except when it was absolutely necessary. And when we played 'house' and there happened to be any boys left after each house-keeper was supplied with a 'man,' they were immediately given a girl's name and were obliged to be a sister to some doll (and sometimes they even had to submit to the humiliation of having hair-ribbons tied to their hair). Which must have been humiliating enough for the boys, but I don't remember that they ever complained. But their lot was infinitely better than that of the poor lad who was chosen to be a 'man.' He had practically no say in the management of his household. His 'mama' (which really meant his *wife*) would send him off to work in the morning and the poor fellow would really not get much out of the whole game at all.
>
> Once in a while a girl would be beautifully unselfish and let a boy have charge of the butcher shop. Weed stalks cut in short pieces were sausages, and large weed-leaves were beefsteak after the butcher had pounded them with a stone."

This afternoon I made three sketches of Thusnelda. In drawing medium light hair that has just been washed, one puts Indian red where the sun strikes it, and then a sort of yellow ochre in streaks. For the dark parts one puts brown and green and much purple.

July 30, Thursday
Rain.
And no thoughts worth mentioning.
And too dark to draw.
And nothing else to do.
And no letter from Armand.
And that's all.

July 31, Friday—10:45 p.m. At grandma's.
I have been beautifully Myself. Oh, it's nice to be able to be One's self entirely. I have just been outside to see the wonderful, silent mists. I sat in the swing and swang high. The world seemed wrapped in a summer snowstorm. I felt the quintessence of "Hloopsies" within me, and everything was so *unheimlich* and yet so absolutely fascinating and enchanting that I wanted to stay all night and swing high, and walk in the dewy Everything.

August 3, Monday

Last Friday I got a letter from Armand. It was full of things that made me want to have a long exciting talk with him. I absolutely leaped for joy for I have been having so few interesting things to think about

(which sounds bad enough, but sometimes one *cannot* find much to think about) and his letter set my mental machinery going at full speed again.

He seemed quite tickled that I had whacked him so soundly on account of his saying that about Chambers, and said he would have been disappointed if I hadn't "come back like a fighter." He said he liked the Hloopsie picture because it was "natural, truthful and sincere" and that it expressed more movement than any of my drawings that he has seen. But he did not criticize the rest of them. And by now he has received a second batch of drawings. He'll never get them all criticized.

I have written him:—"In towns Myself stays wrapped up most all of the time that I choose to have it so, but when I am down here where everything is free and green and purple, Myself just takes a big leap out of the blanket and it *just stays out*."

Last Friday I discovered that Tussy is rather good-looking. Especially from the front. That night I did a river-scape, "Blue, Pink and White." And another picture or rather a design, "Dangling Branches."

I have been allowing myself to forget to think for a while. Which isn't nearly as pleasant and as interesting as thinking; but I am glad to let the thing take hold of me for a while. I feel that a mental rest is what I need.

Last night I went to the park concert with Mr. Gray. Mr. Gray is a college Sophomore who is working here during vacation and who stays across the street. He is very musical. I had a nice time. We talked about school and college days, discussed Les Miserables and many other things. He wants to come and see some of my sketches some time. I told him that I was trying to eliminate "Gee" from my vocabulary but that I couldn't find a substitute for it. He was in the same boat. His expression is "Gosh." I told him about my eighth grade teacher who said to Ione Dekker and me, "Why do you say 'Gee'? Why don't you say something prettier, like 'Oh Pansies!' or 'Oh Roses!'"

I decided that I was going to say "Oh Geraniums" hereafter, which is handy because when I find myself starting with "oh Gee" I'll just end up with "raniums." He decided on "Goldenrod."

Last night I dreamt that Donnie was here on a visit. I dreamt, too, that Armand had written me a lattice-work letter. He wrote it in pencil and tinted the writing with pastel in such a way as to accentuate the thoughts he was expressing.

Aug. 4, Tuesday

Yesterday evening I went to an Ice Cream Social with Mr. Gray. On the way home we met Stella and Judy, so we walked around—it was a perfectly grand evening—and sang all the songs we could think of. It is easy to see, I suppose, that I am still allowing myself to "forget." It is very resting. Mr. Gray, like Jack Alden, diverts one's mind beautifully. I mean he diverts, without taking one out of one's sphere. He has fine eyes. Blue, with dark lashes which curl upward in a most artistic manner. He has a good voice—tenor.

Aug. 7, Friday

Wednesday evening there was an ice cream social at the Lutheran school-house. As not any of us girls had any money, we told ourselves that it was too cold to eat ice cream anyway and amused ourselves in other ways. Stella can make her jacket look very old fashioned when she adjusts it a certain way, and she would stalk around in time to the music (the music at the ice cream social) looking for all the world like some vaudeville actor. When we would be where people could not watch our antics, I would invent new ways of walking (also in time to the music). It was really a cross between walking and dancing.

Tussy took it all quite matter-of-course-ly, she being used to Stella's and my outbursts, but Tussy's friend, Susan, must have thought us decidedly foolish. Which does not bother me in the least, for Susan lives so much in the things that *are,* that she does not need such unwindings and therefore cannot be expected to understand their usefulness.

I say *unwindings* because, when I *think,* I'm winding things about me and about me, and (not being experienced enough to choose only the things I need) I am continually winding things I *don't* need, along with the things for which I will at some time find use for. These unnecessary things sort of churn about inside my mind causing rather more confusion than I can very well stand, therefore it is up to me to get rid of them. So you see unnecessary actions become necessary thru the very fact that they eliminate things which are unnecessary.

Last night Mr. Gray came over and talked with us for a while, (our conversation consisting mainly of slams and flat jokes). He always makes me believe things that aren't so. To tease me. Gravity and solemnity are not his predominating characteristics, to be sure, but he can be beautifully quiet and serious, and he has a laugh that makes one's heart glad, it is so wholesome and true. He is surely very nice.

I am by no means at the height of happiness, altho I am happy. There is all the difference in the world between the happiness that comes of "forgetting" and the other kind of happiness. I much prefer the latter but the former is decidedly soothing by way of variety.

All I do now-a-days is to wait for the evening.

I got a card from Armand the day before yesterday (he was the last person I ever expected to get a *postal* from). There were also a few lines from Dr. Lang. They are both in Montana now.

My letter to Armand is scarcely progressing at all. That comes of "forgetting"—one doesn't think much, therefore one is not constantly being driven to write. Stella and Tussy cannot understand why I should consider it *absolutely necessary* to write when I feel like it, but I am letting them wait until they go thru the same thing.

Aug. 9, Sunday

Last night Mr. Gray met me up at Turner Hall Park. We talked of the war. Almost all Eurasia, it seems, is at war. And as matters stand, it seems that Germany and Austria are going to be pretty well beaten. I hope the United States doesn't enter the field. Some people that I like might have to go to war.

I promised to go to the band concert with Mr. Gray this evening. He dances too promptly and obediently to my whistling, which is too bad for I should not like to have myself get tired of him.

I am surely "forgetting" with a vengeance. I know just exactly where I am. I am living very naturally indeed—I mean it isn't me-stuff that I'm wrapping myself up with. I mean, I'm like a nut. What I'm show-ing is true enough but it isn't the *kernel*. Now during the Springfield Spring I was happy, and thought that that way of being happy was, after all, *the* way. Just now I know well enough that after I have given my poor bewildered and overtaxed brain a rest, there is a much more beau-tiful happiness than this in store for me. Just now I am gliding over the top of things. This is the way I go now and here are all the dips and curves my mind usually makes.

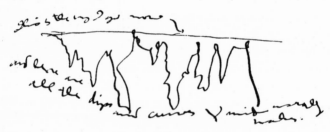

Sometimes I weep stormily because I am allowing myself to "forget" but then I quickly make myself forget again.

August 10, Monday

Yesterday evening Mr. Gray and I went to church and then to a movie and then for some ice-cream and then home. Exciting, wasn't it? Soon people will be saying that that Wanda Gág might be doing something different than running around with that young man. They would not believe it if I were to tell them that I am giving my mind a vacation.

But I think its vacation will soon be over. As soon as I have a good talk with Paula, or as soon as I can stormily un-weep myself, my mind will have to think and solve and puzzle itself again as of old. As a matter of fact I think I am fast beginning to think again, for just a minute ago, the blue in the sky——.

August 11, Tuesday

I have just been wailing to Armand again. I believe I am beginning to "think" again. I wrote:—

"Am I not the most inconveniently constructed creature you ever saw? When I have much to think about, I become bewildered; if I have nothing to think about, I am worse; and when I force myself to stop thinking, I want to think again after a few days."

Also:—

"I have a hard time imagining, or rather remembering, that you *are*. You might as well be some creation of my imagination, something intangible which *exists*, but which exists in the way Myself exists. Perhaps one might say that X is the only part of you which I retain or feel."

August 15, Saturday

Mr. Gray seems to take it as a matter of course that I should spend all my spare evenings with him; and I, in turn, give him all my spare evenings as a matter of course. I am not used to giving all my leisure to one man, but the unusualness of the thing rather appeals to me. It's just as if I had made a new girl friend and I were continually stepping around with her. Next to Armand's set, I like Mr. Gray. I suppose people will think we have a terrible case on each other which is certainly not the case. He is simply a very nice friend to me and I hope he will remain, as he is now, simply a friend. I think the time is ripe for introducing my Platonic friendship ideas.

Wednesday Paula returned from St. Paul. I was quite wild to have her back for I had begun to miss our confidential unburdenings very much.

Tonight Mr. Gray complained about the fact that our way of amusing ourselves was always the same. He said he had tried to rent a launch or canoe or an auto but that he was unable to get one. Just think, they do not rent autos to people here in New Ulm. They say they want to sell autos, not rent them out! I am to set my imagination going and plan some original way to spend tomorrow evening; but I can't think of a thing to do. I'll bet Armand could help me out. I think he could find interesting things to do if we were on the Sahara desert.

I have not heard from Mr. McWhorter and I am becoming decidedly worried. I am just *existing* now but I shall want to *live* presently.

August 17, Monday

Last Friday Mr. Gray informed me excitedly that he had finished his job and was to leave in two days. He seemed to feel very badly about it. He declared that if I would be at St. Paul next winter he should want three evenings out of every week but I said, "Oh, is that so!"

Sunday morning we went to the park where we had some very interesting discussions. Here are some of the questions under discussion:—

1. Does Emotionalism or Intellectualism rule the world?
2. Should one follow one's reason or one's feelings?
3. Would you class Myself under *reason* or *feelings*?
4. Would you class Love under *reason* or *feelings*?
5. Is Intellectualism a result of Emotion, or does Emotionalism grow from Intellectualism?

We both thought Emotionalism ruled the world but disagreed on a great many little points on the question.

Mr. Gray thought that, since one's feelings were continually changing and one's reason is stable, one ought rather to follow one's reason. He admits that no person should try to rule another person by his (the first person's) reason, because one person's reason may differ so widely from another's. In confirmation of this I gave a brief synopsis of "Richard Feverel" which shows so well the danger of *Systems*. I rather think one should follow one's reason to a great extent, but that one should make the rule elastic in order to make proper allowances for *being human*.

Mr. Gray would put one's Myself or conscience under *reason* but I did not agree to that. Of course since I insist that Myself is stable and since one's feelings are not, you couldn't put *them* to-gether very well either. But somehow I can't help thinking that one's higher feelings *are* stable and can therefore be made to coincide with the Myself in a person.

In a way Myself and my conscience seem to be the same, and in a way they seem to be different. It seems that my conscience is the better part of my reason, and Myself is the better part of my feelings. Mr. Gray thinks that one's conscience is caused by, and is a result of, one's feelings.

He was inclined to class love under reason too—at any rate he made it *more* a matter of reason than I would. He admitted however, that he was not making that a rigid statement, seeing that he had had no experience in the matter.

He thought Intellectualism was a result of a great number of Emotions. I was rather vague on the subject. I don't like to make statements unless I have something worth while to back it up with. I might have made some statements which might have sounded plausible enough at first, but they would have been only clever and could not have stood much serious investigation. So, thank goodness, I didn't say them.

I thought it was high time that I gave my customary lecture on Platonic Friendship. You couldn't very well call it a discussion because I, being more interested in it than most people are, talked more than my share—and he, not being interested in the subject, it seemed, said less than his share. He thought it existed but rather between people who were of different ages than between those who were of about the same ages.

He said that he'd send me a present after he had returned to Cedar Falls, and asked me whether there was anything special I'd like, a ring or a pin or something like that. It was all I could do to keep from rolling right off the bank with surprise and consternation, for of course I could not accept jewelry. I said hastily that I really didn't care for jewelry which is very true, and that I'd get much more enjoyment out of a book. But he seemed very unwilling to give up the idea of something on which I could have my initials.

It would be just like Armand to think that I am not writing just because he isn't. Which certainly is not the case. I am not writing because I'm not writing, that's all.

That night Mr. Gray came over and we went to the park concert. We seated ourselves on the grass and planted a circle of smoking punk all about us, and then we talked of many things. I told him about the three stages people had to go thru in becoming acquainted with me—it's really only a matter of becoming used to my different moods. He declared that he was pretty sure that he would escape the second stage. I said, "Well, they all say that" and assured him that he had no more chance of escaping the second stage than anyone else—seeing that even Paula had been obliged to go thru it. This last statement seemed to convince him, so now he is in a great hurry to get thru with it so that he'll have it over and done with, and so that he may glide serenely on to the third stage.

He said, "I'd like to know you." I said, "Well, you know me now, don't you?" And he said, "Yes, but I want to know you well." I told him that would take a long time because I was such an almost insoluble riddle even to myself. Whereupon he gravely informed me that he liked riddles.

He said, "There is so much to you. One finds out something new about you all the time. There isn't much to me. People can tell what I am like as soon as they meet me." Which is not so. One finds out more and more about him as one goes along altho, being as frank and sincere as he is, one's first impression of him is usually correct.

He asked me what my greatest aim in life was. At first I was going to say "To marry happily," but then I said, "To get all that out of me which is in me," which includes the former; for I guess I could not accomplish the latter without the former.

I told him about my ideas on magazine illustration—for instance that I thought it was a crime to give the public bad pictures even tho they demanded it. Surely it is wrong to give a child candy and candy and candy when its stomach is out of order as it is, *from* candy. I told him that I thought it was my duty to give the public the best that I was able to do. I said if all illustrators were conscientious enough to do that, the public would gradually grow to appreciate good stuff. Therefore I thought it was my duty, altho I would play such an almost insignificant part in it, to be conscientious and refuse to cheat the public even tho the public would slash me a little (or much) for doing so.

He said that I have the funniest laugh of anyone he ever heard. It's like this:—"Tsh-sh-sh-sh." I said, "I didn't know I laughed like that." That is not the only way I laugh, tho. I guess I must have about fifteen ways of showing my joy, merriment or mirth—you can't call it *laughing,* I haven't anything that could be called by that name. He described another one of my laughs as sounding like a bird—just beginning to sing. Not sentimentally, I'd have you know. He isn't a sentimental fool, for which, thank goodness.

He asked me what my belief was. I told him I was very undecided but that I certainly did not believe that our existence ended with this world. He said that he, too, didn't know exactly what to think. I said I did not think I would get much satisfaction out of simply being an angel and having a golden voice—I thought it would be nobler to be a soul, and watch and help some struggling mortal whose lot was much the same as mine had been while I had been on earth.

I do think that much of the Bible is taken too literally. It's just, for instance, as if people would take literally what I said about my talks with the sunset or anything like that. It does not happen just exactly as I tell it but what *does* happen is more wonderful than I could ever tell.

While we were in the midst of this discussion Stella, Judy and Paula came over and sat down. After the band concert we all walked for a long while and sang just about every song we could think of. We are so used to having Mr. Gray's voice in there now, that I am sure we shall miss it very much for some time to come. Mr. Gray insisted that I get up in the morning to say goodbye to him. I told him I would if I were awake.

I did wake, and just as the clock had finished striking four I heard our signal whistle (which he had discovered a few days before). It was still dark so we didn't exactly see each other but I whistled twice and then he said, "Well so long." I said, "So long" and I saw two figures move up along the street. There was a heavy mist thru which the stars and moon glowed dimly. The mists were almost as beautiful as those which I had seen down at grandma's only these, instead of clinging to the earth, floated about sixty feet or so above the earth and folded themselves about the church spire. I indulged in a variety of Hloopsie sensations, taking deep breaths of the dark, sweet air, and gazing greedily at the east which was slowly becoming lighter.

After a while I went to bed again but was not able to go to sleep for a long while. I wanted badly to cry, altho I don't just know why. For Mr. Gray, I guess. Not because he was going. To tell the truth, I was rather glad that he was not going to stay until September. All the same I see no reason why I *shouldn't* want to cry for him. I really love him. I suppose it seems funny that I should love a person without being, or even thinking of being, in love with him. But you see I love Theresa and Paula but I am not in love with *them* either. The point I want to make is, that I have not been going with Mr. Gray simply because I like to have a man to step around with, or that I might increase my knowledge of human nature (which Armand accused me of doing last fall) but because I sincerely liked him and because I felt a fine strong bond of friendship between us.

As a matter of conscience, I showed Mr. Gray much of Myself last Sunday. I felt that I would be deceiving him if I did not show him some of my deeper layers. I thought perhaps he would be disappointed in me if he saw that I was not simply the laughing, irresponsible creature that he had found me (you remember I had just decided to "forget" when I met him) but he liked Myself best of all and wants to have nothing to do with my Me's. He took to my Me and Myself idea with a promptness that was beautiful to see. That always raises a person a number of pegs in my estimation directly.

August 21, Friday

Tuesday I got a card from Mr. Gray and to-day came a letter—just about the kind of letter I expected him to write, altho I must confess I wasn't prepared for such a frank statement of his feelings as he did send. It seems he is missing me a good deal and does not hesitate in telling me that he is so blue that if you'd hold him up against the sky you could not see him, and altho *he* is having a good time, *Himself* is lonely. It seems he is in the habit of sending Himself down south (which of course means no farther south than this, our little German city). I have never told him how I send *Myself* about on visits so he deserves the credit of being an apt and rather satisfactory disciple of what bids fair to become my favorite theory—"that that is, is not, etc."

Last night I had a fierce drawing-fit. I stayed up until 2:30 a.m. I made eight sketches in black and white and pastel:—

> "Tilted Nose"
> "A Child's Laugh"
> "The Tussy In Me"
> "The Shadow of a Curl"
> "Abominable"
> "I, with a French roll"
> "The French roll again"
> "Curves in Pencil"

They are all of myself. I don't believe any of them are clever, I was thinking so sincerely and earnestly and vigorously while I was drawing. This morning I did a pastel sketch, "Tussy's French roll and green and purple." It is easy to see, I suppose, that French rolls are my latest fad. I try them on everyone that comes along (almost). I am wearing my hair that way to-day and I rather like it, altho I looked "mouskinny" when I wore them that way last night.

Yesterday we went to a quilting picnic at Hershl's. We made three quilts. Afterwards we told our fortunes with the newly-made quilts. It turned out that I was not very much in love, that I was going to be en-gaded before anyone else present but that I was to be an old maid and that there was absolutely no hope of my ever marrying.

I sent off Armand's letter to-day too. It is three weeks since I wrote last. I am afraid my letters to Armand have been very waily. He told me once that I was a nuisance. I am just that. I often wonder that I have any friends at all. I always expect so much of them. I mean I expect them to take so much of me. I force my diary extracts and letters on them whether they enjoy them or not, and bother them with my good and bad ideas all mixed. I mean it's as if I gave a basket full of peas to some one for a present, not sorted. It isn't that I don't take the time to sort them but that I haven't had much experience in sorting peas and am afraid, therefore, that I'll throw some away that ought to belong to the present.

Oh I want badly to be back at St. Paul. I have written to Mr. Mc-Whorter again. I want so much to be down there by the first of September but I don't suppose it can be managed. I don't feel like doing anything, simply because everything is so uncertain.

I don't know where I am. Coming back to my old fault of thinking, that's certain. I wish someone would come and shake me, so that I could be sure that I am in the same world in which I have been living until a short while ago.

I wish someone would come and whack me if I am not doing what is right and best to do.

I wish someone would come and say, "Keep it up" if I am doing what I ought to do.

August 24, Monday

I have written to Armand:—

> "Somehow I don't feel much like writing to you lately. I always have the feeling that I'm not writing to any person—you seem so very abstract to me just now.
>
> "Do I seem like a *person* to you, or do I seem just like some mental creation which you in some wild flight of fancy have fashioned? But surely in even your wildest flights you couldn't (or perhaps I should say, *wouldn't*) fashion a creature so troublesome, bewildered and *oh everything*, as I am."

August 28, Friday

Much has happened, at least enough for a while. Last Monday I got a letter from Mr. McWhorter—a very nice one. I am to have a position at some designing house, but for the first part I am to have only $3 a week and it's up to me to raise my salary. I am going to start work Monday I guess, and am going to St. Paul to-morrow morning, early.

Mr. McWhorter said——

Aug. 29, Saturday. About 7 p.m. St. Paul

——I don't remember what he said. I'm in St. Paul now, at the Y.W.

I wrote Armand and asked him to let me know whether or not he could come to the depot, so that I could ask someone else. And he never wrote at all about it. Which was certainly inconsiderate, for I could not ask anyone else of course, after waiting until Friday afternoon for an answer, and I nearly collapsed with all those packages.

I was glad enough that he didn't come for it made things more convenient all around, but I do think he might have written a few words to the effect that he would not be able to come.

I wonder what excuse he'll have. I suppose he'll have it scalloped all around with silk and decked with perky velvet bows. And he'll present it to me on a silver tray like a butler, sort of, these little considerations arising not out of chivalry but from an intention to direct my mind from the real excuse, so that I will unconsciously look over that little infirmity which so many excuses suffer from. Lameness.

To-night he called up and asked if I would be home Monday. Monday. Monday! I told him that in all probability I would be at work. Monday noon he is coming to call on me. At least he said so. I won't believe it until he is actually there.

If he isn't a pieface, I'd like to meet one. If he isn't, I want to be spared the meeting of anyone who comes nearer to it than he does. The worst part is, I can't dislike him even if he is a pieface. In fact, I'm sure if he weren't one I shouldn't like him very well. Be it understood that I am not referring to his not coming to the depot. He may have had some plausible reason for not coming, but I can think of no excuse that he may have had for not letting me know about it. It isn't the nicest thing in the world for a girl to come in the depot of a large city with no one there to meet her or to greet her. It isn't.

Now that I have this off my mind I can probably recollect what it was that Mr. McWhorter said.

And Monday! when I am here this very minute all bottled up and bewildered with the thoughts that have accumulated for three months.

———

7:45 p.m.:—Mr. Gray just called up from Cedar Falls, which was nice— oh very nice. He telephoned to see whether I had arrived safe and sound and said he'd be here sometime next week. It makes me so happy to think that someone cares how I got here.

Only about a week ago it seemed to me that I wouldn't be able to keep myself from pinching Armand to make sure that he really *was*. But he's real allright; ding real.

Aug. 30, Sunday evening

I've been with Timmie Frendel to his home for supper, and after supper he came down to the Y.W. with me, where we have been talking of many things. Timmie brought a note from Armand who is still out at Lake Minnetonka. It seems I wrote in my letter that I was coming Monday and put on the back of the envelope, "I *might* come Saturday." When he read this it was too late to answer and he sent me a telegram (which I never got).

Aug. 31, Monday

Armand has been here. Armand and a mustache—at least the beginning of one. Armand and a mustache. Young men and mustaches rarely go together as it is, but *Armand!*

It was a lucky thing that he was looking down when I first saw the old thing, so he didn't see the expression on my face. I felt like saying to him, "Goofie! Goofie!" I said nothing about it however. It makes him look weak and foppish *and* unaesthetic. It spoils his profile entirely by making his chin seem to recede. I mean his face looks sort of like a pennant from the side.

I told Armand that I had discovered a number of characteristics thru his letters. He asked me to enumerate them, and I told him that he was too egotistical and that he was not considerate enough in little things. He accused me of being introspective and asked me whether anyone else had called my attention to it, to which I replied that Timmie had said just that last night. It seems my three worst faults at present are:—

1. Selfishness
2. Interpreting the world thru Myself (instead of me thru the world, perhaps) and
3. Jumping at conclusions as far as actions of people are concerned. (Saturday, for instance.)

Oh why does he have an old mustache? When I look up at him unthinkingly and see his face the way it is now (having expected to see it the nice way from force of habit) I want either to set my teeth or look away. I know he is just about dying to know what I think about it.

I said, "Oh I found the best name for you this summer," and when he asked me what it was I said, "Pieface." He wanted to know just how I would describe a pieface, and suggested a number of adjectives which were so far wrong that I know he hasn't the slightest idea of what pieface means. I told him I couldn't think of any adjectives applicable to the word but——

"But you mean," he said, "that if anyone wants a good definition of pieface, they should look at me." Which was true enough. I did tell him that one applied neither "good" or "bad" to the word pieface—that it was more a *character*.

Sept. 1, Tuesday

Well I have started working at Buckbee Mears to-day. To be perfectly frank with myself, I do not like it. Of course I only practiced today but it has been practice for what I am to do later. I drew superficial ladies' heads and finished them up with some wash of a very exact and thankless nature.

I do not like the work for four reasons:—

1. I do not know whether I will be able to make a success of it—it being so different from anything that my nature inclines to.

2. The hours are from 7:00 a.m. to 5:30 p.m. with only 45 minutes intermission for noon—and unless they give me work which calls for originality, I do not know whether my nerves will be able to stand it. In doing work like I have been doing to-day, I cannot get rid of the amount of Myself-stuff that I have to get rid of every day. And I dare hardly draw after I get home after having drawn all day. I will have to take care of my body, and will not be able to sit up nights and draw because I'll have to get up in time to get up to work every day except Sunday.

3. The woman who has charge of me does not tell me *definitely* what they want, and seems afraid to hack away. And I am anxious to get over the *learning* stage.

4. It is a greater strain on my eyes than anything I have ever come across. If I should have to do this very stuff for one month my eyes would be absolutely ruined by the end of it. They are so tired to-night that I can scarcely look without half-squinting.

And oh, when will I get time to read?

I am so disappointed and disgusted with myself. I know I shall just be a burden to my friends all winter. I do not want to, I will try not to, but I am so afraid I will have to. Here I am with $30 to my name, and with no position except one which will wear upon me physically; and with much, oh much, that I must get rid of with neither the time nor the means to get rid of it by.

Sept. 2, Wednesday

To-day the work was a trifle more agreeable. My eyes were overused again of course. I suppose I'll have to get glasses—as soon as I can afford to do so. Miss West, who has charge of me, seems to be very nice which is very comforting. I took a fling to-day and started a full-length figure of a woman in evening dress. I want to try pen and ink on it to-morrow. I don't like to do wash-drawings. I always get them so ding stiff.

The thing that is bothering me most is that I shall probably have to be working for a long time without pay*—Miss West told me that she had to do finicky catalogue wash-drawings for *years*. If I were not aiming farther than a position for life with Buckbee Mears, I wouldn't so *much* mind doing old wash drawings *for years,* but as it is—glory I'll have to earn money *soon*. I need new clothes, almost an entire new winter outfit, and aside from that I'll have to live.

Last night I cried.

Which just reminds me that Monday Armand said, "You said in your letter 'I can't fight alone.' " I agreed. He said, "You can." *He said "You can." Alone.* I told him I could not for any length of time without "forgetting" every so often, and that I might get to the stage where it would be necessary to forget oftener than was good for me. He said, "Do you mean that someone is to take half of your burden?" I said I meant that different people should take different little portions.

He has easy talking; he is a man. If he were a slip of a girl with no money-making abilities—not even in art, ding it—he might have to turn to other people too.

The mustache does not bother me so much, for the reason that I can scarcely imagine it now that I haven't seen it for two days. It seems as if it had been only a bad dream, in the way that I used to dream that Mr. Doom and Mr. Winkler were growing mustaches. I have now about a dozen points against the mustache, and at least ten different and very effective methods of presenting them, and they are all so good that I don't know which one I am to take. I suppose I'll take none of them and say whatever comes in my mind when I do say it, and I suppose it won't be at all effective.

September 5, Saturday

I had lunch with Mr. McWhorter last Thursday. He just saved me from tumbling over the brink of something—discouragement, perhaps. He told me not to worry about not having enough money until I earned some at Buckbee Mears. He told me it would all come out all right in the end, and if anything was the matter I should just tell him all about it. Which was very nice of him. He is getting to be nicer to me right along. He told me that he was going to be my Uncle Mac, and explained that meant he was going to do all he could for me.

* By this time I had discovered that I was not even to receive the $3 a week I had expected.

Armand took me to "The Whip" last night. I had a fine time. The play was so ridiculously melodramatic that we hooted practically thru the whole performance. At first I was going to talk about the mustache, but I knew right after I saw him that I wouldn't. Once, in calling my attention to something in the play, he put his hand on mine and left it there for a very short while. My first impulse was to draw away my own hand immediately (I have myself trained so well in that respect that I can do it almost subconsciously) but then I didn't. Perhaps it's silly to be so sensitive to little things like that, but I am reserving those things for my husband, if I get one. And if I don't—oh well, if I don't—then—well, I hope I will. I sincerely hope I will. It's so hard to keep your friends Platonic when you're not married, and it would be wearing to have your Platonic friends continually becoming un-Platonic until you were an old maid.

September 6, Sunday

Last night Mr. Gray came. He thinks he has passed thru the "second stage" but I told him he had not. He thinks too that he has been raking me over the coals in some of his letters for not writing. As a matter of fact, it was more like begging me to write rather than scolding me for not writing. He is going to be at Cedar Falls all winter and is planning on coming up to St. Paul *once a week* to see me.

The poor fellow has been starving for a good long talk with some one, it seems. That's just it, ding it. They find me only too willing to talk of sensible things, and also find it rather easy to confide in me it seems (judging by the way they do at least) and then they think they are in love with me. One thing makes me glad tho. A good many of my latest friends like me for *myself* and not because I draw.

It's too bad about Mr. Gray. Too bad about me too, for that matter. I'd hate awfully to lose his friendship and that is what it will have to come to eventually, unless Mr. Gray has the goodness and sense to come and see me and talk to me even after he knows what my attitude towards him is. It would be rather nice if I could fall in love with Mr. Gray because he is so very nice, but I know I can't, of course. That's Armand's fault. No, I mean it's Armand's fault (or virtue) that I will never *imagine* myself to be in love with Mr. Gray. *Because*—thru Armand's help I have outgrown my former Self, the Self that perhaps would be perfectly willing to accept Mr. Gray.

Now, if I could not adapt myself so easily to different people I wouldn't

Top: Self Portrait in Japanese Costume—Charcoal
Bottom: Charcoal Studies of my Left Hand

Three Self Portraits in Pencil

have so many cavaliers. That's a discovery I made this morning and it's true. I have been able to adapt myself equally well to farmers, a telegraph operator, an engineer, an electrician, (I guess he's an electrician, Mr. Gray I mean) and an artist or two. Also a science student. Also Armand (only he doesn't belong to the cavaliers). Also a newspaper reporter (and he doesn't belong to the cavaliers either).

A fierce characteristic to have—introspectiveness. I was getting along beautifully this last week—I mean I wasn't doing much self-analysis—until I got started on this adaptability-idea. But in a way one gets along much faster in the world. Yesterday, after I had made a pen sketch, Miss West came and looked at it. Before she criticized it I picked out three parts and said these were the only ones worth while. I could see that I had just taken the words out of her mouth. "You know your own work, don't you?" she said.

Last night when I came home I made five sketches of myself so it was about 1 a.m. until I got to bed. I learned something too. That is, I learned to *look* for a shadow which one often finds on the cheek or throat or nose. One makes it darker and bolder than I have been used to making it. The drawings are called:—

> "The Triple Roll"
> "Curved Cheek"
> "Oh Just'"
> "The curves of a Head" *
> "Curling upwards"

This morning I played piano for a good while and got rid of much of what was inside of me. In the afternoon Mr. Gray called and we took the car to Columbia Heights where we played guitar and sang. On the way home, while looking at my Kewpie Ring, I remarked that I had the string wound about it because it was a little too big, and Mr. Gray said, "I guess I'll have to get you one," (still harping on that) whereupon I answered "no" very decisively and did one of my curvey motions with my arm. He said, "You won't take any suggestions, will you?"

September 11, Friday

Monday was Labor Day. In the morning I wrote a letter home and I sketched all afternoon. After supper I sketched again. The first time in my life that I really appreciated Labor Day.

Tuesday evening Armand dropped in unexpectedly. He asked how I

* See illustration facing this page.

was and I told him "Tired." I was, oh very tired. I am not used to being bound down to certain hours of work and it's very hard on my system. Particularly because I have so little time to myself.

After a while I brought some pictures down and also my diary. I started reading my diary, and by the time I got to the *maelstrom* part he had become *electrical* again. That is, his mood was so intense that it saturated and shook the air. At such times I can always tell, before I look up, just how he is looking or acting at the time. Usually he will sit with his body bent forward a little and be staring into space with eyes that are at the same time cold and burning, and with a mouth which is set so firmly that one is afraid it will quiver with the keenness of his determination. Curiously enough, the firm set of his mouth seems to denote his indetermination.

It was very wearing, and finally I got so that I could scarcely talk straight. I was ready to fling the diary upon the table or the floor or anywhere it would go, and tell Armand that I couldn't possibly read any more just then, when Armand himself suggested a way out of the matter. He rose violently and said, "Shall we take a short walk?" I said "yes" and went up to get my wraps.

When we got out we raced—absolutely raced. It was just what I needed. My thoughts had been racing so all week that I felt somewhat relieved when I found the rest of me catching up with my thoughts.

For a long while we said nothing. We had slowed down in walking at my request, but before I knew it I was simply flying along again. Armand called my attention to this and I told him that it was caused by my having to hurry all the time lately. "I have to hurry to work, and I have to hurry to lunch, and I have to hurry back again," I said.

"Too much hurry," he said. Of course too much hurry. Of *course* too much hurry.

Long silence again.

Armand:—"You're allright, girl. You're a brick." Extremely relevant, you'll notice.

Much racing in dimly lighted streets.

Armand:—"You're doing me a devil of a good turn tonight. You're paying me back with a vengeance." Very lucid.

At one time I asked him if he believed in intuition. He said he did to some extent. I said I did too. He asked for an instance and I said that many of the things I said were the result of intuition—"Not intuition alone, intuition tempered with reason."

He said, "There you have it—intuition *tempered* with reason."

I said, "Just now you are tempering reason with intuition, but don't know but that you ought to follow intuition tempered with reason."

He admitted that was so. I knew he would, before I had said more than three words of the statement. At times my mind is so clear that the rest of me sort of stands off and regards Myself with awe and wonder. For of course it was Myself speaking. Oh, Myselves are the most beautiful things in the world.

I told him I had often seen him try to drown X, and that I could just see X in the different stages of going under as his reason gained the upper hand. I can see X give a few final gasps and finally subside.

"You tell jokes, don't you?"

He agreed.

"And play the half dollar game?"

"You're right," he said laughing.

Oh, I know when he tries to push X away out of sight. I know it every time, and oh, to think that he should want to. X is the greatest and wisest thing he has and he puts it into a strait-jacket. No wonder X causes him so much trouble when it does get out.

One difference between Armand and me is that to me Myself is *the* great thing, a thing which I can trust to do what is right—and to him, Himself is something which is to be the making of him but which needs a little bit of systematizing. To me, Myself is that part of me which should rule—and to him, Himself is something which he wants to conquer so that he can merge it with something else—I don't know what.

Perhaps when he raced so that evening it was because he was irritated by Himself, X. A number of times he had a queer look on his face. I said, "Don't look like that. Do you feel *allright,* looking that way? You look as I look when I hate myself."

Armand told me that there were two parts to him. His intellectual Me's were jumping on X, and X was being hurt very much. How I pity poor X. Whatever Myself has to endure, it at least has my approval. To justify himself he said that if he would not drown X he would say things which would harm both him and me. And of course he harms neither of us by saying what he says now—*oh no!*

We talked of Mr. Gray too, and Armand said, "What's the matter? Is he in love with you?"

I said, "He thinks he is."

Armand:—How do you know he isn't?

Wanda:—(unfolding a theory she has cherished for a long time) Because I don't believe that one person can love another without the other loving him in return.

Armand:—I think that's possible.

Wanda:—I don't. Not *real* love.

Oh I don't want to believe that! Oh I don't want that the world should be arranged so sadly.

By this time we were back at the Y.W. again so we shook hands. Armand said, "Thank you. You did me a world of good."

Thursday evening Mr. Gray came. I rashly promised once that I would give him a sketch of myself, and now he is bound to have a big one which he can frame and *hang up in his room*. I do not want myself *framed* and hung up in his room. I felt so guilty when I came home last night. I feel that I ought to let him see how I feel about the matter and yet that would seem so ridiculous—I mean it would look as if I were taking much for granted. I am so careful not to say anything that might be interpreted to mean that my attitude is other than it is. *Because* that is hard on the other person—said she, speaking from experience.

He has a kodak picture of me in his watch. "So it won't get lost," he explained. He telephoned to-night and asked me when that sketch would be done. I said I'd make the sketch on one condition, the condition being that he will not frame it.

Sept. 12, Sunday

Yesterday afternoon Armand called for me and we went to Como Park. We sat down on the grass and then I read part of my diary to Armand. I said, "Would you like to hear what I think about the mustache?" He said, "Yes, go on read it." So I did. He hooted thru the whole thing and said, "When you're finished, I'll tell you how I came to grow one." Which he did. He said he just happened to be shaving one morning when his cousin came in. She said, "Armand, why don't you grow a mustache?" He said, "Allright" and immediately started growing one and forgot all about it. He said he left it on because it was so interesting—about half of his friends liked it and the other half didn't. Timmie said he looked like a butcher. Which is true. Funny I didn't think of that. Armand said he was inclined to side with Timmie and me, and said he'd "chop it off" pretty soon. Oh yes, some of his friends even declared he looked *aesthetic*. I'd like to see those people!

We returned to the topic we had started to discuss the other night. I asked him if he really believed that one person could be in love with another without the other loving in return. He said he did. I said, "Oh I don't like to believe that. I don't think that is so. Not *real* love."

Armand asked, "Well, what is real love?" and I replied, "I don't know." "That's a good definition," he said.

Just think, he says love, even real love, is not lasting. He says it may be a matter of a few hours or perhaps fifty years duration. Which I do not believe, ding it, *which I do not believe*.

He said something to the effect that a man could love and outgrow it after a while. *Which I do not believe*. That isn't the right kind of love. I say it isn't, ding it.

We talked of affinities. I aired all my old opinions in the matter and named the Brownings as an instance of "perfect love." I admitted that such perfect cases were rare.

As to his theory—he upheld that by a rather neat argument. He said, taking me for example:—"Say you have a capacity of four quarts (of intellect, emotion, education etc.) and Mr. Gray, for instance, has one quart. Now you have just that quart which satisfies Mr. Gray, which completes his quart, *but* you have three other quarts left—therefore he can be in love with you even tho you are not in love with him." Which is logical enough but I refuse to change my idea on the subject.

Armand said, "So you expect to meet your affinity—run into someone who has the four quarts which correspond to and complete your four quarts" and I said, "Yes. At least I hope so."

At least I hope so.

He said, "I wonder what would happen if I'd fall in love with you?" I don't see what he says such silly things for. "Not that there is much danger," he said, "but—" he wondered what would happen to him if he should join the ranks of cavaliers. The old pieface! Knows he could never be a cavalier!

He said by keeping a shell around oneself one was spared a following of sentimentalists. I said that I liked people so well that I couldn't keep in a shell, and that it seemed many boys misinterpreted my friendship for that reason. I mean, I am not ashamed to tell them that I like them or certain things about them, and as most girls are rather in the habit of making off they do not care for boys at all, they imagine that I feel towards them as they feel towards me.

He began analyzing the reasons why people might get cases on me. I don't remember them all. Intellect perhaps, and the ability to adapt myself easily to different people, "and you're attractive—don't wince—that has much to do with it and you know you are by no means homely."

I said, "Oh but I have such irregular features."

He said, "That doesn't matter. You are pretty sometimes—devilish pretty. If you don't know it, you might as well know that you have that——"

"—Fault?" I said.

But he said, "No it isn't a fault, I'd rather talk to a pretty girl myself, than to a chair with one leg off."

On the way home he wrote in the back of this diary something to the effect that there was more between the lines of this diary than ever was written in them. Of course there is. It would be a sad thing if these angular words, phrases and sentences did not convey more than just what I wrote. Of course there is. I am so frank with myself that when I come to my diary with my feelings in a nascent state, things cannot help but get into the diary some way. Seeing that I have not yet the ability to express the things adequately *in* the lines, the stuff goes between the lines.

Armand kept condemning poor Mr. Gray, sending him to the unpaintable Inferno etc., and said that he wished he could see him. He said he thought that there were some of his qualities he did not like. Perhaps not. On the other hand I am certain that there are a number of Armand's qualities that Mr. Gray would not be particularly wild about either. Nor would I blame him.

On the way home I sat at the car window and looked out, *and* I could have wept with very little trouble. Armand asked me what was the matter to which I had to reply, of course, that it was Mr. Gray. He said, "Don't worry about it, Wanda," and told me that as long as I acted merely as a friend to Mr. Gray it was not my fault if he would have to be disappointed—it was his own doing. Which is true I suppose, and it really comforted me a good deal to think that.

He said that my not getting paid was worrying him considerably. It is beginning to worry me too, for I have only about eleven or twelve dollars left.

I should not have let Armand know how *little* I cared for Mr. Gray. Here I have been wishing since last spring that someone would get a case on me for just that reason, and now I don't even take advantage of it. That's just it. Whatever I may not be, I am at least honest, not only in things that people see but in little things which only I myself know about.

September 14, Monday

Yesterday I had my first great *bawl* of the season. Glory I wept. I wrote diary in the morning and after dinner when I returned to my room I found myself flinging myself upon the bed and sobbing and sobbing. And writhing in anguish. I enjoyed it tho, in a certain way. It felt so good to be able to get rid of so much without having to unfold myself to anyone.

I—oh I cannot help how I am. I do my best to be what I am not—I try so hard to act the way I ought, and I find now that the reason why I can't control these things is (aside from being the result of my strong Myself) a great *outside* force in which I just swirl about helplessly. I feel myself being swept on either one way or another.

September 15, Tuesday

To-day I looked at myself in a triple mirror and glory I looked shabby. I was ashamed to go on the street.

Yesterday Armand called and said he'd meet me at the door of Buckbee Mears at 5:30. Which he did. We went to the Y.W. As I entered the door I saw, to my great surprise, Paula. I rushed over to her and then we all went into the Lounge where we talked of the war. I said I didn't side with anyone, and Armand said he didn't side with anyone either. I said I had almost come to the point where I did not think it the noblest thing in the world to do, to go to battle. And now I am there good and proper. I became quite heated over it, and ended up by saying that I didn't think those men had to fight in a war which the kings and kaisers and those old piefaces had started.

At the mention of piefaces Armand started out to tell Paula that I had said he was a pieface, and Paula, leaning back in her chair, nodded complacently and said, "Yes," and I said, "She's heard that before."

Oh yes, I said I didn't see any sense in shooting so many, many men on each side (of the war I was talking, you know) when it would serve the purpose just as well to kill, say one man on each side instead of 1,000 on each side. I said, "Why can't it be like a game, say that each country puts up 1,000 of their best men and then whoever wins, wins?" Whereupon Armand gave some logical but not convincing (to me) reasons why that would be impossible. That is, they were convincing enough, but oh ding it, I don't believe in that war, I don't believe in that war.

After he had left, Paula asked whether he always smiled so much. She said that he always seemed to have such a *freud* over the things he said. He *was* queer. Not facetious but as near that as a person can be to it without being it.

September 16, Wednesday

Paula is staying at the Y.W. until she finds a permanent place.

Last night I cried. Hard. I don't know why, but perhaps because I want neat-looking clothes (suit hat shoes). I wonder if I wail too much. If I do, I don't to my family at any rate. They do not know that I am not getting *any* pay at all. They think I am getting along allright and I want them to keep right on thinking that. Goodness knows I am an unhandy enough relative as it is.

I am so silly to-day. That is, I am silly in my own eyes. Most people don't notice that I am silly when I am. Paula does. I can always feel *Herself* boring thru my mood and saying to me, "Oh, Wanda, just why?" And she knows that it's only one of my clever Me's that says things which make other people laugh and think I am a funny little thing.

Getting introspective again, Wanda, aren't you? Don't. So I will close the diary.

September 18, Friday

Armand does not show nearly as much of himself as I do. He, half the time when he does make an opening, plasters it up soon after and puts on a label: "Forget this. It was a mistake."

In order to be less introspective, in order that I may think less about myself, I am analyzing other people's characters more. As a result of this I have found that Paula is about the most unselfish person I know. Also that Armand is not selfish but is not exactly unselfish either. To me there is a distinction between not being selfish and being unselfish. I am—but here I go again, forever analyzing myself.

Yesterday evening Armand called. He asked if I could get my hat and coat in one minute—Timmie was going away in a few minutes and we'd have to hurry if we wanted to get to the depot before the train pulled out. I did get my wraps in a hurry. We flew out of the Y.W. across the street and raced the entire length of a block to the car-line. Armand said he supposed people would think we were eloping.

After we got off the car we raced about two blocks to the depot. We must have been a funny sight. No wonder people stood and looked and whistled. I jammed down my hat so that it might not fly off and my cape streamed behind me, and Armand's coat flew as much as it could (it was a rather heavy one [and new I guess {and rather good-looking}]).

Armand said, "I suppose if any of my friends would see me they'd say, 'Well, Emraad has married at last.'"

We got to the depot in plenty of time.

Timmie asked me if I had had my salary raised as yet. Raised. If there'd be any to *raise* I'd be almost satisfied. He told me to be commercial and "keep to the eye" whatever that meant. Timmie is going to New York.

September 19, Saturday

It's a lovely world. Sunshine, and noises, and people.

There is not a pieface in all the world for me to-day, just now. I am not a pieface. I am a girl who—there I go again. I must say this about myself tho. Sometimes I am afraid of my eyes—because they know more than I do.

I have a bad cold. I stopped working at 3:30 yesterday on account of it. I was fuddled, and nervous and irritable. I don't think it's so much the work, as the working for nothing, that makes me nervous.

I am wearing my beloved plaid dress. Sunshine, crisp autumn air and a plaid dress make me want to race and jump and skip in spite of my cold. I don't believe I'd be afraid to meet the King of England in that dress—I feel so very natural in it. Aside from the way clothes look, I like them for the way they make me feel. I don't mean whether they're comfortable or not—I always get clothes that are comfortable if I can in any way help it—but I mean the things they make me feel, the thoughts they give me while I'm wearing them, the height to which they make my spirits rise. I like white stockings and black slippers but the slippers have to be pumps or "baby-dolls."

September 20, Sunday

And to-night—oh to-night I am suffering the agonies of unshed tears again.

Paula and I have had a serious, serious talk. Judy Dekker told Paula that so many people in New Ulm, lately, had asked with a sort of suspicious air why Mr. Weschcke wasn't paying my way this year too. They inferred that I had not made good, that Mr. Weschcke had been disappointed in me or something like that. First when she told me about this I laughed, sincerely and heartily. But after a while it occurred to me that it was not so funny after all. Not that I suffer much by it—I know so well that I am doing only what is right that it did not hurt me. But whatever I am blamed for, my family suffers by. Perhaps not definitely, but indefinitely. *And* suffering *indefinitely* is sometimes worse than suffering definitely.

Oh my darling, darling people. If it were not for the fact that I know I will ever be I, and You will ever be you, and that no one can take from us the only thing in which we are rich, I would scarcely be able to stand it.

They (people) have been in a most terrible suspense all the time for fear that I wouldn't get to the point where I would earn money. (I forgot to say that I am getting $5 a week now.) Paula reminded me of the time she had told me to draw magazine covers and said that was the result of hearing some remarks.

They expect me to make a great deal of money and, sort of along the side, to become famous. And when I want neither fame nor money. Ding it, ding it, ding it. I wish I had iron to bite or wood to gnaw or logs to chop. I know I need the money but I can't sit here serenely listening while they lose sight of the—of *the* thing.

I am afraid I shall have to disappoint them. If I were to become a popular magazine illustrator they would undoubtedly say, "Wanda has made good," whereas if I turn my art over to Life and win no fame, they will say, "She had talent but she didn't use it in the right way."

There are some whom I do not include here. They are the ones who say least but do most. If I ever do anything for New Ulm, it will be for these people (for them I respect and love and appreciate more than they will ever know perhaps) and for its woods and brooks and flowers.

Whatever people may feel towards me, they are afraid to tell me things face to face. If they only would. I know that I could justify anything I have ever done and I could explain to them just why I am taking the course I am taking. For four years, at least, my aim has been to go to Art School so that I could turn that part of me—the only part which is worth while—into money so that my sisters and brother would not have such a hard time getting an education as I had. The trouble is I am not a big, strapping, husky individual. I cannot work so very, very much. Even two weeks of work has made me more nervous than I have ever been, I think. And I am not commercial.

When I worry I do not worry nearly as much about myself as I seem to—I mean I often worry about myself but it is because of the family that I do so. If I had only myself to manage I should soon be in a position to do that satisfactorily, but that would not be noble.

Mr. McWhorter told me that as geniuses could not take care of themselves, it was the duty of other people to do so. *Because* genius belonged to the world. The individual who has been chosen as a sort of receptacle for it had no right to control it absolutely because it was not all his own. I do not mean to infer that I am a genius. Be I what I may be, I do know that there is much within me which is not all my own. That is why there are so many conflicts within me. Myself reminds me that I have no right to sacrifice it for anything, and on the other hand there is my family.

Even Paula did not know how well I could justify my present course. She said too that it made it hard for me. I asked, "Just why?" and she said that I could not even marry if I should choose to do so (or have occasion to do so, I thought) for a number of years. Which is true enough. I could not dream of marrying until I had them comfortably settled.

I must go to bed. I should not have written tonight for I am to go to an oculist tomorrow (Mr. McWhorter has made arrangements) and I am supposed to have my eyes rested.

September 25, Friday

I am having my eyes treated and can see things only in blurs, and now I am almost mad with the unwritten thoughts and feelings which are churning about within me. I guess I had better stop writing until I can see plainly again.

September 27, Sunday

I am still having my eyes treated but I can see enough to write, altho it is still almost impossible for me to read.

Tuesday Armand called. I had just started having my eyes treated and could not see plainly at all. He talked to me. Nice things about humanity. I couldn't for the life of me tell what he said but I absorbed it all.

By Saturday I was in the floor-pacy stage again—simply because I had been unable to read or write or draw all week. I called up Armand but I couldn't get him. Sunday, ditto.

At about the middle of the week I wanted badly to be a boy. Girls are such fools. I think girls are fools, and I as big a one as any.

Paula and Nina and I had a terribly exciting time at supper one evening last week. We discussed Woman's Suffrage and I was the only one *for*. I became quite excited of course. It seems to me that most people who are against suffrage don't exactly know what suffrage is in these days. I would never be a Suffragist if I still held my old view of what suffrage is.

The next evening at the supper table Paula, Rose Luedke * and I had a German talk. We are trying to improve our German, and as we can't very well talk on intellectual subjects with absolute seriousness in German, we make off that we are *Deutsche Hausfrauen* and we tell all about our husbands and our family matters.

My husband is always "Mein Bonifacius," his chief characteristic being the squandering of all our money in buying *Sanct Jacobs Oel* which he lavishes on his rheumatic joints.

Paula's husband used to be *Schuh-wichser* for the king but, because he did his work so well, he has now been appointed *"Herzog's Kanonputzer."*

Rose's name is Frau Schimmelpfennig, *vor der Hochzeit* Wiederkuchen. Upon being asked whether she had ever been in America she declared *"Oh ja, öfters"* but it transpired that she had never come further than Ellis Island for some reason unknown to her. She is absolutely killing. She can assume the narrow-minded views of people and also the *Klatschweibisch* attitude and expression to go with it. She declared that her husband had been *Strassenfeger* but that he had had a little habit of stealing brooms which resulted in his losing the position. The family seems to be *feginglich* inclined for her husband is now *Schornsteinfeger,* and after her husband had succeeded in bringing so many brooms from the street to their house, she took in *sweeping* just as some people take in washing. It's all kinds of fun.

It was the same evening I believe that Paula gave me a lecture. She told me I was too self-centered. I could not deny it, I am. I'm trying very hard to get away from my introspectiveness. She told me that I talked to people of myself. I had not realized this before but after she called my attention to the fact, it seemed to me that I did that. She thinks I do that in order to make people interested in me. She thought also I thought so much about myself and talked so much about myself and wrote (in my diary) so much about myself, because I thought so much *of* myself; because I considered myself a very interesting person.

* Mr. Weschcke's secretary, staying at the Y.W.C.A.

Which is not so at all. I think so much about myself because, good-night! I've got to think about something always, and I have myself with me all the time which makes it handy—it's for the same reason that I draw myself so much. I talk the way I do, not because I want to show people that I am interesting, but because the things inside of me almost make me mad if I don't spill and spill and spill. I write so much about myself and do so much self-analysis because I have to do much within the next few years and—well it may be wrong and injurious in many ways to be too introspective, but the better you know the relation of yourself to the world the faster you get along.

She said that my friends might get tired of me on account of that. I should not think that my friends would adjust their liking or not liking me by my faults. That's what other people do, but not one's friends. One's friends are those people who know one's worst faults and who stick to one in spite of them, even on *account* of them, I should say. *Because* the more faults one has, the more one needs friends. Not only *real* faults, but also the more faults one has *in other people's* eyes, the more one needs friends. I hope I do not like one person better than another because he or she has less faults than the other. You cannot list people's faults and virtues and judge them accordingly. *Because* faults and virtues are of different sizes and weights, and oh, things would never balance.

After that lecture of Paula's I loved her very much. I knew she was saying all those things for my good, and I knew she was justified in saying much of it. I took it meekly enough and went to my room de-nouncing myself vehemently and raking myself over innumerable tons of coal. I could not go to sleep for a long time. I tossed around and could not rest because my faults seemed to glare out at me all the time. And still I was glad, rather glad, that I had them. I mean, I thought it would be so interesting to try to eliminate them.

By the way, this lecture, I rather think, was the result of a talk between Paula and Nina. I know that Nina influenced Paula in several things because I could see her views filtering thru Paula's arguments—I know Nina thinks I think too much of myself. She said once, "Well, Wanda, you can't deny that you are a child of fortune and that things have come your way. Oh you deserve it allright but you haven't *worked* for it."

I said, "I *have* worked. Does it matter whether one works with one's mind or one's hand?"

She said, "Yes, but working with your mind is talent. It is not work."

Talent—not work! I have noticed that so many people think that artists and writers and musicians don't have to work and that their talent does it all. Of course talent helps. But it is certainly a fact that talent will bring you nowhere and will not keep you anywhere without much work.

September 28, Monday

My darling Theresa came today.* At supper we talked as we did of old. After supper we sang all the old songs and then we took Nina over to Art School. Raymon Bowers met us just as we were going on the elevator, and both Theresa and I forgot entirely about introducing him to Nina. After Raymon had gone she made some sarcastic remark about its being very polite of us to do as we had done etc.

I said, "Nina, now don't be sarcastic, because I can't stand it."

If she wants to be sarcastic she may as well know right away that I will not stand for it. I absolutely refuse to have sarcastic friends. I can tolerate selfish or egotistical friends, I do not love my friends the less for being absent-minded, I can even stand enigmatical friends, but *sarcastic friends* is a contradiction in my opinion.

If she had said, "Now Wanda I think it was very ill-bred of you not to introduce me to Mr. Bowers," I wouldn't have minded it. Goodness knows I am a big pieface in a conventional or society way. I can go thru performances again and again, and when the next time comes I have no more idea of what the approved form of meeting it is than I ever did before. It doesn't mean anything to me, therefore I cannot remember. I am doing my best to get over it. Time and again I have even *known* what was the correct thing to do and I haven't done it, I don't know why, I'm sure.

After we returned from art school we were caught up in a little social whirlpool and swirled around for some time. Finally Theresa and I were left alone. I had not many confidential things to tell (only about Mr. Gray and the ring etc.) but Theresa had much. She and her Bill are as much as engaged and have been having nice serious times together.

September 29, Tuesday

We had a discussion about Egotism to-night. To-night I like people who are egotistical. I know it is one of my pendulum ideas again and of course I'll slow down a little later, but just now I can't help liking

* She was taking another year at Art School.

those people better who have too much self-confidence than those who cringe. I see no reason why one human being should cringe before another. I told them my idea of egotism differed somewhat from the definition given in the dictionary but, for lack of a more adequate name, I had to use it.

Nina thought that Armand was much to blame for this egotism in me and that my diary was to blame for my introspectiveness. To her, egotism, selfishness and introspectiveness mean practically the same thing. Not to me. She said that being introspective and self-centered made me selfish—which is true. I know I am selfish but I repeat, I repeat, that it is only with the most unselfish motives.

Paula says that of course I am interesting, but that I ought not to think I was the only one of only a few who were interesting, because one could find a Myself in everybody if one looked long enough. If one looked long enough—yes. Why are people such cowards—why don't they show *Themselves?* I believe that what Paula said is quite true, but I cannot at present go around and look for the Myselves in people who do not interest me, when there are a good many Myselves at home who will soon need my help. I would like nothing better than finding the Myselves in people and I intend to do much of it, but just now I have enough to keep afloat myself.

October 2, Friday

Paula and Theresa and I had another discussion last night. It was caused by a certain Miss Perkins insisting on reading parts of her love-letters to us. Such funny letters. She calls her beloved either "the kid," "my he-male" or "my friend."

I don't know how this led to the subject of Platonic friendship but it did. I suppose I was responsible to a great extent for its happening. Yesterday I read about Victor Hugo and Juliette Drouet in Harper's Bazaar. They published some of her love letters to him. They are certainly nothing extraordinary. It seems that after Victor Hugo was married he fell in love with this Juliette and he requested her to write him two love-letters a day even tho they met often. It seems also that his wife never complained and that she was very nice towards Juliette, bearing her no malice whatever. Now it seems to me it would have been infinitely more interesting to have read his wife's letters or diary or something like that.

Paula said that she should call her relationship to the boys we graduated with, Platonic. I certainly should not. I said that Platonic, to me, did not mean only *dispassionate*—it meant even *affection* in a certain way. It doesn't even mean that it should be emotionless. I think that even with Platonic friends there is emotion. To me a Platonic friend is a person in whom you are intensely interested, whom you like very much, but one whom you cannot marry because he is not your affinity.

Paula stated that if she were married she would never want her husband to go anywhere with another woman nor would she want to go anywhere with another man. Theresa and I differed. By this I do not mean to infer that Theresa and I would consider it perfectly allright for our husbands to go chasing around with other women. We want him for our very own, just as *much* as Paula does, but we do not intend to wrap ourselves up in our husbands alone and expect our husbands to wrap themselves up in us alone.

Paula says that she would want her husband to love her so much that he would be jealous of other men. Theresa and I want our husbands to know us so well that they need have no fear, which is akin to jealousy it seems to me.

Also I believe in partnerships: I should want my husband to be strong sometimes and pull me across the line, and I should want to be strong enough myself sometimes to draw him over in certain things.

I wonder if I will be an old maid.

Paula says she cannot see how I can *write* all I do in my diary. She said that she could not see how I can sit down and calmly analyze my feelings. I said, "Calmly, Paula? Calmly! With the tears rolling down my cheeks!" She said that they had learned in Psychology that as soon as one began to analyze one's feelings they became less intense. I said, "Well, then it's good to write them down." But she did not seem to think so.

I told her, too, that sometimes when I sat down to write I was perfectly calm, but that as I would go on I would become so worked up about a thing that I would have to stop. When I said that about the tears rolling down my cheeks, she said that my diaries didn't *sound* as if I had been calm, but they sounded as if they were written by a *third* person in the first person.

I told her that when I wrote most intensely I was by no means analyz-ing—that in such cases I had no idea what I wrote, which is true, for often when I have read over what I have written before, I have been very much surprised to see what I had written. I said, "One does not think. One simply feels, and your hand does the rest. It's just as if I were drawing. When I draw I simply feel—I do not think of what kind of lines I am making."

I told her too that I did not think she understood what my diary means to me. "It is not a book," I said, "it is part of me," and I explained how my diary seemed just another of my minds.

She thought writing things would spoil the "sacredity" of things. She seemed to think that one would *want* to *keep* those things in one. I tried to explain that even tho I wrote and spilled, there would still be all that in me which I could not express.

She told me that she thought the only test for me (to see whether I truly loved a man) would be to make me choose between art and love, and *then* if I chose love I would truly love the man. She said of course it would be impossible for me to give up drawing entirely, therefore she would arrange it this way: She would make me choose between the man I loved (if I loved one) and my drawing materials, because without the materials I could not draw even if I felt like it. I said as to that, one might tell her to choose between giving up sleep entirely and the man she loved.

She said of course that plan about the materials was impossible and merely a supposition, but I really don't see much sense in bringing an impossible supposition into an argument when it is of no consequence anyway. I have no right to give up drawing (or else why was that talent given to me?) and surely no one has a right to suggest that I should choose between it and love. Of course Paula does not mean at all that she would have me give up art, she merely says that IF I were encountered by such a problem, I would have to choose love just to show that I really appreciated love. If I really would have to choose between the man I loved and drawing, I should probably die on the spot, for I couldn't help loving and I couldn't help drawing.

I have not seen Armand since Tuesday a week ago. Armand said once in a letter that his friends had his sword, and his money, and something else, I forget what it was. Well, they certainly haven't his *time*.

Just pure common sense might have told him that, seeing I could not read, write, draw, sew, play piano, or even go walking in the sunshine, I would need to talk. Of course there are others: Paula, Theresa, Nina and Rose, and occasionally people I don't know so very well, like my eye doctor, Dr. Beaudoux. But I need all I can get. He might know that, seeing I had nothing to do but think and eat (and eating doesn't take up much of my time or thought) for about eleven days, I should want to talk, especially at about the time I had the egotistical streak. The girls had no patience with me when I talked on that subject, and Armand and I would have gotten along beautifully for once.

He's an old *humje* that's what he is. (One pronounces it *humptje*.) Since he insists on trying to analyze "pieface" I shall call him something which has the two advantages of being immune to analysis (seeing I've invented it) and of having a rather definite meaning in my mind.

Goodbye dear diary; Wanda.

* * *

October 6, 1914. Tuesday

I suppose Stella began teaching school yesterday. I hope she is getting along allright. Stella is unselfish—so beautifully so that she does not know she *is* unselfish. She does not wail as I do; she is much braver in that respect. She has a fine, big heart, and a marvelous insight into character (marvelous in that she has seen so little of the world).

I do not know what my attitude towards Armand is now nor do I know what his is towards me. I am calmly letting things take their course. I have been trying to act as he obviously wants me to act—as a sexless creature.

October 8, Thursday

Friday evening Mr. Gray came and we took the car to Lake Harriet. It was absolutely deserted so we sat on the pavilion and sang. After almost two weeks of *not seeing* him I was rather glad to see him again, and acted more friendly than I had been (for really, his frequent visits and phone-calls had begun to weary me).

Saturday afternoon Armand and I went to the football game. After the first inning we left and sat on the Knoll. I read part of my diary and we had a nice talk.

When I read about his labeling his openings "Forget this. It's a mistake," he said, "In about" (I forget how many) "months that will all come true again" and that it would be like living with a wild Indian to have him around then. I tried to find the appropriate thing which was in my mind but I couldn't find the words to go with it.

Well anyway, *he needn't say those old things again.* HE NEEDN'T SAY THOSE OLD THINGS AGAIN.

He declared that he did not think that I talked to people about myself in order to make them interested in me. Which made me feel very much better of course. Finally he got up very abruptly, and threw his coat over his shoulder so vehemently that it swang over towards me and nearly knocked my hat off. Then we walked over to the carline.

On the way home I read him some more of my diary. When I read the part in which I call him "humje" he said, "I see I'm growing—a pieface and a humje." I explained that he was making a mistake in trying to analyze the word "pieface" because it could mean almost anything. "I see," he said. "It's like putty. It fits itself to anything you stick it on to." And that's about as good a description of the word as you can get.

Once he said to me, "You will always have friends. There is something about you that makes people believe in you."

6:40 p.m.:—I just got a letter from Stella. The dear people have been worrying about me. I had not intended to tell them about my eyes until I should be able to work again, because I didn't want them to worry— and Paula didn't know this, and wrote to her mother. I have always told them that they needn't worry if I didn't write, because I'd write if anything serious occurred. "But," wrote Stella, "This time there was really something and you didn't write." It about makes me cry to think that I have caused them so much suffering, and yet it makes me glad that I have people who—oh, who suffer for me with love.

To-day as I was racing home from the doctor's I suddenly saw Armand a few feet in front of me. I ended up my run with a sort of leap which landed me beside him—on my feet. I mean I didn't fall as the sentence might suggest. Last night I wrote him a letter about Egotism and Myselvism, and I asked him whether he had received it. He said he hadn't. "You'll get it to-morrow," I said. He said he hoped it would be a nice long one because he needed it. He said one of these days he was going to send me one too. By the way he said it, I could see that it was going to be *some* letter. He said it was going to be a vehement one. He was going to show me that a man couldn't control all his inside feelings as I seemed to suppose.

This is part of what I wrote to Armand on Egotism and Myselvism:—

"Do you know I am getting over the Egotism idea again? I find that I do not believe in Egotism but Myselvism. I think my definition of an egotist would be: 'A person who thinks *he* deserves credit for what he does.' It's one's Myself that deserves the praise, and the greatest characteristic of Myselves is that they belong to other people. No doctor or any other man has a right to say, 'If it hadn't been for me, this might not have been possible,' because he could not have done what he did if it hadn't been for someone else, and that someone else might not have done what he did if it hadn't been for some other else, a great many other elses perhaps—and so on back, and back, and to each side too. He is only a link in a chain. The world joins hands and doesn't know it.

The difference, therefore, between Egotism and Myselvism is that Egotists are selfish but Myselvists are *Myselfish* which is unselfish, for Myselves belong to other people."

October 9, Friday

I was happy to-day. I got my pay and they paid me for the week that I was absent too. I thought this was so nice of them that I worked with a will all day. You see I loved to do things for them after they had been so nice to me.* Just now I like my work. I am very much surprised but I like detail pen and ink drawing. There is much that I can learn from this Commercial side of art. I told Miss West that my friends were quite surprised that I was able to become so commercial in my drawing. She said I did change surprisingly fast. She thought it was because I was analytic. So you see it pays to be introspective to a certain extent.

I told Armand about this too. He said that I had made enough progress in introspectiveness now for a while and that I had neglected the social side of things. I said I was just beginning at that, as indeed I am. He said, "Yes I've noticed that by the way you're ripping it into your friends. That's always a good sign." He said also that something was taking hold of me. I told him that I had no idea that anything was taking hold of me but he said there was.

He said he'd come Saturday at 1 p.m. I hope I can remain neutral, as Paula calls it, for a long time.

Mr. Gray called up again to-night and is coming over. I don't see why it should be, but as soon as a man likes me too much I get tired of him.

October 11, Sunday

Yesterday noon I got a letter from Armand—a very nice one. In it he justified his "overbearing" attitude, saying that each man must in a measure make himself master of his destiny, declaring that one had to crush one thing in order that another might live. He showed me too just about where I am at present, a thing which I have wanted him to do for a long time. He said that I have been regarding myself as a spectator

---

* Years later I discovered that they were not paying me a salary. Mr. Weschcke was supplying it, with instructions not to tell me about it.

regards a drama, (which coincides to some extent with Paula's remark that my diary seemed to be written by a third person) that I called to the unknown and took *all* that came, being able only to stand off and *wonder* at that which constitutes Myself without calling it into action. Yes, for half a year I have been looking only, and wondering.

A nice letter.

That afternoon Armand came and we took the street-car out towards the river. We walked along a free, free, autumn road and Armand whistled the Musetta's Waltz from La Boheme that used to proclaim the visits of X last summer, and he said that all during the summer whenever he had thought of me he had found himself whistling it at all times and places. I like to be remembered by that tune, and I would never think of connecting anything but Armand with the melody. We walked thru sunshine and air and autumn colors and—oh, happiness— along a narrow winding whimsical path which led us up and down and along the most unexpected curves. I could not walk. I skipped and ran and spread my arms horizontally—a sure sign of hloopsie-joy.

Finally we sat down on a plank. I asked Armand if he had received my letter and he said he had. He said also that he had known, before he read the letter, what it was going to be about—namely, Egotism, Dr. Beaudoux, and some whacks at himself.

The letter led to Armand's lecture—the lecture for which I had been waiting for so long. I was so relieved when I found him going on and on. I leaned against a tree and looked at the sunshine slanting thru the trees, and dreamt in the violet cushions of distance, and listened. Not exactly listened either for I remember very few words—one might rather say I *absorbed* the sounds of his ideas in connection with the purple and gold and green which I saw, and with Armand's mood which I felt. I cannot tell, therefore, what he said. I might have listened more closely so that I might have received his words and thoughts more systematic- ally, but I should not have been able to get the *idea* so forcibly. I mean by simply absorbing, I was more susceptible and receptive to "that that is not, is" etc.

In the main his talk was much like the letter. He declared that up to now I had been standing off watching myself—the time was at hand in which I was to begin to act. I am to dash courageously into the prob- lems that confront me—whether I fail or succeed does not make a great difference, for the great things that lie hidden in one (if there are **any)** *cannot be born* except thru the "shock of victory or defeat."

I was not giving *reason* a fair chance, he said—reason is necessary, system is necessary.

Armand has said repeatedly that after a thing has been given expression it is dead. I can see that too, altho I can feel that I have not been able to realize the full significance of it. This I know however: it is the feeling or idea that is awakened by a thing which is expressed for me that counts, rather than the expression itself.

In explaining to me that one had to crush some things in order to let others live he said, "It is the law of Nature," and said that an acorn fell and became submerged in the earth. It was its duty to fight in order that it might *see the light* and *grow,* it was its duty to fight for itself even tho many other things were crying and struggling for the same thing, it was its duty to fight even tho these other things had to be crushed.

Fully half of that which he told me that day I had known before, part of it indefinitely, part of it very definitely indeed. Some of the things he said were just what I have been trying to say during the last month or two. I mentioned two of these—my unselfish selfishness or selfish unselfishness, whichever way you want to put it (this is not *clever*— it's true) and something about Myselvism. Armand said rather dubiously, "Yes, perhaps," Not *"yes, perhaps."* I'm certain of that. I may have expressed myself so angularly that neither he nor anyone else got the idea I meant to express, but I know what I meant to express and it was just what he said. It is that way with so many of the things I find in Ibsen or Shaw or Dickens, and in the things Armand tells me—they are not new at all to me, I hail them as old friends, only I have never seen or heard them *expressed*. Then, as soon as someone has *crystallized* them for me, I can *use* them. I suppose I use them before that too, sometimes, *but* I can use them more confidently after they have been crystallized.

To-night Theresa and Paula and I had a discussion again. We started out with Myselves & Me's and I tried in vain to explain just what constituted the Myself in a person and what constituted Me's.

Paula thought that Me's were clever actions or speech which were conscious. Conscious clever actions and speech are Me's *but* Me's are not always conscious actions or speeches. The sad point is that so often one is *not* conscious of them until it is too late. I said it was often very difficult to decide whether it were one's Myself or one of one's Me's that was *egging* one on to a certain action.

Paula thought one ought to be able to tell in this way: If it was right, it was Myself that was speaking; if it was not, it was a Me. Which is true of course, but you have to know whether it is Myself or Me before you can tell whether it's right. She still seemed to think that one would have very little difficulty, in all cases except love, to determine what was right and what was wrong.

As an instance of a case which would not be included in love, I mentioned the magazine illustrating argument. I told her that in that case there seem to be two right sides. I explained too that I knew now (since working at commercial art) that I would have stood a very slim chance, if *any,* of gaining anything by it because I knew practically nothing of how things were reproduced.

October 18, Sunday

Armand's lecture is taking effect. I should fight, I should fight.

I rather think Nina thinks I am too egotistical. I don't pretend by any means that what I have is so extraordinarily much. I hope I am broad-minded enough to know that I don't even know how *little* I know; *but* what I have, I realize and acknowledge and *study* and try to *make the most of.* I have no doubt but that there are people at our art school, for instance, who have more talent in them than I have, but perhaps no one will ever know that they have even as much as I have just for the reason that they draw, and forget to *think.* They do not realize that art is sorrow, love, *Life*—considering it merely a matter of putting their pencils to the paper and making marks. How can they ever hope to use their talent for what it was given to them for, if they are not willing to cut part of themselves out of themselves and put it on paper—how can they expect to make other people realize *love* if they themselves are not willing to put their love into the drawing—and how in the world can they ever hope to touch a chord in other people's beings unless they themselves have suffered, and are satisfied to have suffered if only for the reason that it may make others feel better?

Why is one given a talent if one does not put one's entire self into the development of it—why do things churn about within one, and make one spread one's arms, and clench one's hands in pure joy, and stamp one's feet, and pace and pace, if not to warn us that it is not ours to keep, that it is our duty to give to the world what we have?

"Art for Art's sake" gives me a pain. No one will ever get anywhere with that motto. I am using my life for Art's sake only as far as using, in turn, Art for Life's sake. That is, I am using Life for life—but Art as a medium or tool.

Not that I mean to infer that I see my way clearly, or that I will never make mistakes. I am making mistakes now and shall continue to do so for the rest of my life, but that doesn't necessarily mean that I am doing wrong. It does not even mean that that would be failure. Failure and success viewed in the right light are not so very different after all. Failure regarded in a broadminded way is more often than not a step towards success, because one has profited by it. As Armand says, it doesn't so much matter whether one succeeds or fails in an undertaking as long as some good is born of it. Every time I take a wrong path and realize that it is wrong, I have advanced inasmuch as I shall never be deceived by that path again.

In my work at Buckbee Mears I am continually spoiling a drawing. I will come across a thing which will make me think, "Can I do it this way?" I try the way and most often it is wrong. But I will know after that, that just that way can never be used. Those things have helped me as much to learn as those cases in which I have been able to carry out my idea effectually.

What I do know is not so much thru joy or success, as thru suffering and failure. This refers not only to drawing but to everything.

Friday I was so happy. I don't quite know why either. The brightness of the sun caused much of it I guess. I went to Dr. Beaudoux and came away so happy that I could scarcely contain myself. I don't know how I got home, but with Hloopsie hops and gasps and some of the other ways I have of demonstrating my joy, I managed it somehow. I had not gone to supper when they told me I had a caller, so I raced downstairs. Armand. In a terrible hurry. My happiness was still bubbling so fast that I'm afraid I didn't talk very connectedly, and I was continually looking past Armand's face because I wanted to see *all and all,* and because I was afraid that there might be a dab of powder on my nose. Well we decided that I was to leave at noon the next day for the "U."

Then I went up to supper with a song in my throat where Hloopsie gasps are. On the way up I looked out at the sunset and that mad, exquisite joy seized me, one moment of which always makes up for weeks of suffering or sorrow or bitter fighting. One sees the new cathedral from that window—a mass of purplish gray, and I defy anyone to tell me that at such times it is stone and mortar and steel. It is its

Myself then, and Myselves are not made of such things. It is not a thing by itself for it is so much a part of all.

When one eats one's supper in a Cafeteria one cannot very well do Hloopsie demonstrations, and one has to set one's teeth and plant one's feet firmly on the floor in order that one may keep from doing so.

I was so ding happy that I couldn't go to sleep for the longest time. I would curl and uncurl with pure joy, and stretch my limbs and *type* my mouth (that's a new one—one has to set one's teeth, and the lips are parted. It expresses joy which is so keen that it is almost painful) with the intensity of my emotion. This sounds funny enough no doubt, but I'm serious.

And then came Saturday. We were both the same amount late so it was allright. We walked down to the river beyond the "U" campus. I walked behind Armand part of the time and I made sort of vixenish grimaces at him. Somehow I felt that I was getting the better of him in some way. He was almost out of sight because he was carrying both my big cape-coat and his coat, and I could race along without anything to carry.

We selected a shady place and flopped down. At first we said scarcely anything. I didn't feel like talking so I didn't. I wanted to think, but not deeply that day. So I sat and thought, not deeply. It seems when I think, I raise my eyebrows (an action which Armand calls distinctly Viennese) and make other facial expressions. Armand always described them in musical terms such as *Legato* and *Andantino* etc. I laughed finally of course, so it was *Scherzo*.

I don't know exactly how it started, but before we knew it we were acting a little *Drammer*. We were in a little *Dorf* in Austria, and I was "Mirzli" and Armand was "Rudi." I had turned him down whereupon he had gone to *Kirchweih* with "Anna," a friend of mine. I was trying to convince Rudi that I didn't care for him any more, but that I loved "Peter" who had black hair and blue eyes, who had more money than Rudi, and who was beautifully tall.

Rudi would try to convince me that I didn't really care for Peter, that I was lying, and I would pout and declare that I did too love Peter. *"Hast ihm net gern,"* he would say rather fiercely. *"Hab schon,"* I would say, not looking up however. Whereupon Rudi would demand that I look him in the eyes and repeat it. Then Mirzli would shoot a glance at Rudi, saying, *"Hab den Peter doch gern!"*

I would rake him over the coals for having taken Anna to *Kirch-*

weih whereupon he would explain that he had done so out of sheer desperation, seeing that I had turned him down. I told him that I had turned Peter down at least four times but that he had never gone to *Kirchweih* with any other girl, therefore Peter was more desirable than Rudi.

I told Rudi that he could have back the ring and the comb which he had given me, for I had a ring from Peter now. I hadn't promised to marry Peter however.

Rudi declared that he was going to Wien. *"Mit wen gehst du da zu Kirchweih, hm?"* I asked half-accusingly, half-scoffingly, to which he replied that he wasn't going to *Kirchweih* at all. I told him that something awful would surely happen if he stopped going to church but he declared that he simply couldn't help it.

He would repeat that he was going to Wien, and I would say, *"Na, geh doch."* He said, *"Meinst du's wirklich, Mirzli?"* and I would say *"Ja."* So he got up and said *"Adje."* I didn't say anything so he repeated it. I mumbled, *"Adje"* and he walked off, only to return and ask whether I really meant to say goodbye. I said shortly, *"Adje,"* so he went off.

That was the end of Act I.

At the opening of Act II four years have elapsed, Rudi having been in Vienna all the time. I have been in the village all the while, having grown to be quite the belle of the place, and am now really engaged to be married to Peter.

As the curtain rises I am seen sitting on the grass, playing idly with flowers at my feet. Rudi enters and makes a remark. I look up, and when I see him, clasp the vicinity of my throat with my hand (denoting extreme surprise) and gurgle, "Oh Rudi!" Rudi is dressed very stylishly and has quite the air of a gentleman about him. I steal looks at his attire and he walks with a swagger so that I may feel how rich and important he has become. I do feel it, and as he talks about his many possessions my curiosity gets the better of me and I ask, *"Na, wie viele Anzüge has du eigentlich?"* He says lightly, *"O, so zehn oder zwölf."* This makes me gasp of course and I ask him what he needs so many for, and he explains to me that in Vienna one needs a great many suits because one goes to theatres and parties and concerts. He murmurs something to himself about some Countess, which infuriates me so that I turn on my heel and walk off. He calls to his servant Johann, talks with him, and then follows me and asks if I don't want to take an auto-ride with him. Since I have never had an auto-ride in all my life before, I soften and tell him I'll go with him. So we step into the auto and Rudi manipulates the thing, knowing all the time that he is making quite an impression on Mirzli. Finally we reach a pretty spot so we step out of the auto and seat ourselves on the grass.

He tells me that Peter is telling everybody that we are already married, whereupon I become indignant at Peter and declare that now I wasn't going to marry him at all.

Then Rudi tells me about his experiences at Vienna. He says that first he was trampled under foot and made fun of, but that after the first year he began to become rich and popular, and that Wien had given him all that he wanted, *"nur die Liebe nicht,"* and he says that he has come back to claim that.

"Gehst du mit mir nach Wien, Mirzli?" he asks. I say, relenting, *"Ach, nich nach Wien!"* inferring that I'd just as soon go with *him*. He says *"Mit dem Auto?"* That appeals immensely to me, and I say, *"O, mit dem Auto?"* We go on in this manner for some time, I giving in more and more all the time, until finally when Rudi asks whether I will give him the love he has come for, I look happily and dreamily into the distance and murmur *"Ja."*

That's the end.

After that Armand got a very melodramatic streak and did a sort of relentless Rudolf act which was highly exciting.

After that we imagined ourselves to be vaudeville actors. There was a ledge of rock which, being slightly elevated and decorated with trees and grass, made a very good stage. Our first act consisted of Armand's telling me jokes. For instance he would say with an English accent, "Did it ever occur to you that you are devilish pretty?" I would answer expectantly and demurely, "Why, no I had never thought of that." He said, "Well it's a good thing you didn't—because you're homely!" at which he would laugh and laugh and say in a confidential aside to the audience, "That was a clever one." Afterwards we did some dancing, separately but at the same time, and at the end of our act we received an encore of course, so we had to step out and bow to the audience etc.

After that we suddenly became serious. We were standing on the grass-covered ledge of rock. And it was twilight. Brilliant blue mists were folded among the trees in the distance, and a grayish-violet haze was rising all about us. And the river was—oh mixing itself up all over and it had a calm band of silver dividing it in one place. Things were rising and joining hands and hearts and souls. Myselves dropped their veils and, as Armand expresses it, "curtains rolled back."

We stood in silence for a long time watching. Once Armand said, "Well, spill it out" but truly I had nothing I wanted to spill, and I told him so. I was *absorbing*. Armand became quite emotional and paced back and forth, and no wonder, for the evening was enough to make anyone pace. As he walked he recited some of his poetry. I remember one particularly about a leaf, which I liked very much. In German. I usually like things Armand does in German because he always seems to be so un-irritating when he thinks in German. It was about a leaf which fell at his feet and laughed joyously at him. It wished to have him laugh with it, but it caused him only pain. Something to that effect.

Finally Armand grabbed my arm and made me pace up and down with him a number of times, after which he steered me along on our homeward path. It was rather gracefully done. He set me on my car with some money to go home on, and I left.

I surely went over to Armand's side of the line after he gave me that lecture about fighting for one's self, and I have been there more or less since. I am still holding my own all the same I think—the present relationship between us, which is very happy and convenient, makes that possible.

Oh yes on that afternoon at the river Armand whistled things, running into the La Boheme air. When he stopped he said, "Do you know what I said?"

I didn't.

October 25, Sunday

I got a card from Mr. Gray the other day. He had been gone for two weeks before I heard from him. Second stage, Mr. Gray?

During all of last week I have been designing book covers at the shop. I liked it awfully well.

I went over to school one night. When I got over there, Miss Bonta came fluttering out and gave me such a darling kiss. Mr. McWhorter came out too, and said that he had been having good reports of me. He asked me too, how I liked Dr. Beaudoux, and I said, "Oh, we have such interesting talks." He impressed it strongly upon me that I was not under any circumstances to overwork, and that I must not let myself run into a rut, allow my art to become too commercialized, you know.

After that I went over into the Design room where I saw Raymon

Bowers. He and I do have the most interesting talks together. He is one of the few men over there who possess brains. He is a nice man.

The art school is going to have a house party at Bald Eagle the end of the week and I guess I'll go for part of the time. I never know how much I miss school and the school people until I get over there and see them. There, at least, is a place where you can be unconventional, broad-minded, and Yourself.

Paula and Nina were in my room last night. I ripped it into Nina again. She allows boys to take little liberties. I thought I had talked her out of that but it seems I haven't. I said I was saving all that for the man I would marry, and that I wanted to be able to give myself to him "un-hugged, un-kissed, and un-clasped" which sounded so funny that we all had a good laugh, but I meant it all the same.

I was at the Symphony concert last Friday with Paula. The first number, "Les Preludes" by Liszt, appealed to me more than the others. In one place it ran into minor keys (I guess that's what you call them) and then it piled itself up, minor keys on minor keys, until it almost reached the point of realizing, and making one realize, the eternal. One was afraid it would do so and make one die as a sort of penalty or recompense. I found myself following it, mounting and *delving,* and as I felt myself getting nearer and nearer to a great Something, I found myself clutching the arms of my seat and rising tensely. I set my teeth with a most wonderful mingling of painful ecstasy and happy sorrow—and then the music changed. High time too, or I would have fainted (this is no joke, I mean it) or have done something equally sensational.

I love to follow a thread of melody as one would a path. I will be leaning back in my seat following it as long as it goes straight ahead, broken only by the quirky little flower-by-the-wayside notes that slip in and out of this note-thread. Then it begins to curve and I find myself leaning forward—ding it, Wanda, introspective again, aren't you? Stop it. What difference does it make how you acted in connection with it? *It* is the thing that counts.

October 27, Tuesday

There is so much beauty in the world. In sorrow, in sordidness, in poverty there is *beauty.* For example I saw a little girl selling newspapers down on Tenth street. Auburn hair which was trained, not by precise brushing and combing, but which seemed to have curved as it did because it had been brushed back by the child's hand. Blue eyes with a child light in them, a baby mouth already moulded interestingly by the *un-smoothness* of life, and an outstretched hand with a paper in it. A little life crying for Life—the outstretched hand and the appealing look and the paper being only its mediums or weapons or tools or whatever you may wish to call it. I mean one did not get the idea that she was trying to sell you a paper but that she wanted to live.

One has to *feel* beauty as well as see it.

At any rate I have reached the stage where I can satisfy myself to a great extent by seeing and feeling and absorbing beauty without want-ing forever to be capturing it with my pencil. It would be funny if I wouldn't turn out to be an artist primarily. I could never stop drawing of course, but I feel just now that if I should ever do anything worth while (and I think I can do it if I want) that it would not necessarily be by art. Lately I have been appealing to people more by reason of my mind than by my drawing.

October 28, Wednesday

There is much beauty in a city. Buildings and streets and multitudes of people, and big buildings being built, people building them, smoke, lights dripping and popping out all over; sadness, sordidness, joy, love, pain, badness, goodness all being *swept along to-gether*. The beauty of a city lies mostly in a big slice of it.

October 29, Thursday

I had such a funny dream last night. I guess I'll put it down simply to show how absolutely pointless and inconsistent it was. Some one said, "Oh I know a good new joke." And this was it:

Some Sicilian soldiers, who were here in America, wanted a carriage—a domestic science carriage, to be specific. So a carriage was brought. As it came towards one it looked exactly like a stocking very old and worn, but afterwards it was a four-wheeled vehicle. The Sicilian soldiers were evidently not prepossessed with its appearance for they asked, "Well, what is this?" There was a hen inside of the ambulance-like vehicle. The people who had brought it said, "A domestic science carriage. Just what you want. No Jessie, no James, the girls are all dears, I have all my darlings around me, AND angel's food! What more can you want?"

Isn't that the limit? The "no Jesse, no James" part was exceedingly pungent, and it worked up most effectively to the grand finale of "AND angel's food."

The other night I heard William Jennings Bryan speak. I enjoyed it very much. I liked to see the effect he had on Humanity. Even Bryan resorts to cleverness, and flatters and compliments in order to impress the masses. I knew every time when his speech would make the people clap. I like him very much.

I started a letter to Mr. Gray to-day for the simple reason that I felt like writing to him. I didn't hear from him for almost two weeks and I rather hoped that he had found some other girl. And then again I didn't. And now again I do.

Next Monday Miss West is going to Winnipeg to do some drawing and I will be the only fashion artist in the whole establishment. I am rather scared.

This evening Armand called. He said that he had been going thru quite a metamorphosis, he was gaining in wisdom, and I said, "I'm changing too." He said, looking rather past me, "Yes, you are changing." I certainly am. I can feel it so well.

He said, "My prophecy is coming true."

I said, "Which one? You have made so many." He said that one in which he had prophesied that our views would some day differ so widely——

"——that I'd lose faith in you," I finished.

"Not lose faith," he said, "I didn't say that." But I told him he had said that our friendship would cease and that was the same as losing one's faith.

He said, "Well I said our friendship would cease temporarily," and I said, "No you didn't. You said that you thought there would come a time when I wouldn't even look at you even." Which he had to admit. I told him diverse opinions in matters certainly did not make me lose faith in people, and that there were only a few people, of course, whom I really considered my friends.

He said, "May I feel honored—?"

"You're one of them," I said.

He declared that he was sorry he had said that about my losing faith for so slight a reason as diversity of opinion, and said he really shouldn't have said that. And that sort of gives me the victory for that long, exciting discussion we had last spring on that subject.

I said that I had written him a letter but hadn't sent it because I hadn't received any satisfaction out of writing it. I didn't feel as if anything had gone out of me, therefore I didn't think anything had gone into the letter.

He said that he felt another lecture, as I call them, coming on. He told me too that he was going to spill over to me in the near future or thereabouts. I told him, "And I feel that I am going to become enigmatical. I will be bringing packages to you and piling them all out for you to see, but I won't open them. You always do that, you know. You come and pile all your packages on the table but you don't open them." He said he did open them, but I said that if he did he only looked into them himself and didn't let me look in at all. I do think that I shall presently become enigmatical—not deliberately—I mean I just feel it coming on. And now, little Armand, you are rather on my side of the line.

So he wants to spill. Well he needn't. He always spills such bewildering things.

November 2, Monday

Saturday noon Armand called. I don't know whatever possessed me to do so, but I appeared in my hat and coat and found myself handing my sketching materials to Armand as he entered. Armand rather gasped. I found out afterwards that he had intended to start the afternoon by playing piano. He finally managed to decide that we go to Como Park.

After we had seated ourselves on the shore of the lake we talked of various little things of little value. It seems Armand had a desire to swoop into my hair and tousle it up. Also to *paw* around (on the ground). He started a ridiculous story, about a man "folding his still warm and palpitating heart into his check-book" and wanted me to take part, but as I was not inclined that way that day, he soon dropped it too. I told him that if he had started it the day I heard Bryan I might have taken part with pleasure for I was continually talking like that.

We played the half dollar game with a quarter.

We talked about the First of May—or rather Armand talked. He said it was a wonderful day and a perfect one. He suggested that we have an anniversary of the day next year, weather and other things permitting, going to the very same place that we had last year.

We acted a little drama too. My name was Maggie and I clerked in "the five-and-ten," and Armand worked in a garage and his name was Jimmie. Jimmie is very much in love with Maggie but Maggie is very anxious to get a proposal from "one of them Orpheum players." She says Jimmie hasn't got much money and not enough politeness. He tells her that he is earning $50.00 a month now, at which Maggie brightens up considerably. This, and the fact that Maggie insists she doesn't care for him, pains him so much that he shoots himself.

Of course I didn't quite know how to meet this part of the drama at all—it came so suddenly. For a long time I just sat. I also tugged at his coat a little and wept a little, but ding, he couldn't expect me to act the rest out really. Just you wait, Armand Emraad! I'll get even with you in our next little *drammer* if I possibly can. I shall faint or something like that.

On the whole, the afternoon would have been rather wasted if it had not been for the trees and sky and things, and it might have been a glorious rest if I had not had much that I wanted to say, and if I had not felt that Armand really wanted to talk solid stuff even tho perhaps he didn't realize it at the time. Now two Saturdays before that, it was entirely different. Not one bit of the time was wasted.

On the way home Armand started a poem—a German poem about eyes. He said he'd send it to me when it was finished, and said also that I was the cause of it and that the poem was going to be Myself.

Nina and I left for the Art School House Party on the 5:40 train. When we arrived I found myself tumbling into Doris' arms, and before we knew what we were at, we were jammed into an auto and being swept thru autumn woods of no color (by reason of the night, you see) to the cottage. As I entered the door I saw three things—a fire-place, candles all about, and expressions of people's faces all about. All this filled out with patches of darknesses, making a regular patchwork quilt of light and liquid darkness. The only face I saw distinctly was Theresa's, and even in that case it was not her face that I saw but her radiant Myself. It all made me so happy, I wanted to do a series of Hloopsie-hops right on the threshhold. But since that was out of the question, I disposed of my wraps in some way and sat down to supper.

After supper we danced a little. Pilchie gave a solo dance, so when they called on me to give one of my impromptu quirlings I did a "spook dance." We sang for a long while after that. *Ich war wieder einmal aufgedreht* and put all kinds of little quirks and quirls in the secondary parts I was singing. When the boys had gone to their cottages we flopped down our hair and drooped and dreamt about the fire-place and toasted marsh-mallows. Great stuff.

The next day was so happily spent that it needs not to be written up. Towards evening I sat at the fire-place and looked at the fire. I didn't even think. Mr. and Mrs. Zeigler sat down beside me. I have the darlingest mental picture of Mr. Zeigler bending forwards a little in his chair and smiling with a "my-soul-has-been-wakened-to-dreams" sort of a complacence upon his face. At about eight o'clock Theresa and I went for a walk, and when we returned we found our cottage the center of much excitement. It had suddenly been decided that we were to go home that evening instead of staying until the next morning, so everyone was packing their suitcases, or looking for their silver, or helping to dispose of the food in one way or another.

Finally we were all ready to go and before long we found ourselves walking thru the glorious moonlight night. Nina kept railing all the time because our former plans had been upset so suddenly. Said that there hadn't been any system about the whole party anyway, and that things should have been arranged so that everything would have gone off without a hitch. I said that she was not dealing with machines but with human beings, that she ought to make some allowance for art students (for they are beautifully human on the whole) and that besides I thought that the party had been an absolute success *in every respect.* She said sarcastically, "Well I'm glad you can see it that way."

I said, rather more to myself than to Nina, "Even tho human nature changes, Nature is always constant." You see, by this time the almost sombre glory of the night was bringing me to the verge of Hloopsie-ism. Nina kept on whining. I said fiercely and incoherently, "Nina, please don't say those things any more!" and before she or Katharine [a new art student] could recover from my white flame of a remark, I had fallen behind them and was walking alone. I was not going to have the night spoiled, that was all.

I was rather glad I could walk alone. The night and I were one. I gave little jumpeties and Hloopsie-gasps and enjoyed myself intensely. I was glad, oh glad, that we were *walking* to the station that night—it was the most wonderful night I have walked thru for a long time. Mists nestling in little hollows, draped in among trees, and rolling and unrolling along stretches of autumn that were steeped in moon-spun silence and wonder. The air was like spun silver, and fragrant to the sight. *Ich wollte beinahe vor Freud vergehen.* I lived much in those ten or fifteen minutes that I walked by myself. I learned much that I do not remember at all, but which I have for good.

Finally Nina, undoubtedly feeling somewhat guilty, said, "Come on, Wanda, walk with us. I won't talk like that any more." So I walked with them. It was almost amusing to see how virtuously Nina tried to talk of "That that is, is not" etc. in order to please me. It didn't amuse me however—I was too gloriously and seriously wrapped up in the night and the millions of things that people it.

Oh well.

We got on the train. I sat next to the window and spent about half the ride home in looking out of the window for the concluding chapters of my soul-night adventure. One passed a sign, "This is *not* the road to the Pavilion." And one passed water in grey sheets with cubic-nesses of lavender mists pressed upon it. And one passed sweeps of landscape with long, flowing, scarf-like fog-nets fluttering above them. All this with the moonlight filtering thru it.

I wish Armand and I would take a jaunt some evening once, some moonlit fog-drenched night, instead of always in the daytime.

Nov. 12, Thursday

Somehow I am so funny. I mean I *feel* queer. As if I were going to change radically in the near future, or that something in regard to me or on account of me was going to change. I don't believe much in presentiments but often what is considered a presentiment is not really that at all but simply unconscious reasoning. I mean different things happen along the path of your life, they leave impressions which you absorb unconsciously and after a while all these impressions unite and, without knowing that you are doing so, you reason a little this way and reason a little that way, eliminate, set two and two to-gether and draw your conclusions. And there you have your presentiment.

There is so much to one's philosophy of life. Little parts of mine are beginning to pop out from my Myselvian recesses and it's so interesting to find out little by little the things which make up your philosophy of life. I don't suppose one ever finds out what one's p. of l. is—but one finds out little parts of it, perhaps *all* of the little things which are important, only one doesn't know how to set them to-gether. If one would be able to do that we would know too much to be happy. Instead of seeing Eternity for one moment as one does at times, oh, as one does at times, one would have a part of it for ever and ever, and that would be too much.

Eternity to me means all the great, good, wonderful *Unmeasureless* and *Un-explicable*. It means that which mortals can in rare moments catch a glimpse of, but which they can never never fathom or entirely understand. If a person *would* be able to fathom or understand Eternity they would no longer be mortals. I can well imagine, however, a mortal *grasping* Eternity and dying the next moment.

Last Saturday afternoon Paula and I became rather hungry so we went down town to get something. First, however, we went to the library. As we were going up in the elevator—I don't know what in the world possessed me to do so—but I said calmly, "I'll bet nobody would think I were Russian." Paula was too astonished to speak, besides before she *could* have spoken the elevator-man said, shooting his head backwards in the meantime, "I'll bet you a dollar you ain't!" We said nothing and stepped out of the elevator most matter-of-factly. But as soon as we got into the library rooms we absolutely exploded. Paula kept asking what under the sun had made me say that. I was wearing a little toque which, being accentuated by my big cape,* truly does look Russian, but I've worn it many a time before and have never been moved to make that remark. No one could have been more surprised than I when I had said it. When we went back into the elevator we acted quite naturally, and I guess the poor elevator man doesn't know to this day whether or not to believe that I was really Russian. In fact I rather think that he is sorry that he made that rash remark. Paula said that I said it so naturally and seriously that she nearly fell over.

We went to try on some suits (which I have been doing for some time) but could not find anything suitable. They are all too big for me, ding it. We were feeling decidedly unconventional, and ate our cookies on the street. "What's the difference?" said Paula. I said, "What do we care? Nobody knows we're Russian." And this remark has become our latest.

Down at the shop they are sending out circulars, about 5,000 in all. These had to be folded and put into envelopes, and as I had very little work to do all week, a great part of this intellectual piece of work fell to me. I have often wondered what I would do if I had to do something so purely mechanical and something which called for so little brain-power, and now I know. The first thing I did was to think of the fastest way to do it. When I had accomplished this to my satisfaction, I amused myself by reading the different addresses, which was very interesting indeed, but soon became tiresome. By this time I was able to operate the thing so mechanically that I could think of entirely different things. So for a while I philosophized. I found out accidentally that my movements were becoming so subconscious that I could *read* at the same

---

* I had no coat and was wearing papa's Austrian *Lodenrock*.

time, so since then (we did this for a week) I have been reading Shaw, Thackeray, Rosegger and Heinrich Heine. It's queer, but towards the end I became so used to doing the enveloping *in combination* with the reading, that when I'd stop my work I'd find myself reading over a line again and again without being able to absorb its contents.

I wrote Mr. Gray a letter not long ago, and yesterday he answered. A slender little letter. "Dear Friend" it started, and was beautifully un-love-sickish all thru. I guess I vanquished him pretty effectively the last two times I went out with him. I feel so free now. Just think, not a single cavalier to bother my head about. Not a single cavalier, not a single cavalier, tra-la!

It's a shame one has to let such nice friendships dwindle off like that, but one has to.

I'm waiting patiently for Stella to send me some money. I need a suit very badly.

Last night I felt so funny. I felt as if I were not a *person* and that the people about me weren't persons. I wasn't feeling at all well and after supper I cried without any reason whatsoever. Usually when I cry I don't know why I cry but there's always a reason; but last night I cried simply because I lost control of myself. I'm not naturally nervous either. I got over it tho.

I finished reading "Captain Brass-bound's Conversion." Now I am reading "Vanity Fair."

Wanda, go to bed.

Wanda, go to bed.

November 14, Saturday

I have just selected my suit. It is dark blue and quite Russian. Paula bought herself a skirt and Nina bought a dress. We have been racing around a good deal in stores and I saw so many pretty dresses. As it's style to be slender and narrow-shouldered, nearly everything fits me to a T, and oh I want so badly to have pretty dresses while I am young.

It seems to me Armand had intended to take me to the foot ball game but I haven't heard from him for two weeks or so. I can't help wishing that I had about three or four friends like Armand so that one of them would be dropping in every few days. It would do my mind so much good. This way I always have had about four or five or six moods and pendulum-ideas by the time Armand comes around, and of course it isn't nearly so nice as when you can un-talk your mood just while you are in it. And then it would be so nice to get the different opinions of these different people.

I look different on every picture that I sketch of myself, but I look different to myself on different occasions. Sometimes my chin looks more pronounced, sometimes my mouth looks very large, at times decidedly small, and sometimes my face looks much rounder than at other times. To-night for a few minutes the expression on my face was like that of a woman of forty—indeed as far as age is concerned, the expression on my face ranges from that of a child of ten to that of a woman of forty.

I don't see what will happen to me if I don't get a chance to spill over to Armand or someone equally satisfying. When I want so badly to talk and be talked to, a sort of quiet frenzy rages within me. I talk my head off to Paula and Nina and Theresa, and I scribble and scribble in my diary and talk to many other people whom I happen to meet, and still I don't get rid of enough to make me feel calm. It isn't that I think I have so much more in me than other people, but some people are just born to spill and others aren't.

I have been reading Ibsen's "Ghosts" but do not find it nearly as depressing as I expected it to be. That is, it is depressing enough, but it didn't affect me so very badly. I find Stella's letter more depressing, I think. My darling Stella is having her first real fight alone, and it hurts me so to see her struggle so without being able to help. She is going thru the very stages that I went thru. The dear children are all growing up and I am so busy trying to keep myself afloat that I can't help them grow up as much as I want to.

I am crying so heart-breakingly tonight that—I don't know how to express myself.

I can't stand it to be bottled up for weeks at a time. I can't stand it, I say, *I can't stand it.*

I don't feel like Wanda Gág, I don't feel like a person, I feel so abstract. I do not know where I am. I do not know who I am.

November 17, Tuesday

Goodnight, I was lachrymose at the time of my last entry—tears splashed all over it! Since then I have written Stella a long and take-it-from-your-big-sister-y sort of letter. Which made me feel much better.

Sunday we worked the Ouija board. Of course I know that it's one's mind that makes the thing move, and that however unexpected the results may be it must be one's mind, conscious or subconscious, that does it, but it certainly is interesting. It struck me as being almost uncanny a number of times.

November 18, Wednesday

Yesterday evening when I came home from work I had a card from home telling me that Dehli was very sick. I went up to my room in a sort of trance and flung myself across my bed, for I was entirely unstrung. On my dresser was a note saying that I was to move into my new room 415 that evening. It was about the luckiest thing that could have happened for it gave me a chance to work off some of my anxiety and worry, physically. I was in a trance most of the time I guess, and when I wasn't that, I was weeping. I thought of all the girls of about Dehli's age that had died, and it seemed to me that they mostly did die easily when they were about as old as she is.

She has been growing very fast and is very tall and thin. Tussy wrote that she had stomach-trouble and that they had the doctor twice. She wrote that they were afraid that some kind of boils would develop and if so, she would have to have an operation. "But we are hoping for the best," she wrote, "and if she gets worse we will write immediately."

After I had moved into my new room I sat down and wrote a note to Armand. I went to bed at about seven for I could do absolutely nothing, but I did not go to sleep until about nine, for every time the telephone rang I would sit up and hold my breath, thinking that the people from home might have called.

The next morning I left word at the Y.W. that they should call me up immediately if I should receive a letter from New Ulm, and so whenever the telephone would ring at the office I would go thru the most awful suspense. I had a job too that day, a girl smiling and holding a can of "Dairy Maid Milk Hominy." The irony of Fate—to have to paint a smile, with your heart hanging like lead somewhere inside of you.

At about eleven there was a telephone call for me. I went out to the office trying to brace myself for the worst. Fancy my surprise upon hearing a man's voice. Armand. A very nice Armand. He asked how Dehli was and what was the matter with her, and asked me whether I could be at the Y.W. at five. I left work at 4:30 and when I asked for mail at the desk they told me that there was no mail, but someone in the back parlor for me. So I blew in there directly. Armand asked me to tell him as much as I knew of Dehli's illness which I did. He said he thought it must be "Gastric ulcer" and told me not to worry because she had a good chance.

Oh yes he noticed my suit too, and said, "It's pretty. Getting prosperous." Oh yes, $5 a week and Prosperity are synonymous. How I ever manage to live on that amount and get shoes and a hat and a number of other things into the bargain, is more than I can understand. But I do it nevertheless. I have a $7-a-month room now which makes $1 a month less expense.

That day I said he could read part of my diary himself. "Oh not all by yourself," I added, "I'll be around somewhere but I'll let you read it." Armand laughed and said I said it as one might say, "Here Fido, have a bone." I suppose it seems awfully queer that I should not trust Armand all alone with my diary. It isn't that I don't trust him, for I do very much, but he might *accidentally* run across passages which are not for his eyes. There is no reason why he should see things which no one else sees either.

November 21, Saturday

Today I got a letter from home. Dehli is still pretty sick and very weak but she seems not to be quite as bad as she was. Tussy says that she is so very patient and does not complain at all. Oh I hope, I hope that she will not have to have any operations while she is so very weak. I started writing her a letter today, and I shall buy her a birthday present and if I have to go without dessert for a month.

I'll finish up Wednesday's conversation later. I am full to overflowing with a new one altho I do not know whether I can write it—it may be one of those cases in which I absorb and use, but cannot express. Armand called this afternoon. He was at the piano playing when I came down, and I stood beside the piano and stood *fastened* there. I felt as if I would be obliged to be *fastened* to it for a long time. Armand said, "What's the matter?" but I didn't know.

We went in one of the parlors and sat down. All during the afternoon my eyes would go off somewhere and part of me would go with them and think, while the rest of me (which was left) kept on talking and thinking as if part of me weren't gone at all. I can't explain it at all. And it's uncanny. I am going thru some very great change but I have no idea what it can be. Armand said, "Maybe you're falling in love," and I said, "Oh no, I don't think so." One has to have an object for that.

I told him that it certainly felt good not to have any cavaliers whatsoever. He said he had often wondered what I would do if he should become one. He said he had wanted to try it just to see what I would do. I said, "No, for the love of soup, don't." He said that the reason he had not tried it was because he thought I'd see thru his little game. I said I thought I would.

He said that I seemed to have stepped out of the mediaeval ages when he met me at New Ulm. He said that I had gathered that part of New Ulm which was worth something—the *Deutsche Märchen* atmosphere—and that I still suggested mediaeval ages.

He told me about Beethoven's Fifth Symphony, comparing the first part (dom, dom, dom, da) to a rather pessimistic vein of life, the second to the man's analyzing in some respects and the acknowledging of love to some extent, and the third to the man as he comes to his conclusions: "I don't know why, but the world is rich and worth the living." Armand said that we all had to go thru that symphony but that all did not end it up as happily as that.

Armand thought that, altho I loved human beings, I did not feel and realize their suffering and love. I said, "I think I do." He said something perhapsy again and I said that it isn't so very long that I did, but I did now. He said he knew I loved them as a whole but was not so certain whether I would be able to limit myself to one person.

He said that I was less introspective and that I seemed to be *afraid*. And ding, I am sort of. I'm afraid of myself—rather in the way that I was afraid of my eyes one day because they knew more than I. I know more than I have yet *realized*. And I keep on *knowing* new things and I can't learn to *realize* fast enough. It's very bewildering and wearing, and really almost maddening. I am living almost too intensely I guess, but I can't help it. When you have once reached this stage, Hloopsie will come, and pain will throb thru you *ecstatically,* and you can't see things the way you did before you "realized the sun." It may be *ecstacy* to be torn around as I am but it isn't *fun*.

I told Armand that my latest thought was that perhaps I wouldn't be an artist at all, and explained that there would be side issues like art and things of a similar nature, but that perhaps my *best deed* would consist of something not tangible.

I *am* afraid. I am afraid perhaps, that I have seen too much for my age. Perhaps I have been paying too much attention to Myself so that it has grown too strong and wise and experienced in proportion to the rest of me. I do not like to be introspective but I do not see how I can stand it much longer to be *under something* and not be able to find out what it is.

I got a letter from Timmie Saturday, a very nice one. He has been getting only $5 a week too, but has been fired because he couldn't work the typewriter as well as the rather brainless fellow who is going to have his place. I wrote a letter to him to-day and in one place I wrote, "I have been obliged to step mercilessly on certain parts of Myself so that they are now numb." Timmie will probably never know what I meant, but I do. I cannot say that I am in love with Armand. I do not know. I have deliberately checked my thoughts whenever they went in that direction. I never knew that I would be able to do it so thoroughly.

I wrote Armand a letter to-day too. A queer sort of letter, I suppose. I told him he had put me on a horse and that it was beautifully wild, and I liked wild horses, but that he would have to hurry up and teach me how to manage it so that it would not run away with me and throw me off. I said too that either part of me was going too fast or the other part of me too slow, and that it was like being lame.

After a while it becomes very wearing to live on $5 a week. One has to think so very hard and so very much about old financial things in order to make both ends barely touch.

To-day I got a letter from Mr. A. J. Russell (Editor Journal Junior, Minneapolis) who wrote to me while I was teaching school. He remembered his offer of lending me one of his books "Phantastes—A Fairy Story for Men and Women" which, he says gravely, he has read about 500 times. He said that if I got it, I "got" it; if I didn't, I didn't and it would mean that I did not have "fairy blood" in me which my drawings would indicate.

I wrote Mr. Russell a rather *effervescing* letter but I couldn't help it. It made me very happy to think that he had not forgotten me. He wrote once that if I ever came to Minneapolis he would like to meet me personally, and I should certainly like to meet him too.

Last night as I was cleaning my glasses one of the lenses broke right off the fixtures, which was unfortunate because of course I am poor enough as it is.

Later:—I really don't know what to do with myself—I feel so very queer.

It is almost eleven o'clock and I am very tired, so I guess I had better go to bed, altho I am so very much bewildered that I do not know what to do with myself. It's almost eleven o'clock. Wanda, Wanda, go to bed.

November 24, Tuesday

This afternoon Armand called and I read him the letter which Mr. Russell sent me, and he seemed quite interested. He said he knew just what that man looked like. He said that he looked at one with his head rather lowered, and that his glance was either quick and nervous or else far away (I said I thought the latter) and that he would smile much of the time (to which I did not agree).

He came back to the letter I had written him (Armand). In regard to the loving humanity business, he said, "So you don't agree with me," and I said I didn't. He said that he thought in about two years from now I would agree with him and see that at present I do not love and feel for the people about me as much as I think I do. Gr! Grr! Grrr!

He had told me the Saturday before that he knew I loved humanity as a whole but was not so sure whether I could ever settle down to one person. He didn't know whether one person would be *sufficient*. So even he thinks that—leaving me, perhaps, as the only person who thinks otherwise. Just because I have not the power of showing my love, and *have* the power of choking it, drowning it and hiding it for long spaces of time, they think I haven't it.

He said that I regarded him objectively ("Because I've made you do it," he said to himself rather than to me) and that he regarded me subjectively. Out of this a very interesting problem seemed to develop for him, for he set it on the window and smiled at it and cocked his head first to one side and then to the other in intellectual amusement and interest. I suppose as a result there will be an addition to his system, which I don't think I'll mind. I've gotten so that I take the system for granted.

He said, "Well at any rate it's nice that we get along as well as we do in spite of that."

"Queer, *I* think," I said.

And he said, smiling half-thoughtfully and half-gleefully into space before him, "Well yes, *in a way!*"

He said, "About this idea of your being an artist or not. That you have genius, I know now—I told you from the first I believed in you— but whether you will use this in a broad way, thru actions and deeds and in this way influence the people about you with your personality; or whether in the other way, putting things on canvas, I do not know.

You have lived in a small town all your life and now that you come into contact with big things like art, literature, music, drama, you find that you respond to all of them. And you don't know which to choose."

He said that I being young, my experience and knowledge of life was deficient, which of course I cannot deny. "But whether you will get this knowledge thru experience or necessity," he said, "I do not know." Whether I will plunge in, he meant, or whether I will be drawn in. I said I thought that depended on circumstances—I might be drawn in before I had a chance to plunge.

He said, as we were getting into an argument, "You are not a person of decisive character," which I did not even deny, ding it. I don't see why I didn't flare up at that. In fact, I don't see why I didn't throw things at him upon a number of occasions that afternoon; not because he deserved it (for he gave me a good pull out of the hole into which I was sinking) but because it would have been the thing to do.

After that he fired questions at me thick and fast and, as he said afterwards, I did not meet them bravely. I avoided a definite answer. Why, I cannot tell. I knew at the time that I wasn't doing what was natural for me to do but somehow I could not do otherwise just then. I imagine it was because I was so utterly bewildered. He ended up by declaring, "Will you say as Carlyle did, 'It is in me, and by God, it will out'? Or will you go on drivelling (that wasn't the word, I guess, but I can't think of the other) as you have been doing this last year?"

Now I knew very well that I have *not* been drivelling or anything similar to that, but I said, "Well if I have been drivelling" (agreeing that I *had* been) "it was because——"

"Don't agree with me!" he cried, and, finding myself in a bad net, I remained silent for a while.

I thought to myself, "Wanda Gág, say what you think. You haven't been holding your own. Why haven't you? Well, don't bother about that now. Start this minute to assert yourself." So now I said with much decision, "Well I know one thing. There are only two courses open to me now—I will either have to bring it out, or go mad."

He knows I will bring it out if it is in any way possible. I only meant that I might be checked by the fact that my family would need me. He knows—he *should* know—that I have not, as he says, "up to this time been drawn in" but that I have plunged many and many a time. I usually do not tell people when I take a plunge, I never see much reason for burdening other people with my disappointments. Sorrow is a different matter—that's an emotion, it's a state, it can be lessened. But disappointment is an event, an event for which there is no help, and as I have trained myself to bear disappointments very easily, I choose to bear them myself so as to spare as many people as possible. Therefore when I take a plunge I tell no one. If it is not a success I swallow the lesson and remain quiet. If it is a success I let other people know it so they may share my joy. But usually they do not know that the matter had involved any risk on my part. They think that the thing just "came my way."

Mr. A.E., I will endeavor, henceforth, to prove to you not only that I am a person of *decisive character,* but also that I *have* taken plunges and that I will not be afraid to take a great plunge when the time comes for me to do so. To be continually "drawn in" would be entirely too monotonous for a person of my character. I can stand some kinds of monotony, but mental monotony is too much for me, and that is what continually being drawn in would amount to. I have made you come around to a good many things and see if I won't make you come around, meekly, to these.

See if I won't, *see if I won't,* SEE IF I WON'T.

Well Wanda, you've had your little fling. Calm yourself.

He said, "In some things you are far ahead of a senior at college and in other things you are far behind." I know that too. I lack the *training,* the academic part of it. Armand said that he always takes for granted that I have a college education, "Only you haven't." On the whole, I think he manages me very considerately in that respect.

I said, "That is what I meant by saying that part of me seemed to be going too fast and the other part too slow. It would be allright if one part of me went too fast *or* the other too slow, but too slow and too fast at the same time is too much for me. It makes too big a gap."

He said, "You are becoming more complex every day."

I said, "Yes, judging by the way I feel."

He said, "How do you feel?"

I said, "Complex." I might have said, "Complex-compound."

He said too that I caused him more worry than a corn would if he had one. Flattering comparison.

He didn't quite know what to do with me in order to take me out of the whirlpool into which I had been drawn, and contemplated starting me on philosophy first. But afterwards he said, "Do you want to take a course in Rhetoric from me this winter?" I said I would.

He said "I'll have you write themes. Would you like that?"

I said "Yes," rather lifelessly I suppose, for he said, "You don't seem very enthusiastic."

I said "Yes!" more emphatically. So we have decided that I am to write an appreciation of Shaw's "Caesar and Cleopatra," that said theme shall be no longer than 1500 words, and that I would have 3 weeks to do it in.

He said that he would be very severe. I knew that. He told me quite frankly once that he refused to consider me as a poet. I don't think he thinks I *can* write very well. Neither do I. But if it will put me into a position to be able to write up my thoughts and feelings less angularly it will be worth while. It would be worth while even without that. The training will be good for me.

I am prepared to have my work torn from limb to limb. Armand said if I didn't show any originality he would probably wring my neck which, altho it is not exactly gentle, is at least a very original line of action. He told me that he thought he knew what things I was going to run up against. He thought that I would use too many short sentences, and that I would have to fight for unity. "There will be three things," he said, "which I want you to have in your themes, Unity——"

"——Mass and Coherence" I finished, remembering the melody from my High School days. Whereupon Armand said, "You are an apt pupil."

He said that in my theme I should give my opinions—give reasons for every one of them. That, in regarding the characters, I should not say, "That character is badly drawn. He wouldn't act that way in real life," but that I should ask myself, "Is his character consistent with the play?"

"We will not let you go mad," he said. "We will *bring it out.*"

He told me also to write to him just as often as I felt like it, telling him about the things I was reading, etc. He said, "Well I'll have to go—as usual. And thank you." I said "What?" He said, "Thank you. You pulled me out of the dumps."

November 26, Thanksgiving Day

Yesterday I got an answer to my letter, from Mr. Russell. Also the book "Phantastes" which he has written so much about. The letter was very nice. He told me that I was to come over and bring some of my work with me. He understood beautifully about my Me's, and even gave me some new ideas concerning them which suit me beautifully. I have a rather motherly feeling towards my Me-Myself idea and consider it rather as my own child, (altho I am sure many other people have children who look just like it) and usually other people's ideas do not exactly fit my conception of the idea. But I am willing to accept Mr. Russell's thoughts on the subject.

I feel as if, after I had met him, I should want a very very long talk with him. I think I could talk days and days with him because I know that there must be so many things that we agree on. I think he will like me.

I wonder if I am destined to become one of those self-assertive, almost-arrogant people. I do not use these words in the usual sense—I can't find the words I want. I mean someone who is so frank that he has no mock-modesty. Shaw. Byron. Dr. Beaudoux. Armand. Mr. Mc-Whorter. I rather think I will. If so, I know I shall be misunderstood—one usually is. Some of the girls already think that I am too egotistical. I have been trying to explain that I am not an egotist but a Myselvist; but, altho my arguments usually silence them on the subject, I have a very certain feeling that at heart I have not convinced them.

I told Paula what Armand said about his not knowing whether I would do my greatest deed thru my personality or my art, whereupon Paula said quite decisively, "Your art, I think." She does not think that my personality is one which would do it. I said, "Well, do you think you have gotten more out of me thru myself or my drawings?" She said, "Well of course I know you so well, but if I didn't know you well I should certainly get much more out of your drawings." But I have a personality. I know because I have made a number of very interesting tests in that respect—I have deliberately acted natural and watched to see the effect on people. I used to have friends more for the fact that I was clever (ding it!) or because I drew, but all my real friends like me for neither of these things but because of Myself.

I have started reading "Phantastes." A queer book. It is, as Mr. Russell has said, full of pictures. There is also much music, and some thoughts which appeal to me very much. The thing which is predominant, at least from the first reading, is the element of delectable surprise. It's like the things Armand plans. You don't know what's coming but you are sure that it is going to be something you'll enjoy very much, and also just the thing which you least expect.

I had rather a nice Thanksgiving of it. I had dinner at the Y. and a good one. I wanted badly to go to the "Mikado" but the cheapest seats were 50¢ so I went to the Orpheum. All by myself, too, and I enjoyed it. Sketched some interesting characters, did a very satisfying finger-hloopsie-stunt, twisting my fingers in time to the music all kinds of ways, and dissected the performance (I do love to be analytic when I'm seeing vaudeville). When I came back I wrote diary.

I really can't help wishing I would earn a little more. I don't see what I'll buy my Christmas presents with. For the family, I mean. My Christmas presents to other people count practically nothing, but I don't know what I'll do if I can't buy nice things for the family. It would take away half the joy of my Christmas.

Goodnight, and goodbye to this diary. Wanda.

* * *

November 27, Friday

I have just telephoned to Mr. Russell to see whether it would be convenient for him to see me to-morow. His voice sounds much different than I expected it to be, much different than the *Myself* which he shows in his letters. Rather quick, and short. Armand may be right in expecting him to have a quick restless glance.

I made two sketches of myself. I am wearing my hair differently again. My hair is drawn back at the sides and the rest of the coiffure consists of a roll which begins at my forehead and continues across the top of my head and down to the back of my neck. Not exactly pretty, but very stylish. Also rather interesting. I know tho that I would absolutely detest the arrangement if it were not fashionable.

I did some experimenting in water colors to-day.

In my last diary I was seemingly egotistical at the end. I wonder what Armand will think of it. I guess I will let him read it and see if he will put on his sage air and warn me not to think that I know too much.

November 29, Sunday

And now I have seen Mr. Russell. I know him very well. I knew that if I would ever meet him we would not have to go thru useless preliminaries in getting acquainted. We skipped years and years of that and took each other from where we *were* not where we *seemed*. He knows me too. "I can see thru you, just as you can see thru me," he said with a little laugh.

When I came into his office he said somewhat stammeringly, "You are not—Miss Gág?" I said I was and we shook hands. He mentioned something about a telephone being such an impersonal thing, which made me rather glad for he had not sounded very interested the night before. Then he told me to sit down, paced up and down the room several times, picked up a paper and seated himself beside me. "You like poetry, don't you?" he said. I said I did and he showed me one which he thought was exceedingly good. "Perhaps you'd like to read it," he said, "while I get a grip on myself." He explained that he had so much work which had to be done in a hurry that he was rather done to a frazzle.

He paced up and down, and up and down. To tell the truth I didn't read the poem as one should read poems. I read the words and they meant nothing to me. I was too interested in watching Mr. Russell and too excited at his queer ways. He is a slight man, of about medium height. He does not, as Armand surmised, look *up* at you nor do his eyes travel restlessly. He is in fact very frank in his gaze. I do admire his frankness. He makes no effort to conceal his weaknesses, of which he has a number. He makes no effort to *show* them either, for that matter. He's just sincere.

Afterwards he came over and said, "What have you concealed there?" They happened to be the sketches which I had brought so I showed them to him. He seemed to like them very much, especially a pencil sketch of myself which I did on brown paper a few weeks ago (I shall call it "Calm and Myself") and another of a little wondering girl backgrounded by flowers and trees. He raved about them rather to himself than anything else, and—would you believe it?—*typed* his mouth in the way I do when I enjoy a thing intensely, only he did it more mildly.

He said he wanted to show some of my drawings to the Managing Editor, Mr. Jones.* He went to Mr. Jones' office a number of times but the editor was always busy. Then there came two women and a little girl. One of the women was Mrs. Russell and the girl was little Alice Russell. The little girl has light hair, which is bobbed almost severely in a Dutch cut altho I daresay it allows of nothing more ethereal on account of its extreme straightness. Her face is fair, mouth red as a child's should be, and rather small when compared with the eyes which are big, greenish-grey, handsome and fairy-like. After I had been introduced to his wife and the other woman, Mrs. Russell said, "We're going down town to shop and fool around. Will you keep baby here until

* The late Herschel V. Jones.

you go; and take her home?" Mr. Russell said he would and they left. He set the little girl down at the typewriter where she tapped away happily.

He asked me to tell him about my work, which I did. He asked whether they (Buckbee Mears) appreciated—"Well, this for instance" he said, holding up one of my sketches. I said, "Well they consider me only as far as I am profitable or useful to them." I told him too that the greatest thing I had to contend with was my originality. "I have to keep it in check," I said. He does not like to have me be obliged to keep it in check.

He begged me not to let anything stop me from doing "this" (as he pointed to my sketches). He said that art was certainly my *forte*. I told him about my not-becoming-an-artist idea but he seemed to think that, whatever else I might do at the side, art would be and should be the thing which I was to cultivate above all else.

"Oh Wanda," he said sometime after this (he is unconventional and called me Wanda without any apologies, which I liked), "Don't ever marry a man who does not move in your world. You know now—you know there *are* people who *will* respond."

Finally he went over once more to see if he could find Mr. Jones. While he was gone I went over to little Alice and asked her whether she liked to be a little girl. She said in her little child-voice, "Yes." I said we had five little girls at our house. She said "Oh? And mama has only me."

At about this time Mr. Russell appeared with Mr. Jones. The next few minutes are one jumble to me, for Mr. Jones became so enthusiastic about my drawings that I nearly bowled right over. He stood and raved about them. Editors are usually so immovable, so fancy what a surprise it was to me to find him absolutely jumping up and down with enthusiasm as he looked at my sketches. I don't remember exactly what we said, I was so surprised I couldn't think rationally, but I remember that Mr. Jones asked me what I was doing now. I told him that I was working for Buckbee Mears.

He asked, "How much are they giving you a week?"

I said "Five dollars," whereupon Mr. Jones turned around, there to meet Mr. Russell's eyes, and they both gave a sort of snort. At least Mr. Jones did. It was a "Listen-to-that!" sort of snort.

Then he turned around to me and said abruptly, "Do you want to go to Art School here in Minneapolis with all your expenses paid?"

It didn't take my breath away, as one might be led to expect, for it was said in a tentative way. I said, "Well of course I want badly to go to school again, but it's this way. You see we all draw, and there are six younger than I who will soon need educations in order to get that out of them what is in them, and I want as soon as possible to be in a position to earn the money which will be necessary for that."

Mr. Jones said "Well, I'll look into the matter."

Mr. Russell was quite tickled to see that my drawings had taken such effect. The matter really didn't make much of an impression upon me. I have learned not to bank on any statements like that—not that I think people are not sincere in making them, but that they are so busy that such things are soon drowned in the many other things which crowd into their lives. The main reason why I forgot this so promptly, however, was because my mind and heart and soul were so taken up with Mr. Russell. I like him so much. He is so nice and considerate and fatherly, and calls me "Wanda" in such a tender way as my own father might have done—as my own father *did,* in fact.

Then he and Alice took me to the car line. He asked whether he could pay my car fare but I said I thought I had enough money. He said quietly and almost wistfully (altho I don't see how the wistful part came in) "Will you let me?" I couldn't resist—there was a look in his face that seemed to tell me that I would be hurting him much if I refused, altho I don't quite see how that could be either. But then, he is different from the common run of people and one must not consider one's self equal to interpreting all the outward manifestations of such persons, for there might be a maze of reasons, set up one behind the other far back into themselves, for one such action or feeling.

December 2, Wednesday

To go on with last Saturday. For the rest of the day, and for the next two days I could not get Mr. Russell out of my head. In the first place he was so different from what I had planned for two years on his being, and then such a "make-you-think" kind of a difference.

Monday I worked, and Tuesday as I returned from *four* jobs at Buckbee Mear's, I found a Special Delivery Letter for me from the Journal. It said that I was offered instruction at the Minneapolis Art School, all expenses paid, room and board included ("which," they wrote, "are already engaged") so I had to decide fast whether I was going to accept or not. I was, of course, much upset now that the thing had really come to pass. I didn't know quite what to make of it. Mr. Jones had only talked to me about five minutes and seen some eight or ten sketches, and it seemed almost impossible that he should take me up on such scanty proof of my abilities. I did not dream of accepting until I had seen Mr. McWhorter about it.

I did not know just how to handle the thing so I telephoned to Armand. I told him something exciting, but something nice too, had happened, and I believe I asked him to come down *right swack*. But his mother was ill so he couldn't. He told me to tell him what it was and I told him all about it. When I told him that the room and board had already been secured he said, "Where is the room?" I said, "In Minneapolis." He said, "Yes, but where?" I didn't know that, so he told me to meet him at Donaldson's Tea Rooms (in Minneapolis) the next day so we could go to the Journal and find out.

I did meet him to-day, at about 10 o'clock, and we walked over to the Journal. Armand said that I had better go up alone because it would make a better impression. He said, "Tell them you were on your way to a dinner engagement, so you thought you'd drop in. You *have* a dinner engagement at twelve o'clock—with me."

I went up and found Mr. Russell, who really seemed quite glad to see me again. He introduced me to Miss Kilbourne who said that she was glad to meet me because she was interested in me and had heard so much about me.*

I told Mr. Russell that I had just dropped in to get a brief comprehensive view of the matter. I asked him where the room was and he said in the Woman's Boarding Home which was in charge of the Y.W.C.A. The house had been left as a home for girls by a millionaire, Mr. Dunwoody, and it was on Tenth St. I said it was very nice of them to do that for me, when Mr. Russell said that I was to express my thanks to Mr. Jones personally because he was the one that was doing it. He took me in and left, leaving me all alone, face to face with Mr. Jones. At first I quaked a little about the knees but I thought to myself, "Wanda Gág, it's up to you to make an impression," so I plunged in.

I told him that I had come in to express my appreciation for his offer, and in some way I found myself telling him how I didn't feel that I deserved credit for what I did. I told him that my talent, if I had any, belonged less to me than to anyone else, that it was only put into my

* Another Journal editor. She was a friend of my former high-school teacher, Miss Lee.

custody and that it was my *duty* to make the best of it. "I know I can do something worth while if I want to," I said boldly, "That isn't arrogance; it's a feeling inside of me."

He said that that was the way it should be, and after I had raved for some time he looked at me with such a queer, interested smile and said, "When did you think all those things?"

I said, "Why, I always think that way," which of course is true enough.

He said abruptly and with another of his queer smiles, "Well, are you coming?"

I said, "Why, I can't tell yet. I don't want to accept until I have seen what the St. Paul people will say about it. They have been very kind to me and I feel that, as a matter of courtesy, I ought to see them first."

I suppose he thought it rather queer for me to postpone the acceptance so *cooly*. But I never feel like falling all over people—it doesn't pay to throw yourself against anybody. Besides that would be a form of cringing, and I cringe for no one. If I had had any inclinations of cringing it would have meant that I wasn't able to see the thing in the right light. I never would have even thought of accepting if the thing were being done for *me*. I have too much pride for that, and I'm glad of it. They were doing the entire thing for Myself; and Myself, as I have stated before, belongs less to me than to anyone else. They have as much a right to help develop it as I have.

I know both Mr. Jones and Mr. Russell are glad that I can see the situation in the right light, for when I said things to that effect they brightened up with relief as if I had saved them the trouble of explaining the thing to me. And I have noticed that even tho people *do* explain a thing like that to me, they are always afraid that I am only assenting and do not understand after all. But after I had said all this of my own accord, without the slightest suggestion from them, they could be sure that I was not mistaking their offer for *personal* aid.

After I said that the St. Paul people had first claim upon me on account of their being the first to do anything for my art, what does Mr. Jones do but pop out at me with the following question:—"We accepted your first work, didn't we?" And ding, he was right. The Journal Junior not only accepted my first work, but a ding lot of it too. I must have earned about $200 from them, and who knows how I might have gone thru High School if it hadn't been for that. And that was before St. Paul had ever heard of me.

He said, "You'd better come. I'm the best friend you've got" (and here I smiled a cryptic smile, for altho he obviously was going to be a very good friend, he did not know that I am the kind of person who, when I did have friends, had them exceedingly *good*.) "When I start a thing I put it thru. If your work merits it we will see that you go East where you will have a good chance to get in the magazine field and so be able to help your sisters." This last was quite overwhelming, but I took it quite as a matter of course.

I told him I'd see the St. Paul people right away and tell him of my decision as soon as possible. And so I went out. I met Mr. Russell in the hall where I told him briefly what he had said and he seemed quite tickled that it had gone off so smoothly. When I told him about the East he said that Mr. Jones had a good pull with the magazine people in the East, and of course simply being in the good graces of such a man means much. However, I am not building air-castles in the East and about the East. I have the present to live in.

I met Armand downstairs and we went to see my new home. On the way I told him all that had passed and when I said that about the East, he looked somewhat dazed and said, "It sounds so fishy."

I told him I was becoming so business-like and courageous (whereupon he reminded me that it was he who had drummed that into me) that I was quite surprised at myself. He said, "You'll get along all-right in the world. You were born lucky. It isn't luck either, you deserve every bit of it. I told you from the first that I believed in you."

I took the whole thing quite as a matter of course. I never know just what will flop down on me next, and my life has consisted, for the greater part, of such surprises that I am getting quite used to them.

We saw my new home, and when Armand saw it he said, "It's all-right; you'll be safe there." Then we went to Donaldson's Tea Rooms for dinner. The music suited my mood exactly. When the orchestra started playing I must have gone off in a sort of trance, from which I was awakened by Armand's exclaiming that there was much *"Wien"* in my eyes. We talked of many things, and much of the time we didn't talk at all. I was in a queer sort of mood. I could forget all else that was beyond our table. The music I suppose.

Then we went over to the "U." I don't know just how we arrived at the point but we were discussing marriage. I said, "Armand, don't ever let me marry a man who does not move in my world," and I told him that I was absolutely serious about this. (We hadn't been talking very seriously just before that.) He said that if I fell in love I wouldn't listen to anyone, that if he came and told me not to marry the man, I would simply smile and marry him anyway. I said I was so afraid that I would marry that kind of a person. Armand said facetiously that perhaps in that case he would be self-sacrificing enough to marry me simply to save me from the clutches of such a man.

Armand said, seriously, that I would never be happy with a man who was artistically my superior or even my equal, which of course I have thought out a long time ago. He said that there were only a few men whom I could marry, because there were very few who would be deep enough to understand and interpret correctly my "selfishness." He told me that for a while Mr. Gray worried him. I said, "Oh there was no danger. I knew from the first how I felt about it." Whereupon he said that I might not have *known*. Perhaps I don't know whether I love a man, but I certainly do know when I *don't* love a man.

At the "U" I met Mr. Reed (whom I had seen last spring) and Eleanor Price. She bends too much under Armand. Armand made an engagement to walk with her next Friday. After we left he told me she had good stuff in her but that she didn't know just what it was. He said he was going to find out what it was if it took him all year to do it.

He said, "She doesn't know quite how to take me."

She certainly doesn't know how to take him, and unless he's going to fall in love with her, he had better look out.

December 5, Saturday

The next day (Thursday) Mr. McWhorter called for me at the Y.W. I had told him that I'd like to see him because I had something important to tell him. He remarked that I was looking so well and radiant. He said that he had called up Buckbee Mears the day before and they had told him that I wasn't there that morning, that I had gone to Minneapolis. I said, "Yes, that is what I wanted to see you about." He went on saying that Buckbee Mears had told him that I was getting along fine and that I was making stuff which could be used. It gave me an uncomfortable feeling, his running on so delightedly and complacently and my knowing how soon he would be feeling less so. Mrs. McWhorter has been very ill too, and I disliked like everything to pile some more trouble on top of this. I told him that the news I had was at the same time happy and unhappy. "I'm afraid you won't like it

very well," I said. "I have a letter which I'll let you read." Now I think
that that was quite diplomatic, preparing him for the worst.

I asked him how Mrs. McWhorter was getting along, and he said
that she had just had a turn for the better and was getting along pretty
well now. After I heard that I did not feel so guilty in telling him my
news, so I handed him the letter. He actually trembled as he read it.
He said afterwards, "I trembled. I couldn't imagine what in the world
it was going to be."

He must have read it at least four times for it took him so long; unless indeed he was thinking hard and fast after he had read it once.
He *must* have thought hard and fast, for as he handed me the letter
he said, "Accept it."

He told me he was very glad that I was having such a chance, and
that he had become somewhat worried about my living on so little
money. He said that I should write to Mr. Jones and tell him that I
would accept his offer, and that the Manager of the St. Paul Art Institute was very happy that he (Mr. Jones) was giving me a chance, and
that he was no less glad over the whole matter than I was. Wasn't that
perfectly adorable?

He said that there were some things about the Minneapolis School
which he did not like, and he told me some of the things I was to guard
against, such as too much *academicness* (I can't find a noun to correspond with academic) and superficiality to some extent. He said
too, that they didn't give the students so much of a chance to follow
their own particular bent. He said he was sorry that the St. Paul people
were not able to make me a similar offer but thought that I might even
come back to the St. Paul school later. I told him that I was by no
means going to become disloyal to the St. Paul Art School and indeed,
I see no reason why being loyal to a new school should necessitate becoming disloyal to the old one. He said, "Well, you're coming to the
Twelfth Night Party, anyway." I said eagerly, "Oh may I?" He said,
"Why, you *must!*"

When I told him of my interview with Mr. Jones he laughed heartily.
He seemed to be quite tickled over the way I had acted, and said, "I'm
glad you said what you did. It showed him your real self."

He told me the plot for a story which he said he might write up
some day. This reminded me of the fact that Armand was going to give
me a course in rhetoric this winter.

He said, "I don't like the idea of having Armand for your teacher."

I gasped mentally for I could see no harm in that. I said, "Why not?" I thought perhaps he was afraid that Armand might dominate and influence me too much, so that I would see everything from his point of view and so become one-sided. But that wasn't it. He said that when a man and woman saw so much of each other as we did they would eventually fall in love. I hastened to explain that Armand and I understood each other perfectly on that point, and that we had established a Platonic friendship between us—and (I did not say this, of course) I don't exactly see that people falling in love should be exactly a crime. I suppose he meant that they fell in love and married even tho they were not fitted for each other.

He said Jack Alden had always told him that the relationship between Armand and me was Platonic, but he declared that it was impossible for any man and woman to see each other often without one or both of them falling in love. "It's mostly the woman who falls in love," he said. "Oh do you think so?" I said in some surprise, "I have usually found it just the other way round." I told him, too, that usually as soon as the man broke away from the *Platonicness* of a friendship, I got tired of him even tho I had liked him exceedingly well as just a friend.

He said, "If I didn't know Armand Emraad almost as well as he does himself, if I hadn't known him for many years and known that he was a perfectly good man, I would not have let you go with him as much as you do, without first investigating his character thoroughly, *because* afterwards it would have been too late."

So my Uncle Mac does not believe in Platonic Friendship either. He said there was a psychological reason why it was impossible. He said too that he was going to see Armand about it—he would be able to understand it better than I. He said, "Don't take Armand as seriously as he takes himself. Just have him for your playmate."

I can't quite explain what kind of an effect the whole thing had on me. It was so queer to realize that I had been watched like that, and it was nice in a way, for of course it's very handy to have a man who will investigate the character of the people you associate with—especially as I have no father or big brother. Of course I do feel that I can tell pretty well whether people are good or not, but in some cases one might make mistakes. Not that I ever had any doubts about Armand.

He put the matter into such an entirely new light that I was quite taken off my bearings. He said that it would be allright if I were to teach Armand something in return, but I must confess I don't see how that would help much. I wonder if he will tell Armand, and if he does, what Armand will do.

The next few days I spent in packing and writing letters.

This afternoon Mr. Russell took me over to my new home and introduced me to one of the ladies in charge, and showed me my room. Today he was much less nervous.

* * *

Three Young Artists Start An Art Class
*An incident out of Anton Gág's youth, as drawn by him
in an early sketch book*

Part Five

ART SCHOOL—MINNEAPOLIS

1914

December 11, Friday

Monday I came over to Minneapolis.

I went over to Art School directly and asked for Prof. Koehler. When he came I held out my hand and said, "How do you do? I am Wanda Gág." His face broke out into a smile, and he said, "How you have jainged!" He called me "Wanda" with a German *a* and in such a nice fatherly way that I felt much less strange directly. I was to start in the Girls' Life Class the next morning, so I went home. I found my trunk had arrived so I started unpacking right away.

My room is not very large but very pleasant. It is on the first floor and has a nice big window overlooking a pretty piece of yard. And it is only a few steps away from the dining hall. The meals are good and do not taste Cafeteriary or Boarding House-ish. I am seven blocks from the Journal, two blocks from school,* and five blocks from Donaldson's and Daytons'. Oh yes, and about two blocks from the Walker Gallery.

About the first thing I did after I came to my room was to arrange my furniture more aesthetically. Its former arrangement had hurt my vision. I have a screen covered with green burlap, and I conceived the brilliant idea of pinning some of my drawings to it. I call it my art gallery, and when people ask to see some of my sketches I simply unfold the screen, saving myself the trouble of *wühling* all thru my drawers first. I have a good mirror in my dresser too, bigger than those at the Y.W. As a consequence I have some seven or eight sketches of myself since I am here.

Tuesday I went to school. I had Life in the morning, in which Mr.

---

* At that time the Minneapolis Art School occupied the upper floors of the Public Library building.

Gustav Goetsch gave criticisms. He is a little taller than medium height, wears a mustache and pretensions to a Van Dyke beard in straw color, and has lightish hair which is noticeable by its absence upon the top of his head. Perhaps I should not write of him so, but he *did* irritate me so when I first saw him and had him speak to me. And, disrespectful as it may seem or be, I could not help but think that he looked as "a salamander" sounded.

He didn't introduce me to any of the girls, which certainly wasn't very gentlemanly. He has a satirical twinkle in his eyes and can be extremely sarcastic of speech. I had all I could do those first few days to keep myself from saying something—well, rather forceful—to him. He didn't tell me what classes I was to take nor where I was to take them, nor what materials I needed. The first afternoon he didn't tell me where to sit or what to draw until I asked him, and then he just simply said that I should sit down wherever I wished. And ding, all the places were taken that I could see. So I sat down on a stool and waited for him to come around. More than once I was on the point of saying to him, "I may not be very important, but I'm not used to being treated as a negative quantity." I debated with myself whether I ought to do this and claim the courtesy which was due to a new student and a woman, or whether I was to look over the heads of these petty thoughts. I finally decided on the latter.

I was very much surprised to see that it took me fully three days to mingle with the rest of the students. At first I thought that they were exceedingly snobbish, but now that I think back I can see that I was in a very thoughtful and *un-mixy* mood. I have learned much since I've been here. I am in my sphere once more.

Wednesday I wrote a letter to Mr. Russell asking him what was to be done about art school supplies and other little things that I needed besides my room and board, and Thursday morning he called me and said I was to ask Mr. Jones about it. So that afternoon I went up to Mr. Jones' office, a trifle shaky in the knees. I determined, however, that I was not going to act at all timid. I don't think he likes that. I didn't act timid either. I began telling him how I was getting along, when he asked me the very question I had come to ask him. He said that he wanted to have the thing put on a *basis,* and told me to come the following Saturday morning when we would talk it over.

Then I went and told Mr. Russell how beautifully it had all gone off, and he seemed quite elated over it. He is the funniest man. That day he wasn't nearly as nervous as he had been the first time I had seen him, and was even quite spry. He hops around like a boy. He asked whether I wanted to say Hello to Miss Kilbourne so I did. I told her I had seen Miss Lee.

I had met Miss Lee on the Street Car the day before. It felt so good to see her. She was all eagerness as to what I was doing and had been doing.

She said, "You know I saw Fannie Kilbourne some time ago, and I told her that some of my girls used to send things to the Journal, the Gág girls; and Fannie said that there were some contributing now, Asta and Thusnelda, and that Stella used to too at one time. 'Then there was another one,' she said, 'but we've lost track of her, and we wonder what's become of her.'"

That had happened about a month ago and, as I had received Mr. Russell's letter after that, I shouldn't wonder but that it was the result of this talk between Miss Lee and Miss Kilbourne.

Well, to go on with my saying "Hello" to Miss Kilbourne. She asked if I would be at home in the evenings, and I said I would be glad to have her come and see me. "I wish I could come, but I'm married," said Mr. Russell with a queer boyish twirl on his heels. I believe there was a sort of half-bound, half-jump in connection with it too.

December 16, Wednesday

Friday I really first mingled with the students at school, and felt much better. I am getting so that I talk with most of the boys, most of whom seem to be very nice. I do as a rule get along better and faster with men than with women. Most women are so critical about little things and are often, altho perhaps unconsciously, jealous.

Saturday I went to see Mr. Jones. He said "Hello" when he saw me, which I liked because it wasn't so business-like. It was decided that I was to have an allowance of $2 a week (which, by the way, far exceeded my expectations. Fancy having $2 a week for an allowance when you have been *living* [or trying to live, at least] on $5 a week) and that I was to have a charge account at some art store for my art school materials.

I was so happy! It was snowing silently and beautifully, and for some time at least I would not have to skimp and skimp and *skimp* and skimp, and I would, after all, be able to buy Christmas presents for the dear ones at home.

I guess I'll run to supper. I'm awfully hungry. I notice that since I'm staying here I enjoy my meals more than I do at Cafeterias. I forgot to say that Saturday Mr. Gray called for me at School. As I was not in, he waited for a long time, but left before I returned. He has telephoned twice since then, tho. From Cedar Falls. To-day he called up at School. He wants me to meet some friends tomorrow evening.

I telephoned to Armand at the beginning of the week, telling him that he was to call for his books at the Y.W. at St. Paul, and whether he would be able to go to the Twelfth Night Party with me. He said he thought he could and would let me know later.

I am going to have lunch with Mr. Gray this noon.

Later:—Ding *Ding* DING! After I thought I had him entirely vanquished too! I've had lunch with him, and later when I went over to the house, I saw him coming out of the door of that place. Why does he have to be tagging after me all the time? I should think he could be satisfied to see me this morning, this noon and this evening, without wanting the afternoon too. I don't see that he can't *see* I don't care for him. I didn't answer his last letter *at all,* and I've been so cool and disinterested I can't understand why he doesn't withdraw his hat from the ring.

I want my ring clear of cavaliers, I say, *I want it clear of old cavaliers!* They make me unhappy and peevish and make me want to stamp floors. I like Armand and his friends. They, at least, can like a person without falling in love or imagining themselves in love with one. Mr. Gray suggested going skating tomorrow but I said I wouldn't have time. I should think he might see how I am dodging (like a coward, I confess) all his suggestions. I can't stand to have him look at me so admiringly, can't *stand* to be helped across crossings by him. As long as he was only a friend I didn't mind, it was common courtesy, but I don't like to have anyone touch me whom I can never love, and who cares for me otherwise than a friend. He regards me as sort of belonging to him, or at least his relatives seem to regard me as a future member of the family. Not very obviously—but I can just *feel* it, that's all. And that's enough, to say nothing of too much. I hope he's got the ring-idea out of his head by this time.

December 17, Thursday

I don't want cavaliers any more, *ever!* I want only friends until I find the man I really belong to. I don't belong to cavaliers, and *I don't want them, I say,* I DON'T WANT THEM! Why do men have to turn into old cavaliers, when they have been such beautiful friends?

I saw Miss Lee to-day. She asked whether I was still writing. I said,

"Oh, Miss Lee, I don't think I can write." She said, "Oh yes, you can," and she seemed to be very anxious that I should keep on writing. She told me that she used to enjoy Paula and me so much in her High School classes and said, "You know a teacher can't show to her pupils that she is more interested in some who she knows are really getting something out of it."

I like Miss Lee and I like Mr. McWhorter, and Mr. Jones and Mr. Weschcke and Mr. Russell and Armand and Timmie and Dr. Beaudoux. But I don't like Mr. Gray. After I have turned him down flat and forever, I shall like him again, I guess. Oh I want to stay home and read Browning and cry and listen to music and roam along without rhyme or reason in my diary. I don't want to go and be shown a "good time." It's much more fun to cry. Much more fun, and much more instructive. And much more elevating.

I wish it were style to write stories the way one writes diaries and letters, without unity, mass and coherence. I wonder whether one couldn't. One would explain in the preface that there was no attempt at plot, rather there was an attempt at no plot, in order that the fine shades and modulations of moods would not be interfered with.

I have been reading Browning's "Cleon" which I like, oh so much.

> "Referring this to the gods
> Whose gift alone it is! which, shall I dare
> (All pride apart) upon the absurd pretext
> That such a gift by chance lay in my hand,
> Discourse of lightly or depreciate?
> It might have fallen to another's hand! What then?"

And that is how I have been feeling about Myself all the time. Why can't I stay at home to-night and think like this? I suppose it is, as Mr. Russell says, "the tribute we pay the world into which we are born."

12:35 p.m.:—Well, I didn't have as bad a time as I expected. In fact I had rather a good time. Mr. Gray behaved beautifully, and they were nice people that we visited—and we made candy and talked. I didn't have to haul out my Me's at all. Wasn't that nice?

December 27, Sunday. New Ulm.

I am at home for the holidays. Stella and Asta met me at the depot. Stella has become quite plump and the poor girl has to stand for so much teasing. Somehow I can't get used to the idea of any of our family being plump. She seems to get along better at teaching school than I did. My little Dehli was able to sit up in bed. She is so thin and pale and sweet. She is the most patient creature, and would not dream of complaining or causing us more work than is necessary. Asta, of course, is still as funny as she used to be, gloriously frank and full of original thoughts. We still have to scold Tussy for working so much. She'd work herself to a frazzle if we'd let her. Flavia is as satisfactory as ever. She isn't in the least pretty but she's very interesting-looking. Her eyebrows go up quite originally and her green eyes are charming. Howard is in that stage of development which is rather non-committal, but he is very considerate and marvelously willing to do errands. He is beautifully kind to Dehli.

And mama, as usual, is unselfish and loves us all very much. I think mama, as well as papa, has suffered, perhaps unconsciously, thru lack of the proper outlet of the Myself in her. It has always hurt me so much that she was not able to have the education which she really needed. My mother is a brave woman.

We spent the first evening telling everything that entered our minds of course. Oh it was so good to be back! Tuesday and Wednesday I spent in making Christmas presents and enjoying the darling folks. Tussy told me that I had such a good influence on Flavia because as soon as I came home she became perfectly angelic.

Then came Christmas Eve. Tussy and Stella and I trimmed the tree and arranged the presents. The next morning we were all assembled in Dehli's room waiting for the tinkling of the bell which was to tell that Santa Claus was leaving. Flavia remarked solemnly that Tussy "breathed like sleighbells." She said also that she had dreamt all night of Christmas. Her dreams must have been very vivid if she even got Tussy's breathing mixed up with them. By and by mama remarked casually that she'd have to go down to see how the furnace-fire was getting along, and of course soon after that the bell tinkled. Stella and I led Dehli downstairs, and the rest followed in high excitement. We put Dehli in a big chair which we had arranged beforehand, and wrapped quilts about her. She was so happy. She had wished for days and days that she might be able to be downstairs on Christmas morning, for in our family that means so much.

I sketched Dehli as she sat packed up in the chair. She got tired of sitting up after an hour or two, and I suggested that we move the cot bed down into the front room. We put it in a place where she could get a good view of the tree. She said afterwards that she looked at the tree all the time so that she would have a clear remembrance of it after she went upstairs again. It was rather noisy downstairs, so after the first day she went upstairs once more.

We stayed at home all day and we had no visitors except Uncle Frank and Judy. I was glad we didn't have many visitors, because when I come home, I come home to see my family and relatives. Somehow I just want to stay at home all the time. I am always so afraid that if I go away I'll miss some of the interesting sayings or incidents which our kids are constantly committing. When I see some of our children among other people I always laugh with proud glee inside of myself because I know just what they are like, down *deeper,* and other people don't.

We felt so sorry to think that Dehli would have to part from the Christmas tree, so we decided to decorate a small Christmas tree for her owny-ownsy. We put real candles upon it, and tinsel, cookies, candy, tiny stockings and some other knick-knacks. The tree was about a foot and a half high. When it was all ready I carried it into her room saying, "Tinkle, tinkle," like our bell goes on Christmas morning, and as Dehli saw it she said "Oh," so simply and appreciatively, and with such a happy Dehli-look in her eyes that the tears started in mine, and I had to race over to the other side of the room on some lame pretense. I felt as if she had heaped a thousand thankyou's upon our little efforts. For a long time she was content to look at the tree with her rare smile upon her face, but afterwards she drew it and painted it.

Tussy and Asta are reading "Phantastes" and are just wild about it.

My fervent wish of a "happy, tho not a rich Christmas" was granted.

1915

Tuesday, January 5

I am back at Minneapolis. I came to St. Paul Sunday evening, but as it was rather late I stayed with Paula at the Y.W. for the night. The next morning as I was sitting at Paula's window, I was reminded most forcibly and deliciously of last spring. The air that came in at the window was moist and actually balmy, and I thought of chocolate bars and flowered waists and Meredith and Dickens and peg-top skirts all in a jumble. And oh, I liked it.

I went back to Minneapolis that morning but spent the morning in unpacking. I went to school in the afternoon and learned something about pencil drawing. I am beginning to like Mr. Goetsch pretty well, for he really does know a good deal about art and he is rather philosophical at the same time.

Mr. Dehn (one of the boys at school) and I had a very interesting talk too. I like to talk to him because he does not agree with everything I say, because he has ideas of his own to put into a discussion, and because he is broadminded enough to look at the other person's point of view. I told him he could draw, and told him also to appreciate that because I was noted for giving few compliments. He really can draw. And he hasn't much money, which is good for him I think. I always think that a girl in the city is better off with a little more money than she needs, and a boy with a little less than he needs.

Mr. Dehn is German, brilliant, and has much charm. I told him that, as a rule, I liked better to talk to men than to women because women, however broadminded they might be otherwise, were as a rule *requirous* of too much politeness, and small-minded in general about *small* things. And that makes it big you know. It's like two negatives being equal to one affirmative. I said, "For instance if I'd tell a woman that I knew I could draw she would think I were conceited but a man might look at it more broad-mindedly." I suppose I brought in my Myself-custodian idea.

Mr. Dehn said at one point, "You are quite a thinker, aren't you?" I said evasively, "Am I?" He said, "Well, are you? Now be frank about it—don't you think you are more philosophical than most people?" Whereupon I did answer frankly, "Yes, I think that I think more than the majority of girls do." He said, "There, I'm glad you said that, because you wouldn't have been telling the truth otherwise."

January 7, Thursday

Tuesday morning I had a telephone call over at school. It was Armand and he said he was coming at one p.m. Well, I surmised from the start that Armand was coming to say that he wouldn't be able to come to the Twelfth Night Party, and for the rest of the morning I kept saying fiercely to myself, "If *he* doesn't *come*, if *he* doesn't *come!*" and declared mentally that he was "absolutely and without exception the biggest pieface" I had ever known.

At a little after one he arrived. Near the beginning of the afternoon

Armand said that I had a new look in my eyes which he didn't like. I said, "I thought you wouldn't like it. But I'll get over it, I think, when winter is over. I don't see why it should pass away when winter is over but it just feels that way." I believe I mentioned that something (perhaps the new look in my eyes) was probably due to my wrangling with Reason.

"To hell with Reason!" Armand said, and I nearly fell off the Christmas tree. To think that I should ever hear Armand, of all people, say that!

He informed me further that instead of trying to withstand things, he was letting himself go and allowing himself to be drawn in by the forces about him. "And it's doing me good," he added.

I can't understand it, that's all.

Another thing which I do not understand is that he said, "I knew that that day [December 2] was a turning point in our history" (or friendship or whatever it was. I forget the word.) He's just an old puzzle thru and thru, and altho I am coming to realize more and more that he knows what is best and that he's right in what he's doing, it certainly gets on my nerves.

He said, "Your Uncle Mac called me up and asked how your sister was. He said that he had been quite worried about her." Later in the afternoon he said, "I was sore when McWhorter called me up about you." I said, "What did he say?" and Armand said, "Oh, he asked how your sister was getting along and so forth." I wonder what my Uncle Mac *did* say.

Armand said, "I haven't gone to get those books from the Y.W. either."

I said, "Oh, you know, I put my name in some of them, so that in case they should get lost—and I didn't get time to erase them."

He said with unaccountable and entirely uncalled for vehemence, "Leave them in! And write in them whenever you feel like it. I told you to write into them. Write all over them and write it with an indelible pencil, write it with India ink. Write it with *India Ink!* Write in the margins, write over the print, write on the fly leaves, write on the cover—Tear out the pages! Do anything you want! *I* don't care."

Just what this flood of excitement should mean and what it can have been caused by is more than I can say—perhaps there was no reason either.

He said something, too, about my not having written the theme on

Shaw's "Caesar and Cleopatra." I said, "Well you never came to call for it." He doesn't know why I didn't write it, and I couldn't very well tell him that my Uncle Mac didn't approve of his being my teacher.

Armand said, "For once your hands are clean," but I have been keeping all charcoal, pencil marks, paint, pastel and ink off them most virtuously for the last two months or so. Really it seems that since I am here at Minneapolis I spend half my spare time washing myself, the other half being occupied in keeping my room in order. I told Armand that the trouble was he never came when my hands *were* clean.

At one point I mentioned one of my uncles and he said, "Uncle? That's right, you have uncles too. I never thought of you in that way." He asked how I got along with them and I told him I got along beautifully with the darling people.

Armand said, "Remember you have a date the First of May." I suppose it will rain pitchforks or Armand will be called away or something like that.

For a while we played that we were both notorious thieves, and afterwards we played again that we were German peasants. It was piles of fun and I believe we said a good many funny things altho I don't remember them.

As a matter of fact, Armand did really come to tell me that he would be unable to take me to the Twelfth Night Ball. I said that if it weren't so late I might have asked someone else but I didn't think it would be very easy to get a man *with a costume* at such a late date.

I thought of asking Mr. Dassett, one of the boys at school. The next noon I sauntered into the Antique room, bending my steps Mr. Dassett-ward. I said, "You know I told you about the Twelfth Night party they have at St. Paul every year?"

He said, "Yes?"

I said, "Well, my man was called off very unexpectedly and—would you like to take his place?"

He said "Sure" so promptly that it nearly bowled me right over. "When is it?" he went on.

"To-night," said I, "And it's a costume affair. Can you get one?" and he said he thought he could rake one up somewhere.

Armand had intended to go as an individual of the French Court, which would have been quite agreeable, I think. I went as a flower, in pink, and believe me, it was some costume (said she, omitting all signs of slang). It had an accordion-plaited skirt which I plaited *by hand*—it looked quite like the real thing. Mr. Dassett went as a cadet.

Very near the beginning of the evening Mr. McWhorter came up to me and talked for a little while. Then he said suddenly and with much surprise, "Where's Armand?" I said rather gaily (it was such a victory for me), "Oh I came with another man." My Uncle Mac said not a word. He gave me a surprised and almost reproachful look and turned around—mentally, and perhaps physically, gasping. It was a glorious moment for me. Before I turned to the party with whom my "other man" was talking, I gave a little triumphant glee-ful gurgle. My Uncle Mac will forgive me for this I know. It was so funny to have him feel disappointed because I did *not* bring Armand, after he had been preaching to me about that very individual.

I learned two new ways of dancing the fox trot and three Hesitations. I danced the one-step with Mr. Zeigler and before we knew it we were lame-ducking it because somehow it just seemed to come naturally to us. It was here too that I met Dr. McWhorter of South Dakota (my Uncle Mac's brother). This big, Oriental-looking and exceedingly nice man taught me a beauty of a little Hesitation. It was the only dance he could do, he said, so he was dancing it with everybody. Once as we were tripping and dipping with all the grace of which our uneven heights admitted, we passed Mr. and Mrs. Zeigler who were sitting on the thrones, and Mr. Zeigler said with a wistful look and an amused smile, "I wish I could do that!" Glory, it was funny.

	Fox trot	*Schottische*
No. 1.	4 slow steps, 8 fast. Two step	Both to side. 1—2—3—4
No. 2.	4 slow steps	2 schottische steps
	8 hippety hops	Girl four backward
	two step	schottische
	Then fox trot side by side	Both to side 1—2
No. 3.	4 slow steps. 4 fast	Girl four back.
	Side hop using four beats	Both to side 1—2
	Learned these from Mr. Dassett	Girl forwards 1—2—3—4

I had a pretty good time, altho the fact that I was not *socially* inclined that evening kept me from being as "brilliant" as I might have been otherwise. As I look back I can only imagine myself as walking about in a sort of trance, trying not to be absent-minded and trying very hard indeed to be polite and society-ish. Sometimes I almost think I am too far ever to wear the society mask again.

January 11, Monday

Thursday there was a grand Reception at the new Museum (to which
our Art School will move in time, [we are still at the Library]). The
Art Students were stationed in different rooms as guards and we had
all kinds of fun. I was in the Winslow Homer room and Mr. Moylan,
a youth who has brown curly hair, blue eyes and glasses, began to talk
to me, and we (we!?) discussed drawing moods, pastels, self-portraits
and wrapping paper with much vigor and delight. Later he was called
upon to take the Oriental room, but he was soon supplemented by Mr.
Dehn. We had a good time.

Near the end of the evening Professor Koehler came to me and said
in his nice way, "Wanda, you are wanted. Mr. Jones wants to see you,
and have you meet his wife and daughter." His wife and daughter
seem to be very nice indeed and my little round Journal Man looked
perfectly adorable, all done up in a dress-suit. Mr. Dehn and another
Art School boy took me home.

The next day at school we all related our experiences. We had all
enjoyed seeing silks and satins and throats glide by us, their owners
doing their best to say something intelligent or non-committal about
the pictures. Of course there were some who did know something about
art but I think the majority didn't. One young girl, who was surrounded
by some pink silk etc. (a dress), said to her father as they were standing
in front of a picture, "This is real *aht,* papa."

Another woman said to her escort, "Who painted these pictures?"
Her companion, after consulting the catalogue, said, "Corot." Whereupon the woman said, "Oh then I like them. Let's go on."

I wrote a letter to Timmie (about the Reception)—here are some
extracts from it:

> "I did not try to enjoy the pictures. How could I, with costly (and
> for the most part hideous) gowns sweeping past me and hoards of
> bored men in evening dress standing about with 'I-wish-I-were-home-
> and-in-my-smoking jacket' sort of looks on their faces. When I want
> to look at pictures I don't want to be surrounded by people who have
> come to show off their gowns and throats—for the very pictures on the
> wall seem sensitively to draw their Myselves away from the rude gaze
> or cursory glances of those who cannot or do not understand and
> feel the Soul of such things. There were some people there, of
> course, who could feel and understand, but I believe even these did
> not attempt to really enjoy the pictures to the extent that they were
> able, because of the crowd.

"I like to be all alone with such pictures because then the thinnest of veils is drawn back that we may see the sacred part of the picture which is shown only to one person at a time. A good piece of art, when I am alone with it, sends out waves of joy and pain, and love and sorrow, which heave and subside like a mighty pulsating heart. This is not rhetorical or flowery—it only sounds that way. And all these waves of the Souls and Myselves, which have been caught in the pictures, swirl around me and almost intoxicate me. Wouldn't you rather see pictures with soul-swirls about you, than with satin-and-silk swirls? I would, so instead of trying to draw from the pictures their Myselves, which they had so carefully drawn away, I studied the Life and the *Existence* with which I was surrounded.

"After seeing a night-full of rich people, I feel much richer by comparison. This may seem arrogant but how can I help it if I feel it?"

Sunday I went over to see Paula. It was a glorious night. As I walked my two blocks from the station, I felt that I could walk far into the night for the air was moist and balmy and the sky was of a luminous rose color where it had been saturated by the city lights. I think if I had been a boy I should have walked, alone, just on and on, with a silent song in my heart and Hloopsies fluttering in my throat. Just that, truly.

January 13, Wednesday

Yesterday morning I had a telephone call. I wondered who it could be. Surely not Armand, because I had seen him only a week ago. If it only weren't Mr. Gray.

It was Armand. He said that he could get off at 3:30 that afternoon and asked whether I could. I said that we had no school that afternoon and he said, "Delicious!" He came, a little after the appointed time, as usual. He wore a grey flannel shirt. I wore my new pink *crepe de chine* waist which evidently he did not remark at all, and my hands were so clean that they were dazzling, but not one word of praise, approval or appreciation did they draw from his lips. As I sat down he looked critically at my face, and when I asked him what was the matter he indicated his cheek and said, "Is it natural?"

Hm! What does he think I am, anyway—to infer that the rosy bloom upon my cheeks might not be natural! (I am simply bubbling over with laughter to-night and cannot treat even serious subjects in a serious manner). At any rate he is an old pieface for having said that, and he should just wait!

It was the funniest thing. I sat down and he sat down, and there we sat. Once in a while we said something. I made the most virtuous attempts at conversation, gathering all the news I possibly could, but he didn't even do that. Every once in a while he would make me rather uncomfortable with *"ein durch-borender Blick,"* but I was determined not to show him anything, so I would go off evasively on a little whimsical journey. That is probably why we just sat and played hide-and-go-seek with each other's minds, or souls or Myselves or whatever it was.

The poor man is still troubled with insomnia and I feel very sorry for him. When I taught school I used to lie awake nights. I wonder what he thinks about. I usually invent glowing speeches or lengthy tirades against some of my friends or else I plan my wardrobe for the coming season. The last is the most effective remedy but Armand doesn't plan his wardrobes. He goes to his tailor who says, "This is style. Wear it," and he does. Which is convenient but rather monotonous, I think.

Armand said I was still in the stage which I had been in, the last time he was here. I had supposed I was almost over it but he said that it was worse than last time. It doesn't worry me much. I just feel that as long as I'll have to go thru it anyway, I might as well do it and be over and done with it.

He said that the name "Mugwumper" fitted me as satisfactorily as "pieface" fitted him in my estimation.

Then Armand sat down at the piano and played. He started out with the Armand-tune from "La Boheme" and he came back to it again and again. Then there was another little melody that he played a number of times. He told me afterwards that that melody described me exactly.

At about five o'clock he asked whether I'd like to walk with him to the car-line, so I ran off for my jacket and cap. We talked dialect almost the entire way, and several people turned around and looked at us in such a queer way. Which made it all the more enjoyable of course. *"Der junge Bauer"* had taken me with him to the city. He finally went off in the *G'schupsl* and I tripped gaily off home, to make triumphant expressions at an imaginary Armand Emraad (who was represented by the looking glass).

At any rate I did not fall back even tho I didn't exactly advance.

I sent Timmie another long letter yesterday. I hope he gets it before he returns. He will be here very shortly, I think, of which I am glad because I like him.

I learned a good deal today at school especially in Life. Ding it, one of these days I'll make that school sit up and notice. It seems queer not to be one of the star students, and being considered more of a negative quantity than otherwise. Rather resting, but not an incentive. But I will make them acknowledge me—if I can't, I have no right to feel what I don't seem to be able to help feeling.

In Life all the students are three months in advance of me, and a great many of them are a year and three months in advance of me, but I look at the drawings which the most talented of these accomplish and rake myself over the coals for not being where they are. Of course I can't expect to learn in three weeks what these other people have learned in eleven months, but it's an incentive. Somehow I always find an incentive somewhere. If it's not in praise it's in lack of praise, if it's in neither of these it's in other people's good work; and if it's not in that, there is always Myself.

I have always the uncomfortable feeling that my mind, my soul, Myself (call it what you like) are far in advance of my *hands*.

When I remarked incidentally to-day that I did not intend to stop at magazine illustration, Mr. Dehn asked me what my ideal in art was. I couldn't explain it to him. The height towards which I aim is at the same time clear and vague. It's clear as long as I don't think about it, but as soon as I try to *gauge* or analyze it, it melts away evading my grasp. It's like the color in a landscape. Sometimes a patch of distance looks violet, or a thicket looks terra-cotta-colored, or a twig looks pink. You're very sure *subconsciously* that they are of those colors, but as soon as *you think about it,* their color or *lack of color* baffles you.

It's almost twelve and I must hop to bed. And I hope Armand will not have one of those sleepless nights tonight.

January 16

This morning I finished writing a letter to my Uncle Mac. I talked about that progressive thing, my ideal in art. Funny thing, you know. It's stable and changeable at the same time. You see my standard of ideals is always the same, but as soon as I take one step forward, my ideal does the same.

Yesterday morning when I went to get my allowance I ran up to see my Journal Man. This time he gave me a chair to sit upon while I talked, which is very considerate for a Managing Editor, *I* think. I told him how much I was learning. I told him that I was over-leaping myself, "or rather I should say," said I, *"Myself* is over-leaping *me."*

He said that he was very busy just now, so I was to just go on as best

I could (as if that were very hard under the convenient circumstances he has arranged for me!) and then a little later he would look into my case more carefully. He said, "Well, just don't hurry. Take a year or two of this, and then we'll send some of your things to some of those Eastern people and they will say 'What! Who drew this?' and—" I forget how he ended up, but anyway he said that there would be a great demand for my work. Here's hoping it will be so!

I told him that I would do my part of it by doing my best. "For the simple reason that I can't help it," I said. Which is true. I think I really do my best most of the time, altho it may seem to all outward appearances that I am at times rather negligent. For instance, I talk a great deal in Still Life and draw part of the time only. Usually I talk to Mr. Dehn.

One of the girls, who works like a beaver, looks at me every once in a while as if to say, "That girl might do otherwise than talking so much." But ding, when I draw, *I draw*. When I don't draw, I am studying character or other things and I am sure the time is not wasted. Someone will say, "Yes, but my dear girl, you can only reach your end by hard work." I know that too, thank you. I may be working hard as the dickens when I seem to be doing nothing at all. Aside from that, I am not losing sight of the drudgery part of art. The fact is that I enjoy the drudgery part. I love to sit in Life and study out the lines and proportions and muscles and bones. Stacks of fun.

I think there are some people who learn best by drawing and plugging whether they are inspired or not, but I stick to my old theory that in order to do something worth while *I* at least have to be inspired and *see* things unveiled. People may rake me over the coals if they wish, for having moods, drawing moods and others, but I maintain that—Oh well, I've said it often enough.

I stick to my old idea, that's all.

THAT'S ALL, I SAY.

If others want to draw away without inspiration and produce master pieces, let them do so, *I* don't care. I'll get along as fast as they anyway. I learn as much in one evening from 8 p.m. to 1 a.m. (that time stands for a drawing fit) than they do in a week. I learned more about life drawing one morning last week than I have in three weeks.

Then there is my arrogance which is very useful. Some of the other students may have it, but they are afraid to be frank about it and are therefore unable to make use of it. I don't suppose I ought to call it arrogance for it isn't ordinary, every-day arrogance. My arrogance is mostly for self-defense—or rather for Myself-defense. I refuse to let any one get ahead of me. If they do, I do my double best not to let them. Not because I don't like to see others do things. It's an incentive, that's all.

It's cowardly to be overly modest. In fact I think many artists are modest for just that reason. For instance a man would be afraid to say, "If I want, I can make people sit up and notice my work." He's afraid that he can't live up to it—he's afraid of facing *ignominious defeat*. Ding, what if you don't succeed! You at least don't have to be ashamed of your *Aim*. My *aim* is limitless. That I will never reach it I know, but I'm going to get as near there as I can. That will keep me running all the rest of my life, believe me.

One might contemplate upon the fact that I may not always remain as sincerely Myself as I am now and that I will not even continue to do my best. That would be possible, but acknowledging it as a possibility would only be making apologies in advance. Sort of Peer Gyntesque, you know, always arranging things so that you have something to fall back upon. What does he say? "I am always master of the situation—" something like that. But it is not good to be always master of the situation.

My falls are not sugar-coated either. They're bitter and they leave an unpleasant taste in my mouth. They even make me cry at times, but all the same I realize that one needs falls, however disagreeable they may be. Some day I will make Armand take back what he said about my never taking plunges. I am going to make him take back a number of things anyway. At the same time I shall probably take back a number of things I've said to him. There are a number of things in which I was wrong and unjust, as I realize now. Funny how I come swimming after Armand all the time. I mean, I find myself going thru the same waves (to put it metaphorically) and storms and calms that he has gone thru just a little while before. Some day perhaps I'll catch up with him. I intend to, anyway.

January 20, Wednesday

Yesterday was an event in my life—I started painting in oils. I am rather timid about handling my brush for I am not at all used to the medium, so my study is abominally smooth and insipid. It looks something like the work of that eternal aunt or sister or cousin of everyone you meet "who does beautiful oil studies and has never taken a lesson in all her life." But ding, I have a long road to travel in oil painting.

It seems that Emma Brock (a former student who did some good illus-

trations last year) has returned. They say she doesn't care about eating
either.

I am beginning to like Mr. Goetsch and I think in a short time I shall
like him very much indeed. Only some fine day we will have a good hot
little discussion, I think. You see he thinks himself smart about some
things, and I think myself smart about some things, and some day we'll
both think ourselves smart about the *same* thing. I don't know how he
found out I was an artist's daughter, but yesterday during sketch class
he looked at my crumpled wrapping paper and absolutely impractical
method of holding the whole drawing outfit, and said, "Tz! Tz! Tz!
And *you* an *artist's* daughter?" I said, "Well, that just proves that I am
an artist's daughter. Artists aren't practical." And he laughed and went
on.

I made a sketch last night which I consider rather decent but to which
no one, up to this time, has taken a fancy to. I like it because it is bold
and simple, and I think that I have successfully hidden the fact that it was
studied out very carefully in the first place. I mean it looks as if it had
been dashed in, only it hasn't. (Feb. 6. Armand agrees.)

I am taking Color Harmony now and have stacks of make-up work
to do.

January 23, Saturday

We had no school Thursday afternoon, for we are moving to the new
Museum. Thursday evening we had a Farewell Spread at our old quarters and there were toasts bad and good and clever. In this case the clever
toasts were also *good*. After the spread we danced. Mr. MacDonald
taught me the Pose Waltz. As we finished it he said, "You want to get
Dehn to dance too, he's sort of timid about starting."

I said, "Allright."

Mr. MacDonald said, "Hey, Dehn!" and as Mr. Dehn turned around
I said, "I'm going to teach you to dance, whether you want to or not." He
kept saying that he didn't know the first thing about it, that he had never
danced before in his life, and that he would be very awkward. We went
into the Art Gallery where I taught him a Hesitation. He learned it very
easily, and as soon as he had proper control of his steps we floated into
the Antique room. He seemed to enjoy it very much and would have
liked to dance the dance over and over again for an hour or so, but I
thought he would appreciate it more if I would make him wait for a
while. Besides I wanted to dance with other people.

One of the night students taught me a new and perfectly adorable Hesitation. We combined this with the Hesitation which Pilchie taught me, and it worked so beautifully that everyone was watching us in order that they might learn it too—Mr. Goetsch being one of them. It nearly bowled me over to see that he danced all the new dances.

I had a happy time. Mr. Dehn was very thankful to me for teaching him the dances—so thankful, in fact, that he saw me home.

Hesitation Steps (to waltz time)

Learned this I. Tap outside foot to front
from Mr.   Then to side
Giantvalley   Then to front
               Then to side, *dip*

        II.   Hop with outside foot
              Then with inside foot
              Then pull inside foot up to outside foot with turn of body

Learned this III. Tap inside foot to front
from Dr.   Then to back
McWhorter   Bring it back in front but just before you touch the
                ground, bring it back and *dip*—face to face

Learned this IV. Slide step for 4 measures
from   Hop with outside foot
Pilchie   Hop with inside foot
                Walk two steps
                Dip with outside foot to front
                Dip with outside foot to back
                Walk two steps

Friday evening about sixteen of the Art Students went to the Met. to see "High Jinks." It was very funny and pretty too. Mr. Dehn took me home. Pretty soon I shall grow tired of him, I think; altho he is very nice indeed, and is original and a man with big possibilities.

I have made myself a little velvet cap—a little artist's cap. And to-day I bought myself a pair of stylish shoes. I lost my class pin and a nickel at the Met. last night. Now all three of my little pinlets are gone and I can't look intellectual until I get my Palettite pin! They have a club over at school which goes by the name of "Exalted Order of Palettites." It is in the shape of a Palette—the pin, I mean.

January 26, Tuesday

Yesterday we moved into the new Art Museum and I started Illustration. As to the Illustration-work, both in the St. Paul and Minneapolis schools, I wish to remark that the composition is for the most part excellent, the draughtsmanship and execution very good indeed for students' work but that they lack *soul*.

In the Minneapolis school they go at things more methodically than in St. Paul, especially our teacher, Mr. Phoenix. I don't know but that he is a trifle too methodical. However I don't think I am in danger—I believe too sincerely in what I am fighting for, and I fight no less sincerely for that which I believe, to be drawn dangerously far from the Myself-track. For half-artists his method may be good—I mean for people who can never hope to go beyond a certain limit in art and people who have not enough good sound originality to lead them into the right paths. I don't know but that it is best for such people to follow the sign-boards faithfully and stick to the beaten path. But then there are the ¾ artists, and ⅘ artists, and 9/10 artists, and ⁴⁹⁄₅₀ artists—people who have talent and originality but who either do not know it or who have not the strength to be Themselves. They will probably rely on the signboards and on them only, and thus be prevented from taking daring little jaunts into the hundred-and-one little by-paths and nooks which they meet with.

In the St. Paul School they give you a few rather vague directions, call your attention in a hazy but gripping way to the goal which you are to strive for (and it's a ding high goal too) and then let you fight your way to it. The trouble is—only a handful are artistic and ambitious and far-seeing enough to see the goal. Oh well—a handful out of every school would make a number worth while.

The Minneapolis school does thoroughly what it does, but it neglects to push the students' aim farther than they can ever get. It's a good thing to have a higher ideal than you can ever attain. They encourage studying the great artists who have gone before us, they point out helpful things about these artists' work, BUT most of the students, as far as I can determine, do not aim much further than magazine illustration.

Taken all in all, the two schools balance pretty well. Personally I like the idea of going first to one school and then another, choosing the best points of each and absorbing them, and profiting by their shortcomings.

I wonder whether I will have to have people get used to me all thru my life. It becomes rather tiring at times. I can adapt myself to my surroundings to a certain extent (to a greater extent than I ever wish to do, for that requires me to step out of Myself-bounds) but fundamentally I'm *a nut, Myself, an artist*—call it what you like, the name doesn't matter— and other people will simply have to do their part in fitting around me as I do my best to fit around them. The Minneapolis School has never seen me in a heavy thoughtful mood nor in a mood of bewilderment or anguish. And when these moods return (I am rather expecting them altho I can't say I'm exactly hoping for them) they may have to revise their opinions of me to a certain extent. To-day during Illustration I talked a great deal with Mr. Moylan. He said he wished he had my ability to see color. I told him I thought it could be cultivated to a certain extent. He takes kindly to any abnormal ideas which people have and that's a good sign.

During the last few weeks I have talked with four of the boys (all of whom, with the exception of one, can draw) who have told me that they didn't know whether they had enough talent to make their studying art worth while. Toward the one who can't draw I remained silent, to the other three I railed mildly, half-vehemently, and vehemently respectively. Mr. Dehn received the most violent lecture of the three,* the one I gave Mr. MacDonald was short but sharp, and the one I handed over to Mr. Moylan (he is a gentle sort of creature) was mild and given in the form of encouragement.

Paula came this afternoon. We went to a movie after dinner, at which they gave some historical story, the scene being laid in France during the time of Louis XV reign. The costumes were so ravishingly artistic (velvet breeches, white stockings, buckled slippers, cocked hats AND capes—the most glorious, swirling, drapety, droopety capes) and the movements of the people so aesthetic that I fairly jumped up and down in my appreciation of them. I wish men would dress more artistically now-a-days. Really, when you consider the matter, it's only custom which makes us forget that they are not very pretty.

January 29, Friday

I continue to talk with Mr. Moylan during almost the entire period of Illustration each day. We get along beautifully together.

To-day we had Theory of Color again, which I like. I don't know whether or not I have explained it in here before. They are trying to bring color harmony down to a science just as has been done with music. It's very interesting and requires just enough brains and swift, skillful

* He was thinking of giving up art and going to college the following year instead.

reasoning to keep one's interest up at a rather high pitch. Some of them seem to have rather a hard time understanding it and some acknowledge that they are entirely at sea. I find myself—to my own and everybody else's (no doubt) surprise—quite brilliant, for I understand not only what we take up each week, but I find myself able to look far ahead and anticipating all kinds of things which I *know* will come to pass.

Just now I am rather wondering whether I am a very talented individual or whether I am only laboring under a delusion. That I have *stuff* I know—the question is, will I be able to *get it out?* Of course, it is needless to say I will try hard to do so, but perhaps I wasn't *meant* to get it all out. Perhaps I am only a medium, as many people are, of transferring a talent. I mean perhaps I am able to cultivate it only to a certain extent after which it is to be handed on, to a child of mine perhaps, or a grandchild, who will then *do* the things which almost scare me. You see the Thing may not be *ripe* yet.

This noon after lunch I went up into the art gallery all by myself— which I like almost better than anything I can imagine, except going with Armand or Mr. McWhorter, perhaps. I wandered around in the most hloopsie-esque bliss; and as it was too early for many people to be there I could gasp with joy and talk to myself and make any movements which I wanted without being stared at. Once as I was looking at one of Millet's pictures, I caught myself gazing deep into my own eyes in the reflection in the glass, and without knowing it, I said to myself, "There is no reason why you can't. What reason *is* there?" I cannot help it if my eyes tell me those things, *I say I cannot help it.* I have tried often enough to make myself think that it is wrong to let myself think and feel such things, and I have tried very hard to choke down all such ideas, but——.

And if the feelings are false? Great Caesar! there must be *something* in me—else how could I be the way I am? Oh surely God is not so severe as to put things into one which one is destined never to give out——.

And these are the things I weep about, now-a-days.

Later:—Well we have been to see the exhibit.* For a while I wandered around with them and explained the pictures to them in the every-day guide manner, but when we came to the Corot-Millet room and when I found myself in a corner in front of a marvelous painting by Heinrich

* Some acquaintances from out of town had asked me to accompany them.

Zügel ["The Oxen"] I flopped right back into Myselvisms, became oblivious of the people about me, and *lived*. I don't know how long I stood there.

I caught up with them in a Japanese room. I heard the guide explaining something to them so I sauntered up and asked, *"What* is it?" The guide said it was a lantern and explained just where the light would be placed so that an artistic effect might be secured. I said, "Oh that's pretty! Only," I added half to myself, "I wish they wouldn't have the tag hanging there." The tag hung right over the opening where the light was to shine thru, and it rather disturbed me. The guide looked at me and said, "Well you're an artist—you *must* be one!" I said "Why?" and he said, "Because no one else would notice it. You're the first person who has remarked about it." Then he said with the quaintest mixture of pride and modesty, that he could understand that because he did a little drawing himself. (This was interesting. Usually it's only the aunt or cousin or brother who does the drawing, but here I had that wonderful and ubiquitous creature before my very eyes.)

I said, "Oh is that so?" and asked him just what line of art he followed. He had been in the art business he told me, twinkling his blue eyes happily at me—enlarging pictures with an air-brush and crayons. I wandered on but he followed me step by step. I know only too well how it feels not to have anyone to spill to for a long time so I let him talk on and encouraged him to tell me his art-history. He was the only one in his family who had had artistic inclinations and he wanted badly to study art. But his father saw no sense in it and wouldn't let him. Then as he grew older he drifted into "art" because it was his "natural bent." Nice, funny old man with twinklety blue eyes, a choked talent and thwarted ambitions. His name is J. F. Miller. "Almost like J. F. Millet," he said, "I lack only one letter of being a great artist."

February 1, Monday

Saturday afternoon Miss Jones (the daughter of my Journal Man) called on me. She is very nice indeed. I took her to my room and showed her some of my sketches, and by the things she said about them I could see that she really understands something worth while about art. It was a great relief to meet someone who would not constantly be remarking that my sketches did or did not resemble me. Ding! That isn't what I draw them for. She understood beautifully that it was the expression or the spirit of the thing which I tried to catch.

After dinner, I went over to the Y.W. at St. Paul. Theresa and I had the afternoon and evening all to ourselves and I was glad of it, for I haven't had a good talk with Theresa alone, since last September. She let me read part of her diary which is frank and wholesome and noble, just like Theresa herself.

On the way to St. Paul I suddenly became rather car-sick so I took one of Armand's books and began sketching on the fly leaves. I sketched an old man who had sort of rolled himself up on a seat, and as I was doing so, a young man who sat beside me said, "That's very clever." It was plain that he was really interested in the drawing but I just turned around, looked at him rather stiffly and went on sketching. A number of other people noticed too that I was sketching, which I did not like very much, but I felt that I would rather be notorious than car-sick so I kept on.

The man at my side talked to me a number of times, and altho he was perfectly civil and gentlemanly, and tho I should very much have liked to talk to him about sketching and human nature, I realized that it would have been entirely too unconventional and that my unconventionality might be misconstrued, so I said little or nothing. He was a very nice looking man and wore, aside from other stylish and good looking things, a coat with the sleeves and everything in one (I noticed that before he ever saw me sketch, and the folds afforded me much delight and pleasure).

He asked whether I would give him the picture of the old man, but I said, "It isn't my book." So he handed me a post card and asked if I would sketch something on it for him. It would have been narrow-minded to refuse (besides hadn't I sketched a picture for Armand once, without any introduction whatsoever?) and as I like all humanity, I said, "All right. I'll sketch this man who is black all over." It was a man who evidently delivered coal to people's houses and he was chewing tobacco with all his might and main. So I sketched him, chewing tobacco and all, and gave it to the adventurer beside me.

He handed me his card upon which was his name, Will Baines, and some words informing one that Will Baines belonged to the U.S. Department of Agriculture, and that he examined cows. I guess it was cows. He said he'd be at Washington, D.C. in two days, which I took calmly and without a word. He suggested that I might send him a postal after he had arrived there but I said, "I don't think I had better." "Perhaps you'd like to get one from there?" he said, but I said "I don't know you," which I considered conclusive. He had a sister who painted, he said. (Ye gods, *another!*)

As I left the car he said, "Well, you can drop a postal to Washington if you should feel like it, and then you'll get one from there." But I only smiled a cryptic smile and left.

I don't know just how this sounds written down, but—ding, a man can talk to almost anyone with impunity, and just because we are women we can't, however much we are interested in human nature. Oh yes, I forgot to say that I put my signature to the picture, but in such a scrawly way that it was almost unrecognizable.

Ships that pass in the night—and he was very nice and sensible.

Today I turned out a very poor sketch in illustration and as a consequence I feel less arrogant than I have.

It was nearly five o'clock when Mr. Phoenix announced that I was wanted, and as I opened the door I saw before me Timmie, Jack Alden, and Armand. Timmie said, "You don't have to work any more, do you?" I said, "No, I've just finished my sketch," and indeed I had. I flew around for my drawing materials and wraps and then we all left the building.

I was awfully glad to see Timmie again. He said that he had wanted to whoop when he heard of my going to school again; and asked what I thought about his decision of coming back to take Medicine. I told him I hadn't decided what I thought about it. Altho he was cheerful while talking to me, it was evident that he was down in the mouth. Jack Alden, as usual, was shy and retired into the background with his characteristic smile.

Timmie and Jack went directly to St. Paul so Armand said "I'll take Wanda home," and then Armand and I got on the car. Up to this time I had been so taken up with Jack and Timmie that I didn't notice Armand much, but after we had been in the car a few minutes I noticed that something was, or had been the matter with him. I believe he explained that it was self-disgust and that it had been far from pleasant. It worried me considerably. The sad strain in Timmie worries me too. Armand said that he (Timmie) was in a hole and that he (Armand) was pulling him out.

I told him about the treatise on Sketching that I had started to write, and he said he'd like to see it. He doesn't like my little velvet artist's cap. He doesn't like the angle at which it flops and he says I look like an Italian milk-carrier. Hm. He looks worse than that sometimes. An

Italian milk-woman may even look picturesque, but a pennant-profile—
never. Anyway I like the cap and so does nearly everyone else.

I said that I had developed a new characteristic but that I wanted to
see if he could guess what it was when he heard my diary. I meant
arrogance, and what some people might call conceit but which is not
that at all. He said that he had called me up the Saturday before but I
had not been at home. He said also that, unless his new schedule prevented it, we would go and see the Exhibition Friday morning.

I wonder what under the sun he has been going thru.

February 3, Wednesday

To-day in Life I made a pastel study and I enjoyed it immensely.

I posed in my Maid Marion costume for sketch class. I posed four
different ways during the hour with no rests, to which they were not
used at all. But as long as I was not tired I saw no use for wasting a
lot of time in between. Tomorrow, at the request of several of the boys,
I will pose again, keeping one pose the entire hour.

February 4, Thursday

This morning we had three 25-minute poses in life and I did them
all in pastel. I had just the best kind of time. As I was doing the last
one Mr. Goetsch came and told me to make more use of my paper—
use the *tone* of it as part of the color of my sketches. He said, "You
might just as well be drawing on white paper for all the use you make
of it. Have you looked at those sketches by Whistler upstairs?"

I said, "Oh yes, I've looked at them time and time again."

He said, "Well why don't you draw the way he does?"

I said, "Why—I'm not Whistler."

He laughed at that and went on criticising. It was a mighty good
criticism too—believe me. He repeated what he had told me in Still
Life once—that I was just a little bit wild.

I said, "Oh yes, I realize that myself."

He said, "Well, why don't you keep yourself in check?"

I said, "Why, Mr. Goetsch, I spent six solid months last winter in
keeping myself in check," to which he said, "Why don't you do it now?"

I said, "Oh, I do! If you would only know how my work would look
if I weren't keeping myself in check!" To which he laughed again.

Mr. Goetsch took our Life class thru the Exhibition. I admire Mr.
Goetsch for having original and bold opinions about the different

paintings. He has enough arrogance to be a real sizzling artist. He likes Whistler very much, and I certainly do too. It almost makes me mad with ecstacy to look at his two pastels, "Writing on the Wall," and "Rose & Red—The Little Pink Cap."

As I expected, Armand called me up tonight and told me he wouldn't be able to go to the Exhibition with me to-morrow. He said that he might go Saturday afternoon. Gee, I was sore, because I've set my mind on seeing the thing with Armand—and as likely as not he won't be able to go Saturday or any other time. Saturday is the last day. I have formed my opinions about so many of the pictures, and I'm awfully anxious to see what he thinks about the different ones. I know of nothing so nice and so irritating as to have Armand for a friend.

February 8, Monday

Armand had said that in case he would not be able to go Saturday he would telephone Friday evening and every time the telephone rang I felt almost sure it must be for me. Also I had planned to give him a good hot reception when he did call. I was so thoroughly prepared to be furious that I couldn't plan anything very definitely, but I decided to say very cuttingly that he "couldn't even spare one afternoon to see the exhibit with someone who really cared and knew something about art," etc. It was going to be short but spicy. Bye and bye I got so that I was almost disappointed because the telephone didn't ring for me. When I had almost given up hopes of its ever happening, there was a knock on my door and the secretary announced that I was wanted at the telephone. I stormed quietly out into the hall (if you can imagine that) snorting, and with eyes ablaze. (I know they were, because I could feel it.) I took up the receiver, and said shortly, "Hello!"

"Hello, little mouse!" came in honeyed and soprano tones from the other end of the line. Paula.

It was too much for me. Here was I, all wound up ready to spring—and then to be obliged to undo all this winding, and talk rationally to my love of a Paula—I couldn't do it, that's all. Neither could I talk straight nor think connectedly nor hear correctly; and it is still a mystery to me that I cleared myself sufficiently to gather that Paula intended to come over to see me Tuesday. In spite of the fact, however, that I was much disappointed at not being able to fly out at Armand, I was glad that he didn't telephone because I really and truly wanted to see the Exhibition with him.

He was supposed to come at one, which he didn't, but he called me up most virtuously to let me know that he wouldn't be able to be there until two. Before we left for the Museum I showed him some of my new sketches because I was just a little bit afraid that I might be becoming clever again. Armand said I was improving and said also that I was drawing by elimination. Also that he thought I would in all probability go to an extreme in just this. Which I don't doubt in the least.

I pointed out to him how I had succeeded in making the shadow-side of the cheek round, and also in making the shadow transparent and neither hard nor muddy. I was highly elated over this when I accomplished it. I don't know how I did it but I think I can do it again when the occasion presents itself.

On the way to the car-line Armand said, "You have an incipient sense of humor. Cultivate it." Hm. He's only getting used to it, that's all. You usually have to get used to a person's style of humor before you realize the full extent of it. I used to think some of his jokes were awfully flat, and sometimes they still sound pretty flat, and I guess sometimes they *are*.

I told him that he swore altogether too much and he said that I was to remind him of it every time he did so that afternoon by "familiarly pulling his hair," which struck me so funny. I imagined to myself how it would look if I were to do so, and how surprised and shocked the people would be, because at the rate he is accustomed to indulge in strong, and what they call "ungentlemanly" language, I would have been obliged to administer the reminder about every half minute or so.

It felt good to be at the Exhibition with someone who had much the same tastes and appreciation that I had. It was quite a relief after I had been practically killing myself trying to explain my thoughts to others and endeavoring to make them respond.

Armand pleaded exhaustion after we had covered about three rooms so we went down into the Antique room where I read him some diary extracts. When I read him about "Is it natural?" and my consequent indignation, he laughed very much. I told him that I had seriously planned to say to him, "Is it natural?" pointing to his nose.

After that we went back to the place of my abode where we seated ourselves in our favorite corner. I told Armand that I was still well and happy, but that I was on the brink of a hole. Armand raised his eyebrows and asked what the trouble was. I told him that it was because:— (1) here in Minneapolis I didn't have anyone to whom I could really spill, (2) because Myself was overleaping Me, and (3) because I was powerless to express what I knew and felt.

Armand still thinks it would do me good to write themes. And he does not know why I didn't write the other one. He said he thought he might be able to get off one morning every two weeks this semester, which he would use to give me a chance to unspill all my superfluous thoughts. Now I hope he'll do it. Goodness knows I need it badly enough.

February 9, Tuesday

I have just read the first and fifth editions of Omar Khayyam. He is certainly superficial. Also very frank. But not as happy as he thinks he is, it seems to me. It impresses me as an unhappy sort of happiness—a kind that reminds me of Nina's pathetic hilarity. He continually advises one not to think of the Whenceness, Whyness and Whitherness of things and yet, as I leave his Rubaiyat, I carry with me his eternal questioning. His arguments are clever enough but by no means always sound. I like him for his big views of things. I like the Pot and Potter part—and I like the last two stanzas.

Poor man.

Of course I may be wrong. I have not reasoned those things out at all. I come to this diary straight from Omar, with my mind in a sort of trance, and with the mood which he gave me still upon me. These are the nascent sensations which I received from the book tonight.

Timmie's new attitude towards things worries me. There is something about his state of mind which it hurts me to see—because I feel that it shouldn't be there. He is too analytic, for one thing. He tries to get to the intellectual bottom of things, which is allright if done in moderation and for a valuable purpose; but he does it simply for the sake of proving a point, whether or not the point, when proven, will help him to live or understand Life better. I think Life is too short to waste one's time in proving things, the proof of which does not take one a step nearer to what one is striving for.

Later:—I *see* first, and then I *do*. I have noticed lately that so many people *do,* or try to do, more than they *see*. They can't do it of course, and the fault lies not in their inability to do or see—it lies in the fact that they do not realize that it is *not* unprofitable to use some of your time in seeing.

They work and work, and plug and plug, and expect to reach their goal in that way.

I am blamed for not working when I am not inspired. Now, I know that the word inspiration is a hackneyed sort of thing, and the worst of it is, it's *mis*-hackneyed at that. When I talk of waiting for inspiration I do not mean to infer that I sit in a vacuous sort of mood, waiting for some divine feeling to enter my being which will make me do wonders. I *think*—so that when next the veil is drawn for me I will be able to comprehend and to touch that which is shown to me when the veil *is* drawn. So many people forget to cultivate that delicate sense which tells one when there is a rift in the curtain; and, not happening to look up at the right time, they are so busy *doing,* that they miss that which would save them hours of useless grinding.

Yesterday I asked for a criticism in Illustration. Mr. Phoenix gave me some advice which he told me to work with. I liked the advice but I didn't feel quite ready to use it, so I went off on a delightful and profitable little think. When Mr. Phoenix came around again after about five or ten minutes, I was still gazing into space, having done nothing whatsoever to my sketch. He asked whether I had understood all he had told me, and I said that I had and that I was only thinking. He said, "Yes—but don't think too long about it." Now I know that I would only have made senseless lines if I had tried to put in my clouds then. I would have LOOKED more as if I were accomplishing something, because I would have been diligently drawing and erasing and drawing and erasing, *but* would I have been *doing* more?

It has occurred to me that I am very much alone since I am at Minneapolis. There is no Paula or Theresa or Nina to talk to, there is no one upon whom I can thrust my discussions, my diary and my pictures. There is no one with whom I can warble, no one with whom I can play duetts, and no one to play piano for me. There is no one whom I can rip it into, and no one with whom I can share my fruit and candy. Oh there are plenty of *people*—I talk to the girls here at the house and I go to shows and concerts with them and they look at my pictures. At school there are boys and girls galore to whom I talk, to whom I show my drawings. But they do not know me. I have to explain myself all the time and all the time, and I am so weary of it.

Ding it all, I can't help it if Armand is the only person that I can really and truly spill to. It's not my fault that we get along so well together—it's his own. Why is he so absolutely satisfactory? Why *does* he understand me better than anyone else? Why is he the only man I don't get tired of? That's what he gets for being so beautifully irritating. That's what he gets for being a pieface.

The worst of it is that I cannot blame Armand. I don't suppose anyone with a kind heart would be able to let such a poor creature as I am, suffer alone if he knew that he understood her better than anyone else. Even tho it is dangerous. I wouldn't mind going thru years of pain, if only it would come out all right in the end. It is the termination not the interim that I object to.

That was an anguishy weep. My eyelids burn. I am ashamed of myself, for I am almost a coward—I am afraid to put things into my diary because I am afraid that later they will be painful to me.

I wonder whether a life-time of this would seem very long, and very hard to bear. I could always stand it in fall and winter—even in summer —but when spring comes, I cannot help but live over all the joy and pain of it, the mad happiness, the rich anguish and the happy madness.

Friday night I cried very much. I cried because for so long a time I had not had a chance to spill to people who really knew me, and it had to come out some way. Perhaps the main reason why I cried, tho, was the fact that Myself is overleaping me, because I can see so much farther than I can reach at present, and because I can feel so many things which I am powerless to express. To have things churning about within you which you can feel, can see, and can even *grasp* to a certain extent, but which you cannot express—to feel things which you feel you have no right to feel—it's enough to make anyone sob, *I* think.

Last night I planned a long discussion which I intend to have with Mr. Goetsch. I hardly trust myself to speak to him for fear that I will start a very *un-studently* discussion with him. He always blinks at me so arrogantly with his little eyes. I rather think that he is laboring under the illusion that I am a coquette. For the simple reason that I talk so much with the boys. He does not know that I talk more with the boys than with the girls because they are more broad minded. Neither do the girls know this. I guess the girls don't quite know what to think of me. Sometimes they probably think I am saying things for effect when in reality I am in dead earnest. For all this, they are perfect darlings, and I do not mean to do them any injustices whatsoever. I am merely stating facts and conjectures in a very mixed sort of way.

I am catching up and in some cases almost overcoming some of my rivals over there. *Wanda Gág, you old pieface, will you shut up?*

I can't say that I addressed myself very elegantly but I was aiming at something forcible rather than at something elegant. I think I'm an awful pieface and I'm sincerely ashamed of myself, but ding, I have to go thru that stage, that's all.

This diary, it seems to me, has been a queer sort of thing. Very little adventure, less introspectiveness than usual, an appalling amount of arrogance and a gratifying scarcity of cleverness. I leave this diary with perfectly good feelings towards everyone, even Armand and Mr. Goetsch. The excuse for one is that he knows me, and for the other that he does not know me. Goodbye dear Diary. Wanda.

* * *

February 15, 1915. Monday

Yesterday I read over some of my old diaries, and really my writing is so bad that I am afraid I will be unable to read it later. The trouble is that as soon as I try to write legibly, I forget to think.

This morning I awoke with tears in my eyes, for I had dreamt about papa. Usually when I awake crying, it means that. My dreams about papa are always very much the same. He has been gone for a long time, usually because he has been very sick, and his coming back means that he is just a little better but not nearly well. We always feel so glad to see him but we don't talk to him nearly as much as we mutually understand each other. Papa always stands somewhere, tall and loving and kind, his eyes burning with his love for us, and that part of the Myself in him which he was never given a chance to unfold—and which he finally gave to me—all folded up, all folded up. Sometimes he brings pictures with him and we look at them and last night I showed him some of my latest sketches.

The reason why I cried in last night's dream was because I felt that even tho papa had been well enough to come and see us, this would be the last time he would be able to come back. And it had all been so real that when I woke I really began to cry in earnest. I sobbed and sobbed because of that patient, uncomplaining look in my father's eyes.

There is a new exhibition at the Museum now, and Thursday morning I skipped Anatomy lecture and went up to the gallery all my myself. I was met in the hall by Mr. Dehn who asked me to come into the Antique room with him to criticize his drawing. I did so but it was fully an hour

Anton Gág—Self Portrait in Oil, 1903

Top: Pastel Sketch on Brown Wrapping Paper
Bottom: Flavia—Lithographic Crayon on Brown Wrapping Paper

before I left that room, for we wandered from one subject to another and it really seemed that we would never get thru unburdening our minds. I knew that Mr. Dehn had the most virtuous intentions of finishing his cast-drawing so I gradually moved towards the door, he following all the time, and both of us talking just as fast as our tongues could wag. I went out of the door and he followed, and before we knew it we were stationed outside of the door discussing religion and other things. It was almost four when I finally started for home. Mr. Dehn said, "I've had a happy afternoon. I felt so gloomy this morning but after this talk I feel much better." It had done me much good too for, as I have said before, Mr. Dehn is very nice indeed to talk with. Next to Armand, I like to talk to him I think. He also has one over Armand because he is not so irritating.

Paula called on me that day and I certainly was glad of it. I had become quite homesick for her. Glory I love Paula. She is just too darling for anything. Saturday morning I went to St. Paul with her so that I might go to Weschcke's in the afternoon. Which I did. They have the darlingest new home—just the kind of home such absolutely adorable people should have. I had a nice time there. Mr. Weschcke was quite tickled to find another person who was noted for talking much. It seems he is that way too.

I spent a miserable Sunday. It was half-raining, half-sunny outside. I felt dumpy, my drawing mood had left me, my diary was filled (and as it was Sunday I could not get a new one) and I wasn't even artistically inclined enough to plan my spring wardrobe. I read Milton for a while and then, in sheer desperation, I tried to write a letter to Armand, and really I believe it's years since I've written such an abominably empty letter as that. If my drawing mood has left me for a two month's stay (as it has a little way of doing) I shall go right plump down into a hole after a week or so. Who wouldn't, I'd like to know.

February 16, Tuesday

An unsatisfactory sort of day. My drawing mood really seems to be gone in earnest and as a consequence I am down deep in a hole.

It's the most discouraging kind of a feeling. No lines tempt your fingers to draw, no colors sing out to you. You are unable to see *niceties* in light and shade. Or if by any strange chance you are able to *see* a lovely line, a happy color, or an interesting shade, you find yourself unable to put down on paper what you see. Now as a rule, in sketching, I have very little trouble getting proportions—I let my eyes see prudently and my mind connect swiftly; my hands fly about the paper a few minutes and I have my guiding lines all ready. When Mr. Phoenix comes around, he tests these lines to see if they are consistent and to see whether they make the proper allowance for the figure underneath, and they are most usually satisfactory.

But to-day when I sketched, my proportions would be all off. I would get one arm much too long, the set of the head would be expressionless, and the body would not stand firmly. I could *see* well enough that they were wrong after I had put them down, and I knew just what was the matter with them, but I seemed powerless to make my fingers do what I pleased. This is a new phase of the matter. Up to this time I have contended that it was not because one couldn't make one's hands do as one pleased, but that one couldn't *see* correctly, which caused bad drawing; and indeed up to this time it has been just that. Now it's just turned around, altho I feel bound to add that I do not see nearly as *brilliantly* and comprehendingly as I do under a drawing mood. Luckily Mr. Phoenix didn't come to criticize to-day.

I am hungry. When there isn't anything else to do I would just as soon eat. No wonder some people are wild about eating. Perhaps I would be too if I didn't like thinking, drawing, reading and talking better.

February 19, Friday

I went over the brink of the hole yesterday, and am of course still there. I wrote a letter to Armand last night, very inconsiderately. It was not a wail—it was worse than that. A wail is weepy and a trifle whiney, but this was a mood of dry tears in words. It had been one of those days which must come sometimes and in which you smile and joke and are a "good fellow" all around. In regard to this I wrote to Armand, "My smiles are as ghastly to Myself as the grin of a death's head." Also, "I feel to-night that I have fallen short of so many things which I should have come up to." Those two sentences express my mood.

This evening I occupied my mind, as well as my hands, in mending and sewing etc. It made me feel a good deal better but I feared for the latter part of the evening. I heard them dancing out in the hall and one of the girls called to me to join them so I did. I taught my favorite Hesitation to a number of the girls who had never danced before. Glory, some people have little control of their limbs—one of the girls could not even control her legs enough to make the left foot hop and then the right. Then we sang for a while, which was a good deal of fun. I became quite foxy and acted out parts and did little stunts. I don't think they were Me's. As a consequence of this evening I have cleared myself temporarily of much that is heavy and depressing.

Timmie called on me last night and it felt good to be able to talk to an inhabitant of my sphere again. I showed him some of my sketches. He looked at them in such a queer way. For instance, of my two latest pastels he preferred the last one to the one before it, because it was *prettier*. I am afraid Timmie is in a hole—and a deep one at that. It worries me considerably. He is so analytic and scientific; too much so to my notion. He thinks that just now I need college more than Art School. I certainly need college. On the other hand, I do not see how I could get along without Art School for an entire year or two, because in that case my comprehension of art would over-leap my technique and ability of execution. So there you have me. I need *two* things at the same time, and Time isn't *wide* enough to allow of any such arrangement.

I see where Armand gives me a chance to unspill every week or so! I guess I'd better not bank on that. I don't know what I'd do if I hadn't Mr. Dehn to talk to at school.

February 21, Sunday

Judy Dekker * has been here and we had a nice talk. We talked about New Ulm. Judy said that people did not know how intimate she was with me so she heard things about me by the carloads. It seems that Mr. Groos made some sarcastic remark to her, something to this effect: Judy, upon being asked how I was getting along, had replied that I was getting along very well indeed, whereupon Mr. Groos said, "I suppose she has some *good friend* again who is helping her." The words sound harmless enough but Mr. Groos knows how to put venom into sentences which, as far as words are concerned, are bland and innocent.

I know I am a fool to care, knowing that I am good and that my behavior and principles are irreproachable, but I do care, I do care. If I hadn't a darling family there, it wouldn't matter so much.

And it is all because we are poor.

And to think that I should have to cry *hard* about this. I thought

* She was now studying in Minneapolis.

I was too broad-minded but I forgot to allow for the fact that I am human. Sometimes I think I can't stand it, that's all. It's all right to say "Don't worry" and "Don't mind if you are misunderstood." But I am weary of having to explain myself and all that goes with me— and besides, it isn't so much the fact of being *misunderstood* that I mind, as the fact of not being *understood*. I can't stand it much longer, that's all.

I must go to bed and sleep off the painful throbs and sobs so that I may be ready for the same old fight to-morrow.

February 24, Wednesday

Monday we had a Party here at the house. I had a good time but it wasn't Myself that had it. Myself had slumped into a hole, and there was nothing but an empty shell left to have a good time. There were even a few Me's, ding it. They said I danced like a bird, like a fairy—. Well, there is no reason why one should dance badly just because one is moving to the tune of false laughter and silent sobs within one. After the party I sat down on my bed and remained there for a long time, staring into space.

Yesterday at school I could absolutely not draw. There was not a single line which meant anything so I flung the paper away in desperation. I tried to pick up an argument with Mr. Goetsch for excitement but he gave me no opportunity. During the noon hour I talked with Mr. Dehn. In a sudden burst of generosity I offered to give him the sketch I had made of him and which he has wanted so long. In return for the picture he gave me a promissory note which runs something after the following manner:—

"I, Adolph Dehn, do hereby solemnly promise to give to Wanda H. Gag any sketch of herself which she shall deem worthy of her possession."

He doesn't look any more like an Adolph than I do. I think his name ought to be George.

After lunch I sat around in the Illustration room until I was weary of having people say good naturedly, "Wanda, get to work," when I packed up and went home. I cried very hard for a while and then I fell asleep. I almost overslept myself for dinner. After dinner I read Peter Rosegger until about eleven. I finished up with an anguished weep for Dehli's patience before I went off to sleep. A restless sleep at that.

Well, such is my state.

I knew that I would not be able to work any better at school than at home, so today I decided to stay at home. I rearranged the furniture in my room and, as the sunshine fairly flooded me with brightness every time I walked in its path, I became quite cheerful. I saw interesting lines in things, and pretty colors; and altho I never found myself picking up my pencil and paper to draw what I was seeing, I thought that, perhaps after all, I might be able to do my illustration if I truly set about it in earnest. I planned to do it in blue and orange, and after having put in the main lines I began bravely to lay in the colors. I did not seem to be accomplishing anything very wonderful but I worked on. I had soon spoiled the whole thing, and anyone who thinks that this mood is merely imagination or lack of ambition, is urged to look at the five drawings of "The Miser" which I have failed to accomplish.

Monday morning I got a very long letter from Stell and one each from the others. As I had not even answered Stella's last letter I felt very inconsiderate and heartless so I wrote her just as nice a one as I possibly could, using three and a half hours in doing so. The letters from the other kids were so darling that as soon as I had finished lunch I began writing a separate letter for each of them, but after I had written one to Dehli, one to Howard and one to Flavia, my fingers ached so much that I decided to write mama's, Asta's and Tussy's in one.

Mrs. Marietta Fournier asked me to come out to her house Saturday and I have accepted. She said a club (consisting of a number of Art School boys) was going to meet there that evening and she wanted me to be there. Here's hoping I will not be Me-ish. It must be the club which Mr. Dehn was telling me about. It's a very informal sort of an affair and it does not seem to have any definite organization. One just meets and spills, that's all.

I wish Armand would bring me some new books. I always like to have at least five books on hand which I haven't read so that I can choose my books to go with my different moods.

February 25, Thursday

I accomplished absolutely nothing at school to-day. I started a little portrait sketch which was what we used to call *"grad weg,"* meaning neither good nor bad and therefore uninteresting. When Mr. Goetsch criticized it he said abruptly, "You have something which is very, very good." He explained that it was a big general conception of the thing, and that it was not so much that my drawing had it but that *I* had it.

He said, "Now that's all right. Don't lose it. Keep it—*but* there is also something which you have not got which you must work for." By the latter he meant uncertain and superficial execution, due to my lack of knowledge of execution, which fact of course I discovered about a year ago.

I said, "Yes, but I don't understand *what* it is I have got." He explained the thing further but I am not any the wiser for it.

This noon four of us girls looked at the pictures in the Museum. The rest soon had to go back, but as I had no class I decided to stay for a while longer. After they had left, and as I was occupied in draping myself over one of the radiators and gazing at Orpen's gorgeous self-portrait, a middle-aged man who was also in the room and had been listening interestedly to us a little while before, said, "I wish I could paint you that way." He looked nice and intellectual and humanity-loving-ish so I said laughingly, "I'm afraid it isn't a very graceful pose." He said that he'd like to paint my head. I said with genuine curiosity, "Why?" and he said that my face was so typically Spanish!

He told me that he was going to have an Exhibition of his paintings at Beard's Art Galleries next week, and gave me his card. "Charles Paul Gruppé." We wandered on to the Millets and when we came to "The Spinner" I said, "Oh, I like that. I wept before that one day," at which he gave me a quiet look that was at the same time surprised and unsurprised. That look, by the way, seems to be very characteristic of him. At about two he left. I had talked with him for about an hour, and it made me so happy to have found another inhabitant of my sphere. I do not remember all the things I said. He would raise his eyebrows and look interested at the most unexpected places. His son is a celloist.

Mr. Dehn said to-day, "I think you are rather—"

"Fatalistic?" I asked.

He said, "Well, not just that. But you just let yourself be controlled by it" (the un-drawing-mood you know). "I think you rather enjoy it." Not that I blame him for thinking so. I would myself, if I were anybody but myself.

Now I am coming to the stage where I feel as if I were no person at all but simply an *expression* walking around.

Oh, the torture, the bitterness, the utter despair of sitting down, pencil in hand, before your paper. I said—"sitting down, pencil in hand, before your paper." I said that, because *that's all*. You don't get any farther. Even if you put your pencil upon the paper it makes only meaningless lines, if indeed it moves at all.

All thru the day I tell myself that it is only a fancy, and that the next thing I attempt *will* turn out into something presentable if I only try, and every evening I tell myself that I can't stand it much longer.

I can't stand it, I say, *I can't stand it,* I CAN'T STAND IT.

Later:—I have just been reading over some of my old diaries, and I find that last year at about this time I was also minus a drawing mood, and was weeping and wailing even as I do now.

There is one thing that is very interesting about Armand M. Emraad and that is the regularity and dependableness of his non-visits.

Wanda go to bed.

I forgot to mention that I had a flash of a drawing-fit last night, for I sketched diligently and happily from 9 p.m. to 1 a.m., the result being nine action-sketches.

February 26, Friday

Another unsatisfactory day. I did not sketch in Portrait at all. I read poetry until about eleven, when I went upstairs to look at the pictures in the Museum where I ran into Mrs. Brown, one of the Art Students. Mrs. Brown advised me to just simply stay at home for a while. She thought if I'd do something *just the opposite from drawing* I would soon feel like coming back to school and working. She gave this as Mr. Koehler's prescription. After lunch I went up again, and after wandering around alone for a time I accidentally came upon Mr. Dehn and Mr. La Londe. As it was Friday (which meant that I had no class until 3 p.m.) we remained up there until about two o'clock, discussing the different pictures and also drawing moods. Joe La Londe agrees with me that sometimes one simply cannot draw, while Mr. Dehn insists that one can force one's self not only to draw but to draw *well*. It is gratifying to recollect that very few Me's (if any) were allowed to make their appearance during this talk.

February 28, Sunday 7:15 p.m.

Yesterday afternoon I sketched myself about six times—action poses.

Some of them are rather good in action I think, but they are too crazy to show to anyone.

At about five Mrs. Fournier and I went to her home where we had dinner. After dinner, Mr. Dehn, Mr. MacDonald and Mr. Holton came. We have started a club. It is called "The John Ruskin Club," its purpose being "Rambles thru Art, Science and Literature." We elected the officers and to my lot fell the office of Secretary. I don't know the first thing about writing minutes and I suppose they will be something like my cash account. (My cash account is full of digressions and "thoughts-by-the-way.") Mr. Holton is President and Mr. Dehn is Vice Pres. Mr. Dehn wanted to resign, saying that either Mr. or Mrs. Fournier ought to have that office but I told him he needn't be overcome with the honor of the position because at Washington D.C. they make that person Vice-Pres. whom they want to get out of politics.

Mr. Dehn gave a talk on John Ruskin which we all enjoyed. I like the way he talks. He manages to talk informally and still keep his subject in order. After that we discussed things which had come up in his talk and, as is our rule, rambled on into other directions.

Some of them did not believe in *genius*. That is, genius in the accepted form. Mrs. Fournier thought that with proper conditions and surroundings, genius would become universal. She is a socialist, and attributes much to environment. I took the other extreme, declaring excitedly that genius was a thing which was lodged in only a few people who saw much further than ordinary people and were here to teach others and to prepare them for what was coming. Mr. Dehn agreed with neither of us, both of us being too extreme for him, but he admitted that if he were bound to choose either one or the other side, he should have to take mine.

This is only a sample. We said much more on the subject, I being in the thickest of the fray. I naturally would, when the subject dealt with "genius" and "inspiration" etc.

At one time Mr. Dehn and I were having a little argument by ourselves. Mr. Dehn had just said, "Well, at any rate you will have to admit that Ruskin was a greater man than Whistler," at which I flew up with a vehement, "I should say not!" I said it hastily for I had never made a point of gauging the abilities of both these men, but altho I did not mean to infer that Whistler was *greater* than Ruskin, I could not bear to have him pronounced *less* great. I said, "Well, *I* think that Whistler was a greater man than the world realizes even at the present time!"

By this time the rest of the company was all ears, and the fact that I was obviously so interested in Whistler led to the suggestion that I give a talk on Whistler the following week.

I guess it just tickles Mr. Dehn to pieces to see me get excited in discussions. He can just about tell when I'm going to fly up and he always shoots a half-amused and half-challenging look just when I am ready to pop out with something.

We are trying to get Mr. Phoenix to talk to us some evening, and also Mr. Goetsch.

I spent the night at Fournier's. They have the darlingest and most unconventional home. This morning I went home, the happier for having been in a *home* once more, the richer for having read Shaw's *Pygmalion,* and the lighter in mind and soul for having been able to talk with glorious freedom to nice people. The sun was shining outside, children were playing all about (I see so few children now-a-days) and there was a happy Sunday calm over everything. Glory I was happy.

I sketched joyfully all afternoon. Action sketches again, some six or seven. Funny that I should be able to draw that kind of thing and yet be able to turn out nothing worth while in Illustration or Theory of Color. And yet—doing an old Miser, when that lanky and eternal Mr. Neal poses for it. It seems to me we have him all the time—for Life, for Illustration, and for Portrait. He's out of work I guess, and he does look a little better without the mustache, but Great Scott, he hasn't an iota of grace in him and his body is so unaesthetic that one loses all desire to draw when one sees that one has him for a model again. One of the girls said, "He is so lanky that we can't make a study of the muscles, but he has just enough muscles to cover the bones so we can't make it a study of bones either." Well, so much for the poor "Hinglishman." All I can say is I hope that his wish will be fulfilled—he wants to earn enough money to go back to old England.

The John Ruskin Club saved my life. I was slumping faster and deeper right along and there's no telling how far I would have gone had not Mrs. Fournier's invitation pulled me out of such a dangerous hole. I am out of the hole, temporarily.

March 1, Monday

Only ten more days of "being twenty-one."

I am becoming a regular hermit. I don't care to go to parties, I don't like to be invited out to dinners, I lock myself up in my room so that

I may draw and read and think and cry in peace—and when I walk, I usually prefer to walk alone because then I can act just as natural as I please.

If I can't be radical in drawing, I have to be eccentric otherwise; and when I am for any length of time placed in such a position as to be forced to be conventional, I become extremely radical in drawing. That, of course, refers to the present. I don't suppose I will continue to be that way throughout my life. At least I hope not. I think that in case I never marry, I shall do something extremely radical in art. For the reason that, under such circumstances, I would not be mixing up anyone else in the experiment and that would make me more daring.

I have not been at school to-day. I have a bad cold and this morning I woke up with no less than seven cold sores on my upper lip.

I got "The Whistler Book" from the Library. It is by Hartman and is very inspiring reading, I think.

Last night I made seven _hand_ sketches. I put a good deal of conscientious study upon them.*

I dreamt tragically of Mr. Gray last night. First Donnie and then Mr. Gray—great Caesar, if I am to dream of the whole string, I might as well cultivate insomnia.

March 4, Thursday

Ding, I like Mr. Dehn. There is a perky arrogance about his comments which is quite captivating.

Today I went into our Life room where I sat by myself for a long time, thinking and not thinking as the case might be. I must have fallen asleep, for about an hour later I found myself waking up. I believe I have the grippe. It has just dawned upon me that the reason why I seem unable to concentrate myself upon anything might have been due to the fact that I have such a cold. I think it is more languor than lack of inspiration which prevents me from seeing things in a way which will tempt my fingers to draw.

It was scarcely three o'clock when I put on my wraps and left for home. On the way I met Professor Koehler who, after greeting me cheerily, asked me why I was going home so early. I told him that I thought I had the grippe and he said, "You poor child," and told me that I should just take a good rest and take care of myself. I told him

* These sketches are shown facing page 264.

that I had had a cold for the last two weeks and that I had come to school, hoping to accomplish something but that I hadn't been able to do so. He said in his kind way, "No, no, you can't do anything when you aren't feeling well." It made me quite happy.

Tuesday morning while I was peacefully dreaming I received a telephone call. Armand. I was too sleepy to be duly surprised. He asked whether I could cut class Wednesday afternoon and I said I could. Yesterday afternoon he actually came. I still marvel at it. He asked how I was and I told him I had a terrible cold. We had dinner at "The Nook." My thoughts were badly scattered. I would be telling something and would stop suddenly because I had mentally wandered off into something else. It was due to my cold.

When we came back to the W.B.H. or O.M.R. (Old Maid's Retreat), whichever you wish to call it, Armand sat down at the piano and played. He played my favorite air from "La Boheme" and also the one which he had told me was the best description of me he could find. I enjoyed them exquisitely. Later in the day it affected me differently—I stamped my feet and addressed the mirror indignantly with, "He needn't play those things! He shouldn't play those things! He has no right to play those things!" meaning, of course, that they would only cause me pain anyway.

After that we sat down in our corner. Armand talked poetry to me. He said that he finds he is an "Impressionist" which I had thought a long time ago. I said, "Do you remember my writing to you last summer, 'I know just what kind of poetry you are going to write in the near future'?" and he said "Yes. Did you mean this kind?" I said, "Yes," and he asked how I had known. I told him I could tell by his last summer's poetry that he was leaning that way, and he said, "Yes, that was when I began."

He decided I needed physical exercise so he suggested playing the half-dollar game with a quarter. We had a good time playing it too, but somehow when I think of it now I find myself crying.

He had a Bergson book with him and he said, "I wish you could draw something into this before I go." I told him that the only thing I could draw offhand would be children, and he said he thought that would be all right. The idea was to get a picture which was irritatingly unrelated to the subject matter so I made a few sketches of dancing, irresponsible-looking children.

He also gave me a letter which he had written but which he had not sent because he was four blocks away from a stamp. I saw him to the station, and went home and read the letter—two sides long and about flowers and sidewalks.

I think Armand must have determined, before he came, that he was going to stay on his side of the line—for he did stay there.

March 5, Friday

I just had a telephone call. I said, "Who is this?" and the voice replied, "Why this is me."

I said, "Well who's *me?*"

"A.D."

"Who under the sun is A.D.?" I asked.

"Adolph Dehn," which was nice, and cheered me up immediately.

He said, "I was wondering, seeing that the weather is so bad, whether I hadn't better see that you got out there allright to-morrow night"— meaning the Club meeting. I told him that there would be no Whistler talk, and that I didn't know whether I would be able to go on account of my cold. I asked him whether he would be able to call me up to-morrow afternoon because I would know then whether I'd feel well enough to go. He said he would do that, and believe me, I'm going to try and get well.

I have not been at school all day. I have been in bed because I really didn't feel spry at all. I spent the afternoon in dozing and in reading my Artistic Anatomy.

March 6, Saturday

I am ashamed of myself. Without realizing it, without wanting to— in fact, deliberately *not* wanting to—I find myself thinking that later in my life I can if I want, do work which is above the usual standard. I suppose one of these days I will receive such a blow as will knock this arrogance out of me.

I am also guilty of what other people, if they saw it, would call self-exploitation. It is, of course, only Myself-exploitation so I am really not *guilty* at all. Myself-exploitation is inevitable and a necessity. It is more than that—IT IS A VIRTUE. Whistler is accused of self-exploitation, but I'll say right here that the poor fool who makes a statement to that effect is simply stultifying himself because he lays bare his ignorance.

If Whistler had not fought tooth and nail against the mediocre and Philistine statements and opinions of men of *acknowledged ability,* he would have gone mad; if he had not smiled a superior and tolerant smile at the multitudes who not only *not understood* but *misunderstood* him, he never could have lived to do what he did; and if he had not exploited *Himself* as arrogantly and untiringly as he did, his art would have been stunted, if indeed it would not have been choked entirely. This last is a strong statement for me to have said, because I contend that genius *will out*. But after reading a number of books on Whistler, including his "Gentle Art," I cannot help but marvel that he survived at all.

And I don't think for one minute that he took his controversies and caustic correspondences as lightly and sarcastically as he pretends to do. To me there is a pathetic strain underneath all of his sayings. He must have been very lonely as far as his Art was concerned. And brave! Great Caesar, he was brave.

When I read the Catalogue of his Art Exhibition, in which he has quoted his critics, I want to stand with my back against a wall and fight and scratch and bite. One can always forgive unpretending Philistines for saying things which show their complete ignorance of a subject, but when men like Tom Taylor, P. G. Hamerton, and F. Wedmore say things like the following, one feels more like cutting someone's neck than anything I can think of.

"I ought to have remembered that your penning, *like your painting,* belongs to the region of chaff."—Tom Taylor.

"By having as little to do as possible with tone and light and shade, Mr. Whistler evades great difficulties. . . . Mr. Whistler's figure drawings, generally defective and always incomplete."—P. G. Hamerton.

"Form and line are of little account to him. . . . Years ago James Whistler was a person of high promise."—F. Wedmore.

There is something more than contempt and humor in the way Whistler ends up his catalogue:—

"We grope for the wall like the blind, and we grope as if we had no eyes; we stumble at noonday as in the night.
"We roar all like bears."

Of course one laughs over the whole thing now—Whistler overpowered them so splendidly with his shafts not only of wit, but of wisdom. But I'll warrant that at times Whistler was weary of playing with geese. And if Whistler had, say in the middle of his career, given up the fight—for geese do not play *mildly*—they would have pounced upon him and pecked until—oh well.

It is said that Whistler carried on these *amiable* causticisms because he knew it would be good for his art. Great Scott! what if he did? It is better to *do* than to *die*. Surely he can not be blamed for proudly holding aloft the best in him, instead of crawling around in mock modesty among those who did not understand him anyway, and in this way holding out to destruction the Myself in him. Besides, *what else could he have done?* I certainly should never consider a man a coward for protecting and fighting for the best in him. I think Whistler was a hero for fighting in what he believed, and believing in that for which he fought, in the face of all, *of all.*

March 7

I have just written an exceedingly disagreeable letter to Armand— twenty sides long at that. It almost breaks my heart to think that I should have written a letter in such a hypocritical spirit, and it hurts me even more to think I am actually going to send it.

I feel very guilty lately as far as my treatment of Armand is concerned. I want badly to be as nice to him as I *feel,* but I dare not. It isn't that I don't want to, and it isn't because I can't—it is simply because I *must* not. How queer this world is. One *must* not do things even tho one ought to do so in order to be honest.

It's almost ten and I guess I'll go to bed.

I cried for Whistler today. As I have written to Armand, I wonder whether anyone has ever cried for Whistler before.

March 10, Wednesday

I am quite miserable again, today.

Last Monday morning I got ready to go to school, but felt so tired that I stayed home and read Hamlet instead.

Tuesday morning I felt so badly that I stayed at home again. I was in bed the entire afternoon and I didn't feel, as I usually do in such cases, that I was wasting valuable time. I was only too glad to lie down and do nothing.

This morning, urged on by a sense half of guilt and half of desperation, I went to school. I made an abominable life drawing, and was in consequence thoroughly disgusted with myself. I feel lifeless, listless, and seem to have no energy at all. I have been asking myself whether I am lazy or whether I am really ill. But I guess it's the grippe allright. Of which I am afraid. Some six years ago I was laid up with the grippe for the entire winter and it started exactly the same way this is doing. I am so appallingly indifferent. The fact that I haven't the *slightest desire to draw* almost drives me mad. Even "Hamlet" didn't grip me as it would have done under other circumstances. Music is the only thing that remains as potent as it does under ordinary circumstances.

This afternoon I went into the Still Life room where we had a discussion on religion. It was highly exciting. And no wonder. Joe La Londe is Catholic, Mr. Holton is a Seventh Day Adventist, Gertrude Schaffnit is the daughter of a Lutheran minister, Miss Magnusen is a Presbyterian I believe, I have no definite religion as yet but am not a skeptic, Mr. Dehn was brought up as a Lutheran but is now an agnostic.

Joe La Londe, who has obviously never run up against opposition in the matter of creeds, demanded with flushed cheeks and flashing eyes of Mr. Dehn, "What *do* you believe? *Do you believe in a God?"*

Mr. Dehn, who labors under the difficulties of being at the same time frank and very considerate of other people's feelings, said with a candidness and delicacy that I could not help but admire, "Well, I do not know. I certainly believe in some great Guiding power which plans life—you call it a God? Yes, I do believe in a God." It was not so much what he said, as the manner in which he said it which won my approval. He does not challenge them as a skeptic would, with a view of overthrowing their principles. *He sincerely wants to know.* He is going thru the stage that I suppose every person who thinks has to go thru.

Mr. Dehn and I have many views in common. His face looked very interesting today.

Later:—I have the most aggravating manner of saying to myself, in the midst of my thoughts and inner arguments, "Hm?"—as if one part of me were warning me or explaining something, and the other part acknowledged it by a questioning and half reluctant sigh. I caught myself doing it fully a dozen times today and it makes me nervous.

The girls in St. Paul are going to give a spread for my birthday tomorrow, so I am going there in the afternoon. I hope it will do me good.

I am almost frenzied with being alone so much, and there are so few people to whom I really want to talk.

March 11, 10:30 a.m.

I did not go to school. I saw no use in going.

Yesterday I got a flat birthday package from home upon which was the warning, "Do not open until Thursday." I was very curious to know what it might be, and seriously contemplated staying up until twelve and opening it as soon as Thursday had arrived, but by the time twelve o'clock came I was sleeping soundly.

Very early in the morning I awoke. Almost the first thought that occurred to me was, "It's Thursday now. I can look at the package." I put on the light. It was four o'clock. I rather expected the package to contain an embroidered dresser scarf or some tatting-edged handkerchiefs which would have been very acceptable of course, but not nearly so much so as that which it actually turned out to be. A little booklet, the contents and grey cover tied together with red ribbons by loving fingers. In red and delightfully amateur letters was the legend, "Family Incidents. By Thusnelda and Asta Gag."

And then I read the booklet thru, laughing and crying alternately over the carefully written and decorated pages. The frank and veracious method of treatment was refreshing, amusing, and touching. Tussy is a Senior at High School and will be ready to enter upon the duties of a rural school teacher this spring but she is still so beautifully a child.

I cannot tell how glad it made me. If Paula or Armand or anyone else who labors under the delusion that I am incapable of love, individual or otherwise, had seen me reading that book I am sure they would have changed their minds.

The other day I sent a long letter to Mrs. Weschcke. I told her that some day I wished to discuss the meaning of "genius" with Mr. Weschcke because the Club insisted that I give a good definition of it. This morning I received a little note from her, explaining that Mr. Weschcke wanted her to send me the little booklet she was enclosing.

The booklet (which is written by the Pres. of the Theosophical Society, Mrs. Annie Besant) is called "Do We Live on Earth Again?" and its main purpose is to show the Superiority of Theosophy over other religions. The reason why he sent it, however, is that it contains a number of passages on Genius which he thought might prove interesting and helpful to me. And he was right. I enjoyed the article very much, especially because it treats of "original sin" and a number of other things which we were discussing yesterday in Still Life.

I will quote a number of the sentences which appealed particularly to me:—

> "Dare you say that that man (speaking of a congenital criminal) will have a future of everlasting misery when his earth life has been misery from cradle to gallows? . . He is not fit for Heaven—there is no doubt about that. It is not right to send him to hell. What will you do with him?
>
> "Ignorance is the only original sin, and it is not *criminal,* but *inevitable.*"

Another sentence which I like was this:—"The *genius* marks the high water mark of the family." I had so often thought how queer it was that the children of great men were very rarely famous, and this explains it very simply and satisfactorily.

March 13, Saturday

Thursday afternoon I went to St. Paul. As I was walking Y.W.-wards, what should meet my gaze but the eternal Mr. Gray emerging from The Orpheum Theatre. I tried to be deeply interested in the St. Paul Hotel across the street but he had seen me, and before I knew it I was shaking hands with him, he was asking me how I was, I was telling him that I had a cold, and he was informing me that he had had an attack of pneumonia.

"I was just going on to Minneapolis," he said, "but I guess I'll stay here now!"

I said mercilessly, "Oh I'm going over to the Y.W. where the girls are giving a spread for my birthday," at which his face fell.

"I think I'll write again—if I may," he said.

"I didn't tell you you couldn't, did I?" I said.

"Well you see, I hadn't heard from you for such a long time that I didn't know what was the matter," he said.

Great Caesar, man, when *will* you know what's the matter?

He said also that he was coming back to Minneapolis in two weeks, and might he come to see me? I could think of nothing to say but "Yes," so I said that. He kept saying that he was awfully glad to have seen me again, and I kept saying lamely that I had certainly been surprised when I saw him.

After I had left him I stamped my feet fiercely. If the deepness of love were determined by *blindness* it would surely be true love in his case.

At the Y.W. I found Paula who greeted me with a darling middy blouse for my birthday. And then came Nina and then Theresa. When Dorothy Spriess had arrived we went up into the private dining room where we had the spread. The girls had bought me half-a-dozen lovely yellow jonquils and it was quite festive. Some of the girls wore their prettiest waists for the occasion. I never knew before how nice it felt to have people dress up for your especial benefit.

"Look!" cried Paula, drawing me around to one side of the table, "Mama Hershl's birthday present." It was a big platter full of *Berliner Pfannkuchen*. Theresa had sent home for a cake too, and it was good, Oh it was nice all around. Theresa gave me a pretty hat pin, one which she made at school.

The girls prevailed upon me to spend the night with them. That Y.W. has entirely too many rules. One gets all tangled up in them. The latest is that one is *not allowed to gargle!* It's overdoing it, that's all.

March 14, Sunday

Thursday evening I received a phone call. "This is one A.M. Emraad," said the voice at the other end. He asked how I was feeling. I said, "About the same. I've been a good deal worse since you were here last." "The devil!" said Armand eloquently. He told me that he and Timmie would be over in twenty minutes. They were just about on time, probably due to Timmie.

I told them of the talk I was to give on Whistler. Timmie said, "Well of course you know that Ruskin was a much greater man than Whistler." I gave him a challenging look, and he continued, "As an artist, of course, Whistler was greater—but as a *man*?"

"As a *man*," I said.

Armand said, quite to my surprise and certainly to my joy, "Mr. Frendel, I take up my arms for the opposition."

"Mr. Emraad," said Timmie in his quaint inimitable way, "One might expect as much."

Armand sat down at the piano. At first he played rather turbulently but wandered on to calmer things, and after a while I found that he was playing the tune which he considers a description of me. Which made me want to sit and dream, but Timmie felt disposed to talk.

Timmie said excitedly, "But Ruskin did so much more. Whistler only gave us art——"

"But art isn't *Art*!" I shot at him with much earnestness.

Armand turned around and said, still playing, "She's right."

Soon after this Timmie gravely felt my pulse and asked me a number of questions, after which he said, "It's the grippe, allright."

"You ought to go to bed," Armand began.

"Get a hot water bag," advised Timmie.

"Oh you can do that if you wish," said Armand tolerantly, "but it isn't necessary."

"But really," insisted Timmie, "It's very good. I've gone thru all that myself."

"Drink some hot lemonade," said Armand, "and then wrap up warm so you'll get good and hot."

"But I can't get any hot lemonade here," I said.

"Oh, I'm sure you can," said Timmie. "This is a Christian place, isn't it?" and he looked at the doorway, the curtains and the ceiling.

"—and then you go to bed and cover up well," Armand was repeating, "and stay in bed all day tomorrow."

"*Ach!* I don't want to stay in bed all day."

"But you must."

"And Wanda, do get a hot water bag if possible," added Timmie, as he went out into the hall to put on his rubbers.

At this point Armand came up to me and said, "Now Wanda, I ask you as a friend, please stay in bed all day to-morrow." So I said, "All right."

Then I went into my room, and prepared to follow the advice of my nice doctors. It had made me so happy that somebody cared how the grippe and I were getting along. I stayed in bed meekly all the next day writing a 22-sided letter home and reading Whistler as usual. Sleeping part of the time too, I believe. I didn't go to the Club that night.

March 15, Monday

Sunday afternoon I received a telephone call.

"Is this Whistler?" said the voice, "this is John Ruskin."

I said, "Yes, this is James Abbot McNeill Whistler."

"Would you let John Ruskin take you somewhere to-night?"

"Why yes, I'll let him," I said. "Where are we going?"

"Why I thought you'd enjoy it more if it came as a surprise," said Mr. Dehn.

He arrived at a quarter after seven. "We're going to church," he said, and explained that he had heard me say once that I rarely went to church and that he had just thought to himself, "Now I'll make her go."

So after talking excitedly about inspiration, dumps, and Whistler (of course), we went to the Unitarian Church where a Seventh Day Adventist is giving sermons for a few weeks. As I had known practically nothing about Seventh Day Adventism before, I found it quite interesting.

After church we went to have some ice-cream and we discussed, among other things, Mr. Dehn's plans for the next two years or so. He will have to earn his way thru school, and we exchanged ideas as to what would be the best thing for him to do. He also suggested that I go fishing with him sometime this summer. He thinks it would be interesting to see me fish. I told him I supposed I couldn't fish unless I happened to have an inspiration in that direction.

This morning on my way to school I met one of the girls. She informed me that I had 19 sketches up at Concours [the Monthly Competition Exhibition].

I think the girls must think me an awful nut. I always take my bench into a corner all by myself, so that I can draw and think and act as I please. Really I do very little that is good at school. I just go there to learn, and then I go home and *do*. At school I think and analyze and absorb criticism and feast on the good pictures at the Museum. Then I go home and use all this subconsciously.

Tonight Armand called up to see how I was, and Timmie talked to me too. It made me feel good to have people ask how I was getting along.

March 18, Thursday

Last Tuesday when I came to school, Mrs. Fournier congratulated me on the fact that I had so many pictures up at the Concours Exhibition. She said, "You made a hit with Mr. Breck * that time," and said that he had practically chosen the pictures.

I have been going to school every day. I have been working very earnestly in Life and have learned much. I am thoroughly disgusted

* The late Joseph Breck—at that time Director of the Minneapolis Art School.

with myself as far as the execution of my charcoal studies is concerned. My mind and hands are most obstinate in trying to master the technicalities of it. I have done two little pastel sketches of the model which are better than my big study. Yesterday I fixed them and the Fixatif simply ate the color right up. I felt so badly about it that I nearly cried.

Yesterday evening Mr. Dehn and I went to a Movie. It happened to be a particularly good one, so we had little chance to criticise, which was what we had been looking forward to. We had a Sundae and we talked about Theosophy, Atheism and Orthodox Christianity, so you see we covered the entire field of Religion.

Mr. Dehn thinks I am not democratic enough. He objects to my speaking of mediocrity. He disagrees with Paula and Armand in that he thinks I am capable of individual love, but thinks I do not have the right attitude toward the masses. Referring to my mention of mediocrity, I told him that I did not necessarily mean the lower class of people, and that there were many people who had gone thru college whom I considered mediocre whereas I might easily come across a working-man whom I did not consider as such. As a matter-of-fact I can tolerate the working-man kind almost better than a person who makes pretensions to knowledge and hasn't it. I am bent on proving to Mr. Dehn that I do love humanity as a whole.

I have several drawings which I ought to hand in to Mr. Phoenix, or rather I have *not* got them. I have "The Miser" and a cursory sketch of the Valley Forge Soldier, but they are so utterly bad that I refuse to hand them in. Not that I am a coward, but that it would be a crime to my Muse. The things are absolutely empty. There is one good thing about them—I did not use cleverness to hide their emptiness. I showed my faults, or rather my absolute lack of good points, in a frank manner which is almost a joy to behold.

If we had good models in life, I think I should like it very much. I like to draw muscles—especially the pectoral and deltoid muscles. I like to draw shoulders and knees. The sternum is interesting too, providing the model has enough muscles to show their attachment at this bone. But shoulders, I think, I like best.

I am very enthusiastic about elimination of detail, and find that in one- or two-minute sketches I can pick out the most important lines rather quickly.

The honorable Joseph Breck came into sketch class yesterday and when he saw that Dallas Hodgeman was working in pastel he said,

"It's fun to work with these, isn't it?" I couldn't help wishing he had said that to me. I would have said swiftly, "Yes, but that isn't what I'm using them for." I would so have enjoyed to have seen him bowl over.

March 26, Saturday

The other day at school Miss Canteeny said, "Well, Wanda, you're getting to be the star of the school," to which I replied with unusual modesty, "Oh no."

Last Saturday afternoon I began definitely organizing my Whistler talk. I said it over three times from beginning to end, and by that time I had memorized most of it. Mr. Dehn called for me again in the evening—that is getting to be a regular institution it seems—and we went to Fournier's.

I gave my Whistler talk, not saying anything against Ruskin (to their surprise, and possibly to their disappointment) and as much good and as little bad as I could of Whistler. Mr. Holton, for whom facts count exceeding much, orally proclaimed himself a champion for my side, and the others declared they had never known how important Whistler really was, etc.

I have a confession to make here. Part of my success was due to the fact that I picked out the things which were in Whistler's favor. When any of his weak points were mentioned in the consequent discussion I admitted them, of course, but there were a number of things which I might have said which would have been a trifle detrimental to my side of the argument. I excuse myself in this wise:—In the first place I was expected to prove that Whistler was as great as Ruskin, and they were supposed to uphold and prove the reverse; therefore the whole thing was conducted in the spirit of a debate. And in debates people serenely disregard the points which are not in favor of their side. In the second place it was an experiment. I wished to see how much one could accomplish by picking out and presenting the favorable arguments, and leaving out and even *leading away from* the unfavorable arguments. I have found that one can do a *good deal*.

To myself I admit that Ruskin, as a man, was a *bigger* man. *Bigger,* to me however, differs from *greater,* which last is the word which we used in our arguments.

Mr. Dehn, I know, is not by any means convinced. I suppose he could not help but acknowledge that Whistler was a much greater man than he had ever supposed him to be. But all the same, I could see that

Self Portrait on Brown Wrapping Paper

Elf—An Attempt at Popular Magazine Illustration

A Page from the Diary, February 3, 1915

My First Printed Cover—Tempera

he was not as ready to proclaim me victor as some of the others. I still believe the things I wrote about Whistler in this diary, March 6.

Sunday morning, to my great surprise and joy, I became very much interested in my Theory of Color problems and really accomplished two of them.

Tuesday noon, as I came out of Life, whom should I see in the hall but Mr. Gray. He wanted me to have dinner with him that night, and as I had no other engagement I had to accept. I fumed most of the afternoon, and when sketch-class came I scratched fiercely all over my drawing with sorrowful rage. We went to dinner and I cannot say that I enjoyed myself exceedingly. Suffice it to say that Mr. Gray informed me that I hadn't by any means seen the last of him. I believe he knows I do not care very much for him but he absolutely refuses to be shaken.

Wednesday Paula came and had dinner with me and we went to a Movie. We had a good time. I am getting so that I need my friends more and more. The "glass door," of which I have not spoken for many a day, has been fully opened to me at last. I love people for the sake of loving them, and they love me for myself and not for my work or any other thing.

Thursday evening Mr. Dehn came. We talked about Theosophy. He brought me a story called "Little Sister" which he wanted me to read. It was about a seventeen-year old youth in the amusing state of his first crush. From this I drifted very naturally to some incidents about my very early cavaliers. They amused Mr. Dehn immensely.

I said at one point, "I have turned down all my cavaliers now, because I intend to have nothing but friends for a couple of years——"

"Good!" said Mr. Dehn characteristically.

"—Except one," I continued. "I've turned him down too but he simply won't stay turned." I gave a brief account of the Gray-Romance. Mr. Dehn said that he admired him for being so persevering.

We had some interesting little arguments all thru the evening and he said a number of things I liked very much. He has a quiet little smile which is very charming.

He asked, "What is Paula like?" I said, "How do you mean?" and he said, "Well, is she exceptional like you?" I said, "I'm afraid you're flattering," but he declared he wasn't. I was very much surprised to hear him say that, because he always thinks I am too arrogant as it is, and is not in the habit of saying things which might tend to make me more so.

Yesterday morning I received a telephone call. Armand. He said he

had no class until 3 p.m. and could I get off? I said I could and re-
paired myself directly to the W.B.H. where he arrived at a little after
eleven a.m. I didn't enjoy his visit very much at all. He was a pieface good and proper again, and I don't know whether I wanted more
to cry or grab him by the hair and shake him. I told him all the news,
which included, of course, Mr. Gray's latest visit. He always acts funny
when I mention Mr. Gray. At one place he said, "Oh that sentimental
Gray."

I said, flaring up, "He's *not* sentimental!"

Armand said, "Well he would be, if he had the chance."

I said indignantly, "He would not!"

Armand said, "That's good. It's nice of you to stick up for him." I
may not like to have Mr. Gray come to see me etc., but I shall certainly
defend his character, which seems to be very good indeed.

I told Armand too, how my Whistler talk had come off. He said a
number of things about Whistler which would be as effective as poisoned
arrows in the hands of my adversaries. I had known these things too,
but he enlarged upon them so provokingly. His main argument was that
Whistler was great only when he forget himself, that his art was limited
and that, had he been *exceedingly* great, the driving force within him
would have been so great that there would have been no room for his
"petty" causticisms and clevernesses. Also that he was selfish and not
Humanity-loving enough. These were the things I had evaded in my
arguments.

He said he would bring me "Jean Christophe" to read, which he considers about the greatest novel ever written. Now I wonder what he
wants me to read that for. He always has a purpose.

We took a walk. We serenely ignored lunch. We went to a movie.
In one place it was so funny that I rocked back and forth in silent mirth.
I would look up, to see Armand just turning around as I had expected,
then we would look at each other for one moment and follow up the
look with an "outburst" as Paula and I used to call them.

At one place Armand remarked that Timmie liked to "chatter." I
said, "Don't you?" and he said, "No."

I said, "Do I?" and he said, "Yes, I think you do."

I said, "I chatter, but *I don't like it.*" I told him that he chattered too,
and when he wanted to know upon what occasions, I said, "You chatter
when you are thinking about something else. Sometimes for a short time
and sometimes for an entire afternoon," which he could not deny.

Once, after thinking of magazine illustration and the darling family at home, I found myself running my hands thru my hair—emotionally, one might say. Armand asked what was the matter, but I didn't answer. He asked gently, *"Was ist los?"* but still I didn't answer. I managed after a while to state it very angularly. When I think of those things I become so worried. I seem so small in comparison to my problem. Sometimes I wonder how it will all turn out. Of course Stella is earning a little now and Tussy will be teaching next fall, but I cannot bear to have them teach school for any length of time. I would so gladly do more if I could, but I think for being such a slip of a girl as I am, I have accomplished a good deal. A great deal in a way, and so very little in another way.

April 1, Thursday

It is becoming more and more necessary for me to have friends simply so that I have people to love and be loved by. When I taught school I didn't seem to need people's love so much, last year I had so much to learn that I quite forgot about it, but this year I am beginning to feel—in a material way—the absence of my darling folks. Besides, last year I had the girls at the Y.W. and at school—but this year I see so little of these people and I have not attached myself to any of the girls over here.

I have a number of boy friends at school out of whom I get a good deal of satisfaction, but Mr. Dehn is the only one whom I should call an *accepted* friend. In a way I can be more frank with Mr. D. than with Mr. E. because Mr. D. has no old system-ideas. The worst he does is to take that side of a discussion which is opposite to mine, just to see me get excited and to see what arguments will be forthcoming. And one doesn't mind that so much.

I have been telling myself that I was a very foolish little creature for having taken Armand's last-spring remarks for what I did. I find myself on the point of saying things of a like nature to people for whom I have nothing but a friendly dispassionate regard. One says those things in a broader way than a little foolish girl would naturally take them.

I don't know quite how to act to Armand. I am always afraid that he will misconstrue my remarks and that he is afraid that I will misconstrue his. The reason why I am *afraid* is because I usually do misconstrue his—I mean, I cannot help construing them the way he seems to be afraid I will do, altho I try very hard not to show it. I try so hard to have the attitude that he obviously wants me to have.

If it is a foolish infatuation on my part why are not my eyes opened to the fact by this time? If he does not care for me and never will, and if I read all these diaries over, will I be ashamed of these things that I have written? *Must one be ashamed of loving the wrong person?* Or is it possible that it's all a mistake and that some day I will find someone else. Some one else? Some one *else?*

If this is not real love, what is *real* love like? Perhaps I am a sentimental fool.

I have drifted unconsciously from Armand's visit. After the movie we went back to the house, Armand playing the part of an extremely polite and stupid Englishman. He does get the drollest expressions on his face, and the fact that he happens to be on the street while he acts out these parts doesn't bother him in the least. Afterwards I saw him to the car-line and on the way he acted like a sort of every-day sport who tries to be very proper while walking beside a young girl. He would walk along, dutifully looking straight ahead of him but giving me an occasional and greedy sort of look out of the corner of his eye. Then he gave a sort of imitation of a dog, licking his chops as he sees a particularly tempting bone. He looked just awfully funny. That man has too many accomplishments. It seems to me it's enough if he is a musician, a poet, and a short story writer, without having abilities in the vaudeville line. I was peeved after he left. I mostly am, lately.

I broke my glasses again. $1.50. Easter bonnet $2.98. I sketched myself three times in it. Wanda go to bed.

I had a ghastly dream last night. I dreamt that men with death-heads were always racing after us. I always have such bad dreams lately. And now I must go to bed.

April 2

In Life I do rotten work. I cannot handle charcoal and charcoal paper. I know very well what is expected of me to do, but I can't do it. When I take a scrap of wrapping paper and a few pastels I come very much nearer to doing the right thing than the other way, but I need the other sort of training.

During the last six or seven weeks I have handed in only one problem each into the Illustration and Theory of Color Classes. I don't know whether I am right or wrong in being negligent about those things. I intend to talk it over with Mr. Goetsch very soon.

I am afraid of going into Mag. Illustration. I am afraid that I will have to do Soldiers and Misers and Animals and interiors. I would not be so much afraid if I could do only the things which I like so much to do.

Saturday evening Mr. Dehn called for me, as usual, to go to the Club. A man gave a talk on the Reproduction of Drawings, which I found very satisfying because I have always been intensely curious as to how pictures were reproduced.

April 4, Easter Sunday

Wednesday Mr. Dehn called on me. We talked about the usual subjects. Religion, of course. Mr. Dehn is so much at sea upon the question of immortality at present that we discuss it just about every time we meet.

I believe in immortality—I don't know just what I think its nature is, neither do I care, but I can't see how anyone with a big mind and heart can think that our souls die with us. *Matter* is endless, *space* is endless— why should we consider the *soul* mortal?

It makes me tired to have materialists come in with their man-made arguments and proofs, trying to refute such a big and super-human thing as immortality of the soul. If they can find the soul, hold it in their hands, make it tangible, dissect it and analyze it materially—they will have a right to apply material and scientific tests and arguments to it, and not before.

Where does space end? If it is endless, how can it be? If a thing can't be endless unless it goes in a circle, and space goes in a circle, what *after* the circle? In what is the circle placed? In space again. And after *this* space?——

Time must be endless, for even if it stopped, there would have to be something in place of it after it. It must have begun somewhere. But what before the beginning?

When I think these things and realize to a certain extent how absolutely too small we are to comprehend things like that, I am ready to believe almost anything. Those things are so big and wonderful that we should have no trouble realizing that we can never fathom their mysteries in this life. If there are such things, why shouldn't there be a life big and wonderful enough to conceive them?

There was a time when I was practically a skeptic or an atheist. Mr. Dehn is in that stage now. I told him I thought that he would get over that in time. You know when you first hear the cold, bare facts which scientists assail us with, their arguments (being so material and therefore entirely within our conception) seem to brush away all possibility of anything intangible, and we doubt all but that which can be explained in our own feeble, human way. Then, great Caesar, when you get to the point where you feel that you are touching sunsets, and are part of curves in trees or stretches of landscapes or of a bird's trill—then you realize how small and insignificant and nonconclusive are cold, man-conceived proofs. Let them prove our *material* existence by science, but for the love of soup, let them leave the Divine and unfathomable to the Soul.

It's enough that we have to be material. I do not mean to condemn matter or infer that I don't appreciate it. I am glad to be alive, to be able to feel the sunshine-laden breath of spring, and to be able to delight in purely physical demonstration of my feelings—but even these things would not be so enjoyable if they were not linked with something greater and more mystical.

Oh Tush!

I believe I could doubt anything more easily at present (and I hope *always*) than immortality. It's only part of "Being is not; non-being is." It seems to me that the person who does not finally come to that is more beast than man. For me, I thank God that I have a soul, a Myself (call it what you like), and that I have the light to acknowledge it and have faith in it. The nature of a hereafter, or of our God, does not worry me much. I cannot conceive of either the conventional hell or a personal devil.

Right and wrong, and the causes of them, are so bewilderingly mixed in this world that I sometimes doubt whether there is such a thing in the usual sense of the word. Or perhaps I should say "good and bad." I don't know which to use. Well anyway, it seems one might substitute instead of "right and wrong" or "good and bad"—"doing one's best or not doing one's best."

On the other hand (said she, unchronologically) Christians as well as materialists are too material. So many of them take the Bible so literally. What if the Bible has contradictions? Why can't people take it for what it is, whether it be an accurate history or not? It's a good and an uplifting piece of literature. The people who wrote it, whether they exaggerated or not, at least were big and un-philistine enough to "see the sun." Having become capable of this, and rejoicing in their ability to see thru the veil, they did the most natural thing in the world. They tried to show it to others too. So they wrote the Bible. I suppose they wrote the Bible for the same reason that an artist paints a picture. The divine spark in them moved them to tell the world. I am getting off my subject, I'm afraid.

History is valuable, it seems to me, only inasmuch as it teaches consequent generations to understand life. It matters very little to me when things happened as long as they happened at the psychological moment, and as long as *something* is born of the experience or incident.

Whether in Bible Days there were miracles or not, doesn't seem to me to be of much consequence. But there was *Light* and there was *Good,* and those things are worth recording.

Whether we descend from Adam and Eve or whether we are only an improvement on apes, doesn't matter much to me. That's past. I thank goodness that I am as far removed from apes as I am. If I have ape-blood in me—I don't care. So has everybody else then. If I have upon me the mark of original sin, I am not responsible for it, and besides if *I* have it so has everyone else. The only thing to do is to be as sinless as possible—I mean, adding as little sin to the original sin as possible.

There is nothing better for us to do than to take ourselves as we find ourselves and make the best of ourselves. If I find myself, as I did, the daughter of an artist who has left me with broadmindedness and a conveniently strong character to resist temptation, I take myself from there and accomplish what I can. If a little slum child finds itself with a heritage of ignorance and crime (which words are almost synonymous) you cannot blame it for not getting as far as do I with my advantages. In the same way, I have no right to pride myself upon my virtue, my chastity or my broadmindedness. I do not even deserve praise for doing my best, for that is my duty and I deserve rather to be blamed for not doing my best.

Of course, there are some people who are born with rich heritages but who, thru misfortune or some other reason, fall down. And perhaps they cannot even be blamed for not having done their best. Or perhaps they *did their best* but fell anyway.

I am wandering off again.

I do not know how much of the Bible I actually accept, I do not know what part of the Christian doctrine I accept. I don't care much how much other people accept—as long as they can *realize the light.*

It seems to me that the trouble is that Church people as a general rule underestimate *this* life, while materialists, atheists etc. over-estimate it. I do not chafe under *having to BE,* physically, as I used to; but I take such ecstasy in actually living because the material part of our life is linked with something bigger.

You little pie face, you little pebble, you little, little dot—talking for pages of Eternity——

Last night Mr. Dehn came again and we went to the Club. Mr. Holton gave a talk on "The Meeting of Prophecy and History." On the way out Mr. Dehn accused me, with a cryptic smile, of a delight for "tall talk" and a tendency towards affectation. I became exceedingly excited as may be imagined, denying it and trying to explain in what way he was mistaken. I have a sneaking notion that he did it only to see how I'd take it. In fact I'm almost sure of it. But not quite. So I must ask him seriously whether he really thinks that there is any danger of my doing so.

This morning I went to Church and I liked it. When I go to church of my own accord I like it. And I like to go to church with Mr. Dehn because he looks at the matter from a different point of view than a regular church-goer would.

I have just finished Arthur Pinero's "The Benefit of the Doubt—A Comedy in Three Acts." I fail to see where the *comedy* comes in. I am reading "The Blue Bird" in German.

April 5, Monday

Mr. Dehn was here again last night. We talked again of immortality. At about nine we went out for a walk. A glorious evening—so I was glad I had someone to walk with and talk with.

He said that he could not understand how I could write things and draw things and not know at the time that I was doing so. That thing being so frequent with me it seems quite natural with me. He said that he had long ago admitted that I was different from most people in thoughts and ideas but that, as he saw more of me, I continued to show much more exceptional-ness than he had ever expected to see. So much, in fact, that at times he had a hard time understanding me. That is, he does not *mis*understand me but it takes him a while to recover from the unusual-ness of my thoughts, ideas, and feelings. I told him I would get worse as spring came on, and said that I became absolutely crazy with delight when I was "among nature."

We discussed briefly Platonic Friendship. We agree so well on the subject that no discussions arise.

He said he liked to hear me call him "pieface." It seems I called him that the other night when he accused me of "tall-thinking" and affectation. By the way, I found that he said that simply to get me excited and to see how I defended myself. I told him that I had become quite alarmed over his accusation because I feared, altho I could scarcely believe it, that I might be leaning towards cleverness again. I asked him, with much earnestness, to be sure to tell me immediately if he should detect anything of the sort in either my work, actions, or speech. We decided that each of us was free to criticise the other after this. He said that if I ever needed someone to take me to or from any place, or any other sort of assistance in anything, he would be glad to do all he could. This moved me to ask him for his telephone number which he gave to me.

To-day was a glorious day and I walked over five miles and sketched many little children.

April 8, Thursday

Last Tuesday, being thoroughly disgusted with my Life drawing, I said, "I wish Mr. Goetsch would come and say, 'This drawing is absolutely rotten.'" At this I felt a sort of gasp going around the room so I looked up to see what was the matter. Mr. Goetsch was in the room himself, and said with one of his queer smiles, "What?" I repeated it quite to my own surprise and certainly to everyone else's. He smiled and said nothing and the class subsided.

After the rest period Mr. Goetsch came right over to my bench altho it wasn't nearly my turn. He sat down, looked at the drawing and said, "Miss Gág, this is *very good.*" That's the first time he's ever said that of any of my life drawings, so after I had recovered from my surprise, I found myself being quite tickled. It makes me so happy to think that I am finally beginning to grasp, however slightly, the technique of charcoal drawing.

I have gathered my sketches for the next Concours Exhibition and I have exactly seventy.

I heard nary a word from smarty Armand E. during Easter vacation. I am becoming impatient. If we are *friends* why can't we be as frank and unconstrained as of old? The worst of it is that I cannot blame Armand for acting as he does, and that however much I may be humiliating myself, I cannot help but feel as I do. If I only knew whether what he says is *part of the truth* or the opposite of it. If this is not love, why do I suffer as I do—why don't I find the real thing—and why do I feel always, in spite of my efforts to the contrary, that I cannot understand how it *could* be someone else?

Spring is here and with it all the memories and associations of last year. And my heart is almost smothered with all the things I have to gird about it to keep it prudently silent.

> „*Alte Erinnerungen wehen mich an,*
>   *Vergessene Träume, erloschene Bilder*
>   *Qualvoll süsse, tauchen hervor.*"

The "La Boheme" air has been running thru my head all day. And I keep thinking of meadow larks:—

> „*Wer hat euch das Wörtlein gelehret,*
>   *Ihr Vöglein in luftiger Höh?*
>   *Schweigt still! Wenn mein Herz es höret,*
>   *Dann thut es noch einmal so weh.*"

April 11, Sunday

Last night I took Paula with me to the Club. Mr. Goetsch gave a talk on "Student Life in Paris." He leaned leisurely back in his chair and related different incidents with much grace, giving us a general idea of his life in Paris. He knows several very well-known artists.

After Mr. Goetsch's lecture, we discussed, among other things, Woman Suffrage, Socialism and Selfishness. At one time there was a little pause in the conversation, of which I took advantage by asking Mr. Goetsch what his definition of Genius was. Once started on this, we kept on until we adjourned. There were five of us who took the same car, Mr. Goetsch, Mr. MacDonald, and Paula and Mr. Dehn and I. We kept right on discussing genius all the way home, and with such vehemence that the people in the car regarded us curiously. I believe they thought we were quarrelling.

They all admitted that there was such a thing as genius but no one except Paula agreed with me that there was a definite division between geniuses and non-geniuses. I don't remember all the exciting things we said, but certain it is that I saw a side of Mr. Goetsch's character which pleased me very much. It makes me laugh when I think of the things I wrote about him when I first came to this school, for I do not think any more that he looks like "a salamander" sounds. At least not as much as I used to.

Paula stayed the night with me and she raved about Mr. Goetsch until almost three in the morning. I likewise. Paula said she thought Mr. Goetsch was "perfectly adorable." She likes Mr. Dehn too.

April 14, Wednesday

Last Sunday evening I was sketching away for dear life with my hair hanging negligently down my back when they told me I had a caller. I jumped into a conventional waist and skirt and gathered my hair together, and hastened out to the parlor. Timmie and Armand rushed forward, shook hands and said, "Put on a coat. You have about half a minute to do it in." So I flew to my room, rushed into a coat and jammed a cap upon my head.

In the car were Fred Wing and Armand's sister. We all piled in for a fine little spin. Timmie and I had a little conversation concerning Whistler. Armand, at my side, said little and when he did, it was exceedingly polite. I said, "How polite you are!" He said, "Yes, I'm always polite when I'm irritable." To things I related (my latest school experiences etc.) he responded with a mirth which was as uncalled for as it was unnatural. It sounded, to use his own words, like breaking glass.

He said he had received my last letter the day before. He said that as soon as he saw the envelope he said, "She's mad." He declared that he had been frightfully busy. "I've had to do a great deal of the kind of stuff I don't like to do." When we returned to the house Armand took me up to the door and said he'd probably call me up sometime during the next week. Which I may as well doubt. I like his sister very much. She is so quiet that she is exceedingly interesting.

Monday Mr. Dehn called. I read him part of Hueffer's "To Heaven" which he liked. We walked to Loring Park as usual, discussing the usual topics with the addition of new ones.

This afternoon, just as I had finished my sketch for Illustration, the door opened slightly and I saw Timmie out in the hall. I went out and he asked whether I had time for a little walk so we set off for Lake of the Isles.

Timmie is too conventional for my taste. He said that conventionality was the price we paid for having been allowed to reach the present high state of civilization and intellectuality. I said it was allright to have to pay a price, but I saw no use for paying a price which was of so little value to humanity. I said I didn't see why it couldn't be something more useful. I also stated that I disliked it because it caused so much hypocrisy.

Armand's outlook on life is broader than Timmie's. Last fall when Timmie used to talk incidentally of Armand (continued in the next diary, goodbye)

* * *

—I used to wonder whether he or I knew Armand better. I always had a comfortable, subconscious feeling that I knew Armand much better, but all the same Timmie has been his intimate friend for so long, that I didn't know but that Timmie might be right. Then Armand would tell me to do one thing and Timmie would tell me to do the other. Each one seemed afraid that I would do what the other wanted me to do. Sometimes I hardly knew which one's advice to follow, and upon such occasions I would follow my own inclinations. I may change my mind, but at present I think Armand's advice was better. Where under the sun that man got all that knowledge of human nature, I do not know, but the more I think about it and the more I compare him with other people, the more I realize that his knowledge of people's innermost selves is not only extensive but beautifully sympathetic. Oh ding it all, Armand is a perfect brick and all his irritating characteristics are but virtues which are misunderstood. I am speaking particularly of those which I deliberately misunderstand. I mean, I know all the time that I ought not to blame him for them, but I do anyway, for the simple reason that I like him too well as it is, even if I look hard and virtuously at his faults only. Great Caesar, it sounds as if I were idealizing Armand, but now that I have allowed myself to regard him in a just light, I might as well be reckless and say the much I cannot help but feel.

Oh it is so hard to know that you have to keep caring when you are trying so virtuously to do otherwise. Even the fact that Armand may not care for me at all, and even tho I may be humiliating myself unspeakably in the eyes of the future Wanda Gág, I write, recklessly, that I love him still. If I were a man it would be different. No one thinks a man humiliates himself by loving faithfully and forever a woman who does not care for him. One even admires him for it. But with a woman it is different. She must choke it down and bear it all in silence. I must just act as if I now believed that it was the *child* in me that had spoken last Spring. Perhaps it was the child-part that spoke, and perhaps I *will* meet someone whom I like better—but I am certainly not anywhere near believing it.

Oh I am reckless to-night. It had to come. I have been trying to lie to myself for too long. Perhaps some day when I know that all is hopeless, I shall be coward enough to tear up all these anguished writings.

Oh Armand, you think I regard you objectively. ("I have *made* you regard me objectively," he said with some satisfaction, I remember.) If this is only objective—what would *subjective* be? If he did not understand me so very very well, and if he were not so absolutely indispensable to my poor groping Myself, I should almost wish I had never met him. But I'm glad I did, anyway.

I have sobbed so hard to-night that at times it seemed that either my head or my heart must burst.

Oh, Wanda, go to bed.

April 18, Sunday

It has been a quiet Sunday. This morning simply melted away. I hung different pictures upon my walls again. I change them when I have drawn out all that I can (until some further date when I can bring newly-added experiences to the thing). Funny. First I draw myself into them and then I draw myself out of them again for consequent use. I suppose it is because so much of what is in my pictures went into them independent of my own volition or certainly without my knowledge. And then a few days or a few months or even a few years later when I look at them again, I shake hands, so to speak, with the part of me with which I had never been really acquainted altho it may have been lodged within me and sent out a long time ago.

I find a thought, feeling or experience in a tree or a tilt of a head or the turn of a cheek—I translate it onto paper, then later I take it out of there and make it into, or add it to, a thought, feeling or experience again. And this again will have a noticeable effect on my consequent method of expressing myself. It goes in a ring, only the ring grows wider and wider and is therefore a sort of spiral affair. And we do not know where it will stop or how long it will go—with me, I mean. Of course it will keep going on because my influence, whether it is good, bad or indifferent, will make a difference in other people's spirals.

April 19, Monday

Only twelve days more, and then the First of May. I am so afraid that it will rain or that Armand will forget all about it.

Saturday afternoon Timmie came and we went to the Walker Art Galleries. The pictures are hung so closely that one detracts from the other, and they were all covered with glass which gives me the Willies. We talked of many things, Selfishness, Art and Marriage, Science and Art. Timmie sometimes forgets that I have not had a University Education. Funny and nice Timmie.

Saturday evening Mr. Dehn called for me as usual and we went to the Club. An old lady talked on "Artists I have known." One of the artists she knew when she was young had spent almost an entire summer with Whistler. In speaking of Whistler she said, "That ridiculous man who wore shoestrings for neckties," and of course she didn't know why that remark was received with such applause.

April 24

Today I sent in a sketch to the Northwestern Artists Exhibition. It may not even be accepted but I want to convince myself that I am not afraid of making a plunge. Besides it will do me good to have the thing turned down. It is a black-and-white sketch of myself.

I have taken a plunge. I have decided to throw myself into magazine illustration with a vengeance. It is the only way, I think. I shall study magazine covers with much diligence in order that I may get used to all their little tricks and devices. I shall use my brain to analyze half-tones and zinc plates and all the other things, I shall use my eyes to see nature and the people about me as magazine illustrations. But it hurts so to say goodbye to the other things even if it is only for a few years. And Armand, the only person who can really see my point of view, is so busy with his own affairs that he will doubtless let me fall over the brinks of holes and to run into ruts. He is so eternally busy. I wonder if he is really so busy, or does he want me to change the attitude towards him which he must almost know I have?

If he forgets the First of May it will break my heart.

April 25, Sunday

It will break my heart if he forgets the First of May.

It has been a queer day. I have been designing a dress and listening to good singing and dreaming myself into one or two of Anderson's

Fairy Tales in German and going off into trances and telling myself that I shall grow tired of Mr. Dehn if he comes to see me four evenings a week.

I don't care if that sentence is long and unbalanced. I don't care, I don't care, I don't care.

April 26, Monday

One beautiful day after another drags on.

Sometimes I even go so far as to think that Armand may have grown tired of me and my thoughts, and sometimes comes the painful and almost unbearable thought that he may be going around with some other girl. I do not like to have him take long walks with Eleanor Price because she has good stuff in her and he wants to bring it out. Being only a "friend," I have not even a right to object to such a thing.

Sometimes, there have been a few times like that, I have found myself wondering that I should ever have had any doubts; and at other times, and there have been many such, I have wondered that I could ever have felt in the least sure. Sometimes—and there have been many, many such —I have felt absolutely certain that my words to Armand last spring were not those of a foolish child; and at other times (but these have been exceedingly rare) I thought that I might have been mistaken.

Of course I was young last spring, and I am only a very little bit older now, but I do not think it at all strange that I, who am so frank with myself on such matters, should have been able to judge myself correctly. Oh, if I should be doomed to go thru this every spring——.

Sometimes I think that I ought not to write these things down because they may be so painful to me later, but it would be painful whether I had recorded it or not.

April 28, Wednesday

I am so happy. Yesterday morning I received a telephone call. Armand. He said I was to come over to the "U" directly, and he said also that we would have to take our annual walk on April 30 instead of May 1. He had an exam he said.

On the way to the "U" I hoped and hoped that I would say neither too much or too little—which, by the way, is my usual prayer every time I am to see him. We took the Como Harriet car to the little "First-of-May-Gate" and then we sat on a hill. I don't remember how we happened to switch to the subject of "his truly" but we did somehow. I said, "One day you found occasion to call me a damn fool, and I have felt like returning it a number of times."

Armand said, "Well, rip it into me now," and before I knew it I was railing at him with a good deal of vehemence. I said, "I told you this winter that I was on the verge of tumbling over the brink of a hole and I never heard from you."

He was beginning to rail at himself mentally as I could plainly see, and he said, "It was my fault. I had no right to let you go over to Minneapolis and fight it out alone."

I said, "The only reason I would blame you more than anyone else, would be because you understand me so well," and I told him the worst of it was that, altho some of the things he was and said and did irritated me very much, I could not feel justified in blaming him for them because I always felt that he was either doing right or trying very hard to do the right thing.

"Here you have made me contrite," he said, "and I had no intention of doing so at all." Then he talked long and vehemently about what he had gone thru this winter. He seems to have an idea that he has not made the best use of his powers. He declared that he realized that he couldn't handle the beauty that he saw—"and I won't try to," he said, "until I am man enough to do it." He said that the things he had been building up about him were being thrown right back at him and that was what caused him so many sleepless nights. And like that and like that. I told him I thought he was blaming himself too much but he said I was mistaken.

Once as we were sitting there on the hill, the wind blew Armand's hat off his head and right on to mine. It was so funny and sudden.

Undated Entry

In speaking of our little "drammer" which we acted at Como Park last fall,* Armand declared that he had certainly got the better of me and that he had done it just to see how I'd meet it. He repeated that I hadn't met the situation very gracefully. Which I knew well enough, ding it. Armand said, "Now an original way of finishing the thing would have been to sit down and say with a yawn, "Oh hell, now I've got to go and dig a grave!"

It was the nicest afternoon I had spent with Armand for many a month. And I was happy all the next day. And the next. And the next was The

* November 2 (page 297).

Day, the biggest holiday of my year—only I must celebrate so much of it in silence.

I forgot to mention that when I had the nice afternoon with Armand I heard a meadow-lark for the first time this year, and I was so glad that it happened then.

My sketch has been accepted—at the N.W. Artists Exhibition.

May 4, Tuesday

And then, as I said, came the Annual Walk Day. I woke up somewhere around six o'clock and popped up to see what kind of a day we were going to have. And the sky was blue and clear.

We met at the First-of-May Gate and started walking right away. Along the same road, past the same houses and past the Rose Hill Nursery. Armand had a Sat. Evening Post, from which he read me something written by Mary Roberts Rinehart (who is at the front now) about a gravestone on which was written *"Morts pour la patrie."* Armand said that it had just given him an idea.

We saw a man working in the field, and Armand cried, "Look!" It *was* beautiful. The horses brownish, and the old cart brownish with rich gold where the sun struck it. *Rich,* that was it—all its colors were blended warmly into a rich, mellow spot. I remember I remarked that it looked "toasty, sort of."

I don't see how Armand can have such a subtle perception of color without being an artist who paints. Because it is mainly thru painting, being forced to interpret these colors thru your medium, that you teach yourself to be sensitive to such things. But I suppose it is because he is a poet—for a poet, as well as an artist, has to translate these things thru a medium.

When we came to the place where Armand had given me the lecture last year, we sat down of course. Only there was no lecture this year. Not a trace of one. And the stretch of grass on which my eyes had rested while Armand had talked the year before, was all plowed up, to my disappointment and discomfort. The scene must have made an indelible picture on my mind's eye for I could not get used to the change. I felt just like one feels when one finds that a picture, which has been hanging in a certain part of a room for years, has suddenly been removed. And yet I had looked upon this scene for only an hour or two—and it had been a year ago.

But wagons went past as of old, and in the distance we could hear the

meadow larks singing. Armand called my attention to this and I remarked that last year we had had one in the tree above us. "Two of
them," Armand said.

"Perhaps it was that beastly bird," he had said last year.

As the wagons rolled along Armand said, "Wouldn't it be queer if that
same man would come along on his wagon?" the one who had stared at
us so. This year there was a woman in a car, with a bright pink waist and
a bright green sweater.

I am glad I had a chance to see Heinrich Zügel's painting of "The
Oxen" last winter, for as I saw these carts crawling towards us I could
see that which Zügel had given me—the beauty of the foreshortening of
the horses, the design and rich blackness of the lower parts of the legs,
the glorious dust about their hoofs; the purple, the brown and the blue
of it; the vigor and the weariness, the poetry and the prose, and the
joy and the pain of it.

We played the half dollar game. He has a new trick now. He manages somehow to get the coin on the back of my hand, and of course
I can't get it there.

We went and got some sandwiches, cookies, and very sour pickles,
and returned to the Nursery. We found a nice grassy shady place and
ate our lunch.

In trying to explain to Armand what I had learned about "rope lines,"
I said, "Wait. I'll draw that tree and show you." While I was sketching,
he asked whether it would make any difference if he wrote. So he wrote
a poem. I showed him the drawings in the successive stages and it was
so satisfying to find he knew what I was doing. We finished at about
the same time.

The poem was based on *"Morts pour la patrie."* Armand asked, after
I had read it, "Well what do you think of it?" I said, "I like it."

"Well, criticise it."

I said, "Well you see, I can get the feeling, but I haven't learned to
talk about those things yet." He said that since there was no standard
as yet for modern verse, my opinion was worth as much as anybody
else's, and that he really had no idea where he was or whether his verse
was good or bad. Being impressionistic myself, I *do* get the feeling or
the impression or whatever you wish to call it. The beauty of modern
art is that it is almost beyond analyzation. I mean, the impression con-
veyed is definite enough but you can't just tell how you got it. It just
occurred to me yesterday that Armand writes the kind of poetry he

does because he can see so much like an artist. As an impressionistic artist puts pure colors side by side on a canvas to produce a complex emotion, Armand paints with common words.*

I have liked modern poetry from the start. My first real acquaintance with it was probably when I read Walt Whitman when I was in High School. Some of the High School pupils called my attention to him and laughed boisterously over his irregular unrhyming sentences. I don't remember whether I laughed with them or not. Perhaps I did—for at that time I was still so unassertive and meek that, altho my feelings on such subjects were quite definite, I did not voice them very often. But the point is that they impressed me. I felt sort of guilty when I found myself liking them, because everyone else seemed to think him so impossible.

Armand said that he was sorry but he had to make a class at 3 o'clock. So we took the car back. I had been telling myself a number of times during the afternoon that it was rather tame—against last year especially. We said very little on the way home. Armand stepped off at the "U," and I rode alone the rest of the way with my unfixed sketch on my lap and some disappointment in my heart.

7:30 p.m.:—To-day Sally Peck** blew in and, after reading me a poem, declared she had seen Armand with another girl. I asked, "Who was it?" and she said, "Eleanor Price." I tried to subside as quickly as possible and said, "Oh he's only a friend of mine anyway."

I have been telling myself fiercely that I do not want him to walk around with other girls. And all the while I must remember that I have no right to him at all.

May 5, Wednesday

I am almost ashamed of myself. The thing just about drove me to distraction. I sat around and could not even cry. Perhaps I am a sentimental fool. Sometimes I almost think so. In fact, sometimes I'm quite sure. The funny part is that no one else knows it. They all consider me exceedingly neutral and unimpressionable.

I read some verse by Constance Lindsay Skinner last Sunday. Indian Poetry. She has lived among the Indians ever since she was a child, and has subconsciously absorbed not only the rhythm of their songs but of

* My ideas on Modern Art were still vague and confused at that time.
** A University student staying at the house.

their hearts and souls as well. "The Song of Whip Plaiting" and "The Song of the Young Mother" gave me a queer feeling and another glimpse into the great scheme of things.

> "(Ah—sometimes—thou wilt be gentle?
> Little roots of pain are deep, deep in me
> Since I saw thee standing in my doorway.)

> "I have quenched thy torch—
> I have plaited thy whip.
> I am thy Woman."

"'I am thy Woman"—and I shuddered with joy and fear. That, and the succeeding poem, struck a blow at a number of ideas I have held in connection with Woman Suffrage. Whatever Woman Suffrage will do in other things, it will ever be like this. The woman has to give herself over to the man. It's inevitable—for that is part of the great scheme.

In the second poem:—

> "Strange that pain came with love;
> I knew it not until thy father sought me.
> Yet—what woman would cast love out?
> Gladly in the dusk I waited him—
> None told me, not my mother, even, of the pang.

> ". . . . Darkness . . . and his,
>   utterly, in that dark . . . . .
> None had told me . . . . .

> "Ay, 'tis old, the custom,
> Old as earth is old;
> Ancient as passion,
> Pitiless as passion—
> Ay, pitiless, pitiless, the earth-way for women!
> Bitter it is, as the taste of bright sea water,
> That he, who takes the gift, and wields our weaving of desire,
> Knows not the meaning of the gift—nor can know ever!
>   .   .   .   .
> It is the law of the earth-way."

I may change my ideas on the subject, but I doubt it. It made a tremendous impression upon me. I walked around half of the day in a trance. I realized with a sort of fear gripping at my heart that I would do the same, that I would give myself over—and gladly at that.

Mr. Dehn thinks I am neutral. I have *made* him think that. So you think I am neutral? In many things I am neutral, of course, but in my heart I am a woman.

May 5, Wednesday

This morning in Life, Sarah Aansted said, "I'm afraid, Wanda, that you like to shirk."

I said, "So you think so," and went on to explain that just because I didn't work like other people it didn't necessarily mean that I didn't work at all. Also that I studied art wherever I went.

"Yes but what about criticisms?" she said. "What are the teachers here for?"

I said, "*Ach,* I don't know."

Now I wonder, is she right? I always feel that the best way to study art is to study other things with it. I want to do what is right, and up to this time I have had very few doubts, if any, as to whether I was right or wrong. But when these people pounce on me like that, I think and think about it, and then after a while I don't know.

It seems to me it cannot be wrong to read good poetry an entire morning if you happen to be particularly receptive in that respect, because when you are poetically receptive you see so much of life behind the words. For instance, when I have reached the stage where I can draw for people, I can then illustrate really big ideas because I have not neglected my mind in my eagerness to train my hand. It seems to me that those people who study only art will run up against a blank wall some time in their lives, if indeed they ever get to the place where that sort of thing is to be found. They will be very good as far as they can go but they can't go so very far.

I have been asking myself today, with much earnestness and some alarm, "Am I doing right in letting myself go as I am, or shall I turn around and study against my principles just because other people do so or want me to do so? Is it Me or Myself which is leading me such an erratic sort of race?" Sometimes I almost think that I have not enough stick-to-it-iveness, and then comes the question, "Can I be otherwise?" I feel as if, whatever anyone else may do [teachers, etc.], they can do nothing more than *complete* me. Like this: The apex of the diagram is the original, essential Wanda Gág and people will have to take me from there and fill me out. Those two outside lines *are there* and they will go in the same direction, and it's only a matter of *how far* they can go.

Perhaps I am entirely wrong. Perhaps I can control those things if I only try hard enough. But I am afraid that I will crush the essential part of myself by girding about it the ideas and advice of other people.

Goodness knows it isn't in the least easy to be as I am now. I have to fight and fight, and I am sure that it is not thru cowardice that I am following my feelings as I am. If I am doing wrong, it is not because I am just reckless but because I do not know it. I don't know whether it is my duty to conform to the things about me or to fight against them. Some people are born to fight things, and I don't know whether I am one of them or not.

I must have freedom.

I guess if I ever wish to do anything, I must rely upon my individuality to do it. I cannot bear to think of following in the footsteps of others. And that is what they are teaching us to do here in Illustration. We are doing covers for the Saturday Evening Post, and every one has a Leyendecker cover at their side which they consult and worship while working at their own sketch. Now that's allright if your aim is to be a second Leyendecker, but the Saturday Evening Post surely doesn't want Leyendeckers for the next 50 years. Besides, I don't want to be a *second Anybody*. I want to be *myself*. Perhaps I am too radical. Too radical, perhaps, for one who needs money badly.

I don't know whether I have too little sense to conform to these things, or too much sense.

There is a new fear gripping me. Perhaps I can not be meek, superficial, and mercenary enough to earn money.

Yesterday I received a letter from Armand. It was absolutely the *swiftest* thing I have ever read. I flew thru it, and when I reached the end I was actually panting. He is going thru a new and very vigorous sort of stage. And a very optimistic one, it seems. The panting was *physical*, not figurative, and every few minutes I found myself taking a deep breath.

Mr. Dehn is as regular as clockwork in calling on me on Wednesdays, Saturdays and Sundays. Yesterday evening we went to the Art Exhibit. On the way home I was very sleepy. I remarked facetiously that I had determined to marry no man unless he had invented some kind of breakfast food. Mr. Dehn said he thought he could invent some, and I told him in that case he could consider himself a candidate.

May 10

This morning I received a telephone call. It was Armand. He said he was in Minneapolis and would be down in about half an hour.

I had expected him to be in a good humor, judging from the *swift* letter, but he greatly exceeded all expectations I could ever have had on the subject. I've never seen him so absolutely gleeful as he was this morning, and I saw from the start that there was absolutely no use in trying to get him to talk seriously on any subject. He would laugh merrily at things he saw from the window, and he said the most ridiculous and incongruous things. He said that he had been talking to some people (professors, I believe) about certain things. "And they haven't got it! They haven't got it!" he cried with one of his gleeful looks. He said he felt like a professor who had told him a certain fact and had then said confidentially and joyfully, "I'm the only man in the world who knows this!"

He told me that when his father had read him of the sinking of the "Lusitania," he (Armand) had said, "I wonder if they were eating noodle-soup at the time!" and that he hadn't been able to keep from imagining the noodles scooting merrily all over the place.

There was a woman in the same room with us, and as she got up and left, Armand asked who she might be. I told him that she was staying here and that her husband had been killed in some war. "He must have looked funny!" laughed Armand, and that, you will admit, was almost uncanny.

He was playing with a ring of his when it broke in two and fell upon the carpet. Armand pointed to the ring and then to his forehead—an idea for the poem, you see—and soon he was writing very earnestly. The funny part of it is that, altho he talks so ridiculously, his poetry is very serious. He told me that now he didn't blame me for taking such a keen delight in my drawing moods, and also that some of the best words and sentences in his verse came independently of his own volition.

We talked of Timmie too. He said he hadn't told Timmie of this new stage. He said also that Timmie considers his ideas erratic and too violent.

Just now I happened to remember that Timmie asked me to write something sometime, some kids' stories or something, and give them to him to look over. He would be very severe, he said, but he didn't suppose I would mind that. I told him I did not pretend to be able to write but that I might do as he suggested.

I am more *out* of love, at present, than I have been for a long time. I don't just know why either.

I went to the Club Saturday evening with Mr. Dehn and his sister

Viola. His sister, by the way, is very nice indeed. Mr. Wells gave a talk on Sculpture which I liked very much.

I have been reading Ibsen until I am blue in the face. It has made me sort of gloomy but it isn't an altogether disagreeable sort of gloominess either. I was trying to explain the feeling to Lloyd Moylan to-day. I had been telling him that it made me feel pessimistic. "And yet," I found myself saying, "it's an optimistic sort of pessimism." I have read "Little Eyolf," (which I found more depressing than "Ghosts"), "When We Dead Awaken" and "Pillars of Society."

Oh I'm so sleepy.

Mrs. Fournier told me that she had tried to put in a good word for me in regard to the Palettite Scholarship (which is given not so much on account of the merit as the poverty of the student) but she said she was unable to do very much. They said that I couldn't be in circumstances to need it, because I was so independent. Because I was so independent! As if one couldn't be independent and poor at the same time.

"'Besides,' they said, 'she isn't a hard worker.'"

"Oh isn't she?" Mrs. Fournier said, "I thought she was a very hard worker."   . . .

"Not in Illustration class. She just sits around and doesn't draw."

Now what under the sun can you do with people like that? As long as one isn't *obviously* a hard worker, one isn't a hard worker at all. And results don't seem to count in the least. Great Caesar, I am not to be judged by what I *don't* hand in, but by what I *do* hand in.

May 25, Tuesday

I have been very busy getting all my school problems in.

Lloyd told me that he had sometimes heard some of the students express the wonder of when I did my sketches because I seemed never to be working. It makes me almost want to shoot out very far just to show them how plausible my methods are. I told Lloyd, "The difference between them and me is that I know what I'm doing, and they don't. They think that I am irresponsible, and without aim. They think I simply float along, dabbling a little here and a little there. And the funny part of the matter is that I am following a very definite system of my own and that they, who think they know what they are doing, are floundering."

Sarah said that day, "What about criticism? What are the teachers here for?" Well, certainly not to make apes and machines of us. When I feel that I need criticism, when I feel that I am ready for it, when I feel that I am not going to be endangered by it, I will solicit it and no one needs to worry his or her head about it. I say *endanger* because relying too much on criticism smothers the Myself in you. You see too much as others see, and your individuality is hampered.

I don't mean that my method of working could be used in a school, for instance. Because few people are so sincere, so frank and so merciless with themselves as I.

They can't smother Myself—I won't let them. I would rather die. I have fought for the things I believe in, faithfully and for a long time. And altho I have fallen innumerable times, I have succeeded in rising swiftly. I refuse to be a disappointment to my friends.

I don't give two cents how other people work. Just because every one else works one way, is just the reason why I must work another. An imitation never gets far and, what is worse, no one who is an imitation can be *himself*.

Oh ding why talk about it? And now, Goodbye.—Wanda.

* * *

May 30, Sunday

Stella came yesterday, to my great excitement and joy. In the afternoon we went over to the Museum where our closing Exercises were held. I got no honors except a Second Honorable Mention for the Hinkle Scholarship which made me feel more peeved than otherwise. I had scarcely any hopes for the Scholarship because I was competing against people who had had fully two or three years of art. And my attendance may have interfered—I have done most of my important work at home, but of course they do not know that when I skip school I skip with a good purpose.

But I did want a little more than I got. I suppose it was good for me. The other day I found myself thinking, "It isn't the fault of myself or of my talent, but of the *age*." Which was really too arrogant and I am thoroughly ashamed of myself.

For the first day or so I was rather downcast about it, way down in my heart. I thought that perhaps it would be just as wise to *shut up* about my thoughts and things, and that perhaps the fact that I spent more time training my mind than most of the students did was not such an important thing after all. Here were people winning scholarships and books, and here was I with a dinky second Honorable Mention.

Mr. Dehn carried off the Honorable Mention for the Student Scholarship. He felt the same way about it as I did. I said, "Much good that piece of paper does us," and we amused ourselves during the rest of the afternoon by talking facetiously about our "honors." I wanted badly to have Mr. Dehn get a scholarship. He needs it badly, and deserves one too, but his is the kind of drawing that is too broad and human to make the proper impression. A nice academic, *finished* drawing makes so much more of a hit.

It peeves me so that *character* in a sketch or study seems to make no impression on the people. Now, I do not know—is it that they are unable to *see* the best that I have put into my work, or is it that I am simply laboring under the illusion that I am putting something into them? Ding it all, I may have something which no one has grasped yet. Perhaps I am not able, as yet, to put it down so that other people can grasp it—or if it is not that, what under the sun is it that makes me feel as I do sometimes? They say that it is very natural for a very young person to feel that he or she can do a great deal.

May 31, Monday

Tonight I am rather a jumble of emotions again. And I don't know exactly why either. Of course Mr. Dehn is gone, and I am just beginning to realize it now. And Paula is going and Theresa is gone. Everybody nice is going. Since Stell is here visiting with me I won't be lonesome this week. But by next week she will be gone too. I don't expect to see much of Timmie and Armand because they will undoubtedly be gone for the summer.

I think if Stella were not here I should cry a little because Mr. Dehn is gone. Because I really like him very much. Of course there is nothing sentimental about my attitude towards him, and unless I am very much mistaken his attitude towards me is also only friendly. And I am not the only one who likes him. He is so beautifully himself that everyone seems to like him very much. And that is all I will say about that just now.

No, it isn't either. He was always so nice and considerate that I will miss him very much. When we have picnics or parties he will not be there to take me home. I could always depend on him. And he won't be there to take me to the Club. And when on gorgeous evenings I want to talk, I won't have any satisfactory person with whom I can walk far into the night.

Yesterday we walked to Lake of the Isles—Stella and I, Paula, Mr. Dehn and Garth Howland.* And then we walked home as it became dark. I walked with Mr. Dehn most of the way, but we said very little. Not that there was scarcity of material. There was altogether too much to say. I could not say, of course, that I thought he had been very nice to me, and that—oh well. You see I was thinking of Armand too, and I couldn't say that either. Once I said emphatically, "I'm a ding fool." Mr. Dehn asked why and I said I didn't know. I didn't know just why either, altho in order to have told the truth, all the truth, I would have been obliged to say that I was a fool to be such a fool about Armand. Sometimes I think I am very imprudent to let myself care for him, because he is such a pieface anyway. Sometimes I think he is a poet first and a man second, and altho I admire his unsusceptibility—being a woman, I resent it.

I am very unsusceptible too, I suppose. But not nearly as much as it seems. I am very severe with myself. Perhaps I am almost a prude in that respect. I scarcely allow a man to touch me. If our hands meet accidentally I draw mine away, almost unconsciously because it has become a habit. And yet, sometimes I have all I can do to keep myself in this self-adjusted strait-jacket. For at times I find myself thinking recklessly and blindly, "What does it matter? There is so much love being given and taken in the world. Why should I guard mine so rigidly?" I would so love to run my hands thru people's hair sometimes or give someone a little, little caress. You see I am very conventional about those things. Or perhaps I should say, "I am exceedingly reserved." But I can't help that. Principles are principles you know. Yet, as I have said, sometimes I feel very much like saying, "Principles go hang."

I am not such a cold, flapping fish as I may seem.

June 1st

I am not so very, very young after all. I notice it so much since Stella is here. I am so much older than she is. She wants to be active constantly, she likes the city because there is always "something doing," and there is a noticeable, tho passive and sensible, yearning for romance. Of course I want activity too, but it is of a different kind, and the romance in things which appeals to me is different also. I remember when I was just where she was but that was such a long time ago. Two long years ago.

I have not seen Armand for about a month, nor heard from him either.

* A member of our Club, staying at the Fournier's.

To tell the truth I did not miss him much. I have been so very busy and I have always had Mr. Dehn. But now I am ready to haul him over the coals again. I wonder what he meant that day at Donaldson's when he said, "This is the turning point of our—" (I forget what is was, "lives" or "friendship" or something like that.)

Perhaps I am a disappointment. I refuse to be a disappointment to my friends, *and that's all.*

June 4, Friday

I have not sketched myself for ages. I am taking the Theory of Color summer course now, and I like some of it but chafe under much of it. I cannot bear to have my rules for color all laid out for me. It's so much like being a machine and admits of no real, throbbing, gripping inspiration. You get so that you do your work mechanically, and altho that method admits of production with or without the aid of a drawing mood, the things which are produced are not as spontaneous, and are not as satisfying *to the artist,* as otherwise. And I am afraid that unless we look out, we will train ourselves to rely too much on formulas. I am beginning, subconsciously, to feel a fear that if I keep on relying on these formulae, I will soon become so that I can't tell a good color combination from a bad one unless it is included in our list. It seems to numb my innate perception of color.

The others, however, do not seem to feel that way about it. Whether it is my innate sense for spontaneity in art that is crying out against man-made recipes, or whether it is simply because I am an iconoclast, or an iconoclast in art—perhaps even a fanatic—I do not know. But certain it is, that whether or not the others see danger in the system, I do; and I am going to do my best to keep myself from following such a dangerous thing as a system. For a system is a system, and altho it is good to be acquainted with them, it is not as a rule wisest to impose or follow them. They clash with human nature.

I think if I knew absolutely that it were the right thing to do, I would be strong enough to bind myself down to steady and punctual production as I am gently advised to do. But I have been doing so, very intensely, this week and somehow I don't feel nearly as much as if I had done right, as I do when I sketch fiercely for an entire evening during a glorious drawing fit.

I believe it is not so much that I am unable to make myself do those things as it is that I am unable to make myself believe in them.

I am not condemning the class. It furnishes one with very valuable information, but I refuse to restrict myself to rules which tend to make machines of artists. I am too much of an artist to allow myself to be turned into a machine. I have too much faith in my own originality to follow, step by step, another man's footsteps. I believe too much in freedom to chain my ideas in formulae. They may be reliable but the result looks too studied, too premeditated.

I hope that somewhere within me is something which no one else has as yet, something *new*—for without that, it seems to me, I can hardly be truly happy.

I must have freedom. I will never get anywhere, I will never get out of me what must out, if I try to run myself after other men's systems. If there must be a system, let it be myself that imposes it.

I think Armand, that old *thing,* might come and help to clear my poor mind of all these things—tell me whether I am right or wrong, for he knows better than anyone else what I am.

June 12, 8:35 a.m.

Well the Color Class is over.

Towards the end of last week I wrote a very violent letter to Armand. I was very sorry to find myself writing it and it hurt me even more to send it off, but one day I found myself mailing it. I would be very much disappointed in Armand if he were the sort of person who allowed new friends to crowd out the old ones. I wonder, when he talked of breaking circles and breaking away from old friends in consequence, whether he also meant me. If so, he may consider himself mistaken. For I too am breaking circles and very swiftly.

And now I must go to bed because I intend to go on a hike with Timmie to-morrow morning at 7 a.m.

June 13, Sunday

I did go on the hike. Dr. Owre led the party and there were, aside from Timmie and myself, Eleanor Price and several other students.

Eleanor Price is a very sweet girl, talks low and much in a somewhat unmodified inflection of the voice, and seems a very brilliant sort of person.

I like Dr. Owre very much. He is quaint and nice and dresses pic-

* The late Dr. Alfred Owre, then Dean of the Dental College of the University of Minnesota.

turesquely. We walked about ten miles in all, after which we took the launch across Lake Minnetonka. The water fascinated me more than I can tell. It looked like molten gray silk, with a rich blue bursting thru the long sweeps and tiny flipsies, (that's a new one—it means the little, little wave-like bits of water). I sketched Dr. Owre with a very hard pencil on ink paper and he took the sketch home with him.

I came home very tired at about half past one. Much of the afternoon I spent in sorting wood-ticks from my clothes. I found seven, and I have the uncomfortable feeling that I didn't get them all.

Then I hopped into bed and took a long rest for, with the two weeks of Color Class and Stella's visit, I felt quite worn out. Someone played piano in the parlor, and as I lay there a great calm came over me. I have an idea it was because I had practically renounced Armand but it may also have been due to physical exhaustion.

I do not want to seem ungrateful to Armand. He has been a good friend, one of the best I have ever had. He shared his friends—his very nicest friends—with me, he helped me out of many bewildering situations and gave me books to read which he had chosen carefully and with consideration. And perhaps the biggest thing he has done for me was to smash the "glass door" for me, and altho it threw me into a state of bewilderment, it proved that I was, after all, capable of loving humanity.

And here I am weeping—not for the things I used to weep about but for the kindnesses of the Armand I used to know. However far apart we may become I shall always feel the deepest regard for him. His kindness nearly tears my heart to shreds not so much, strangely enough, because it must evidently cease but because it ever existed. My attitude now is by no means sentimental—I am speaking of him merely as a very good friend. I know only that he knows me better than anyone else ever has and that he has been kind to me. It hurts to lose a friend like that. But I am brave, and as my life seems destined to be one of constant strifes and adventures, I may as well get used to it while I am still flexible enough not to break under these things.

I may as well be moulded with dents—the bumps of the world will then fit in better.

If my old attitude must be eliminated to save our friendship—I believe that even tho it leaves a large void, I would rather have it cut out so that the thing can heal and so that the wound will be prevented from spreading further and deeper. Somehow I find myself taking the thing resignedly. I have a feeling that it was all for the best, that it had to be.

If this has not been real love on my part—if it has only been an illusion, I cannot imagine the strength and beauty of real love.

June 18, Friday

Since I have written last I have been having all kinds of psychological and mental experiences.

Tuesday noon I went to St. Paul. Timmie, looking very captivating in white flannel trousers and a white tennis shirt with a Byronesque collar, met me at the station. We went on a hike, "over the hills and far away." One could not have wished for a day more perfect, and after a happy idle ramble we sat down upon a grassy slope overlooking St. Paul. We listened to the different bird notes—watched the cows, geese and people—and tried to analyze the colors of the different parts of the landscape about us. Item:—I convinced Timmie, after much discussion, that a certain row of bluffs had much pink in them.

Timmie is fine, absolutely fine. He is so considerate about little things.

Yesterday I went to Mr. Russell's office to return *Phantastes*. As he seemed to be not busy at all, we had a nice little talk about friendship. I told him that if I had once put my love and faith into a person, and even tho I would of necessity have to withdraw my faith, I would be forced to leave my love there to the end. He said it was very sweet of me to be that way, but that he thought it would cause me much suffering. He said also for this reason I must not try to put my faith and love too deeply into people. But I told him that after one had gone a certain distance one didn't have this thing under control. It is not that I idealize people. I put my love and faith into them even tho I know they have faults, and sometimes *because* of it.

It doesn't seem as if Armand could, for no reason at all, cease being one's friend. I believe I have solved nearly all of the big "un-understandables" he has confronted me with, but this last is absolutely beyond my comprehension. Surely he cannot consider me as one of those people which he has been forced to leave behind as he broke one circle after another in order that he might enter into wider circles. *I refuse to be considered as one of those who is left behind.* I too am constantly breaking away from old ideas, old conditions, and old acquaintances. But from *old friends?*

Of course I can't blame him if he has become weary of me and my adventures. I know I talk too much, I write too much, I force too many of my drawings and ideas upon my friends—but think how strenuous all that must be to me who am forced to be with those thoughts and characteristics day after day. I have often wondered how I managed to keep my friends in spite of all those disagreeable characteristics.

Then there is also his idea about its being unnecessary for friends to see each other or even hear from each other, because when one had a friend, one had it, and neither need worry about the other's constancy.

Yesterday I felt that I was able to look at the matter in a more broadminded and magnanimous way than I had been able to do before. For the last few days I have been planning a lengthy tirade against Armand to be delivered when next I see him, but to-day I imagine myself shaking hands with him and saying, "It's allright. It's allright." And I rather hope I will be able to present myself in that condition when I see him next.

This is certainly a critical time in my adventurous young life, and I fervently hope that all will turn out for the best.

June 22, Tuesday

Saturday afternoon I went with Timmie to the Art Exhibit. We both found Alex Fournier's "Charcoal Burner's Hut" very much to our taste. The thing which prepossessed us so violently in its favor was a wreath of blue and very smoke-like smoke, coming from a chimney and streeling off into the distance. We returned to it again and again, and finally we took two chairs and sat down before it so that we might look at it to our heart's content.

Timmie invited me to join Dr. Owre's hike again the next day. Which I did. Dr. Owre was as quaint as ever and passed his imported Hopjes around. I felt very happy and light-footed, and hopped and skipped rather than walked.

I am wearing my hair a new way. It is done in such a way that it appears to be bobbed, and I have a very narrow ribbon bound around my forehead (fillet, do they call it?). Timmie's brother picked a long slender blue flag for me and when I walked along, holding it, I felt just like one of Burne-Jones' women. I told Timmie so, but he didn't seem to see the resemblance. But afterwards when he was walking behind me, he said that the style of my gown (which is drapey) did suggest the pre-Raphaelites. He also declared that I had a pre-Raphaelite neck.

Timmie likes my hair that way and so does everyone else whom I have asked. And so do I. It goes better with my face, I think, than my former *coiffure,* for my face still looks very girlish.

June 26, Saturday morning, 9:20 a.m.

I feel free-er and, it seems to me, happier since I have renounced the old Armand. I do not intend, by any means, to repudiate the new Armand. I have decided to take him as he is, and not to let him come between me and my enjoyment of life. And, unless I am mistaken, it is not as hard a thing to do as I had imagined.

The tug-of-war is over. The rope broke and here we are, neither having won, neither having lost.

I continue to take the matter calmly enough. Two violent tear torrents and that was all. What I cannot understand is that I could have felt so intensely towards a being whom I was evidently not meant to love otherwise than as a friend. Of course I suppose the love for a friend can be exceedingly intense and painful, but if I love a mere friend as keenly as that, I shudder to think of what a mad thing my love will be when I really will fall in love with a person who is really in love with me. Perhaps that will never happen.

I have many philosophical, resigned, stoical and comfortable feelings upon the matter, but as ideas they are still too amorphous to admit of being set forth in words, sentences and paragraphs.

In Shaw's "Pygmalion" Higgs says:—"I care for life, for humanity, and you are a part of it that has come my way and been built into my house."

And perhaps that was Armand's idea from the first—to get me started on my path, and then—when I was ready to navigate by myself—to go on his own way as before, confident that he had done his part by me. Well —and that would be very noble, but why was he so enigmatical thru it all? Why couldn't he have told me his plan from the first?

Still, I suppose that would have interfered with the plan. It was thru illusion that I was moved to force myself "thru the glass door," and it was all the doubt and joy (even tho its causes were false perhaps) which made me live many years in a few days, and which made me capable of feeling the big human life-throb. Still, even then, after having accomplished his purpose (which was probably when I got my Minneapolis offer and when he said, "You'll get along allright etc." [and that, perhaps, was what he meant when he said that the turning point in our friendship {or life or whatever it was } had come]) he might have laid the matter out to me neatly and coldly.

Perhaps he thought by staying away for a long time he could impress it upon me in a mute sort of way—but he might as well have told me that point blank. It was the suspense which threw me into all such wild imaginings and into such bitter tears. I respond correctly only to truth and frankness.

"If you knew what I am thinking now, you would fall over with surprise." How often did he say that! Great Caesar, why *didn't* he make me fall over? I would have had the strength to get up and walk on as before. Besides the sooner he would have told me all, whatever that all may have been, the longer a time I would have had for recovering. One can do much recovering in a year or so, and it is over a year ago that he began being so actively enigmatical.

The old cryptic pieface!

The part that hurts me is that Armand may have regarded me as a scientist might regard an interesting insect under a microscope. Now, scientists are very good of course, and we are glad that they spend their time examining and studying insects, in putting them to tests and all that, but all the same——

Still it seems to me that Armand did not regard me as coldly as all that.

Ah well, I forgive him for all that, and I forgive myself for all. And I forgive everybody, everybody for all. Sometimes it almost seems as if we were given reason and intellect simply to remedy or lighten the errors which we, as mere human beings, commit—and to bear and forgive those which our fellow beings, who are also mere human beings, commit at our own expense and theirs.

I suppose all those things are necessary to fulfill my great wish—*to get out of me what's in me.*

2:15 p.m.:—I just got a letter from Mr. Dehn. He is coming to St. Paul next week to work with Joe La Londe [painting churches]. I was so tickled that I almost forgot my toothache for a while. I wonder how he will like my new hair-arrangement.

June 28, Monday

I have been having the most nerve-wracking toothache. I have slept very little during the last two nights, and the continual pain has done me to a frazzle. As yesterday was Sunday I couldn't go to a dentist. I am going today.

I wanted badly to sketch myself last night, but my toothache was so bad that it was impossible to do anything of the sort. It makes me shudder to think of how many teeth I have which ought to be filled. And I have no money to do it with. And it breaks my heart to think of Tussy and the rest having a toothache every once in a while, and no money to have them fixed with. They tell me that to put off such a thing is false economy. But what are you going to do if you have no money?

I must earn money very soon so that the darling folks can all have their teeth nicely fixed up. I had almost forgotten what an awful thing a toothache is, and yesterday I told myself that the dear folks must not be obliged to stand that sort of thing. Goodness knows they are struggling bravely enough as it is.

We are all struggling.

Another thing that worries me very much is that Asta and Stell ought to have their adenoids removed. My ear ought to be seen to, also. I am afraid that if I do not look out it may develop into an abscess or something like that.

I wish that instead of spending a great deal of money for less important things (fire-works on the 4th of July, etc.) each city would pay good salaries to a number of very good doctors and dentists, so that poor people could have their ills and ailments attended to as soon as necessary. That would make better citizens too.

Later:—I am writing this in Mr. Russell's office. I went here to ask him whether he knew of some good dentist who was also *reasonable* and *gentle*. He has called up someone and has offered to run up with me as soon as he had finished writing up his editorial. Everybody is so nice to me that it almost makes me weep. I have no right to say that Armand is the only person who understands me. Of course, at present he understands me more thoroughly than anyone else but that is simply because he has had a better chance than other people.

I have gone to summer school one week.* In three days I made 44 sketches of children. The rest of the time I have spent in landscape and design. I learned a great deal during the week.

Saturday evening Timmie and I went to the Club. Timmie gave us a very nice little talk on Art:—"The Arabesque conception—its relation to Life, and Life's relation to it." He said that his main object was to precipitate a fiery discussion, which object he accomplished.

June 30, Wednesday

I always thought that it would simply be impossible for me to face

* Two new and talented students attended these Summer Classes—Harry Gottlieb in Design, and Elizabeth Olds in Mr. Goetsch's Sketch Class.

the bare fact that Armand did not care for me and that I did not care for him. I thought it would unbalance me. But life is so different from what we imagine it. One thinks one is learning one's biggest lesson in life; but in perspective, and when it is all over, it seems so much more unimportant than one had made it. To think that a year ago last spring I should have felt that I should care to belong only to this man and then to find (after a year and a half of this conviction) that it is comparatively easy to switch around to the belief that I have never really loved. All the same, I feel that I have a rather good idea of what real love is.

Just at present I almost feel as if love is not eternal. It is sincere—I grant that—but eternal? Still, the only dependable thing in the universe is *change,* and in order to keep up with the dependable—oh ding, that was such a silly thought. But then, love is surely the most lasting *emotion,* for when one ceases loving one thing one goes right on and loves other things.

What reconciles me to the whole matter and even makes me glad that it happened is that I have learned so tremendously much by allowing myself to be subjected to it. And the thing which seems so queer is that altho I had false love as my basis, it did not prevent me at the time from seeing things as thru the glasses of a true lover. I am happy now, in a free sort of way, but the magic veil has been withdrawn. I can see with the eyes of an artist or the eyes of a philosopher, but not with the eyes of a lover.

By this I do not wish to infer that I have been in the habit of looking at Nature in a sentimental sort of way for that is too absurd, but the glamour is gone and that is all. The Browning and the Heine of life is so purely objective now.

I wish Armand would come to see me. I am anxious to meet him on this new basis. Is it possible that he does not see that I have reached the point where I can see everything in a broadminded light?

I have learned much thru mistakes, but never as much as thru this incident, which I refuse to consider as a *mistake.* Bit by bit, it was a mistake—a succession of mistakes, in fact—but taken as a whole it is far from being such. Thank goodness I can see that side of it, for else I should feel as if I had been very foolish indeed. I remember that when I became unusually frank in my diary I used to write, "I may be sorry later for having written so much," but that is not the case. The whole affair gives me neither annoyance, embarrassment or shame.

I am dying with curiosity. I want to see the mechanism of the System against which I have been struggling for so many months. I do not mean that Armand is to blame for the System. Much of it he imposed deliberately and with the idea that he was doing the right thing, some of it he imposed unconsciously, and the other part—just happened. But now that I am free from it and no longer afraid of it, I am wild to ferret about among the wheels and things to see the cause of each movement and action which has taken place during the last year and a half.

I feel sane once more, and a year older on top of that. I only hope, in case he will drop my friendship, that he will find someone else to take my place as "coal raker."

July 1, Thursday

Yesterday they told me that a man had called twice for me during the afternoon and at about 6 o'clock I received a telephone call.

"Hello," from me.

"Damn it!" from the other side of the line.

"You old pieface!" etc.

Mr. Dehn of course. He said, "Well, Ego, how are you?"

We talked a long while and he said he'd come at 7 p.m. to see me. Which he did accordingly. He was obviously glad to see me. So was I glad to see him. He looked at my new sketches and then we took a walk. To Loring Park as of old. We kept up a bantering sort of conversation for a while and then he suggested that we stop talking nonsense. So we talked Socialism.

Mr. Dehn told me that he had a pessimistic streak. He proceeded to tell me of some of his troubles, and I did my best to cheer him up. He said he was too lazy to work. It is true he is what one might call lazy when it comes to manual labor. I can not blame him for being *lazy*. It is perhaps simply that he has not found his right course. He says that sometimes he feels as if he would just as soon be a tramp. The life of a tramp is a purposeless existence and that is bad. When he asked just why I thought it was wrong to lead such a life, I told him that it was selfish and that in such a case one was not helping the world.

"What do you think you are in the world for?" I asked. He declared that sometimes he thought we were all here for nothing. In short, he was very deep in the dumps. He was *slipping*. And that is bad.

Armand's sentence came back to me:—"All miracles are possible if you can smile into the day and understand your part in its great symphony. Death lies only in the arrogance of forgetting!" To be inert or indifferent is death. It is worse to be indifferent than to be selfish, for when one is selfish one tries to make the best of at least one of God's creations—even tho that being is one's self. It at least shows life and energy and *interest*. Simply by wanting things, it shows that there are things in the world worth having and worth striving for. But pure inaction! Oh I know I have felt like that myself. I am not blaming Mr. Dehn. After he had left me I saw him across the street kicking at things dejectedly.

I was comparatively reckless myself, but in another way. I allowed him to grasp me by the arm as he switched me over to the other side of the sidewalk. Which is a good deal for me. I even let him hold me by both arms for a moment when he showed me something in a window. He was standing a little behind, with each hand on one of my arms just a little above the elbow. Last night was one of those nights when I almost felt like letting "principles" go hang.

I am reserving the Fourth for Mr. Dehn, altho I do not know whether he will ask me to spend it with him or not. It is too silly for me to call him Mr. Dehn. He calls me Wanda, almost ever since we have known each other, and it is simply because he doesn't look like an Adolph that I refrain from calling him so.

I have not enough outlets for Myself. The things which are churning about within me are too persistent to admit of the slow progress of coming out thru one channel, be it literature, music or anything else. I am going to the library to get some books on aesthetic dancing. Dancing will help some.

July 3, Saturday

I have just been to see my Journal Man. I asked him if he had time to look at some of my drawings, and as he took them he said, "Are you ready for a little lecture?"

"Oh yes."

"This is a waste of time," he said as he came across "The Fan" and went on to the others. I had the two Collier covers at the end and he seemed to like them. "Well," he said looking up with a smile, "I don't think I have as much to say as I thought I had," and he laughed very heartily. And I did too.

I began, "I had a discussion about magazine illustration with my teacher the other day and I asked him whether one absolutely had to go thru the stage of doing this, that, and the other thing, and he said that there was only one way of avoiding it and that was to do something extremely original—"

"Yes," said he, interrupting me, "that was what I wanted to speak to you about. I was up to look at your things and it seemed to me that your things were not as good as some of the others." He went on to say that I ought to do skulls (meaning Antique, I think) and things like that. Things for good, sound, serious drawing you know.

"But I have done that too," I cried.

"Oh did you?" he asked. "How long did you have it?"

"I had an entire year of Antique in St. Paul. I'm past that now."

"Oh I see." As to the good, sound drawing, he went on to say that one needed construction first and then you could handle the picture as carelessly as you wished. I assured him that my drawings had construction, that indeed it was one of my strongest points, and that it was merely experience in execution, the "magazine twang," which I needed.

I wish I had been able to finish what I started to say about my talk with Mr. Goetsch, because I rather think he got the impression that I was afraid of the drudgery of the thing. Which is not so at all. I'll be willing to do any amount of drudgery in private, but if possible I should wish to skip as much of the public part of it as possible. I am glad I had this little talk with him. I know better what he wants, and it gives me a chance to disperse any doubts he may have had on the subject. I would give a great deal if I could have a 15-minute talk with him in order that I might tell him how I had laid out my plans.

I believe I am unusually brave for a woman. Some girls might have felt downcast over the fact that their patron had declared their work was not as good as some of the others. I am so confoundly confident! It almost scares me at times. This morning's episode merely tends to make me more earnest and arrogant than ever. When I strike the earth, like the giant of old, I rise more violently than before. It is true that sometimes when I look at the work of some of the students my spirits fall a little—especially when I view the work of Mr. Aurness and Ethel Claussen. These are my rivals, and I have a mad and unreasonable desire to rise above them. It is too silly to wish to rise above all your rivals but I find myself trying to do it nevertheless. I am not afraid of construction, action, resemblance or spirit. It is the drawing of landscapes, animals and interiors that I am afraid of; and I lack sufficient practice in finishing a picture up and making it fit for reproduction. And that can only come with time.

July 4, Sunday

Great Caesar, Wanda, *eliminate*. Eliminate detail and use the spaces produced to carry out design. I am eliminating continually but not nearly enough. In landscapes, I must remember to tone down the backgrounds much more than one ordinarily sees it.

And I must be original. My ideas are more original than my execution I think. My execution, for magazine illustration at least, is too exact and not individual enough. I have a style they say—a very definite style—but I must constantly be on the look-out for any new and snappy tendencies in my work so that I may develop them. And more than that, I must deliberately *plan* original things. I must not only draw as my eye sees, but I must train my eye to see as my mind has planned.

I MUST DO SOMETHING.

I must also practice pen and ink work. In that medium my technique is unique enough but I have not cultivated it. It is crude and not studied enough. I must also practice drawing *large*. And I must begin right now and study the illustrations of others.

Later:—I believe I have really discovered something new. Not exactly new—but a *plan*. I shall keep on sketching as usual for a while, and when I wish to make the drawings look right for reproduction I shall simply trace them, using a touch and line which comes very natural to me and which is, I hope, snappy and sparkling. I shall trace in this way in order that I may learn in the shortest time possible how the different things about me impress me while using that style—and then after a certain amount of this I hope to be able to sketch right from nature in this style.* This may be faking and I admit that it is *clever,* but I can't help it. Oh I do not care what the world says—I know what I am doing.

This does not mean that it will cut down the amount of work which is usually necessary—it will mean the same amount but in a concentrated form. And in order to do this one must have a mind which can think and analyze and grasp quickly the salient points of everything, and that is what I have been training myself to do for a good many years. How glad I am that I have the habit of subconsciously picking out the most important shadows, the most interesting lines and the most satisfying masses. It will also mean that I will have to be merciless enough to ignore and stamp on things which come my way, it will mean that I will

* An example of this is shown on the opposite page. The drawing in its first stage is shown facing page 355.

have to train my conscience to be numb for a while, for I will have to be *clever*.

I will have to be clever! It nearly breaks my heart. It is a dangerous step to take, because there is danger of my running into such a rut that I may never be able to get out again. But I will try to guard against this—while I am getting ready to cater to the public taste, I must constantly keep in mind the fact that my ideals at present are high and noble. My family must have money and I must make good.

I don't know whether I have mentioned the fact that I am thinking seriously of bobbing my hair in a Castle Clip. I am asking all my friends whether I ought to. One of the girls told me yesterday that I must not. She said, "You'll look freakish. Oh you'll look cute enough—you'll look stunning," but she seemed to think that by doing so I'd attract too much attention. But that is not what I want. I want coolness and ease in the arranging of it, and the ends of my hair are split all over and I thought that this would be a good time to cut it.

If I ever wish to do landscape I must do it in a very different way than is usually seen. I can stand doing people in a rational way, but landscape, never! I say that with much conviction, but it may be merely the conviction of the moment.

July 5, Monday

Wanda, will you in some picture *work out* one figure, manipulating two or three other figures as *plastic* rough masses?

Professor Koehler said at our last Club Meeting that he thought Whistler had been more influential than any other artist of the 19th Century.

As soon as you are no longer in love, or imagine yourself to be so, there are other things which seem as big as, if not bigger than, love.

And then as soon as you again find yourself in that state it is the only thing worth while. It seems so queer that one should be able to switch around so fast. It is almost unbelievable.

Later:—I have just returned from the dentist. He said that I needn't hurry at all about paying my bill.

There is no such thing as a definite line. That is, there *may be* but we never see it as such. Even that which is considered the clearest line—in a silhouette for instance—vibrates. I have discovered that, and now I must discover an effective way of drawing it. To draw a line which we know to be definite but which can never really be seen as being so.

I am reading Rabindranath Tagore.

I am impatient to show my worth. I am wild to get into the magazine field. Not because I feel that it would be more enjoyable than my present stage, but because my family needs money.

Wanda, go to bed.

July 7, Wednesday

I am worn out, and I don't know with what. I believe I need a vacation. The trouble is, even when I am vacationing, I think and read and draw with much vigor. I am no physical giant. I can do only a certain amount and then I go kerflop.

Some of the summer students asked me for criticism on their sketches so I told them all to put their sketches up in front and I criticized them. My latest idea is that I'd like to conduct a sketch class.

I believe I have not mentioned that Mr. Dehn and I had a picnic last Friday. He showed me the sketches he had made at Waterville (where he lives). I criticized them and enjoyed doing so very much. Six of them were really good.

We went out to Lake Minnetonka. I was very peevish when we started out, and after singing "She done it for her lover who was fur, fur away" until both he and I were almost frantic, I was so disgusted with humanity that I wanted to sit down and cry and cry. I don't know the reason for it either. The fact that two feather-headed couples were walking before us may have been responsible for part of my disgust. They would fool around, grabbing each other's hands or managing to touch each other as if by accident, and it irritated me. Of course I know it is old as the world is old, but just that afternoon I couldn't bear to think of such a thing as physical attraction. There are times when I hope violently that I

am never physically attractive. I nearly always wish that, but sometimes I wish it so much more vehemently than at other times. Not that
I would despise a girl for allowing a man to take little liberties—I suppose
it isn't her fault that she is so primitively constructed. But that day it did
seem so irritatingly *"animalisch."* As I sat there I was filled with revolt at
the thought of any man except a relative touching me. I don't know
what I would be like if I were a man. If my feelings would be the same
as they are now, I certainly would be able to have good morals.

Then Mr. Dehn picked up a snake and also a little turtle. Which irritated me some more. I couldn't understand my disposition at all and I
apologized a number of times for my peevish manner, but Mr. Dehn told
me that I didn't act nearly as disagreeably as I imagined. We sat down
and talked seriously about art for some time and soon I was feeling more
rational again. By the time we were ready to go home I was just as
agreeable as I ever was.

Mr. Dehn ought to be told that he must not call on me so often. I do
not know how it is—here is a young man who has sense, talent, a good
heart and a fine brain, and yet I fear that if he comes too often I shall tire
of him. He wanted to come to-night but, as one of the girls asked me to
go to a movie with her, I did not wait for him to call up. When I returned, the secretary told me that I had had a great many calls while I had
been gone.

"Different people?" I asked.

"No, always the same one," she said. "A man."

Which of course was Mr. Dehn.

July 16, Friday

Sally Peck is back. She returned Monday and we talked until about
3 a.m. about friendship. She is perhaps the happiest person I have ever
met.

We have been planning all kinds of things this morning. One plan is
that I will draw a portrait sketch of both Sally and Ruth Clark, and they
will act as my "press-agents" over at the "U." I have also told Sally that
I would be willing to make a few sketches for the Minnehaha [a college
magazine]. She said she could in that case get a friend of hers to put
in a little write-up in the same paper. All this for advertisement.

I am very much run down and have been in bed yesterday and to-day.
Sally is very sweet and considerate and brings my meals to my room and
does up my bed and everything.

I spent the last week-end at Mrs. Fournier's. She is—oh so very kind. I had a fine rest. Miss Frances Cranmer* spoke at the Club. She is very nice indeed.

The other day I made a black and white sketch of myself—I may send it to the State Art Exhibit. The same day I made another big one in Sepia crayon.

Not long ago Mr. Dehn and I went for a walk. We were talking about characters and I found myself asking him whether I ever irritated people. He said, "Well, not exactly that—" and then stopped, groping around for the right expression. It seems that much of the time he is with me he is unhappy. "It's funny," he said, "sometimes for the entire evening I don't enjoy your company at all, and still I want to come again." Which is funny; and I can't understand it. I told him that perhaps I was too serious for his taste.

He was here again Wednesday and I criticized his new sketches, some of which were exceedingly good. I pointed out to him the fact that some of the draperies on his figures had no texture and that his construction in some places was vague. This is particularly true of the shoulders of his figures. He is learning to eliminate beautifully. I just love to criticize sketches.

Mr. Dehn looked at my new sketches too. (I made over 30 kid-sketches last Tuesday). Their main virtue is graphic simplicity of line and color. Mr. Dehn marvels at the fact that I can put down my lines with such confidence and accuracy. In both the St. Paul and Minneapolis schools they have warned me that unless I "blocked in" the entire figure first (using about 4 or 5 lines) I would not be able to get the correct proportions and the action. For a while I actually believed it but I don't any more. I know that for most students that is the best way; but I can get the action and proportions very well, in fact *better,* in using my own method, which is just drawing carefully in charcoal, starting at the head and going downward, and then taking a general survey of the whole. In a general way I do my blocking piece by piece, and that is what Mr. Dehn marvels at. The reason why I like my method is because, in follow-ing it, I have each of my lines meaning something very definite as I put them down one after the other.**

---

* Now Frances Cranmer Greenman.

** This is not very clear. What I meant was that I did all my "blocking" in my mind, so that whatever lines I put on the paper would be spontaneous.

I have just written a very nice letter to Armand. In it are some very arrogant passages:—

"Great Caesar, I am impatient with being a girl. I have more courage and self-assurance than many a man, and yet I am treated as a mere wisp of femininity. A girl has so much harder a time of making good as it is—she has not so much vitality. To have always more enthusiasm, ideas, and ambition than you have energy for, and to run continually across obstacles which have been deliberately placed in your path *because you are a woman*. I tell you I will not let that come in my way. If I accomplish nothing else I mean to surmount that difficulty at least. I shall not rest until men are willing, *and glad,* to regard me as important as they (and with my hair hanging down my back in curls if I choose!)

But I must fight forever. I have that within me—call it principles, standards or whatever you like—which is Myself, and consequently *right*. Part of it conforms with the world as it is, but the other part conforms to the world as it should be, and that is the part which I will fight for, to the end."

Yesterday after reading some of Armand's old letters I nearly cried. It seemed so cruel of the world to have shown me a person who understood me so supremely well only to take away the companionship of that person in a year or two. Armand's letters are really wonderful. There is a coherence and unity about them which is very calming, and they are full of the things which fill up my life. Well, Armand *is* a brick, that's all, and I like him as well as ever only in a different way.

July 23, Friday

We (the class) are out at Fort Snelling and I ought to be sketching. I find that I look at landscapes, not as an artist, but as a poet does. This is due to the fact that I have done so little landscape, I suppose; but it does seem queer that I am able to look at people, seeing them as they would look on paper, and to be unable to apply this faculty to trees, clouds, bridges, etc.

July 24, Saturday

I am very happy to-day.

Timmie has been here. I showed him my latest kid-sketches, over which he became quite enthusiastic. He wants me to illustrate some children's book and try to sell the drawings to a publisher. "I would be willing to finance a thing like that," he said rashly.

He advised me to show them to my Journal Man too, and to tell him that they were good, and to tell him also about Timmie's suggestion about the children's book. Timmie always bewails the fact that I am not business-like enough. He declared that if he only had creative power, he would be a wonder. Timmie is becoming a finer friend day after day.

July 30

This from a little story by James Oppenheim:—

> "In all save myself life was released. It uncurled from the trees in little crumpled leaves, it burst from the orchard in a storm of pink, it sang in roaring cascades, and in the throat of birds. But in myself it rose and found no outlet, it made me feverish and wild . . . . . But all at once the truth came, wonderful and dazing. To what did Siegfried wake Brünnhilde? Not to a life of love, for soon he left her. No, he was merely the instrument of her awakening . . . . . Now I knew, I must be Brünnhilde. My love for Siegfried had wrought its wonder. It had awakened me. It had set the tides of life in motion; and now I must put aside all vain yearning, and pour my power into life—life itself."

I have been sketching a good deal this week—seven portraits. It is not a path of roses, but it brings the dollars.

Today has been the last day of summer school. I brought some of my sketches for the final exhibition, and Mr. Koehler and Mr. Goetsch declared that I had so many drawings that I ought to have a screen for myself. Professor Koehler said that he wanted one of them. They selected a bunch of sketches, intending to eliminate therefrom, but they didn't seem to know which to take away so I have a good many more sketches up than any other student.

Mr. Dehn was here last night and he gave me a very nice sketch as payment for losing the bet about the 4th of July weather. I hope he does not like me too much.

Sally and I have been reading aloud to each other, a trashy novel by Marie Corelli. Whatever possessed us to do such a thing is more than I can explain, but the fact remains that we did it. Not having read anything of the sort for many years, it was interesting to study that sort of fiction from a psychological standpoint of view—I mean, to see what means the authoress employed to work upon the minds of her readers. I read only about ⅓ of the book, which was about all I could stand. Sally bravely read the rest of the book and gave me a synopsis of it afterwards. The name of it is "Wormwood." Thank goodness I am far enough ad-

1915

W·G

Child in Garden

vanced to read Ibsen, Sudermann, Browning, etc. I must run to dinner
now. She will say "fish or beef" and I will say "beef, please."

August 2, Monday

I have just been down to the Journal. I ran in to say goodbye to Mr.
Russell. He said that if he were young and handsome and twenty he'd
be chasing me. "Because you certainly made a big hit with father," he
said, laughing, "but it's too late now." "You know, you're something
like a fairy," he said. He is so funny and nice. He asked me whether I
had made any nice friends this year and whether I had any nice special
man. I said I hadn't, but that I had some very nice men-friends.

I also went to see Mr. Jones. He returned from his lunch, all done up
in a rain coat and looking very plump and twinkly. "Like a pudding, he
was a pleasant sight."

He said "Hello Wanda," which delighted me.

I said, "Well, I'm leaving for my vacation to-day so I thought I'd run
in and say goodbye." At this point I sat down upon a chair without being
asked.

"And when are you coming back?" he asked, twinkling up at me in
the most delicious manner.

"Well, I don't know," I said. "Am I to come back in the fall?"

"Oh yes—yes," he said in a matter-of-course drawl which nearly sent
my heart up to my brains with joy. It was so perfectly grand of him to
take the thing so for granted. He said that they might start me on a cover
or so next year, and I said perhaps I would try one or two during the
summer. It was that same day, I believe, that Mr. Russell told me that
Mr. Jones thought it was his duty to act sort of stern about my drawings
once in a while.

August 8, Sunday. New Ulm

I am very much in love with my family. I came home Monday night
and it felt so nice to be among mama and the children once more.

Tuesday and Wednesday I sketched and enjoyed the folks, and Thursday Tussy and I went down to grandma's. Grandma is getting old and
walks very slowly, but she has such a sweet, calm, smiling look on her
face.

I sketched and read, rested and ate. I can enjoy eating when I am out
in the country. It must be fun to be that way all the time. In spite of hay
meadows, the big stretches of sky and the almost perfect weather, I was

not exactly happy. To secure this state of mind I ran the phonograph and read Stevenson, but altho I was not sad I could not become ecstatic.

But to-day I am happy. I suppose it is very foolish but I dare scarcely to acknowledge my happiness for fear that it may switch back upon me. But oh, it is fine to have a mother, a brother, five sisters, a grandmother, and aunts and uncles. I am so proud of the children. Not that I consider them so exceptional but they are *mine.* Think of the joy and endless interest in watching five sisters and a brother grow up.

Poor Stella poisoned herself while out in the country.*

Tussy is going to teach next year (that little wisp) and will earn $50 a month. It seems almost incredible. Stella will get $55 a month this year. Asta is just beginning to grow up. Her conversation is artless, but racy and humorous. Dehli is able to be up and about again, but as she has grown very much and very fast, she is tall and very slender. She is becoming really beautiful. Her dark eyes are very soft, expressive and comprehensive (should I have said comprehending?). Her features are good and her hair is a joy to behold. Howard is still very *non-committal* as to his "natural bent" but I always have an idea that his mind will run to inventions or some such thing.

Flavia is a queer little morsel. She reads marvelously well, has a fine little brain, and draws much. She sketched me to-day and I was surprised and delighted to find that, at the age of eight, she had already discovered that things must be drawn as they *seem,* not as they *are.*

"I can't see all of your eyebrow," she remarked, "but I'll draw it just the way I see it." She got a foreshortened view of my drawing pad. "It looks so funny when I draw it just the way it looks," she said, but she did not draw a square as most little children would have done. She drew what she saw, and succeeded, in her baby way, to secure the effect of foreshortening.

I got a letter from Mr. Dehn, a nice long one.

August 14. At grandma's.

Yesterday morning I got a letter from Paula. I sat out on the swing and wept a number of tears as I read it. I love Paula from the bottom of my heart. She is so good and so sympathetic and so constant. She says that she does not know whether she loves Larry Morse in the way she thought she did, and that she was afraid she was growing bitter and loveless—as tho she ever could!

* Ivy-poisoning.

August 22, Sunday

Just before I left Minneapolis I got a letter from Mr. Gray. A very docile taking-nothing-for-granted sort of an epistle. When he is gone I like him quite well, altho of course my attitude never exceeds the friendship mark.

I got a very nice little letter from Timmie the other day. He asked me to be sure and write him one of my long, illegible, scribbly, "feelingful" letters.

I am sending four pictures to the State Art Exhibit. They are called:

"Allegro"
"Elf" *
"Ego"
"Studien-kopf"

I like the world, but we are so poor. The things which are bothering me are the taxes, the sidewalk to be laid, coal and things like that. Also the dentist work that the kids ought to have done.

I think little, read less, and draw only a little more than that just now. (I have done about 60 sketches during the last three weeks tho, which isn't so bad after all.) I do housework, and talk with the kids, doing my best to give them as much of the culture I have acquired as possible. I am teaching Dehli, Asta, and Flavia the little that I know of music. Next week I may sew. I may rest instead, or I may even mingle with people outside of the family for a change.

It may sound silly for me to say it, but I do wish there were some nice unsusceptible young man to walk with and talk to. Being a normal girl, I like men. I am only exceptional in that I admit it openly.

I got a very nice letter from my Uncle Mac. He told me that I must be prepared to meet disappointment (in magazine illustration) very often. It sort of put me into the dumps that day because I was afraid it might be many years before I could do for the family all that I wish to do.

We have been rejuvenating the attic room, and I like it more than ever if possible.

I like the world, but altho it is kind, it is merciless. Propagation seems to be the big idea and all must conform to it. They may be miserable if they do; but if they don't, they are too.

My supply of wrapping paper came to an end to-day and I hadn't drawn all I wanted to.

* Facing page 376. This was one of my attempts at doing the popular magazine illustrations which I so despised.

September 7

I wrote Mr. Dehn a letter the other day.

Today, by way of variety, my pictures look pretty good. So far I have done 123 sketches since I am home. And I have been home five weeks now. Yesterday Flavia raked together a pile of fallen leaves and came to me, magnanimously offering to pose for me. She would run for a short distance so as to get a good start, and upon reaching the pile she would flop down into it in a haphazard way. She posed about four times in the apple tree and, so that the thing might be as realistic as possible, she insisted upon tying a big apple into one of the branches. She is absolutely tom-boyish, and one can't do a thing with her. She isn't mean but she is so very full of exuberant feelings.

Today I secured a shadow effect which delights me very much indeed. It is dark and yet lightish and transparent. First I put on blue pastel and a little dark green, and then a thin even coat of charcoal.

Only one glimpse of "Hloopsie" all summer. I worry too much, and that prevents me from appreciating all the glorious sunshine and wind that we have been having.

* * *

Part Six

LIGHT AND SHADE

1916

(NOTE:—The diary covering the intervening five months is lost. My return to school in September marked the beginning of a busy year, for aside from my school work I did much outside drawing. I continued to do sketches for newspapers and made pastel portraits at one dollar each. A young man connected with a paper company (referred to in the diary as "my Paper Man") became interested in my work and gave me art advertising jobs, supplied me with the brown wrapping paper I always used for my pastels, and bought many of my sketches. As my own expenses were being paid by Mr. Jones I was able to send home all my extra earnings; but Stella and Thusnelda, who were both teaching school, were the chief breadwinners at this time.

I was contributing regularly to the University magazine, *Minnehaha*. Adolph Dehn and I worked together on posters, and magazine covers which we kept sending to New York, and which always came back.

In order to be closer to school, I had moved to the Woman's Christian Association Club at 1619 Stevens Avenue, where I met a new art student by the name of Lucile Lundquist.* We became good friends immediately. Lucile was an accomplished pianist; we played duets together and she played Bach to me by the hour. We walked and talked and worked together, and this, in addition to my heavy work-schedule, kept me so occupied that I had much less time for diary entries than in previous years.)

February 18, Friday

I have written nothing about my Christmas Holidays as yet. They were most joyous. I visited only Paula and Daisy and stuck at home with my dear family to my heart's content. Phil Becker was in town and we inveigled him to come and visit our family. He took a special fancy to Flavia and Stella. Phil and I are only friends now and I am not at all afraid that he might change his present attitude. I like him and I did not try to hide it, because I took it for granted that we had both gotten over our school-day attitudes. He said to Daisy, *"Die Wanda is trustworthy. Sie is so a faithfuller kleiner Puppy."* Flavia took an awful fancy to him too. She said, *"Der Phillip, der is gelung. Der is anyhow gelung!"*

And now I come to my latest upheaval. Last night Adolph called on me again. I was rambling on, telling him all the news, but when I would

* Now Lucile Blanch.

428

happen to look up I would find him looking at me intently. This was a trifle disconcerting and I would always run on hastily with my talk. At about nine we went to a movie. I knew I would be cold and reserved that night. And I was. I gathered all my little prudishnesses about me and there I sat as cold and cruel as you please. This is silly but it's true; he had had his hair cut again and that was responsible, to a small extent, for my attitude. His intent looks may have had something to do with it. It was obvious that he hadn't come to the movie for the movie's sake. He wished to talk and he wished to have me talk. "Say something," he said.

He spoke again about my treating him as a "nameless creature." I told him he was justified in objecting to the way I omitted his name in speaking to or of him, that it was foolish of me to do so, and that I was sorry to be hurting him so. He said, "Yes, but that's all the further you will go. You admit that you are sorry but there you stop." He thought that I evidently didn't consider him a good enough friend for that, and I could see he was most awfully hurt. Towards the end of the movie we said nothing at all. I slipped into my wraps very silently and we walked for blocks and blocks without talking. It was not until we got to Twelfth Street that he talked at all.

I said, "I think you're super-sensitive about this name-incident."

He had evidently been doing some tall thinking, for he said, slowly but without hesitation, "Well, I suppose I ought to tell you what my attitude towards you is."

My heart quaked within me, and I didn't know whether I ought to let him go on or not. He continued to talk but I don't remember what it was. The next thing I remember is that I heard him saying, "But the truth is, Wanda, I'm in love with you."

I knew neither what to do nor what to say. I said, "Oh you aren't!"

He said, "Perhaps I shouldn't have told you this, and I really didn't intend to say it for a long time to come, but it just seemed that that was the only thing that was left for me to do."

I said, "Well, I'm glad you were so frank about it."

"Didn't you know how I felt about it?" he said.

"No I didn't."

"Well, it seems to me that you aren't as good a reader of character as you think you are then."

I told him it was so hard to tell where the Platonic attitude ended and the other began. He said he thought it sort of gradually developed from the beginning.

"As to my own attitude," I said, feeling the question, unasked, in the air, "I will tell you frankly that I don't know what it is."

He murmured something to the effect that he was glad I didn't know. Which was a funny thing to say but it may have been said in the manner of a hope. He said that he would try very hard to get over it and perhaps some day he might, altho he was dubious about that. One always is. I remember when Armand told me I was mistaken I said, "Yes, I suppose I am," but for many months after that I felt just as sure as ever that I had not been mistaken.

I said that after having been fooled so thoroughly once, I was afraid I would not be able to tell when I met the right one.

I said, "Have you ever been in love before?"

He said, "I know nothing about it."

I said, "Well, I suppose all one can do is to let it think it out for itself," and that I hoped this incident would not interfere with our friendship, and this seemed to cheer him up a little. That foolish man had been afraid that after his confession I might turn him down flat and forever. I told him that he was a striking exception to the usual rule, because all the others had simply faded away after finding that my attitude was only Platonic.

We walked for quite a while, discussing the matter with a frankness which was beautiful to see. I told him that I had felt rather guilty about letting him come so often because he might regard my actions as encouragements, but that I had liked his company too well to deny myself the pleasure of it. He declared that he, on the other hand, had felt equally guilty about coming so often, knowing all the time that his attitude was different from what I perhaps thought it was, but that he just simply couldn't help asking again and again. He said that often when he had been grumpy to me and had said things to hurt me, he had done it purposely to keep himself from saying the opposite. He told me that he liked me better than any other girls he had ever met and that he had found me most satisfying to talk to. I told him that I considered him my best pal at present.

I told him, as we neared home, that altho I sometimes acted very cold I was that way only because of my principles. I said that I didn't allow little familiarities, not so much because I objected to them but simply because I had strict principles and wished to live up to them. He said, "I have always admired that in you," which made me very happy.

As I went in the door I said, "And let's be pals."

He said, "We'll be better friends than ever!" and this hurt me more perhaps than anything else which he had said during the evening.

It made me awfully nervous and worried—the whole thing.

The next day at school we acted just as usual, thank goodness.

March 1, Wednesday

Oh dear, my ideals have taken such a leap away from me and I am down in the dumps, oh, ever so far. It isn't that my work is getting worse but that my ideals are getting better. Another thing that contributes to my misery is that for once other people have more sketches in Concours than I; Lloyd Moylan and Mr. Aurness. I have only 1 big life drawing, 3 compositions and four dinky sketches.

With the realization of my incompetence gnawing at my heart all day, I was facetious yesterday. I wanted badly to talk, so I told Adolph he could walk home with me and talk with me until dinner time. I didn't say very much tho, because whenever I'd approach the painful subject I would find myself on the verge of a weep. Consequently I spent most of the time fighting off tears.

Adolph said, "Why don't you cry? I wouldn't mind if you did. It might make me appreciate your sincerity more." But it was too near dinner time and besides, people were always running in and out of the sitting-room. I said I was almost certain I could become a popular artist if I wished, but if that were all that I were capable of, I would rather not have been born an artist at all.

Dear God, suffer me to fight all my life, all my life; but do not let me stop at being a clever illustrator.

Perhaps I wasn't supposed to be a real artist. Perhaps I am only a secondary creature who goes around and does the thinking for more successful people. As I sit here, writhing and weeping, my pictures smile mockingly at me from the walls. Whereas otherwise their good points made themselves manifest to my eyes, their defects now take great pains to call my attention to themselves.

I used to delight in my mental perspective, my broadmindedness and my imagination. I have reached the place where I ask myself, "And to what avail? Those whom I have been picturing as running up against a blank wall some day are steadily advancing." Even if my prophecy about the wall should come true, would it not be possible for them to *scale the wall?*

And yet I must remain the same. My desire to do things differently, to illustrate differently for instance, comes not from the desire to be exotic. I chafe under much of present magazine illustration. I have become so meek tho, that I feel bound to add that perhaps the reason why I chafe under it is that I am not educated up to where I can appreciate it, as for instance Lloyd and Ethel. They do such conscientious and un-wild things. If such radicals as Adolph and I do not look out we shall be rapidly dropping out of the Concours exhibits entirely. I do not expect any prizes at the end of the year for the same reason—namely, that I am still untamed. Lloyd, Ethel, Mr. Aurness and Louis Rasch have evidently never needed taming. They have been sensible from the start.

A thing which worries me greatly is that if I make such a lack of a hit with the instructors, how can I expect my Journal Man to retain faith in me? Financially, I believe I ought to be able to make good bye and bye. I seem to be able to get rid of more of my work than any of the other students.

Later:—Well, I had an anguished weep. Then I took a nap and then in desperation I read Oscar Wilde—"The Importance of Being Earnest." He is so confoundedly clever.

Adolph continues to come—and I continue to treat him namelessly. It is so hard to all of a sudden call him Adolph.

My cover for the Paper Co. has been accepted. $8. The other day I won a second prize for a poster contest. $7.50. I like money to come in hunks like that. Adolph submitted two drawings for this contest. With one he captured first prize ($10) and for the other he received $3. He said it seemed like thirteen million to him.

Lloyd Moylan, Louis Rasch and Mr. Aurness are getting to be so ding good in Life. And in Illustration too, for that matter. Ever since I have come to Minneapolis, my "spoiled-little-artist" attitude (of others, to me) has been receiving nothing but bumps, and glory, it's most gone now. If the Minneapolis Institute of Fine Arts should ever be accused of over-appreciation of Wanda Gág, I shall jump to its rescue—they are not guilty! My sketches may be very defective, but I think it is largely a matter of their getting used to me—I'm sure that if some other student had handed in some of my sketches which they neglected to exhibit, they would have hailed them with delight. Of course I suppose I ought to rejoice that I am improving in Life. (They kept two of my big drawings last month.) But so is everyone else. I know that I have learned a great deal about construction as a result of my serious application, but I have nothing that I can show at the end of the year to show that I have learned it. Mr. Phoenix knows what I have learned, and I do, but no one else does.

The new *Minnehaha* with my *First Cover*, my first *printed* one, is out, but I haven't seen it.*

Mar. 4, Saturday

And now I have seen the Russian Ballet. Adolph, Lucile and I had $2.50 seats. It was evident that, on account of the strict laws of Minneapolis, some of the things had been tamed down a little—"The Faun," for instance, and "Scheherezade." This was the only thing in which I was disappointed—I did so wish to see Bakst out-Baksting himself. Of course the majority of people might not have been able to stand it, but I am sure that altho they would have gone to the wildest extremes—in costume (or lack of it)—I should have been able to maintain my moral and emotional equilibrium. It was wilder in St. Paul they say. Would I had been there. Several of the girls at school thought some of it was vulgar—these eternal prudes get on my nerves. It makes me suspicious of their fortitude against things *Satanique*.

"Prince Igor" was for the most part a barbaric swirl of color. Lucile said that on account of the similarity of costumes in the different groups there would be a color-pattern of movement, a circle of blue-green, purple and gold, winding and unwinding itself. Lucile almost rose from her seat in excitement. "The Faun," splendidly grotesque, was so primitive that it gave one a sort of choky feeling. He would walk across the stage like a spotted animal, with his toes upturned; and the essence of primitiveness was reached, it seems to me, when he turned the corners with his knees slightly bent. "Scheherezade" was the wildest of the four. I was wild about the impassioned barbaric antics of Adolf Bolm who played the favorite slave. The color of the negroes was delicious. In "Le Sylphides" Lydia Lopokova danced to a waltz [the Andantino] by Chopin. The tune clings to me like a fragrant memory just as the air from "La Boheme" has always done. We emerged from the entire performance in a sort of trance. Or rather we didn't emerge at all. When a big thing like that gets into your system it isn't so very easy to get it out. Not that we wanted to get it out either.

Undated Entry

The next morning I secured a pass for entering behind the scenes that

* Facing page 377.

day. Adolph and I went. Arnold Blanch and Joe La Londe were also there. We sketched a little but there was so little room that it was almost impossible. We stood in the wings and watched. Massin and Tcherni-cowa stood right beside us in the wings. Massin has the most wonderful eyes and he is very handsome. Adolf Bolm ran into me! Of this I am very proud. Massin ran into me too. I got a quick sketch of Serge de Diaghileff. I am very glad to have it.

By the time this performance was over, I was completely saturated with the Ballet Russe. I had allowed it to enter my system and there, for many days, it surged full force. Lucile was affected similarly. To calm ourselves we played piano but whenever we played duetts we saw those figures dancing daintily, madly or sadly before us, and when that mad-deningly delicate air from Chopin would sing itself within us there was no hope for peace.

Perhaps I am too intense. In fact I am quite sure I am. But what can I do?

I have become alarmingly thin. I have been eating virtuously and am keeping good hours at night, but it seems to help me not at all. Yesterday I went to see my Journal Man about it. When I got down there I found that he had sent me a letter to come down and hear the New York verdict. They had written advice etc. on the backs of my pictures. Mr. Jones said, "They said you had ability but that you didn't finish them up enough."

He said, "How do you think you are getting on?" I asked him what he thought of it and he seemed to think we weren't (that is, *I* wasn't) progressing very much. I asked him if he thought I didn't work enough but he said it wasn't that. He said I didn't concentrate enough, I scattered too much, and that I did too much of the scratchy lines on brown paper. I told him that I wouldn't have much to show at the end of this year be-cause I had been working at fundamentals, construction, etc. all the time. I said too that the reason why I hadn't finished anything up to that time was because to *finish,* one must know a good deal about construction.

He said, "Yes, I told you that the other time, and you wouldn't believe me."

"You were right," I said contritely.

It seems he wished to have me come to see him oftener. He said, "I'm your guardian and your advisor, but you never seem to need advice." I told him that I always needed it, and that I should be only too glad to come to him for it if he wanted me to do so. I try so hard to do what is right but most of the time he isn't entirely clear as to what he wants me to do. He said that he sent me to school in order that I might support myself bye and bye. He declared that he was making it too easy for me, that I shouldered no responsibility. He said this sort of thing wasn't good for one's character. "And I don't want to hurt you, I'm trying to help you," he said.

Shouldering responsibility? I have done that ever since I was fourteen. Oh, Mr. Jones is so kind to me but sometimes he does not quite understand. I think his patronage will end with this year. And what can I do then? If I were a buxom sort of person I might work and go to school both, but I have all I can do to keep up my school work. I try so hard to get to the place where I can earn money for myself and the family, and my Journal Man thinks that I am not trying very hard. I told him that I was nothing but a half-baked fish and that I needed much advice.

He said that children seemed to be my long suit, so I was to apply myself to child illustrations.

I told him that my real reason for coming was because I was getting so thin. We talked it over a while and he sent me to a Dr. who has given me a tonic. It tastes very bitter but I am glad I have it. I was beginning to get worried. Nearly all the bones of my body seem to be in evidence. My clavicles, scapulae, ribs and so forth are far too noticeable. I can't help but pity myself when I look in the glass.

Undated Entry

I saw Lohengrin. I got two tickets from Delos Lovelace so I took Lucile.

Sometimes I get sort of used to myself but every once in a while I can't help standing off and looking at myself in bewilderment.

I seem to be too chaste for the city. It never struck me that way particularly. I always took chastity as a matter of course.

Last night I had a "Backward, turn backward, Oh time etc." sort of a feeling so I went over Stevenson's child poems. I had to grow up into a young woman (or into the *age* of one at least) before I was half thru being a child. The feeling is very strong within me, and I certainly can't be blamed for wanting to paddle in pools and to run and skip and kick and think like a child.

I have been thinking a good deal of Armand lately. Perhaps because for two years he has been associated in my mind with spring. I wish Armand hadn't taken my foolishness so seriously. I am sure if he were to speak to me now he wouldn't have to fear that I cared too much for him now.

I was twenty-three years old a week ago. How can I be 23 and feel sometimes 17, sometimes 25, and sometimes 7? I got two lovely nighties, one from Stella and one from Tussy. Adolph gave me a book by Oscar Wilde:—"Ballad of Reading Gaol."

Pen and Ink Drawing for *Minnehaha*

March 30, Thursday

My Journal Man was right. I do not concentrate enough. I work hard and I am conscientious enough, goodness knows, but as he says, I am scattery. Yes I am scattery. My mind is always in five different places at once.

I am able, now, to settle down in life class and draw conscientiously and *academically*. Of this I feel a trifle proud. I have decided that for the rest of the year I shall confine my illustration work to children.

Last Thursday Adolph and I went to a movie. I had been having an awful toothache. I was worn out and weak and had a headache. I said I was weak. And I was listless. Adolph's hand touched my arm and I hadn't the strength to remove it. I was on the point of taking his hand and laying it back on the arm of the seat where it belonged, and saying, "It is better so." But I didn't. Sometimes one just doesn't, that's all. I finally disengaged myself however. He said, "Why do you object, Wanda?" I said, "Because I'm a prude."

On the way home he said, "Are you angry with me for that?" and when I said "No," he said, "Goody!" He's such a little boy at times.

The following evening we walked a while. As we were going thru the park, he caught my hand again and fancied the arrangement so strongly that he did not wish to discontinue when I asked it—which was immediately. At school they call him The Untamed One on account of his sketches. It was this that made me say, "You are so untamed." He said, "Well, then I might as well live up to my reputation!"

He told me at the door that I was very cruel. Of course I am cruel, but I would rather be cruel with a clear conscience than temporarily gracious with a troubled one. The night of the movies I objected merely on account of the principle of the thing, but this night I objected to being treated as if I belonged to him. I don't belong to any man, and neither Adolph nor anyone else need expect me to tie myself down and to be the possession of some man for some time to come at least.

He told me that coming to see me was his only vice. Some vice—to sit in the parlor of the "Woman's Christian Association" with old maids either present or scurrying thru the rooms half of the time!

Undated Entry

Well I have seen Armand.

I was at a party at Timmie's last night. We had a good time. During the refreshments Armand sat to my right and Ted Hilton to my left. I talked to Ted Hilton for a long time. About what constituted a good picture in comparison to literature and music. Armand asked me about my work and we landed on the subject of the *Minnehaha*. I said, "I suppose you *loved* my work." He said for about the first hour he was furious but that he calmed down afterwards. I said I knew the work was rotten but that I was doing it because it gave me a chance to see my work reproduced for nothing.

He said, "I called you up the other day but was unable to get you. I suddenly remembered that it was almost May," then turning to Ted he said, "You know, Wanda and I have a queer arrangement. Every year we take a day off in May and go for a jaunt."

"Any special day?" Ted asked.

"What day is it?" said Armand to me.

I said, "I don't know." Of course, I know it *ought* to be the *first* day of May but what I meant was that I didn't know whether it would always be that. Last year it was the last of April.

Armand was wild about the Russian Ballet too—especially about the colors in "Scheherezade." He said, "As soon as the curtain rose I thought, 'Wanda ought to see this!'" He didn't care about "The Faun."

To my great joy I was not at all nervous about re-meeting Armand— nor was I excited during our conversation.

After we had finished eating, we sat down by the fireplace. Armand said, "Well, tell me about yourself." So I told him how docile I had become, how I had found that *grind* was very necessary and not at all disagreeable, and that I was thoroughly disgusted with, and had even been discouraged about, my work at times. He said it was good to be disgusted but that I must not overdo it, because I could draw. I told him that if I could do just as I pleased I should simply grind away at Portrait and Life for five or six years.

I said, "I've said goodbye to a good many of my old theories, ideas, and principles."

"I knew it!" said Armand with what he evidently considered justifiable pride in his perspicacity.

"Of course you know it!" I flared up. "Anybody with sense *would* change their opinions."

At this he laughed tolerantly, as of old.

Later we all went for a walk on the bluffs. Ted Hilton fell in beside me and we had a most interesting talk which ended up with Cubism, Post-Impressionism and the "291." It was lovely on the bluffs. Below in a semi-circular manner the city was spread out—a city of lights in clusters and patterns. It was here that Armand used to go last year in the early, early morning and I suppose it is here that his "Dawn" originated.

Timmie saw me home. On the way he said, "Did you have a nice talk with Armand?"

I said, "Yes, we talked about my artistic fluctuations."

"He's a nice chap," said Timmie. "He's sort of irritating at times, but you can't help liking him anyway, can you?"

I agreed with some indifference. He is right tho. You can't help liking him. The Platonic-ness of my attitude towards him was not spoiled by seeing him again.

A most satisfying evening.

Last Monday evening Adolph came over in order that we might do our page for the *Minnehaha* to-gether. The subject appealed to neither of us but I kept egging Adolph on and finally we finished it.

Undated Entry

Tuesday evening I had a raging toothache again. I have an abscess beneath one of my teeth and am having it treated at the "U" where one pays only for the materials. The next day the ache was worse than it had ever been. I stayed in bed all the time.

Friday Adolph came over to see me. He brought a "Vanity Fair" and the "Masses." I sat in the big chair and he beside me, and a number of times as I was looking thru "Vanity Fair" he would catch my hand. But I fought against it every time and told him to be good. I said, "I'm a little disappointed in you. I thought that *you* at least would be able to resist temptation."

"But it's a legitimate temptation," he said. "Isn't it legitimate?"

"I don't know," I replied.

Goodnight, perhaps it wouldn't be so bad. I had always supposed it to be very harmful, to the man at least, but judging by things I have heard people say lately it may not be as bad as I thought.

He thinks my hands are the most expressive he has ever seen. He likes their length and skinny-ness and can go quite wild about the curve of my thumb and wrist. It is not much that he asks, to play with my hands, but yet—.

I try so hard to do what is right and I don't know quite what is right. Lucile thinks I am a little hard on him and sometimes I almost think so too. Ding it all, why do folks have to fall in love with me so long before I am ready for it? I like the sunshine and I like music, I like to draw and read and take tears over fields and hills, I love children and all sorts of folks—I can't get along without nice discussions and jaunts with men—but why must they always fall in love just when we are getting to be such great pals?

April 25, Tuesday

Yesterday morning my Uncle Mac called up and told me he wanted me to come and stay a day or two at his house and take a rest.

We talked of many things on the way to his home. It seems that when one gets along as far in life and experience as my Uncle Mac is, all the bewilderments of youth do untangle a bit and arrange themselves somewhat logically. This is hard to believe when one is young and tangled up in the myriads of threads about one. Even if I seem to have some of them untwisted and laid out into some sort of a pattern, the pattern turns out to be a wrong one as I grow a little older and see it in perspective. The idea that all these things might straighten out in the distant future is about the only thing that reconciles me to the idea of having to develop into something more than a child.

Mrs. McWhorter is so lovable and says such nice funny things. My Uncle Mac and Mrs. McWhorter went to the opera last night. So did I, of course, only I was behind the scenes. My Uncle Mac took me there and introduced me to Agnini. As I entered I saw Adolph, Arnold Blanch, and Joe La Londe grinning at me from afar. The manager said, "You know them?" so he turned me over to them. I certainly like Arnold. I not only like him but respect him.

I sketched Riccardo Martin. He liked it but told me not to put a double chin on him. "Here," he said taking my charcoal with one hand and holding my hand down with the other, "this is the way you should have it," and he made a mark which gave him a chin with no doubleness to it at all. "Make me as I should be," he said smiling, "not as I am."

I said, "Oh."

After a while we were standing in the wings watching the opera (The Love of the Three Kings) when someone pulled me by the hair. (I had them hanging down in curls.) I turned around and found it was Riccardo Martin.

"How old are you—" he said, "fourteen?"

I said, "Nine years older than that."

"Oh no," he said.

"In years," I said.

"In experience probably, but not in years."

"In years," I said, "but not in feelings."

Then came the ballet. I got a quick sketch of Pavlowa from the back. She brushed into me and said, "Excuse me." Isn't it childish the way I hoard up all these Bumpings-into and brushings-past, and "Excuse-mes"? A man who evidently knew Pavlowa very well showed her my sketches. "Klink" is doing a statue of Pavlowa's partner Volinini. The ballet was "Snowflakes" from Tschaikowsky's "Nut-cracker Suite." Pavlowa and all the dancers keep themselves very much aloof from everybody, even from the opera people.

Adolph behaved very nicely.

Undated Entry

I have Armando Agnini's card so I am at liberty to enter thru the entire Opera Season. The following evening (April 25) they gave "Pag-

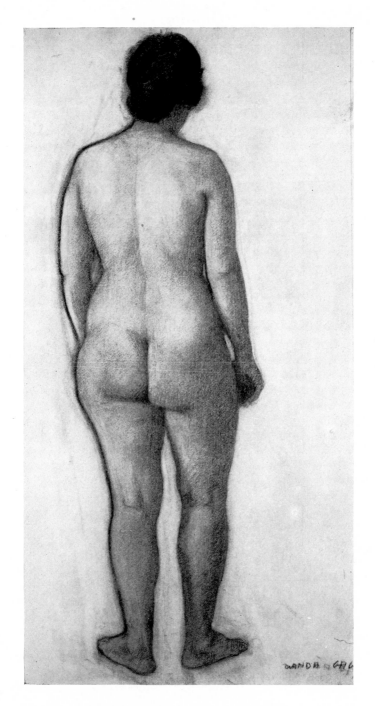

Life Drawing in Charcoal

Grand Opera Singer—Pastel on Wrapping Paper

Five Minute Sketch of Lucile, 1917

liacci." Giovanni Zenatello asked if I would sketch him and I did. I sketched also Pezetti. He is a funny little person with a twinkle in his eye and a most captivating and sardonic twist to his mouth. By this time all the Opera people knew me and would nod cordially and greet me. While I drew they would stand around and say, "Nota Bene!" "Multo Bravo!" "Magnifique!" etc. They are such child-like folk. What I like about these singers is their utter lack of snobbishness. I sketched Robert Moranzoni, Luisa Villani, Maggie Teyte, Jose Mardones, Puliti and many others.

During the performance of "Walpurgis Night" Adolph caught my hand and kept it. I could do nothing. I tried to get away but could not resist very forcibly lest I should call people's attention to me. So I gave in. Oh Wanda, Wanda, you are becoming quite worldly. Ding it all, I didn't mind it much either.

My Uncle Mac came to call for me and had also watched me draw. On the way home he told me gently that I was not drawing correctly. He advocated the blocking-in method, you see, and I was putting lines down just as they impressed me, working in what Mr. Phoenix would call my "patch-work" way. I told my Uncle Mac that I realized it was wrong, that I had been doing it the right way all year, and that I did it this way simply because it was quicker. I felt quite guilty. He said one couldn't do big things with that method. This was the last straw. Mr. Phoenix, Lloyd and Adolph had been hounding me all year as to that, and I had still held on to my dear bad old method. And here comes my Uncle Mac.

At my present stage of development I must choose either my dear bad patch-work method and character—or the good cruel blocking-out method, a little more accuracy in proportions, but no character. Ah Wanda, you have a big hill to climb over. Oh, must I say goodbye to my dear, satisfying, impractical patch-work method? I would gladly give it up for all else, but for quick sketching it seems that I must put down each thing the moment that impression is made upon me. When I go to work at blocking-out, the first impression—the part of the thing that is most virile to me—becomes diffused and gets lost. It is for this reason, and not because I am afraid or obstinate about learning a new method, that I cling to the old.

I could tell that Adolph was somewhat disappointed in me that evening. He thought my head was being turned by my popularity. I knew this was not so, but this and the thing I have just finished mentioning kept me awake until 2 or 3 a.m. *Goodnight, how I despised myself!* I felt badly to think I had let the Me's pop out. I had, you know. But thank goodness, Myself ran on serenely and firmly as an undercurrent to the froth of the Me's. The praise of the *artistes* had not upset me, I think I can truthfully say that. What I want is the praise of my instructors and people like that.

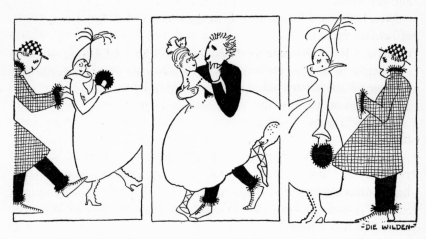

Minnehaha drawings—Girl by Wanda, Man by Adolph

The last evening came "La Boheme." My beloved "Musetta's Waltz" sang thru all the second act. I nearly jumped out of my seat with ecstasy when Musetta gave her harmonious little shrieks. That night I went back to Minneapolis.

May

"Klink" is posing in our art school now. Poor fellow. He has to earn some money so he can hire a model.

Some time ago Adolph and I went to Loring Park. We sat down on a bench and found ourselves on the topic of "Familiarities." He asked me a good many questions to which I had to say, "I don't know." For instance he would say, "Well there's nothing bad about it, is there?" and I'd have to say, "I don't know."

I asked him whether it wasn't allright to be prudish. He said, "Of course it is, Wanda, and I have always admired you for it. In fact I like you all the better for it. That's the irony of it!"

The whole thing, to-gether with the coolness of the evening, made me tremble a good deal. I said, "Oh I don't understand the world at all!"

On Thursday Armand called up. He asked me to go with him and Timmie to see a college play the following night. The following afternoon I met Armand at the "U." We flopped down on the grass and talked. About anatomy—nice muscles and things—the Russian Ballet, and my work.

"Yes, I suppose I kept it up a little too long," said Armand in speaking of holding up to me high ideals in art and the *"That that is not, is"* sort of thing. "But I was determined to brand it into your soul."

It began to rain so we raced down to the car line. While we were waiting for the car we talked about our "May Jaunt."

"It rained on the first this year," said Armand.

"I should say so," I said. "Besides I couldn't have gotten away. I was too busy."

Armand said it had been the same with him. He remarked about our progress since last year. "Last year," he said, "school could not have kept us from going."

"Oh!" I said, "It kept *you*. We had our jaunt on the day before because you had a quiz."

"Well," said he, laughing, "I was just a year ahead of you then."

On the street car we talked of many nice things. Armand took me to Timmie's where I had dinner, and then Timmie, Armand and I went to the play. Timmie was always telephoning to someone, or something, and that left Armand and me by ourselves a great deal. Well, in this as in our former meeting, I found myself very calm and unconcerned— and dispassionate. I enjoyed his company very much—it was just like old times except that there was a little more freedom somehow, owing to the fact of our change in attitudes.

A few weeks ago Adolph and I went for a walk out to Fair Oaks. Adolph actually tried to embrace me but I fought hard. Oh dear, if it had been only a matter of disliking it I should not have objected so strenuously. Oh Wanda, Wanda, where is your cold and prudish outlook upon the world?

This is the first time he has fallen in love (or imagined it, as the case may be) and when he says, "It isn't bad, is it?" I haven't the heart to say it is bad because, altho I always have the idea that it might be harmful, I am so afraid of interfering with his pure-mindedness. I am afraid I might put ideas into his head of which he seems happily to be without.

I have told him that he shouldn't like me for outside reasons but for the more spiritual part of me. He said, "Yes, but Wanda, the two things are so much entwined that you can't separate them." I said, "Yes, of course I have known that before, but somehow as soon as *I* enter into the equation I lose the perspective and I can't tell where wrong ends and right begins." He said, "Yes, I see."

The thing that alarms me somewhat is that altho my principles make me fight against little demonstrations, I have no disgust for them—in Adolph.

I said, "You make it so hard for me. I have to do the fighting for myself and for you too."

He said, laughing, "Yes, I always told you I needed a moral leaning-post. What's the use of a moral leaning-post if you don't need it?"

May 21, Wednesday

Tussy came Saturday morning [on a visit].

In the afternoon we had our school exercises. They read: "*Palettite Scholarship*—Adolph Dehn. *Honorable Mention*—Wanda Gág." All my hopes gone, but to my surprise: "*McKnight Scholarship*—Wanda Gág." I was also Honorably Mentioned for sketches and Adolph received a book for good sketches. We were both very happy.

Arnold Blanch won the Eastern Scholarship.* To my great surprise Ethel was simply Honorably Mentioned for life drawing. Lloyd Moylan got the Hinkle Scholarship.

That evening Adolph, Lucile, Thusnelda and I went to the Met. to see "Bunker Bean." Adolph was good. After the performance he and I walked over to the little park where we waited for Lucile and Tussy who were having a good time hiding from us. I don't know whether I couldn't get out of it or whether I gave in, but I let Adolph play with my hands. Yes, I did—*yes I did,* ding it. Sometimes I get human enough to just submit for a few minutes. Oh ding it, I don't blame him for it. And I think even I may be forgiven for submitting. I like him very much. Oh this is all so new to me and I can't quite grasp it, but sometimes even I, strong fighter that I am, seem to be powerless to gather my prudishness about me and remain cold and icy.

Sunday evening I went with him to get some library books which I

---

* Awarded locally, but providing for a year's tuition in some Eastern art school. The Palettite, McKnight and Hinkle Scholarships were also local awards, each providing for a year's tuition in the Minneapolis Art School.

was to return for him the next day, as he was leaving in the morning. He was almost provokingly good all the time. On the way home we sat down in the little park for a while, and a little later he said rather quietly, "Wanda, may I kiss you?"

I said, "No," and sprang from the bench.

"Well, I won't," he said in the same almost quiet tone.

I said, "I have a record to keep up."

"A record?"

"Yes I have never allowed it and won't allow it."

"Never?"

"Well, perhaps in about 4 or 5 years." I told him it would break my heart if anyone should ever break my record without my permission. When we shook hands I said, "Be nice and good this summer." He laughed a little and said, "I can't very well be otherwise for the next four months."

I went upstairs and told Lucile all. I didn't want to tell her about his request for a kiss but it was too heavy and I couldn't go to sleep, so I had to. I cried a little too because it is almost too much to have to say goodbye to both of those good people at once. That was last night. I said goodbye to Lucile this afternoon. Lucile and Tussy both like Adolph very much. Lucile says he's almost too good to be true.

June 2

Glory but I miss Adolph and Lucile. When I think of dear Lucile I either weep or nearly weep, and when I think of Adolph I feel the same way. Yesterday I got a letter from him. He says:

> "Work hard, Wanda—and concentrate. You must make good. You know that you have as much talent as anybody—all that is necessary is the development of it. Do it.
> "Now that I can get a sort of perspective on our relationship I can see things pretty well from your point of view. It is the only attitude for a girl to take, especially you who must develop your art to a point where nothing in the world could swamp it. However talented a girl might be, if when she were young she should give in, it might mean the end of her art career. Be good the way you have been. You will conclude that I am a theorist and can't live up to what I say. But I admire you for it."

He asked me to write him another letter so that he could start out with some encouragement Monday morning. He is going to sell books.

I am writing him a little homily about my idea of right and wrong from an unrelated stand-point and otherwise.

June 30, New Ulm

I have been at home for about two weeks. I have been missing Adolph a good deal and have become very home-sick for the company of men in general.

I have written to my Journal Man and am anxiously awaiting a reply. I rather think it will be a very disappointing one. Last night I dreamt that my Journal Man's daughter wrote me a long letter, declaring that I had done very well last year at school but that her father could not finance me any longer because the Journal had gone bankrupt.

I am very much upset by the Mexican War. A bugle call makes me ill. Japan may help Mexico. That would be very bad for us, I'm afraid. Two of my former cavaliers are patriots and have gone to Ft. Snelling—Otto Felz and Walter Gennert.

To-morrow morning at 4:15 a.m. Paula and I are going to Waterville to visit Adolph and his sister. He said we could catch enough fish to pay for my fare. Adolph and Viola have both quit selling books.

July 15, Sat.

No word from my Journal Man. I am worried.

Mr. Gray got married about a week ago. Yu—hoo! They say one can never take gracefully the marriage of a former cavalier even tho one was not so very wild about him. I experience no uncomfortable feel-ings.

Paula and I left for Waterville Sat. morning (July 1). Adolph and Viola were down to meet us, Viola in a cool summer outfit and Adolph in a sport shirt. He is very, very brown. We rowed home via two lakes and a nice shallow winding river. Adolph has a nice cozy *homey* home and a nice, nice family. My regard for him flew up a couple of pegs on account of these. In fact after seeing him at home, I liked him better day after day.

One day he and I went over into the pasture to read a book on Anarchism and Socialism. We read it too, but got very little out of it. For one thing it was written in an exceedingly involved manner, and for another thing he seemed to be much more interested in me than in the book. He made it very uncomfortable for me because he wanted always to sit rather near to me and I, to get out of the way, had to be moving about continually and most of the time I had to sit one-sidedly— I mean, bent to one side in order to get out of his way. Finally I declared I would go home, and got up. He begged me to come back but I refused. "I'll be good," he promised like a little boy, "you can sit on one side and I'll sit way over here." So I sat down again. Usually at this stage he is filled with remorse over what he calls his foolishness. This was the case that day and he raked himself over the coals and remarked about his being so "darn primitive." After a while he turned around and looked at me until I became uncomfortable.

"Why do you like me?" I asked.

He said he couldn't tell definitely. "I like you because you are Wanda," he said.

"Oh but that doesn't say much," I said. "In that way you could like another person because she was Helen, or still another because she was Dorothy."

"You are right," he said and went on to say that he liked me because I was good, and because artistically I could sympathize with him better than anyone he had met.

"So far," I said.

He said, "Yes, so far."

After he had told me the above and a few other reasons for liking me, he asked, "Now you might tell me why you like me—if indeed you do."

"I like you because you can sympathize with me artistically, because you are good, because you have a sense of humor, because you are progressive, and because even tho you have very little money you manage always to look respectable." Oh yes, I said too that I liked him because he was frank. We agreed to be even more frank than we had been.

The following morning we went fishing. Paula, Adolph and I. Paula caught 27, I caught 37, and Adolph caught about 40. It was the first time I had ever fished. On the way home we sold them for $2.00. This they gave to me to pay my train fare with.

Garth Howland came Wednesday evening and at about 11 p.m. we all went for a swim in the lake. Wasn't that looney? But it was fun. Thursday we went fishing so as to earn enough money to buy ice cream with.

Friday morning Adolph and I went fishing again. The fish didn't bite well at all. We tried three or four places and then rowed to Rocky Point where we got off and sat on the grass. We talked of many things, morals mostly.

"Has your attitude changed at all since I told you how I felt about it?" he asked.

"Yes," I said, "I like you a great deal more than I did then, but I don't know just *how* I like you," referring of course to my still being so childlike in my affections. He was glad that I had changed as much as I had.

After a while Garth, Olivia * and Paula came in the boat. As the fish were not responsive that day we didn't try to catch any more but lay down in the grass and made up a foolish progressive story. I started it, something in this manner, "Once there was a mouse, who died. Her astral body took the shape of a strawberry with spikes on it." Adolph related the circumstances of its death as follows—(Note:—my nickname is Mouse): "This mouse had been very hungry and had caught a perch. But the perch was not six inches long, and as it was against the law to catch fish less than six inches in length, the mouse threw the perch back into the water—it liked the perch but, under the circumstances, eating it was against its principles, so it died." No one got the point but I, I guess. It was a good natured little slam at my resisting things not because I didn't like them but because it was against my principles to give in.

Saturday Flavia came. Adolph, who is evidently wild about children, took a great fancy to her and took all kinds of pains to amuse her. Sunday we went for an all day picnic but we were all so blue because of our leaving the following morning. After supper we flopped around on sofa pillows and watched the sun set over the big sheet of water called Lake Tetonka. Then we rowed home. Garth and I sat on one end and Paula and Viola rowed. Adolph sat silently at the other end with his arm about Flavia and his head against hers. I tried to cheer up the company by singing little Bavarian love lyrics. We were all so absolutely blue that Garth got an "outburst." It *is* funny now that I look back.

* Adolph's youngest sister.

It was one of those peaceful moonlit nights. I could not bear to go in, especially since this was to be my last night on the lake for a long time to come. The rest wished to go in—I don't see how they could—so I said I'd stay and go with Adolph to return the boat. The boat belonged to an old bachelor.

Well, after the others left we rowed for a while. It was an ideal night and silence would have gone capitally with it, but Adolph kept looking at me with such appalling seriousness that I became uneasy. "Say something," I said, in desperation. But he declared he couldn't.

Another interval of soft water-plashings, moonlight and that long continuous look. "Why don't *you* say something?" he asked, but I too had to admit that I couldn't. I thought it was high time for us to divert our minds a little so I started rowing to the shore. We slid in among a lacey, fragile bower of willows. I wanted to get out of the boat directly but he begged me to stay a little. So I did. Still that long mute look.

I said, "I wish rather you'd talk a little."

"Why?" he asked.

"I'm sort of uncomfortable," I said. But we continued to be silent. A number of times I suggested that we get out of the boat but he wanted to put it off as long as possible. We finally got out and started to walk home. "May I put my arm around you?" he asked. I did not resist, so he did. I think I may be forgiven for not having resisted. I don't think anybody but the pruniest, primmest, dried-upest, old-maidiest prude would have had the strength and the desire to do so. I might have had the strength but I certainly didn't have the desire. Besides I saw no definite reason why I should object. There is just as much of a possibility of my being in love with him as there is of my not being so, and I certainly would have to know—before I could tell absolutely how I felt about it— whether I could stand that sort of thing from him. I seemed to have no difficulty in standing it.

There was a long puddle which has to be crossed by way of unsteady stones. Adolph took my hand to help me and when, after we had crossed it, our little fingers were still interlocked I made no move to alter the arrangement. I had often wondered what I *would* do when I loosened the reins on myself. I find that my demonstrations are very mild. I curled my fingers around his hand and bent his fingers, one by one. I could see he was glad about it and that he regretted we were so near home. I am not a bit sorry I did it either.

Then he drew me over to the pump. "May I kiss your hand, Wanda?

Just once?" he asked. I said, "No," at first but then I let him take it. I don't care, I think it wasn't very bad.

The next morning we went home. Adolph had given me one of his graduation pictures. I must say I feel somewhat sentimental looking at it.

Undated Entry

I am at grandma's now. Poor dear grandma fell and broke her hip and has to be in a plaster cast. She is so patient and sweet about it.

July 19, Wednesday

It will probably be more than three months before I can see Adolph again. Whether it's a pseudo-love or the real thing, it certainly takes me right with it. I don't care a bit if some of my prudishness *did* go up the spout, *I don't care one bit*.

I am so afraid that he might be merely in love with love than with me. Formerly I used to regard with relief and hope this idea of its being his first case, but lately I am not sure whether it would make me feel happy if he got over it.

I am afraid, after my other experience, to let myself fall in love. If I were not so ding conscientious I would have been carried away entirely in this instance. When I first met him I never dreamed of him being a future cavalier. I remember I distinctly made up my mind that I would never fall in love with him. I had always thought I could never care for anyone who hadn't light curly hair and blue eyes. I also wanted a man a little below medium height and a very musical one. Adolph is none of these and yet it doesn't seem to matter.

Letters—every week one goes and one arrives. They are the one big thing this summer.

Undated Entry

My dear sweet grandmother has died. The funeral was yesterday. I could write a long eulogy on her life which was certainly a good and beautiful one, but I could not do it well anyway.

August 14

Phil Becker has been having a good case on Stella. He is wild about discussions, his favorite theme, however, being love and marriage. He thinks as I do that frankness is the only thing that will make marriage a safe thing to enter upon. He asked what qualities one should look for in order to get a wife of whom one would not tire. I suggested that

he look for a woman who was progressive enough to be always changing, educating herself more and more so that she would be a continual
source of interest and inspiration.

I told him that I didn't consider myself ready to fall in love yet for
a number of years, that I wasn't grown-up enough to know my own
mind. Phil declares that men can't decide whom they really love until
they're about thirty. That would put Adolph on a shaky plank for the
present; or, if you prefer, it would put me on that plank with Adolph
juggling it.

August 24

Finally I heard from my Journal Man. He will pay my board and
room but I will have to see to all other expenses myself.

And now dear diary, goodbye. Wanda.

* * *

(Note to cover gap in diary:—That fall Stella and Thusnelda went back to their school-
teaching jobs. Stella's school was a few miles outside of New Ulm, so she was able to spend
her week-ends at home. I returned to Art School and stayed at the W.C.A. Club as before.

Adolph had only $60 saved but he returned in October, planning to work part of the
time. He was rooming at the home of Hans Schein, a friend of Lloyd Moylan's. Lucile
was not back but hoped to be able to manage it later.)

November 2, Thursday

A month of school is over. Arnold Blanch, Curtis Sprague and Lloyd
Moylan have gone to New York to study at the Art Students' League.
Mrs. Fournier is evidently not coming back. There are a good many
new students, very few old ones. The *charming* Ruby poses all the time.
I work hard even if it is such an unprepossessing model as Ruby.

Adolphe * came the second or third week of school. We have been to-
gether most of the time. Once in a while, when we can make ourselves
believe we can afford it, we go to a movie. Sometimes we go to the
library and look at Art things. Sometimes he comes over to the house
and we combine our efforts and make some poster or picture and in
this way add a few dollars to our little heap (mostly *little*). And we walk
a good deal.

Three weeks ago I went to see Mr. Jones. He said, "I guess I haven't
seen you since I got those pictures back from the East." He said they
said I had great talent, especially in drawing children, and that if I kept
on as I had, there would be no stopping me. Last week I went down

* This was the spelling he was using at that time.

again and when he saw me sitting in the waiting room he said genially and with the old twinkle (which I had not seen for so long), "Hello! Well!" He was very good-natured thru the whole thing, but it seemed too good to be true and I was always afraid he might change most any moment. I brought two illustrations which he evidently liked very much.

"What are you going to do with these?" he asked.

"Send them away," I replied. "Of course they'll be coming back a good many times but that doesn't matter."

"Now you're talking!" he said. Well, it tickled me to find him in such good humor. It always makes me feel good for a whole week just to get one of his nice twinkles.

I showed Mr. Goetsch some of my summer sketches and he seemed to like them pretty well. "I see you've been digging deeper," he said. In Illustration I have been virtuously drawing most any pose that came along, but this week I have lost what three years ago I would have called "my inspired vision." I have been working tho. I am doing a rush order, a Football cover for the *Minnehaha*. Adolphe is doing the lettering for me. We always help each other out on our jobs. I did my second cover for the Paper Co. too. I have sent illustrations to *St. Nicholas* and *Today's* but both came back.

Adolphe does caricatures as of old. Mrs. Appelbaum and I are still his favorite victims altho Jo Canteeny is fast coming into favor too. He is all for Russian literature now and comes to school every day with some Russian book or other.

November 13, Monday

Adolphe acts queer. I don't know why and he says he doesn't know what's the matter with him too. Last night he said he was *simple*. I do not like him so. He is in this state so inconsiderate and surly. And it always makes me think he is getting tired of me.

He draws nice things. Nice decorative things with *colorful* values. No, colorful is not just right either—they look a little like the word *choice* sounds. I love his line.

I rake him over the coals for not studying his anatomy more. He tells me that I have become terribly academic and that I am actually becoming mediocre. A necessary stage. I suffered too keenly from lack of construction knowledge so I had to become meek and modest for a while. Since I have accepted the "approved" method, things are swinging better for me and I am regaining my self-confidence.

Perhaps Lucile is coming back after Christmas. Hooray!

Bernard Flannigan,* Adolphe, and I are impatient with some of the people at school—their wailings and mutual praisings are irritating to us.

It is not kind to be so and I suppose it is more or less transient with Adolphe and me. (I don't know about Flannigan. Flannigan is a taciturn, un-smiling creature who reads Nietsche and Schopenhauer and is all for the modern tendencies in art.)

But Adolphe makes me uncomfortable. He is so brusque in his attitude towards me and everyone else.

November 15, Wednesday

Adolphe continued his surly attitude all day Monday and Tuesday. I've argued with him and almost begged him to try to over-rule himself but to no avail. He denied nothing and agreed that he didn't blame people for objecting to his ways—he declared he was disgusted with himself and that was all the further he would go. He declared that he could not change himself, because to do that one had to have the *desire* to do so, and he was too indifferent to desire to do so. I went on hauling him over the coals, but he retained the half-reckless, half-indifferent air and even tried to laugh some of it off, but in spite of this he looked far from happy. I imagine it isn't very pleasant to be in that sort of a stage. I have been there too but I had sort of forgotten about it. I remember when I felt so desperately indifferent that people couldn't do a thing with me.

* John B. Flannagan, the sculptor.

December 5

Yesterday afternoon Adolphe called up and asked whether I'd like to come over and do the portrait of him which I had promised to do for him. So I went over and sketched until he got too tired to pose. Then we sat and talked in the twilight. About Adolphe's affairs. His need of money and a job, and we tried to plan what he had best do.

Soon the trunk man came to get his trunk for on this day Adolphe was moving. Now he is staying at Merton's. They are rich folks. He is tending their furnace and in return for this service he gets his room free of charge. He is making car cards for a Mr. Smith, and gets paid for little odd jobs he does for Merton's, so you see he is getting to be extraordinarily prosperous. As I eat only fruit at noon and as my lunches include sandwiches, I give him my sandwiches and in this way he has one less meal to pay for. I am rather glad he is boarding himself for in this way he will have to live on a more slender diet, and there isn't so much danger of his getting too plump.

Ding, he certainly can draw. That is, he can't draw so very well now but he certainly will be able to in time. He is at home to-night doing a car card.

I think my picture is going to be in the paper Sunday. I am to sketch at a Society Bazaar and this is to advertise it. I went down to Lee's Wednesday and had my picture taken. With a palette. I should have preferred to have it minus the palette, but they wanted the palette. I don't care much about having my picture in the paper.

Undated Entry

I sketched at the Bazaar. Society depresses me somehow. The whole thing—gowns, affectations, polish—seems so foolish to me; so utterly, utterly a waste of time.

I went down to Donaldson's and had a shampoo and a marcel wave from a Mr. Gans who rejoices in a foreign accent and auburn hair. When I came home and surveyed myself in the mirror I decided that I looked impossible, paradoxical. I looked aristocratic, perhaps even chic, but I didn't look like Wanda Gág, so I hastily destroyed Mr. Gans' structure and built up my own comfortable psyche. I slipped on the net for fear that the Bazaar folks (who had sent me down) would notice what I had done.

All one needs to look societyish is a hair-dresser, a masseuse, a manicurist and expensive clothes.

Undated Entry

Love is certainly a complicated business. Perhaps I am not qualified to judge but it looks like one big eternal, undependable tangle to me.

The other evening Adolphe declared that it must be an awful risk to marry. I have often thought it, but it seems that a woman has more cause to be afraid of marrying than a man has. Adolphe is afraid that one might get tired of the other or fall in love with another, or something. There is that danger of course, but surely that danger is lessened if one chooses one's mate keeping in view character, broadmindedness, intellect, and aptitude for progress.

Well, as I said, this love business becomes more complicated the more one thinks of it. In a way it is really much more peaceful to have a couple of half-cavaliers and Platonic Friends (as long as they last) than to narrow oneself down to one man. When you narrow yourself to one man you are always so concerned about him, about his attitude towards you, and your attitude towards him, etc.—whereas when you have a string you enjoy them all more or less dispassionately and you aren't nearly so sensitive to their words and actions.

It may be due to my extreme youth that these things seem so important to me.

1917

February 14. Minneapolis

Things went on quite as usual after I returned to Minneapolis after the holidays.

Adolphe and I started a big ambitious cover, a Vanity-Fairish sort of thing. We would work on it Saturday afternoons, and one afternoon as I came down for this purpose I found in my mail a letter from Stella. Mama was ill with the grippe, she wrote, and as the children had been losing a good deal of school trying to keep things going, I was to come home immediately and take the place of Chief housekeeper, cook, Disciplinarian to the kids, and head nurse to mama. I knew that mama had been far from well at Christmas time so I was thoroughly alarmed. I was heavy-hearted and in spite of my efforts to be stoical I couldn't help crying a wee little bit every once in a while. I left the next morning just as a big snowstorm was brewing. I felt sad at leaving school and my friends, and I felt sad because I knew I was going to go thru a great deal before I would return to Minneapolis.

I will not tell the details of my stay home. I could see that mama was very ill. She had become very thin and was too weak to even sit up in bed alone. My premonition continued to grow and when, a week after I had come home, Mrs. Diel told me that she was afraid mama would never recover, I was not shocked. It was only a confirmation of my fears. After that I had to keep myself well under control. I tried to be cheerful with the kids, for I told no one of the matter, and I had to be careful not to be over-solicitous towards dear mama lest she should suspect something. I could write pages of all the silent grief I carried about with me, etc., but I won't. I worked so hard that I soon felt I couldn't stand it any longer, notwithstanding the fact that under the circumstances there was nothing I liked better to do than work from morning to night. It was bitterly cold. We froze a good deal altho we nearly ran our legs off keeping the furnace and kitchen fires going.

Tuesday night when I was all alone with the four younger children, mama became decidedly worse. The doctor and Mrs. Diel and Mrs. Spenz were with me when she died, at 4.45 Wednesday morning. I was the only one in the family who saw our dear, brave mother die.

She was unconscious for the most part of the last three hours, but she became conscious twice during that time for a few minutes. Each time she called me. The first time she had already returned to unconsciousness when I reached her bedside (I had gone down to the children for a few minutes) and the second time she told me that it was warm. She was not warm, poor mama—her breath was coming shorter and shorter and she felt the need of air. The doctor told me, as I was watching her during her last hours struggling for breath, that she was not suffering any to speak of, and of course I was glad for that.

And then came the funeral. All the responsibility rested upon me, for of course now I am the head of the family. The neighbors were very kind to us all, and other folks farther away were also kind. I held out until a few hours before the funeral. I got shaky in the knees and I just flopped together and wept.

It seems the news of mama's death was a great shock to Adolphe even tho I had sort of prepared him for it. His first idea was to come to New Ulm. "I wanted to be with you," the dear boy wrote, "because I like you and your family and I thought you would feel better if I were with you." Of course I should have been very glad if he had come. As it was he got the news too late so as to be there for the hardest part (the train service was all tied up in knots on account of the big blizzards we were having).

Well, and now I am back at Minneapolis. I came Feb. 10. I am quite surprised at myself. I never thought I would be so stoical in a thing like this. I thought, for instance, that when I would meet such people as Adolphe, Lucile and Paula, that I would just drop into their arms and cry. But I did nothing of the sort. All my crying happens after I am in bed. Everybody tells me that I am so brave. The trouble is that I am too brave for my own good. It is very wearing to hold yourself in check. The responsibility resting on my shoulders is just about too much for me, and during the last few days I have come nearer to being utterly discouraged than ever before, I think.

Undated Entry

Last night Adolphe wanted to go to a Peace meeting. We thought it would probably be too rough for me to go with him but finally we decided to try it. He had to tend to his furnace first, so we went down into his cellar where he showed me his furnace, how it worked, where the coal was, where he kept his food, etc.

Mr. Goetsch is making us be so neat and proper that we have scarcely time to learn to be artists in.

I was over at St. Paul at the N.W. Artists Exhibition, and had a lovely talk with George Resler, the etcher. He seems to be very nice and timid and wise. He reminds me (pleasantly and amusingly) of corkscrew whiskers—he is so twisty in his attitudes. He told me to study the sketches of Chavannes and Gauguin and some of the other Modernists.

March 21, Saturday

Adolphe and I are working on a new cover together. The other one is almost done.

I have been sick all the time lately, with a cold or toothache or something and last night to top all I swallowed, during dinner time, a big silver tooth-filling. It means more money to be spent in having it re-filled.

Adolphe and I sent some drawings to the New York Art Students' League Competition.

Mr. Goetsch, in looking at some of my little ramblings (compositions), said, "These are more what I call a composition than anything that has been handed in here." * I like to sit down and let my pencil wander around on the paper. I am dissatisfied with my knowledge of composition, however. It is not versatile enough. I wish to solve deeper and more subtle problems.

There is a woman taking care of the kids now. I haven't heard how they like her. The poor kids have been having hard times.

April 12, Thursday

And now I have done it. I knew it would come but didn't think it would happen so soon. I gave to Adolphe my first kiss. Down in the unromantic sewing room (which we use to paint in) surrounded by temperas, brushes and our new poster.

It was all on account of the war. The United States has been drawn into the conflict and there is much talk of conscription and people are very much alarmed. And of course, I am becoming much worried for fear that Adolphe may have to go. He didn't seem to be much worried until about yesterday, and both of us were so concerned about it that we couldn't concentrate our minds on the poster. Bye and bye he began to beg for a kiss. He kept on asking and altho I wanted to very much, I didn't quite know whether I ought to. And then I thought of the war and of how he might be here only a short while and of how nice he was and how I liked *Himself* as shown in his drawing, and then I gave it. I should say there were three of them but he insists that it was one, with interruptions.

* See illustration facing page 463 for one of these compositions.

I had often wondered just what the "first kiss" would be like. I did not feel the thrill one reads about. I should say that the memory is more thrilly than the actual thing itself. There was a faint and almost indefinable feeling, tho, which was connected with the thought that this was the only "first kiss" I could ever give or take and that I was experiencing it now for the first and last time. And right after that, with my head on his rough woolen coat, I shed a few tears about it. I meant to go right up and tell Lucile but I haven't told her yet. I feel and act strangely after it and I wonder whether she has noticed it.

Undated Entry

Adolphe and I have each been awarded a scholarship at the Art Students' League in New York! We are two out of twelve of the entire United States, and I believe this is the first time that this honor has been conferred on any member of our school. It is the biggest honor either of us have won.* My Journal Man should be glad to hear it. And my Uncle Mac. I haven't dared to write home about it. They will say, "Yes but you have no money to live on, and what is to become of us?"

Adolphe is afraid too that if they have conscription he may not even be able to take advantage of the Scholarship. I have spent so much time and energy worrying about this. It interferes with my sleep and it just makes me sick to think of the war. It has driven away my appetite too. Last week I weighed 99 lbs. (with my clothes on). I am trying hard to have an appetite and I am virtuously swallowing Scott's Emulsion.

My Journal Man sent two Kid posters to an Agency in New York. They were sent back without an explanation. I might say much about the war. Naturally it is the biggest topic of discussion just at present. *The Masses* has been suppressed.

April 24

Things are happening thick and fast. Dear Mr. Koehler died yesterday. He died on the street car on his way to school where he was going to give his usual History of Art lecture. We all feel the loss very deeply. What a fine unselfish man he must have been! He gave such a great part of his life for this school of ours to the disadvantage, no doubt, of his own work.

* This was the result of our sending some drawings to the Annual Competition, as recorded on March 21. This scholarship provides for a year's tuition at the Art Students' League.

Mr. Phoenix will not be back next year, having allied himself, it seems, to the Federal School of Art.

And now our big man, Mr. Goetsch is leaving us. Miss Cheney will be Directress of the School next year. The idea of Mr. Goetsch leaving

upsets us all. To think of all he has done, and when he says, "If you will not let me do the best for the school I can, I cannot stay," they calmly say, "Allright." It is outrageous. Mr. Goetsch with his nice, quaint, big original ideas, and with his lovely sense of color and his velvet-and-iron lines which caress the paper, Mr. Goetsch who handles his charcoal so lovingly and believes in the "that that is not" which *is*.

And here I am actually weeping about it.

We wrote a petition to the Board in which we begged that we might keep our teacher. All who were in the building signed. Then we called Mr. Goetsch in order to ask his permission to present it to the Board. He read it. All were silent. He sat down and, being a little bit self-conscious about the tears in his eyes and being also too moved to be able to speak, he wrote in a queer, almost shaky way:—"This is awfully nice of you, but everything has been decided and I am afraid it is too late. But I thank you for your interest."

With his eyes quite tearful and with deep emotion in his face, he handed the paper to the person nearest to him and went very hurriedly out of the room. Some of us shed a few tears over it and all of us were very much impressed. All except Ross who was obviously having a frivolous streak. Mrs. Appelbaum, Gertrude Bergen and Mrs. Curtis went off to deliver the paper to Mr. Chute. It was raining and Adolphe walked home with me. He came in and worked on the lettering of my Baby Poster.

Lucile and I had lunch with the Paper Man. One of these days I must write him up.

The American Art Annual is evidently going to file me and my few statistics. It sent me a blank to fill out, "Who's Who In Art." That is its name. I told Mr. Phoenix I had received something but I didn't quite know what it meant. He looked at it and told me to be sure to fill it out and send it. I wonder how they heard of me, and what basis they have for wishing to file me.

Last week I went to my Journal Man and told him about our winning the scholarship. "Are you going?" he said, and I said I'd certainly try my best. "Well," he said, "I guess I'll have to see to your room and board again." Glory, I was tickled. "We'll skin 'em yet!" he said, and as I left, his "Good luck to you!" was followed by a peal of nice Journalmanny laughter.

Last Sunday to my great surprise I saw one of my sketches and a write-up about Adolphe and me in the Journal. There wasn't enough in it about Adolphe to suit me.

Now isn't that enough happenings for a week or so?

April 29

The Conscription Bill has been passed and oh how much afraid I am for Adolphe.

Adolphe and I decided to take a walk yesterday. As it happened, it turned into a cool, cloudy, dreary afternoon.

"What shall we do?" I asked.

"We might go to the Library," Adolphe replied. "Best of all I'd like to go upstairs." *

We dressed well and walked out to Bryn Mawr. We found a big place which had been used for excavating purposes with many tin cans

* In the W.C.A. Club no men except the girls' fathers or brothers were allowed in the rooms.

about, and new green grass and old brown grass. Here we sat down. It seemed too bad that we should have to go out on a cold dreary day to a tin-canny dumping hollow when right at home was a nice warm room with prints of Old Masters on the wall and many nice books on a shelf. It began to rain so I said we'd have to go home but it took me some time before I could convince him of the fact.

My Uncle Mac wishes that Adolphe and I would be separated for a year or two. He wished him no ill but he did wish Adolphe would not be at New York next year. He is afraid it will interfere with my work. "Certain psychological conditions," he said. Myself, I think Adolphe saves me from a great many troublesome cavaliers. I noticed that last fall (before he came back to school). It made me wonder how many cavaliers I would have if it weren't for Adolphe. I didn't say a great deal to my Uncle Mac about the affair. I did say I didn't intend to marry anyone for a long time to come and perhaps I wouldn't ever marry.

"Oh yes, I think you will," he said. "But I don't think it will be Adolphe." He thought it would be some man, not an artist—a business man perhaps, who would appreciate my work and who would adore me, something like that. I don't want to be adored or idolized or something like that. It savors too much of the double standard. I want a man with whom I can work, and who will know just what I am doing and what I am going thru. I want—oh I want a great deal and I suppose I'll never get it.

When I disagree with my Uncle Mac I usually keep quiet and think my think. But I know he says those things for my own good, and he did make me think. I also discussed my home affairs with him at good length.

May 15

The weather has been lovely and Adolphe and I have been on a number of jaunts.

Joe La Londe and Louis Rasch are back from New York. Lloyd has learned to smoke and also drinks beer and wine it seems. He also has an awful case on a prize-fighter's daughter. Curtis Sprague lives the gay Bohemian life of Washington Square. Stedman has enlisted as an engineer.

I am so worried about the war again.

June 4

Our School Carnival came off May 7 & 8th. The second night I met

Charcoal Drawing of Howard

Drawing—Lithographic Crayon

Composition—Lithographic Crayon

a Mr. Wehle who is an art critic sort of man and is connected with the Art Institute. From Boston.* He bought my "Incense Ladies" and the wild "Faun Picture." I had a very interesting talk with him on the whole. It was Hans Schein who introduced me to him and bye and bye all three of us went and had some ice cream. I sketched at the Carnival. Not for likenesses this time but as a diversion for the public. Miss Cheney bought one of my sketches and so did some more folks.

On Decoration Day my Paper Man called and I gave him a batch of sketches and showed him my Baby Photographs and my Memory Book. But that (as our friend Rudyard Kipling says altogether too often) is another story, and I sincerely hope that I will have time this summer to write up the entire episode. It is really more than an episode now. I like the Paper Man very much.

Undated Entry

A picnic on Sunday. Mr. Wehle was there. I spent the afternoon with him and enjoyed him. After we got back to town we went to a movie. He said in regard to Adolphe, that he understood I was all taken.

I said, "Oh no."

"Oh, that makes it more interesting," he said laughing. We carried on a sort of mock flirtation. With Adolphe to back me up I could afford to do that.

At the final Exhibition Adolphe and I had one panel all to ourselves. Oh, believe me, we were the shining lights this year. At all occasions we and our scholarships were mentioned, and Mr. Goetsch always loves to tease us about our *both* getting one.

All my joys are overshadowed by the old draft tho. Adolphe has decided to register and then, if he is called, to resist. My feelings on the matter—too deep to explain, that's all. I dare not think of it.

Undated Entry

Adolphe, Lucile, Paula, Molly and Johan Egilsrud, and I, all had a picnic at Fair Oaks. We played "Statue" and "Tag" and a guessing game. Lots of fun too, I liked it. On the way back, just as we were all nibbling ice cream cones and playing that Adolphe was our grandfather, we met Mr. Wehle who had come to see me. So we all trotted back to

* Harry B. Wehle, now Curator of Paintings at the Metropolitan Museum, New York.

the W.C.A. Club and showed him Adolphe's and my two "Slender Lady Covers" which was what Mr. Wehle came to see. He is interesting.

June 16, Saturday. New Ulm

I took Lucile home with me for a few days. She liked our family awfully well and thought Flavia was a very "different" child. Her legs are longer than ever. Howard is growing. Dehli looks quite stunning at times and has her front hair banged. I bobbed Stell's and Asta's hair today. I can fancy how people will talk. Tussy bawls because she wants hers cut and we don't want her to. She'd look cute enough but her hair looks so nice as it is.

We have been cleaning house, and *talk* about physical fatigue at the end of every day! We cleaned the entire house of rubbish and painted the kitchen and dining room. We are expecting Adolphe tomorrow. He is coming to help paint our house on the outside.

We are planning hard (foolishly perhaps) on going down to Minneapolis in the fall. The whole shee-bang, except I of course. We hope to find work for Tussy and Asta, and let Stella keep house. I hope we can do it. I am reading plays. Björnson, Strindberg, Lady Gregory, Synge. I like "Riders to the Sea" very much.

June 21, Thursday

Adolphe came Sunday to paint our house. Stella and I in painter's overalls helping him at it. The people stand and look at us, but seem to think it's pretty nice of us to do it.

July 7, Saturday

This is the end of our third week of painting and we aren't done yet. It is certainly a big job. We climb ladders, and really we have worked ourselves to such a frazzle that we're getting peevish all around.

The draft is close at hand and I dare not think of it.

Mr. Phoenix said he did not wish to see Adolphe resist the draft—a man needed experiences and his character suffered if he did not meet them bravely. Oh what an ironical old world it is at times! when it takes so much will power to have our views and maintain them, one is told to do the other thing for just that reason. Adolphe of course has "conscientious scruples." Mr. Phoenix wants Adolphe to enlist in the Government Service. Make war posters. Imagine a person with conscientious scruples having to do that! Adolphe of course has a hard time deciding what he is to do. It's just a question of whether he can convince himself whether it is better for his cause to give himself up (in resisting and being punished) or to keep his life for some Socialistic service later.

It seems that it is not as hard to *do* right as it is to *know what is right*. I find it harder every day to do the latter.

I got a letter from Hans Schein the other day. He told me that Mr. Wehle had the three slender Incense Ladies framed. A man came to the Art Store and saw the picture and declared that that was rather a bold ·thing for a girl to do. Hans told him that the girl had won a New York Scholarship with it and (as Hans puts it) "at that the gink sort of drew in his horns." Hans calls Mr. Wehle "Frater." He said, "The Frater wishes to be remembered to you." The Frater, by the way, wrote me a nice little letter and the other day I wrote him one too.

I believe Adolphe is going to have something printed in the *Masses*. A sketch or two. He got a very nice letter from Floyd Dell. In green ink. He is getting quite a collection of letters. Floyd Dell, John Sloan, Arturo Giovannitti.

We children have about $140 besides our house. There is the insurance—$110, but that will go for the painting bill for the house. Oh I'm getting so desperately tired of being so poor. Really we feel most desperate about it. When young people like we are moved to say that we felt (oh well, I am sorry we said it, but sometimes one just *does*) like just lying down to die. . . . I'm sorry we said it, for I love my life and it was not a brave thing to say. But when one has been brave for years and years, sometimes one forgets to stay so. I wrote to Paula:—*

> "I am too tired even to think much altho lately I am so often impressed, or rather depressed, with the futility of anything or everything. To top all I ran into Tolstoy just at this period. I am given to understand that he gets all cleared up afterwards and becomes quite peaceful and Christian but I have not gotten that far in the book. I suppose this verges on morbidity so I try not to think of it too much but really, Paula, if you have six kids on your hands and about $140 to keep all of them with, it looks pretty blue sometimes."

July 31, Thursday

Well, our house is on sale. I have had to be diplomatic, business-like,

---

* She had graduated from the University and was at that time student Dietician in the City Hospital of Minneapolis. Now she is a librarian, and recently (under the pseudonym, Georgia Travers) she published a book for children, *The Story of Kattor*, which Flavia illustrated.

on the look-out for people who are ready to take advantage of our situation, and oh, all sorts of things. I had practically decided to send all the kids down to Minneapolis this fall, but we can't make it yet. I think

LITTLE CLOUD ATHWART THE SKY,
WHAT'S THE NEWS UP THERE SO HIGH?

From *A Child's Book of Folk Lore*

Stella and Thusnelda will go down there tho to try their luck, the four younger ones living here in New Ulm until next June or so, when I want to go down to Minneapolis with the whole batch.

Adolphe is not included in the first draft and of course we are all happy about that.

I have almost one hundred sketches so far and am learning a good deal about child-anatomy. I have an offer to illustrate a child's text book with twelve pictures. There is not a great deal of money in it, but publicity, practice and much joy. I am going to do it for a Mrs. Rankin of Minneapolis. I have done almost seven of the illustrations now.*

---

* *A Child's Book of Folk Lore—Mechanics of Written English,* by Jean Sherwood Rankin, M.A.

I got a Minneapolis Art School catalogue. A man with an absolutely unpronounceable name is in Goetsch's place [Vaclav Vytlacil].

September

We had a household goods sale and sold most of our trash, keeping enough furniture for the kids to live with. The house isn't sold, the kids will go on living at home as before.

I received a telegram from my Book Lady [Mrs. Rankin] asking me to come down to Minneapolis at her expense to see to the reproducing of my book illustrations.

Stella, Thusnelda and I went to Minneapolis Sept. 22. We stayed at Egilsrud's most of the time and they were so lovely to us. I went to see my dear Mrs. Rankin too. She gave me much valuable advice, information and help. Mr. Rankin lent me $150 for my youngsters in New Ulm to live on.*

Undated Entry [end of September]

My Journal Man wrote and said that he had a room reserved at the Studio Club in New York for me. Happy, gee——.

The Alumni of the Minneapolis Art School took a collection for me—$50 to be used in my New York struggles. I almost bawled over that. As I understand it, it was done at Mr. Goetsch's suggestion—dear old Mr. Goetsch!

I am going thru all the letters I have been saving for about six years, in order that I might throw away those for which I had no use. In this way I had occasion to run thru all of Adolphe's letters. I like them very much. I have been having a deliciously sentimental and weepy time over those letters. Yes, ding it all, I've been doing nothing but dream of Waterville and that irresistible pieface of mine who lives there. I like him so particularly well since I read those letters because so many of his good qualities, which I have just naturally become used to and therefore have become sort of numbed to, have made their re-impression on me.

---

* Stella and Thusnelda did not return to New Ulm with me. Stella roomed with Lucile and got an art airbrushing job. Thusnelda worked for her board and took a Business Course. The following summer we sold the house and moved the four younger children to Minneapolis as we had planned. Before I returned to New York, all six were established in an apartment—the "house money" was used for rent, light and gas bills; Stella and Thusnelda paid the food bills in return for getting their rent free. Asta, now through high school, kept house; Dehli, Howard and Flavia were still going to school. We all *did* get through high school as we had promised ourselves to do.

The letters of my former cavaliers, as I read them, made a very good impression on me. Mr. Gray's humor is so cheery, and Donnie's dreamy qualities are very nice too. Glenn Edgerley's respectful, appreciative letters, ditto. Phil Becker has, of course, his inimitable humor and serious discussions. The Paper Man, Armand—Funny world.

Adolphe, Arnold Blanch and I start out for New York Wednesday evening.

* * *

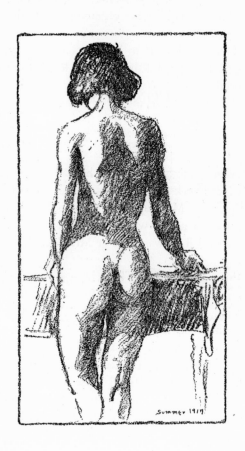

Summer 1917

CONTRASTS

1905 - 1938

Pen and Ink Illustration

"But it was not they, but a
dear little monkey dressed like
a girl."

Top: Illustration by Wanda Gág for her First Full Length Story,
Jocko, 1905-1906
Bottom: Illustration from *Tales From Grimm,* 1936

Interiors

Top: Pen and Ink Drawing from the *Journal Junior,* 1909
Bottom: Grandma's Parlor—Lithograph, 1930

Still Life

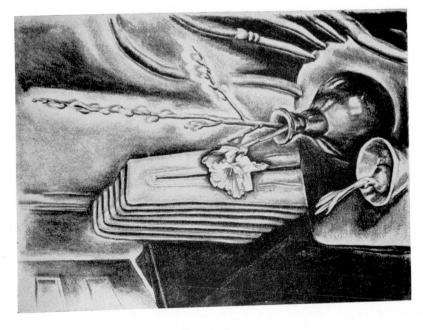

Easter Morning—Lithograph. 1926

Water Color, 1913

Landscape

Spring on the Hillside, New Jersey—Lithograph, 1937

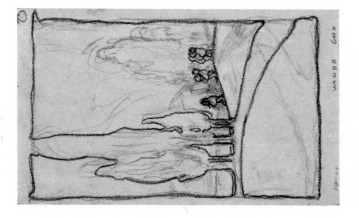

Drawing, Minneapolis, 1917

Plant Life

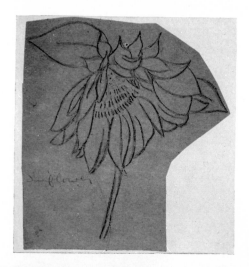

Top: Sunflower—Pencil on Wrapping Paper, 1908
Bottom: Squash and Zinnias—Brush and Ink, 1929

Self Portraits

Top: Pen and Ink Sketch, 1914
Bottom: Self Caricature, 1937

Top: The Crooked Man and his Crooked Cat—Drawing, 1909
Bottom: Illustration from *Millions of Cats,* 1928

More Cats

Top: Siesta—Lithograph, 1937
Bottom: Mutzi Asleep—Crayon Drawing, 1938

Winter Landscape

Top: Houses and Snow, Minneapolis, 1916
Bottom: Ice House and Snow, New Milford, Connecticut, 1927

WHO'S WHO IN THE DIARY

WHO'S WHO IN THE DIARY

For the sake of brevity only a partial list of names is given here. In the New Ulm section, for instance, I have included only people who were closely connected with our every day lives, such as relatives, playmates, school chums and teachers. It may be assumed that all others were friends and neighbors whom we had known all our lives. In the St. Paul and Minneapolis sections I have listed not only the main characters but also such minor ones as were inadequately identified otherwise.

The real names of our family and relatives have been retained; the names of all other people mentioned in Parts One and Two are fictitious. In the St. Paul and Minneapolis sections, however, I have kept most of the actual names, supplying fictitious names for only a few who I felt might prefer to remain anonymous.

In several cases people altered the spelling of their names during the time I was writing about them in the diary, and I have retained these variations. As to our own name, in New Ulm it was pronounced correctly (Gaag) as a matter of course, but when I left home it was usually mispronounced—(Găg). Since ä denotes the sound ah *in the English language, I tried using that for a while, but this was frequently confused with the German ä, which brought it back to ă again. Later when I saw how the photographer Nicholas Ház got around a similar problem, I adopted his system. In order to avoid confusion, I have kept this marking throughout the diary.*

NEW ULM

THE FAMILY

Papa—Anton Gág
Mama—Elisabeth Biebl Gág
Wanda Hazel
Stella Lona
Thusnelda Blondine (called Tussy, which rhymes with *pussy*)
Asta Theapolis (short broad *a* in Asta)
Dehli Maryland (Dehli pronounced *daily*)
Howard Anthony Jerome
Flavia Betti Salome ("Baby")

RELATIVES

"Down at Grandma's"—Grandma
Uncle Frank
Uncle Josie
Aunt Mary
Aunt Magdalene
Other relatives—   Aunt Klaus
Cousin Clara
Johnnie
Nora
Cousin Dolores

FRIENDS AND PLAYMATES

Daisy Becker—a school chum
Phil Becker—a University student, cousin to Daisy Becker
Ione Dekker—a school chum
Judy Dekker—Stella's school chum
Fern Fischer—Stella's school chum
Kurt Fischer—Fern's small brother
Gertie Drucker—a school friend
Paula Hershl—a school chum
Lucy—a school chum
Erna Rosen—a friend living near Grandma's

HIGH SCHOOL TEACHERS

Miss Allen   Mr. Evans   Miss King
Mr. Bredford   Mr. Groos   Miss Lee
Mr. Cheevers   Mr. Heywood   Miss Meadows
Miss Dillon   Mr. Jellick   Mr. Winkler
Mr. Doom   Mr. Jolliffe

ST. PAUL AND MINNEAPOLIS

A

Aanstad, Sarah—Minneapolis art student
Alden, Jack—a young architect
Ames, Phoebe—St. Paul art student
Appelbaum, Mrs.—Minneapolis art student
Aurness, Mr.—Minneapolis art student

B

Bergen, Gertrude—Minneapolis art student
Bergen, Hazel—St. Paul art student
Bergmeier, Etta—St. Paul art student
Blanch, Arnold—Minneapolis art student
Bonta, Elizabeth—teacher at St. Paul Art School
Bowers, Raymon—St. Paul art student
Breck, Joseph—Director of the Minneapolis Art School
Brown, Bob—St. Paul art student
Brown, Mrs.—Minneapolis art student
Brownell, Grace—St. Paul art student

C

Canteeny, Jo—Minneapolis art student
Cheney, Mary Moulton—teacher at Minneapolis Art School
Claussen, Ethel—Minneapolis art student
Clark, Ruth—a University student
Curtis, Mrs.—Minneapolis art student

D

Dassett, Mr.—Minneapolis art student
Dean, Miss—a friend at the Y.W.C.A. at St. Paul
Dehn, Adolph—Minneapolis art student
Dehn, Olivia—Adolph Dehn's youngest sister
Dehn, Viola—Adolph Dehn's sister attending the University
Dickman, Hortense—St. Paul art student

E

Eberhart, A. O.—Governor of Minnesota
Edgerley, Glenn—a young architect
Egilsrud, Johan—Minneapolis art student
Egilsrud, Molly—Johan Egilsrud's young sister
Emraad, Armand—a University student
Evans, Doris—St. Paul art student

F

Farrell, Guy—a young newspaper reporter
Flannagan, John B.—Minneapolis art student
Fordham, Miss—a Y.W.C.A. Secretary, St. Paul
Fournier, Mrs. Marietta—Minneapolis art student
Frendel, Timmie—a University student

G

Goetsch, Gustav—teacher at Minneapolis Art School

Gottlieb, Harry—Minneapolis art student
Gray, Mr.—a college sophomore

H

Hare, Peggy—St. Paul art student
Hendrickson, Dave—St. Paul art student
Hilton, Ted—a University student
Hodgeman, Dallas—a Minneapolis art student
Holton, John—a Minneapolis art student
Howland, Garth—a young man staying at Fournier's

J

Jones, Herschel V.—Editor, Minneapolis Journal
Journal Man—the same

K

"Klink"—a St. Paul art student
Koehler, Professor Robert—teacher at the Minneapolis Art School

L

La Londe, Joe—Minneapolis art student
Lang, Dr.—a medical student at the University
Lovelace, Delos—a young newspaper reporter
Luedke, Rose—Mr. Weschcke's secretary, staying at the Y.W.C.A.,
   St. Paul
Lundquist, Lucile—Minneapolis art student

M

MacDonald, Mr.—Minneapolis art student
Magnusen, Miss—Minneapolis art student
McQuaide, Mrs.—Matron of Y.W.C.A., St. Paul
McWhorter, Tyler—Manager of the St. Paul Art School
Morse, Larry—a friend of Paula Hershl
Moylan, Lloyd—Minneapolis art student

N

Nelson, David—a teen-age friend
Nina—a friend, staying at the Y.W.C.A., St. Paul

O

Olds, Elizabeth—Minneapolis art student
Owre, Dr. Alfred—Dean of the Dental College, University
   of Minnesota

P

Paper Man—a young business man, Minneapolis
Peck, Sally—a University student
Peterson, Madge—a University student
Phoenix, Lauros M.—teacher at Minneapolis Art School
"Pilchie"—a St. Paul art student
Pousette-Dart, Nathaniel—teacher at St. Paul Art School
Price, Eleanor—a University student

R

"Rags"—a St. Paul art student
Rasch, Louis—a Minneapolis art student
Reed, Mr.—a University student
Ross—a Minneapolis art student
Russell, Arthur J.—an editor and columnist, Minneapolis Journal

S

Saxby, Phyllis—St. Paul art student
Schaffnit, Gertrude—Minneapolis art student
Sprague, Curtis—Minneapolis art student
Spriess, Dorothy—a University student
Stedman—Minneapolis art student
Swanwick, Irene—St. Paul art student

W

Wehle, Harry B.—a young man connected with the Minneapolis
    Institute of Arts
Weschcke, Charles—a St. Paul friend and business man
Willink, Theresa—St. Paul art student
Wing, Fred—a University student

Z

Zeigler, Lee Woodward—Director of the St. Paul Art School

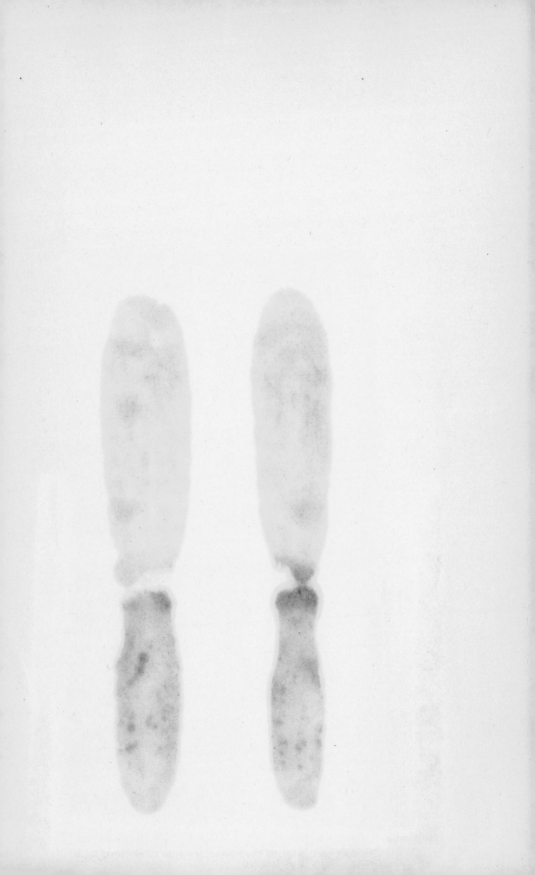